The Missed Encounter of Radical Philosophy with Architecture

Also available from Bloomsbury

Aesthetics and Architecture, Edward Winters

Aesthetic and Artistic Autonomy, edited by Owen Hulatt

Aesthetics: Key Concepts in Philosophy, Daniel Herwitz

Aesthetics: The Key Thinkers, edited by Alessandro Giovannelli

Architecture in Black, Darell Wayne Fields

Art, Myth and Society in Hegel's Aesthetics, David James

Art, Politics and Ranciére: Seeing Things Anew, Tina Chanter

Deleuze and the Schizoanalysis of Visual Art, edited by Ian Buchanan and Lorna Collins

A New Philosophy of Society, Manuel De Landa

A Thousand Plateaus, Gilles Deleuze and Felix Guattari (Translated by Brian Massumi)

Conditions, Alain Badiou (Translated by Steven Corcoran)

Theory of the Subject, Alain Badiou (Translated by Bruno Bosteels)

The Politics of Aesthetics, Jacques Rancière (Translated by Gabriel Rockhill)

The Missed Encounter of Radical Philosophy with Architecture

Edited by

Nadir Lahiji

Bloomsbury Studies in Philosophy

Bloomsbury Academic
An imprint of Bloomsbury Publishing Plc

B L O O M S B U R Y
LONDON · NEW DELHI · NEW YORK · SYDNEY

Bloomsbury Academic

An imprint of Bloomsbury Publishing Plc

50 Bedford Square
London
WC1B 3DP
UK

1385 Broadway
New York
NY 10018
USA

www.bloomsbury.com

BLOOMSBURY and the Diana logo are trademarks of Bloomsbury Publishing Plc

First published in paperback 2015

First published 2014

British Library Cataloguing-in-Publication Data
A catalogue record for this book is available from the British Library.

ISBN: PB: 978–1–4742–4209–7
HB: 978–1–4725–1218–5
ePDF: 978–1–4725–0687–0
ePub: 978–1–4725–0982–6

Library of Congress Cataloging-in-Publication Data
A catalog record for this book is available from the Library of Congress.

Typeset by Newgen Knowledge Works (P) Ltd., Chennai, India
Printed and bound in Great Britain

for Nayere. . .

Contents

Notes on Contributors

Rex Butler is Reader in Art History in the School of English, Media Studies and Art History at the University of Queensland. He writes on both theory and visual art. His most recent book is the edited *Jeremy Gilbert-Rolfe: Art After Deconstruction* (Edition 3). He is currently completing *A Reader's Guide to Deleuze and Guattari's What is Philosophy?*

David Cunningham is Deputy Director of the Institute for Modern and Contemporary Culture at the University of Westminster in London, and a member of the editorial collective of the journal *Radical Philosophy*. He is an editor of collections on Adorno (2006) and photography and literature (2005), as well as of a special issue of the *Journal of Architecture* on post-war avant-gardes. Other writings on aesthetics, modernism and urban theory have appeared in publications including *Angelaki, Architectural Design, CITY, Journal of Visual Culture, New Formations* and *SubStance*. He is currently completing a book on the concept of the metropolis.

Mladen Dolar is Professor of Philosophy at the University of Ljubljana, Slovenia. His main areas of interest are German Idealism, psychoanalysis, contemporary French theory and philosophy of music. He is the co-founder of the Ljubljana School of Psychoanalysis. He is the author of numerous books, including: *A Voice and Nothing Else* and *Opera's Second Death* (with Slavoj Žižek).

Hélène Frichot has recently taken up a new position as Assistant Professor in the School of Architecture and the Built Environment, KTH, Stockholm, in the Critical Studies stream. She has co-curated the Architecture+Philosophy public lecture series in Melbourne, Australia (http://architecture.testpattern.com.au) since 2005. Between 2004–11 she held an academic position in the School of Architecture and Design, RMIT University. Her research examines the transdisciplinary field between architecture and philosophy (while her first discipline is architecture, she holds a PhD in philosophy from the University of Sydney, 2004). Hélène draws predominantly on the philosophical work of Gilles Deleuze and Félix Guattari, alongside other poststructuralist as well as feminist thinkers. Her published research has ranged widely from commentary on the ethico-aesthetics of contemporary digital architecture operating within the new biotechnological paradigm, to the role of emerging participatory and relational practices in the arts, including critical and creative spatial practices. She considers architecture-writing to be her mode of practice. A selection of recent publications include: 'On Finding Oneself Spinozist: Refuge, Beatitude and the Any-Space-Whatever', in Charles J. Stivale, Eugene W. Holland, Daniel W. Smith eds, *Gilles Deleuze: Image and Text*

(Continuum Press, 2009); 'Drawing, Thinking, Doing: From Diagram Work to the Superfold', in *ACCESS*, 30 (2011); 'What Can We Learn from the Bubble Man and His Atmospheric Ecologies', in *IDEA: Interior Ecologies* (2011), 'Following Hélène Cixous's Steps Towards a Writing Architecture', in Naomi Stead and Lee Stickells guest editors, *ATR (Architecture Theory Review)*, 15,3 (2010); edited volume Deleuze and Architecture, EUP, 2013, *forthcoming*.

Graeme Gilloch is *Critical Constellations* Reader in Sociology at Lancaster University in the United Kingdom. He has been a visiting research fellow at the Humboldt University in Berlin, at the Johann-Wolfgang Goethe University in Frankfurt am Main (with the support of the Alexander von Humboldt Stiftung) and, most recently, was a visiting research fellow at the Korean Studies Institute of Pusan National University in South Korea. Working in the area of social and cultural theory, his main research focus is the Critical Theory of the so-called Frankfurt School and in particular the writings of Walter Benjamin and Siegfried Kracauer. He is the author of two monographs on Benjamin (*Myth and Metropolis* 1996 and 2002, both with Polity Press, Cambridge) and numerous articles and book chapters exploring Critical Theory in relation to the writings of other theorists (Roland Barthes, Jean Baudrillard, Friedrich Kittler, Henri Lefebvre, Marc Augé) as well as contemporary filmmakers, artists and writers including, among others, Paul Auster, Orhan Pamuk and W. G. Sebald. The themes of urban experience, memory and visual culture are abiding preoccupations. Dr Gilloch is presently completing a book of essays on Kracauer and an edited collection (with Professor Jaeho Kang of the SOAS, University of London) of Kracauer writings on propaganda and political communication. His work has been translated into French, German, Italian, Polish and Korean and an Arabic edition of *Critical Constellations* is forthcoming.

Mark Jarzombek, Professor of the History and Theory of Architecture, is currently the Associate Dean of MIT's School of Architecture and Planning. He teaches in the History Theory Criticism programme (HTC) of the Department of Architecture. Jarzombek has taught at MIT since 1995. He has published on a wide range of historical topics from the Renaissance to the modern.

Nadir Lahiji is Associate Professor of Architecture at the University of Canberra. He holds a PhD in architecture theory from the University of Pennsylvania. He is the editor of *The Political Unconscious: Re-Opening Jameson's Narrative* (Ashgate, 2011) and editor of *Architecture Against the Post-political: Essays in Reclaiming the Critical Project* (Routledge, 2014). He has previously co-edited *Plumbing: Sounding Modern Architecture* (Princeton Architectural Press, 1997).

Andrew Leach is Associate Professor in the Griffith School of Environment and an Australian Research Council Future Fellow (2012–16). Among his books are *What Is Architectural History?* (Polity, 2010), *Manfredo Tafuri: Choosing History* (A&S, 2007) and the edited volumes *Architecture, Disciplinarity and the Arts* (A&S, 2009, with John Macarthur) and *Shifting Views* (UQP, 2008, with Antony Moulis and Nicole Sully).

Joel McKim is a Lecturer in the Department of Film, Media and Cultural Studies at Birkbeck, University of London. He has been a postdoctoral fellow at the Henry Clay Frick Department of the History of Art and Architecture at the University of Pittsburgh and the Department of Art History and Communication Studies at McGill University. He has recently co-edited an issue of the journal *Space & Culture* on the theme 'Spaces of Terror and Risk' and is working on a book-length project titled *Memory Complex: Competing Visions for a Post-9/11 New York*. His writing on architecture and conflict, political communication and memorial design, and media and architecture has appeared in the journals *Theory, Culture & Society, Borderlands, SITE* and *PUBLIC* and in the collections *Informal Architecture: Space and Contemporary Culture* and *The Politics of Cultural Memory*.

Todd McGowan teaches critical theory and film at the University of Vermont. His books include *Enjoying What We Don't Have: The Political Project of Psychoanalysis* (Nebraska), *Rupture: On the Emergence of the Political* (Northwestern) (with Paul Eisenstein), *Out of Time: The Ethics of Atemporal Cinema* (Minnesota), among others.

Gabriel Rockhill is Associate Professor of Philosophy at Villanova University, Directeur de programme at the Collège International de Philosophie in Paris and Chercheur associé at the Centre de Recherches sur les Arts et le Langage (CNRS/ EHESS). He is the author of *Logique de l'histoire: Pour une analytique des pratiques philosophiques* (Editions Hermann, 2010) and *Radical History and the Politics of Art* (Columbia University Press, 2014). He co-authored *Politics of Culture and the Spirit of Critique: Dialogues* (Columbia University Press, 2011), and he co-edited and contributed to *Jacques Rancière: History, Politics, Aesthetics* (Duke University Press, 2009) and *Technologies de contrôle dans la mondialisation: Enjeux politiques, éthiques et esthétiques* (Editions Kimé, 2009). He edited and translated Jacques Rancière's *The Politics of Aesthetics* (Continuum Books, 2004) as well as Cornelius Castoriadis's *Postscript on Insignificance* (Continuum Books, 2011). He is also the co-founder of the Machete Group, a collective of artists and intellectuals based in Philadelphia.

Douglas Spencer has studied design and architectural history, and cultural studies, and currently teaches on the Historical and Critical Thinking, and Landscape Urbanism programmes of the Architectural Association's Graduate School, as well as co-directing the school's research programme on Urban Prototypes. His research and writing on urbanism, architecture, film and critical theory has been published in journals including *Radical Philosophy, The Journal of Architecture* and *AA Files*. He has also contributed chapters to collections on urban design, utopian literature and contemporary architecture. He has recently completed his study of 'Architectural Deleuzism' and 'control society' for his Doctoral thesis at the University of Westminster.

Richard Charles Strong is currently a graduate student pursuing a doctoral degree from Villanova University in Villanova, Pennsylvania. He received his BA from DePaul University in Chicago, Illinois. He works primarily in the areas of nineteenth- and twentieth-century continental philosophy. At present, his primary research project is an investigation of the social, political, aesthetic and epistemological force of various conceptions of habit from Hume to Bourdieu.

Acknowledgements

I would like, first of all, to thank the contributors to this volume. They took this project seriously from its inception and made the intellectual content of this anthology highly satisfying by their rigorous writings. They helped me immensely along the way. David Cunningham read my introductory piece and offered helpful and incisive comments. He also took time to correct my tortured English and made it intelligible. My thanks also go to Richard Charles Strong who additionally read my own essay in this volume and helped it with his editorial corrections. I should mention my friend Donald Kunze who in turn read my introduction and offered his suggestions for its improvement, for which I am thankful.

My special thanks go to Mladen Dolar who graciously responded to our invitation by granting us an interview. Gabriel Rockhill and I sat down with him in Philadelphia where we conducted our interview. For the memorable and pleasant time we spent with him and for his thought-provoking conversation, I am grateful to him. It was especially wonderful to hear a prominent contemporary philosopher for what he has to say about architecture, who having written on opera and music with so much philosophical insight, modestly makes no claim on knowledge of architecture. I would like to thank Gabriel for putting a lot of time and effort into editing and polishing the text of our interview.

I would like to thank Colleen Coalter at Bloomsbury. I am grateful to her for throwing her support behind this project and for the pleasant time she spent with me discussing the book at its early stage, when I met her in London. At Bloomsbury, I am also indebted to Andrew Wardell for his patient and great assistance in the entire process of editing and production of this book. Also, I would like to thank Srikanth Srinivasan and the entire copy-editing team for their excellence work.

This book is dedicated to my sister, Nayere Zaeri.

Introduction: Philosophy and Architecture: Encounters and Missed Encounters, Idols and Idolatries

Can the art of architecture be a 'cipher for social antagonisms'?[1] This is the question for which the contemporary radical philosophy has failed to provide an answer. This failure is the crux of the proposed title for the present book, which claims that contemporary radical philosophy has missed its encounter with architecture.

Why this missed encounter?[2] From the outset, one, however, is justified to ask: what exactly does the word 'radical' in the term *radical philosophy* signify? At this point, it will be useful to bear in mind that any radical theory must first firmly locate architecture in the nexus of *art* and radical *politics,* and between politics and aesthetics, to which a number of contemporary radical thinkers have contributed novel theories. These theories are mainly focused on the lines of debate that concern not only a 'political problematization of the concept of aesthetics' but also that '*direct politicization of aesthetics*' which was originally the project of the historical avant-gardes in the interwar years of the twentieth century.[3] In our time, radical thinkers have offered complex analyses for a redefinition or '*de-definition of the aesthetics*' linked to redefinitions of 'politics' (Alliez and Osborne, 2013). Alain Badiou's concept of 'Inaesthetics' and Jacques Rancière's of the 'distribution of the sensible' [*le partage du sensible*], to name two prominent cases, are among the most challenging ideas that are being widely discussed today by numerous commentators.[4] If, after Kant, the case can be made that the formation of aesthetics is simply 'the displacement of political desire into philosophical discourse about the structure of feelings through form' (Alliez and Osborne, 2013, p. 8), then the thesis underpinning a contemporary account of aesthetics must be the conviction that any political thinking must a priori be grounded in philosophical thought, notwithstanding the reservation registered by the same philosophers with regard to the notion of 'political philosophy' as a specific discipline.[5]

These critical discourses should have a direct bearing on recovering the lost radical political thought and criticism to be found in architectural discourse of the late 1960s and early 1970s – mainly in the Italian context – which was replaced by postmodern or poststructuralist philosophy imported into the architectural discipline beginning in the 1980s. The effects of this importation (to be discussed in more detail below), in the absence of a politico-philosophical discourse on aesthetics, have brought us to the point in the state of contemporary architecture that can be characterized as a transition from 'aesthetics sans politicization' to its end point, that is, the aestheticization of theory and practice verging on '*anaestheticization*', to use the term described by Susan Buck-Morss in her 'revisiting' of Walter Benjamin's 1936 *Artwork* essay.[6] This aesthetic 'indistinction' blocks the distinction of *aisthesis*, in the sense discussed by Benjamin and Rancière,[7] from the reigning contemporary image industry, which comes to serve the 'spectacle of capital-become-image'.[8]

In the *longue durée* of modern philosophical thoughts on art in the Western tradition, the last significant piece of writing on architecture is still the one written by the 'last' philosopher, Hegel, posthumously published, almost 200 years ago, as the *Lectures on Aesthetics*. Hegel's lectures roughly coincide with the rise of modern architecture around the turn of nineteenth century and the writings of revolutionary architect and theoretician Jean-Nicolas-Louis Durand, the teacher at the École Polytechnique in Paris.[9] By this time, architecture had begun to enter the cultural discourse of incipient capitalism but in the absence of any critical discourse about its role and function, it came to be connected, on the one hand, to radical revolutionary thought, and, on the other, to commodity culture, radical politics and aesthetics. Before Hegel, we find only architectural figures or the 'metaphor of architecture', which go back to Plato and get repeated in Descartes, Kant and Hegel himself. (The case of Nietzsche and his own use of the 'architectural metaphor' is a different case that I will discuss in a moment.) It must be pointed out here that, between the time of Hegel and our present age, no modern philosophical writings on architecture can perhaps compete with Hegel's essay in scope and depth, exhaustive if not exhausting, notwithstanding the various criticisms made against it. It is not an exaggeration to claim that the success and failure of every philosophical thought on architecture by any philosopher has to come to terms with Hegel's contribution, whether in its affirmation or refutation, not to mention in the hostility directed towards his philosophical system from Nietzsche to Gilles Deleuze. Needless to say, the time of Hegel's lectures and of the 'post-Kantian' period more generally, which is replete with philosophical writings on the arts, also belongs to the aftermath of the French Revolution and the Enlightenment, in which philosophical writings were characteristically connected to politics (Alliez and Osborne, 2013).

The 'metaphor of music', so to speak, never entered philosophy before Nietzsche with such intensity as can be found in his writing. It must be kept in mind that the reason for the ubiquitous presence of architectural figures and metaphors in the texts of philosophers from Plato onwards has been tied up with a project of 'grounding and stabilizing otherwise unstable philosophical systems' (Karatani, 1995, p. 4). This 'grounding' is never the aim of the metaphor of music. Nietzsche, and his decisive influence on architecture in the early years of the twentieth century, in this regard, is a unique case. The history of the immediate past, mainly over the last three decades, as regards the influence of philosophy on architecture has been limited to the hegemony of poststructuralist philosophy and Anglophone neopragmatism, which is still exerting an unwarranted influence on architectural discourse in the academy, albeit with diminishing returns and declining influence. Poststructuralism came with those anti-Platonist and anti-Hegelian strands which entered architectural discourse with the aim to weaken or 'deconstruct' the Kantian 'architectonics' of reason and to dampen the '*will to architecture*'.[10] This weakening of 'architectonic reason' is mainly due to the so-called French Nietzscheans. The French poststructuralists returned to Nietzsche and to his claim that 'Plato' is the name of 'sickness' from which one has to be cured. In fact, twentieth-century philosophical projects, as Slavoj Žižek reminds us, were united against Plato and the 'tyranny' of *reason*.[11] Consider what Nietzsche wrote in his *The Twilight of the Idols*:

> If one needs to make a tyrant of *reason*, as Socrates did, then there must exist no little danger of something else playing the tyrant. Rationality was at that time divined as a *saviour*; neither Socrates nor his 'invalids' were free to be rational or not, as they wished – it was *de rigueur*, it was their *last* expedient. The fanaticism with which the whole of Greek thought throws itself at rationality betrays a state of emergency: one was in peril, one had only one choice: either to perish or – be *absurdly rational.* . . . The moralism of the Greek philosophers from Plato downwards is pathologically conditioned: likewise their estimation of dialectics. Reason = virtue = happiness means merely: one must imitate Socrates and counter the dark desires by producing a permanent *daylight* – the daylight of reason. One must be prudent, clear, bright at any cost: every yielding to the instincts, to the unconscious, leads *downwards*. (Nietzsche, 1968, p. 33)

However, the poststructuralist return to Nietzsche overlooked Nietzsche's 'romanticist disposition' (Karatani, 1995). 'In opposition to reason', Karatani writes, 'romanticists regard as essential the manifold and contingency – immanent in concepts like, body, affect, feeling, and the like' (1995, p. 9). The 'French Nietzscheans', mainly Jacques Derrida, Michel Foucault and Gilles Deleuze, accomplished respectively deconstructive, genealogical and vitalist readings of philosophy (Schrift, 1995). In particular, it was Nietzschean *vitalism*, via Bergson, that entered Gilles Deleuze's oeuvre, whose philosophy has since the 1990s been continually discussed, albeit in a problematically reductive fashion, in academic architectural theory. But the current radical philosophy is not obsessed with Nietzsche or his anti-Platonism. On the contrary, the hallmark of radical philosophy today, at least in the work of some of its prominent representatives, including Alain Badiou and Slavoj Žižek, is a re-turn to Plato, contra Nietzsche, letting itself be contaminated with his 'sickness' and no longer seeking a cure! Moreover, there is no pretension anymore in our radical philosophers to be the 'architects of new civilization' *à la* Nietzsche. It is rather a kind of return to the Kantian or Hegelian 'architectonic system' that is becoming the foundation of *radical* philosophy, which is not anymore bent on a 'deconstructive' act of weakening the 'will to architecture'.

Here, we can surmise the main factor that would constitute the element of 'radicality' in today's radical philosophy: It is, characteristically, a 'new materialism' which is combined with a 'return' to Plato, and in various ways, I would contend, to an 'architectonic system' in Kantian or Hegelian fashion. For Badiou, Nietzsche's philosophy is the exemplar case of an *antiphilosophy*.[12] This would no doubt have come *ex post facto* as a surprise to those architects and avant-garde artists in the early decades of the twentieth century who largely embraced *one philosophy*, that is, Nietzschean philosophy. Whereas a host of philosophers have variously influenced architects and architectural critics from the late 1960s to present, it is perhaps not an overstatement to say that it was only Nietzsche who imparted a singular influence on architects and avant-garde artists in the early twentieth century, to entirely different effects. I want to briefly examine this influence in high modernism and its impact on the architecture field. This will help to place the contemporary relation between philosophy and architecture in a larger historical perspective.

For Nietzsche, who was more interested in *Kunstwollen* than the visual arts, architecture was the *first* art because it directly manifests the 'will to power'.[13] In *The Twilight of the Idols*, Nietzsche famously wrote:

> The *architect* represents neither a Dionysian nor an Apollonian condition: here it is the mighty act of will, the will which moves mountains, the intoxication of the strong will, which demands artistic expression. The most powerful men have always inspired the architects; the architect has always been influenced by power. Pride, victory over weight and gravity, the will to power, seek to render themselves visible in a building; architecture is a kind of rhetoric of power, now persuasive, even cajoling in form, now bluntly imperious. The highest feeling of power and security finds expression in that which possesses *grand style*. Power which no longer requires proving; which disdains to please; which is slow to answer; which is conscious of no witness around it; which lives oblivious of the existence of any opposition; which reposes in *itself*, fantastic, a law among laws: *that* is what speaks of itself in the form of grand style. (Nietzsche, 1968, p. 74)

Thus, architecture was for Nietzsche 'the aesthetic objectivization of the will to power'; it is architecture that constitutes 'the ecstasy of the great will': 'the edifice that manifests "pride, the defeat of gravity, the will to power"' (Bothe, 1999, p. x). As Bolf Bothe points out, when it comes to Nietzsche, the topic of art and architecture cannot be discussed in isolation from Weimar culture, 'that "enchanting" town in the shadow of Buchenwald, which ever since Goethe's time has oscillated between extremes of cosmopolitan openness and malignant philistinism. It is a place where "free spirits" have always needed themselves against pedagogues and "yes-men"' (Bothe, 1999, p. ix). Almost all the architects in the early twentieth century, from Henry Van de Velde to Peter Behrens, Mies van der Rohe and his friend and collaborator Ludwig Hilberseimer, to Bruno Taut, Eric Mendelssohn (as we are now informed by Fritz Neumeyer), and above all, to Le Corbusier – who read *Thus Spoke Zarathustra*, the 'Master Builder', twice; first in his early career as painter-architect and later in his old age – adhered to the prophetic words of Nietzsche, which, paradoxically if not contradictorily, were shared by both architects who followed *Neue Sachlichkeit*, or New Objectivity, *and* the so-called Expressionists (Bergius, 1999).[14] No less would the artist at the turn-of-the-century in Vienna and avant-garde artists in Futurist and Dada movements from Raoul Hausmann, Hugo Ball, Hanna Hoch, Johannes Baader, Hermann Finsterline, Kurt Schwitters and Georg Grosz and many others (Bergius, 1999). This period was the time of Weimar Republic and social democracy and radical political movements, the time of rising German industry, affecting all architects. The

Architectural programme at this time in the history of capitalist development was translated into a *social* programme. This was the time that capitalism had already fully entered commodity culture and the so-called society of consumption with its concomitant alienation and reification that saw its Marxist critics in Georg Lukács and others. It was also at this time that Benjamin and Ernst Bloch directly addressed architecture. Furthermore, it was at this time that the discourse of aesthetics entered the discourse of politics.[15]

In the span of time that can be marked from the moment after Hegel's writing to the twentieth century, up to 1960s, we can cite only rare occasions on which modern philosophers encountered architecture; always with brief contributions. In the short list, we might include Adorno, Benjamin, Kracauer, Bloch and Heidegger. With few exceptions, from the 1960s to our present time, the relationship between radical philosophy and architecture has mainly been a case of a missed encounter. Jürgen Habermas, writing in the tradition of the Critical Theory of the Frankfurt School, has devoted one essay directly to architecture and another one in which he indirectly addresses architecture.[16] Similarly, in the philosophical environment of poststructuralism, we encounter only sporadic and brief thoughts from the likes of Michel Foucault, Jacques Derrida, Gilles Deleuze and Jean Baudrillard on architecture. Henri Lefevbre and the theorists associated with the Situationist International and Paul Virilio, on the other hand, represent some exceptions who paid a more serious attention to architecture and the analysis of the city.[17]

Architects of the so-called heroic period of modernism shared Nietzsche's desire for a liberation from the dead weight of history in a total act of purification and 'elimination': 'Nietzsche remodeled historicist architecture into the architecture of present, and he did so as an artist. "He who eliminates is an artist": an artist who can "see no value in anything unless it knows how to become form"' (Buddensieg, 1999, p. 266). The objective was to remove the content from the old architecture, as Nietzsche said, 'What nonartists call "form," the artist regards as content' (in Buddensieg, 1999, p. 266).

Nietzsche constantly engaged in an analogy between music and architecture, especially in relation to the 'grand style' about which he spoke in *The Twilight of the Idols* (as was quoted above). In a letter to Carl Fuchs, dated mid-April 1886, he wrote: 'Forgive me if I add one thing more. It is the *Grand Style* from which decadence is further removed: a description that applies to the Palazzo Pitti but not to the Ninth Symphony. The Grand Style, as the ultimate intensification of the art of melody' (in Buddensieg, 1999, p. 270). In a posthumous fragment he wrote, 'Will to power as art . . . No musician has yet ever built like the architect who built the Palazzo Pitti . . . Does music perhaps belong to a culture in which dominion of men of power, of every kind, has already come to an end?' (in Buddensieg, 1999, p. 270). It is in this musical analogy that pure form or 'emptiness' and freedom from content in architecture are obtained (Buddensieg, 1999). As Fritz Neumeyer points out, Nietzsche's thesis of the birth of art 'from the spirit of music' was instructive and attractive for the architect Eric Mendelsohn: 'An "architectural" feeling for music, which emphasized the importance of rhythm and, with Nietzsche, considered rhythm to be the origin of all poetry, led Mendelsohn to his own "musical" – and specifically rhythmic – feeling for architecture'

(Neumeyer, 1999, p. 294). In the widely cited aphorism 218 in *Human, All Too Human*, Nietzsche wrote:

> *The stone is more stone than before.* In general we no longer understand architecture, at least by far in the way we understand music. We have outgrown the symbolism of lines and figures, as we have grown unaccustomed to the tonal effects of rhetoric, no longer having sucked in this kind of cultural mother's milk from the first moment of life. Originally everything about a Greek or Christian building meant something, and in reference to a higher order of things. This atmosphere of inexhaustible meaningfulness hung about the building like a magic veil. Beauty entered the system secondarily, impairing the basic feeling of uncanny sublimity, of sanctification by magic or the god's nearness. At the most, beauty tempered the *dread* – but this dread was the prerequisite everywhere. What does the beauty of a building mean to us now? The same as the beautiful face of a mindless woman: something masklike. (Nietzsche, 1984, pp. 130–31)

What is crucial to note in this passage is that Nietzsche, the artist-philosopher, regarded himself as 'a kind of architect of imagination' and wanted to see the edifice of his own thought as 'the mind that builds'. He wanted this 'art of thinking' to be synonymous with an 'art of building' in which the verbal noun *building* would be a fundamental human activity in creating form. This notion was not lost to the modern architects of the early twentieth century. As Neumeyer remarks, 'Known in German as the New Building, *das Neue Bauen*, the modern architecture of the 1920s was proclaimed by an avant-garde that summed up its weariness with traditional architecture by protesting the dishonest "masquerade" of fancy-dress facades' (Neumeyer, 1999, p. 286). Adolf Loos had sarcastically called this 'masquerade' a 'Potemkin city' (Loos, 1982). A new architecture thus must not only liberate itself from the past historicist dead weight of history but also must return to the act of building, rejecting 'architecture'. In this sense, the word 'architecture' was associated with 'ideology'.[18] 'In itself', as Neumeyer says, 'the choice of the verbal noun *Bauen* [building] should be interpreted as a principled rejection of *Architektur*' (Neumeyer, 1999, p. 286). *Building*, and not 'architecture', can be associated with the '*disenchantment of the world*' to use Max Weber's term.

In 1919, in the wake of Spartacus uprising, Weber wrote:

> The fate of our time is characterized by rationalization and intellectualization and, above all, by the disenchantment of the world. It is precisely the supreme, the most sublime values that have been recreated from the public life, either into the transcendental realm of the mystical life or into the brotherliness of immediate human relations. It is no accident that our great art is intimate, not monumental, nor that it is amidst the smallest communities, between individual human beings, *pianissimo*, that there pulsates something corresponding to the prophetic *pneuma* that once swept like wildlife through the great communities and welded them together. If we try to force or 'invent' monumentality, the upshot will be a lamentable malformation, like the many monuments of the last twenty years. And

if we try to devise new religions bereft of genuine new prophetic inspiration, the result will be inwardly similar, only with still worse effects.[19]

Irving Wohlfarth, who takes up the above passage for an extensive and stimulatingly astute commentary, asks: 'What, then, might an "honest," truly disenchanted architecture look like?' (Wohlfarth, 1999, p. 144).[20] He seeks the answer in the writings of the historian of modern architecture, Siegfried Giedion, along with Walter Benjamin, both of whom read Nietzsche.[21] 'Under modern conditions', Wohlfarth writes, 'truth in architecture is, from this perspective, more or less synonymous with functionalism and constructivism – that is, with a building style that no longer masks iron girders as Pompeian columns' (Wohlfarth, 1999, p. 144). Further he writes, 'The historicist charades of emerging modern architecture, Benjamin and Giedion argue, faithfully mirror the contradictions of the nineteenth-century bourgeoisie. What holds for state and society at large is also true for art and architecture. "Just as" Napoleon did not, or would not, recognize the functional nature of the state as an instrument of the bourgeois class, "so," Benjamin claims, the Master Builders of his time failed to recognize the functional nature of Iron' (Wohlfarth, 1999, p. 144). Wohlfarth in this passage is quoting Benjamin from his exposé of 1935, 'Paris, the Capital of the Nineteenth Century.'[22] Pointing out Marx's 'architectural metaphor' of sub- and superstructure, Wohlfarth sharply remarks that 'superstructure as a facade served to conceal the (glass and steel) substructure from view. The bourgeoisie *refused*, in short, to consider itself "with sober eyes." Therein lies the essence of what Marx, Giedion, and Benjamin respectively termed "ideology" (or "false consciousness"), "historicizing masks," and "Phantasmagoria," the latter being in turn equated by Benjamin with the "collective dream consciousness and superstructure"' (Wohlfarth, 1999, p. 145). As Wohlfarth continues, 'Functionalism may be understood in this context as a *new* soberness, a *Neue Sachlichkeit*, a *second* disenchantment of the world' (Wohlfarth, 1999, p. 145). Echoing Nietzsche's last sentence in the passage from *Human All Too Human* quoted above, Wohlfarth writes:

At both aesthetic and sociopolitical levels, the dishonesty in question had consisted in a *self-denying functionalism*. The rationalization of social and architectural construction had been accompanied by a tendency to mask the new nakedness with obsolete drapery. The inexorable disenchantment and reactive re-enchantment of the world thus formed a fatal couple. For Weber, as for Marx, honesty consisted, on the contrary, in taking disenchantment at its word. (Wohlfarth, 1999, p. 145)[23]

Weber resists all re-enchantments of the world, Wohlfarth reminds us. Nietzsche would vehemently attack historicist eclecticism. Nietzsche's famous phrase, '*The stone is more stone than before*', according to Wohlfarth, sums up 'the dilemma of building and dwelling in the disenchanted world. The history of modern architecture is a series of answers to the challenge that this dictum poses' (Wohlfarth, 1999, p. 149). But, 'What Nietzsche did *not* care to say is that stone was also *less* stone than before; that its iron and steel underpinning and reinforced concrete made it possible to construct ever-higher high-rise buildings, which, while certainly not calculated to accommodate the Superman, were no longer built on human scale' (Wohlfarth, 1999, p. 149). About Nietzsche's statement in *The Twilight of the Idols,* where he wrote, '[t]he most powerful men have always inspired the architects; the architect has always been under the spell of power', Wohlfarth offers the following astute comments:

> Insofar as the Nietzschean 'will to power' is not always sufficiently distinguished from the power that be, his *Baumeister* [The Master Builder] belongs to a line that extends from Napoleon to the totalitarian dictators of the twentieth-century – master architects who, along with their house architects, have sought to immortalize their imperial order in appropriately monumental forms. To Napoleon III, his Haussmann; to Hitler, his Speer. Such examples are a parody, at once tawdry and searching, of what Nietzsche had in mind. *They confirm Weber's verdict that the twilight of the idols is also that of an architecture built in their image.* (Wohlfarth, 1999, p. 151) [emphasis added]

Wohlfarth's reflections aptly summarize the condition of thought under which the architects in the 'heroic' phase of modernism took Nietzsche as *the* philosopher to 'guide' them in building for the new 'disenchanted world', to serve and fulfil Nietzsche's master architect's dream of casting the 'will to power in stone', notwithstanding Benjamin's reaction to this 'will' with his own notion of the 'constructor'.[24]

With the last sentence I emphasized in Wohlfarth's commentary above, in effect, the idea of building in the image of the 'Idols' becomes the story of a contemporary 're-enchantment of the world', a return to 'architecture' as *ideology*. Let us now leave behind the early decades of the twentieth century and come to the present panorama of architecture and to the contention we are advancing in the present anthology about the missed encounter or the absent confrontation of radical philosophy with contemporary architectural 'Idols' to which I now want to turn. I only add here that Max Weber's verdict is perhaps still valid, even prophetic, for an explanation of our own predicament.

Idolatry has returned to the scene of contemporary art and culture. As Boris Groys has argued in his *Art Power*, the Iconoclastic Enlightenment, which had triumphed over the Christian Iconophilia, was supposed to have driven it out once and for all from our tradition of radical secularism. Hegel had announced this victory in his famous 'art is the thing of the past' (Groys, 2008).[25] But the contemporary culture industry has perniciously brought Iconophilia back onto the scene of culture. In this context, the figures of architecture as new Idols have become the main vehicles for the transmission and proliferation of this Idolatry in affirmation of the libidinal economy of consumer capitalism. The premise of the present collection is based on the argument that while our radical philosophers have generally noticed this return of Idolatry to the visual arts, and while few have seen it only in music, still, all have entirely overlooked its presence in architecture. Within this context, it can be argued that it is incumbent upon radical philosophy to recover or to reinvent the discourse of 'ideology critique' of architectural Idols that are embedded in the current Iconophilia of the digital image industry of global capitalism. Architectural Idols directly participate in and abet this new 're-enchantment of the world' and its phantasmagoria in late capitalism. The master architects of our time, 'dishonestly', as Wohlfarth would say, are once again bent on *immortalizing* 'the imperial order in appropriately monumental forms'.

As I stated at the beginning of this Introduction, the recent radical turn that has marked philosophy – some call it 'revolution' – has yet to take up architectural figures of Iconophilia for a critique, largely because its encounter with an architectural system of illusion, fantasy and fiction presiding over contemporary ideology has fundamentally been missed. In his 1935 exposé, to which Wohlfarth has alluded as seen above, Benjamin wrote: 'Just as Napoleon failed to understand the functional nature of the state as an instrument of domination by the bourgeois class, so the architects of his time failed to understand the functional nature of iron. . . .' If I may, I want to transpose Benjamin's statement into a contemporary analogical statement that can be read like this: 'just as the new imperial authoritarian neoliberal state apparatus fails to understand the functional nature of the State as an instrument of domination of the new financial bourgeois aristocracy, so the contemporary architects fail to understand the functional nature of architectural Idols in iron and glass, that they help to create, as an instrument of cultural domination in the hands of this State.'

Less than 100 years ago, in 1921 to be precise, Walter Benjamin penned an extraordinary fragment titled 'Capitalism as Religion', only published posthumously (Benjamin, 1996). In this piece Benjamin wrote: 'A religion may be discerned in capitalism – that is to say, capitalism serves essentially to allay the same anxieties, torments, and disturbances to which the so-called religions offered answers' (Benjamin, 1996, p. 288). In taking Max Weber to task, Benjamin further argued: 'The proof of the religious structure of capitalism – not merely, as Weber believes, as a formation conditioned by religion, but as an essentially religious phenomenon – would still lead even today to the folly of an endless universal polemic' (Benjamin, 1996, p. 288). Rather than being the secularization of the Protestant ethic, Benjamin argues, capitalism develops parasitically from Christianity in the West: '(this must be shown not just in the case of Calvinism, but in other orthodox Christian churches), until it reaches the point where Christianity's history is essentially that of its parasite – that is to say, of capitalism' (Benjamin, 1996, p. 288). According to Benjamin, three aspects of this religious structure of capitalism can be discerned: 'In the first place, capitalism is a purely cultic religion, perhaps the most extreme that ever existed. In capitalism, things have a meaning only in their relationship to the cult; capitalism has no specific body of dogma, no theology. It is from this point of view that utilitarianism acquires its religious overtones' (Benjamin, 1996, p. 289). Benjamin relates the 'concretization of the cult' to the second aspect of capitalism: 'the permanence of the cult. Capitalism is the celebration of a cult *sans rêve et sans merci* [without dream and mercy]' (Benjamin, 1996, p. 289). And the third aspect is that the cult makes guilt pervasive. The notion of 'cult', Benjamin claimed, underlines the meaning of things in capitalism: 'Capitalism is a religion of pure cult, without dogma' (Benjamin, 1996, p. 288). Capitalist religion is all about *guilt* and not atonement, Benjamin said. 'The nature of the religious movement which is capitalism entails endurance right to the end, to the point where God, too, finally takes on the entire burden of guilt, to the point where the universe has been taken over by that despair which is actually its secret *hope*' (Benjamin, 1996, p. 289). For Benjamin, capitalism is a religion, therefore, which does not offer the reform of existence but simply its destruction. Benjamin further notes that Nietzsche is the first philosopher who formulated this cult of capitalist religion in his conception of the Superman. 'This man is superman, the first to recognize the religion of capitalism and begin to bring to fulfillment' (Benjamin, 1996, p. 288).[26]

In the light of Benjamin's commentary, we must recognize, I want to argue, the rise of a yet *new* religion, a cult of architecture, within contemporary capitalism, beyond Hegel's 'art as religion', that is, the rise of religion of architectural Idols as 'high art', for a deceptive 're-enchantment' of the world. What is the function of these new Idols? Is it possible to subtract this new religion, the architectural Idols, from the contemporary religion of capitalism? An answer may be sought in Marx's famous remarks in his 'Towards a Critique of Hegel's *Philosophy of Right*', and by its transposition I will attempt below. First, Marx's statement:

> *Religious* suffering is the *expression* of real suffering and at the same time the *protest* against real suffering. Religion is the sigh of the oppressed creature, the heart of heartless world, as it is the spirit of spiritless conditions. It is *opium* of the people.
>
> The abolition of religion as people's *illusory* happiness is the demand for their *real* happiness. The demand to abandon illusion about their condition is a *demand to abandon a condition which requires illusions*. The criticism of religion is thus in *embryo* a *criticism of the vale of tears* whose *halo* is religion. (Marx, 1994, p. 28)

I indecorously transpose the above statement that can be put as following:

> 'The demand to abolish the *illusion* of architecture Idolatry as the religion of contemporary capitalism, to abolish the illusory happiness, the enjoyment, in its culture by architectural Idols, is to *demand to abolish a condition which requires this illusion*. The criticism of architectural idols is thus in *embryo* a *criticism of the vale of tears* whose *halo* is architecture as religion!' The meaning of Marx's comments must in essence be understood in these terms: *What must be 'practically' abolished cannot merely be 'theoretically' critiqued.*[27]

And, yet, we must *critically* ask: In the contemporary constellation of ideology, what nefarious impact does architecture have over culture and society? While our prominent philosophers have devoted stimulating and sophisticated writings to the analysis of the ideological impacts of music, literature, cinema, opera, theatre and other forms of arts on contemporary culture, no significant or comprehensive contribution to the analysis of architecture has been attempted. Instead, attention has been accorded more or less exclusively to 'Musica Ficta', to cite Phillip Lacoue-Labarthe's potent term indicating how music, in his view, has now become the dominant ideological mode in modern culture over all other forms of art to which certain other philosophers have subscribed. Our prominent radical philosophers seem to have come to a tacit agreement on the supremacy of music over culture and ideology. Slavoj Žižek praises Adorno's analysis of the composer Richard Wagner by asserting that, for the first time, Adorno 'combined' a Marxist reading of musical work of art as a 'cipher for social antagonisms' with the 'highest musicological analysis' (Žižek, 2009, p. viii). The late Lacoue-Labarthe, in turn, whose influential *Musica Ficta (Figures of Wagner)* (Lacoue-Labarthe, 1994) is dedicated to the critical analysis of the German composer, is exemplary in coining the term 'musicolatry' to underscore his own negative reading of Wagner's continuing influence today. He wrote:

> The fact that, as nihilism has taken hold in the wake of Wagner, music, with even more powerful techniques than those Wagner himself invented, has continued to invade our world and has clearly taken precedence over all other art forms including the visual arts – the fact that 'musicolatry' has taken up where idolatry left off is perhaps a first attempt at an answer. (Lacoue-Labarthe, 1994, p. 115)

Alain Badiou who in his *Five Lessons on Wagner* effectively takes apart Lacoue-Labarthe's anti-Wagnerian stand, nevertheless endorses the latter's notion of 'musicolatry'. He reaffirms that music in contemporary culture has become an idol functioning as a main operator in contemporary ideology. And, yet, Lacoue-Labarthe's thesis that the Wagnerian apparatus is a vehicle – albeit a problematic one – for the aestheticization of politics, as well as Badiou's understanding of 'the transformation of music into an ideological operator, which in art, always involves constituting a people; that is, figuring or configuring a politics' (Badiou, 2010, p. 9), instructively indicate how one might approach this issue in relation to architecture's nefarious role in contemporary culture. The current institutionalized elevation of architecture to the status of 'high' art in the service of a cultural *dispositif* of post-political, post-ideological and post-critical discourses would seem to indicate, to paraphrase Lacoue-Labarthe, an *Idolatry of Architecture*, that can be put in an equally awkward neologism 'architectolatry' (akin to his 'musicolatry') in contemporary culture. I contend that this Idolatry is in a dire need of an Iconoclastic gesture on the part of radical philosophy.

This anthology was conceived to address the lacuna that exists in the writings of contemporary radical thinkers on the Left who have written persuasively on aesthetics, ideology and arts, especially on music, but have failed to thematize architecture's aesthetic-political function. One important fault line can be traced to Lacoue-Labarthe's argument, made in the same book referred to above, that 'Before the invention of photography revealed, with the violence that is well known, the threat that hung over "the work of art in the age of mechanical reproduction" [a reference to Walter Benjamin's *Artwork* essay], music, even more than painting or architecture – in any case in a much more spectacular manner – was the site of formidable technological innovations, which not only affected instrumentation but also worked toward amplification' (Lacoue-Labarthe, 1994, p. xx). This statement would seem to contradict Benjamin's own thoughts about architecture as the 'canonic art' and as 'concrete a priori' means of perception in the technological organization of experience through human sensorium.[28] But does music take absolute precedence over all other forms of art in the so-called technological age? How should we interpret Nietzsche's saying, in *Human, All Too Human* quoted in the epigraph above: 'In general we no longer understand architecture, at least by far in the way we understand music.' Should we agree with Lacoue-Labarthe when he says: 'Music, in other words, carries *aisthesis* to its limit: it gives the sensation, infinitely paradoxical, of the condition of all sensation, as if the impossible of presentation itself, in general, were incumbent upon it'? (Lacoue-Labarthe, 1994, p. 31). But what we learn from our prominent contemporary radical philosophers, whether they address architecture or not, is nevertheless the fundamental insight that it is only in the configuration of politics that aesthetics can be staged. Criticism of art or architecture as 'religion' starts with this insight.

Slavoj Žižek, among the radical thinkers most often cited today – namely, Jacques Rancière, Giorgio Agamben, Jean-Luc Nancy, Alain Badiou, Antonio Negri – is the one to be credited who, in the wake of Fredric Jameson's critical interventions in architecture discourse over the past three decades, has taken up contemporary architecture for a critical analysis, albeit briefly in a chapter in his *Living in the End Times* (Žižek, 2010). Žižek's contribution so far is in step with Adorno's, who devoted only one seminal essay to architecture in his lifetime.[29] But, how much legitimacy is there in Adorno's assertion that music is always the 'unique artistic medium' for the declining bourgeoisie? Can we talk equally about architectural ideology and its role in the libidinal economy of contemporary culture and capitalism? With this question we come back to the question I posed at the beginning of this Introduction: What would be the contour of a 'highest architectural analysis', which can then recast architecture as 'a cipher for social antagonism'? If in the short durée of the philosophical discourse of modernity, the discourse on art cannot be separated from critical-political discourse, in an even shorter span of time from the late 1960s to our present time, the discourse of radical philosophy cannot be divorced from discourses on radical politics and aesthetics. Yet, within the same short period, radical philosophy has failed to take on architecture in any significant fashion on a par with Adorno's great reflections on music. To conclude: As was claimed at the beginning of this introduction, the critique of this situation has been the guiding idea in conceiving this collection.

The contributors to this anthology were invited to address the conspicuous absence of the treatment of architecture in the writings of the prominent radical philosophers of our time. They come from different disciplines and academic backgrounds. From the prominent positions they occupy in their respective departments of philosophy and critical theory, architecture and art theory, cultural studies, literary criticism, film studies and sociology, they all have taken a keen interest in addressing the same question that was posed to them from different angles, offering compelling arguments and novel analyses. Some have gone back to the philosophers of German Idealism, Kant and Hegel, to illuminate and critique the conception of architecture and the city in the work of these philosophers (Todd McGowan and Mark Jarzombek). In one case, we are offered a comprehensive analysis of the relation between art and radical politics, and the encounters and missed encounters of critical thinkers with architecture, within a larger historical view in the twentieth century (Gabriel Rockhill). The vexed question of the relation between art *and* architecture, or art *in* architecture, within the dialectical relation between 'autonomy' and 'heteronomy', in the work of those radical philosophers who did not miss the encounter with architecture in the twentieth century, mainly Walter Benjamin and Theodor Adorno, is discussed and scrutinized in one highly analytical essay (David Cunningham). Still, certain concepts and analytical methods in the work of the same critical philosophers and radical thinkers in the twentieth century who had some fruitful encounters with architecture, prominently Walter Benjamin and Sigfried Kracuer, are adopted as a tool of analysis in the expanded field to discuss certain singular buildings with reference to literature and cinema (Graeme Gilloch). The works of the same radical thinkers are equally taken to task for their analysis of architecture. In a persuasive argument, Walter Benjamin's thoughts on architecture are scrutinized and critiqued, while, at the same time, his conceptual insights are extracted and analysed for their possible applicability to the state of architecture in our own time (Richard Charles Strong). Conversely, those contributors to this collection who come from the discipline of architecture have variously discussed critics, architects and historians of architecture from inside the discipline who are influenced by radical thinkers. One special case is the reading of Mario Tronti in Italy by the Marxist architectural historian Manfredo Tafuri in the 1960s and early 1970s, which is analysed within a highly complex view of 'historical understanding' (Andrew Leach). The philosophy of 'new materialism' is the subject of an analytical study in relation to contemporary thought on architectural 'infrastructure', with a sharp critique of those writers and architects inside the discipline who have failed in their conceptualizations of the same idea (Joel McKim). In another case, a critique of contemporary 'image fatigues' in architecture and architectural education is offered using the notion of 'thought image' in the philosophy of Gilles Deleuze (Hélène Frichot). Yet, the non-serious and instrumental reading of the same philosopher by a group of elite architectural theorists and critics from the inside of the discipline in the academy has been subjected to a critical scrutiny of their relation to the imperatives of a current state of global financial capitalism and its impact on architecture (Douglas Spencer). In this case, we are informed that the advocacy of this group of intellectuals of the work of contemporary critical philosophers does not go beyond so-called applied philosophy to practices of theory and building. They fail in the same way that the architects in the nineteenth century, accordingly to Benjamin in his 1935 and 1939 exposés, failed to understand the relationship of architecture to the structure of power and state, letting themselves be exposed to the *perversions* of capitalism. And finally, in the same vein, the naïve 'application' of philosophy in architectural discourse is discussed under the term *antiphilosophy* adopted from the writings of radical philosopher Alain Badiou. In this case, the same group of critics and architects in the discipline are taken to task for their misappropriation of the critical philosophy they deploy (Nadir Lahiji).

Notes

1   A case has been made for music by contemporary radical philosophy. Slavoj Žižek in his critical evaluation of Adorno's analysis of the composer Richard Wagner asserts that, for the first time, Adorno 'combined' a Marxist reading of musical work of art as a 'cipher for social antagonisms' with the 'highest musicological analysis', see Slavoj Žižek, 'Foreword: Why Is Wagner Worth Saving', in Theodor Adorno, *In Search of Wagner*. London and New York: Verso, 2009, p. viii. Elsewhere, Žižek remarks that Adorno's *Philosophy of Modern Music* is a masterpiece of materialist analysis of the music in the twentieth century.

2   To put the question more precisely: Why has critical reading of architecture lagged behind that of the musical art by the contemporary radical philosophers? Which one of these, architecture or music, takes the pride of the place as the main ideological vector in the constellation of contemporary culture? Is it legitimate to compare only these two forms of art with each other at the expense of the others? I have taken up this comparison further in the text.

3   See Eric Alliez and Peter Osborne, *Spheres of Action: Art and Politics*. London: Tate, 2013. Also see the contribution by Gabriel Rockhill and David Cunningham to this volume.

4   See Alain Badiou, *Handbook of Inaesthetics*. Alberto Toscao (trans.). Stanford: Stanford University Press, 2005; Jacques Rancière, *The Politics of Aesthetics*. Afterword by Slavoj Žižek. Gabriel Rockhill (trans. and intro.). London and New York: Continuum, 2004; see also Jacques Rancière's 'Aesthetics, Inaesthetics and Anti-aesthetics', *Think Again: Alain Badiou and the Future of Philosophy*. Peter Hallward (ed.). London and New York: Continuum, 2004. See the excellent comparison between Badiou and Rancière on this issue by Gabriel Rockhill in his essay titled 'Recent Developments in Aesthetics: Badiou, Rancière, and Their Interlocutors' in *The History of Continental Philosophy*. A. Schrift (ed.), vol. 8. *Emerging Trends in Continental Philosophy*. T. May (ed.). Durham: Acumen Press, 2011, pp. 31–48.

5   See Jacques Rancière's *Disagreement: Politics and Philosophy*. Julie Rose (trans.). Minneapolis: University of Minnesota Press, 1999; see also Alain Badiou, *Metapolitics*. Jason Barker (trans. and intro.). London and New York: Verso, 2005. In this regard Rancière in the 'Preface' of the abovementioned book writes: 'We will be testing the following hypothesis: that what is called "political philosophy" might well be the set of reflective operations whereby philosophy tries to rid itself of politics, to suppress a scandal in thinking proper to the exercise of politics' (p. xii).

6   See Susan Buck-Morss, 'Aesthetics and Anaesthetics: Walter Benjamin's Artwork Essay Reconsidered', *October* 62, Fall 1992; also see Neil Leach, *The Anaesthetics of Architecture*. Cambridge, MA: MIT Press, 1999.

7   See the recent magisterial book by Jacques Rancière, *Aisthesis: Scenes from the Aesthetic Regime of Art*. London and New York: Verso, 2013.

8   In the sense in Guy Debord, *The Society of the Spectacle*, also referred to by Osborne and Alliez in their 'Introduction', 10.

9   Jean-Nicolas-Louis Durand at the end of the eighteenth century and early nineteenth century was a student of Étienne-Louis Boullée and for 40 years taught the principles of modern architecture at the most prestigious and authoritative school in France, the famous École Polytechnique. Besides teaching and building, Durand dedicated himself to theoretical work. He wrote *Recueile et Parallèle des édifices de tout genre* and published a two-volume work titled *Précis des lecons d'architecture* which appeared in 1802 and 1805. The latter title was adopted as a textbook at the École Polytechnique. It is translated into English as *Précis of the Lectures on Architecture: With Graphic Portion of the Lectures on Architecture* and published in 2000, David Britt (trans.), Antoine Picon (intro.). Los Angeles: Getty Research Institute, 2000.

10 I am using the phrase 'will to architecture' in the sense Karatani has discussed in his book, *Architecture as Metaphor*, 1995.

11 Slavoj Žižek in his seminal essay titled 'The Three Events of Philosophy' cites Alain Badiou and enumerates the philosophical trends against Plato:

    '1 – the vitalist anti-Platonism (Nietzsche, Bergson, Deleuze): the assertion of the real of life-becoming against the intellectualist sterility of Platonic forms – as Nietzsche already put it, "Plato" is the name for a disease . . .

2 – the empiricist-analytic anti-Platonism: Plato believed in the independent existence of Ideas; but, as Aristotle already knew, Ideas do not exist independently of sensuous things whose forms they are. The main counter-Platonic thesis of analytic empiricists is that all truths are either analytic or empirical.

3 – the Marxist anti-Platonism (for which Lenin is not without blame): the dismissal of Plato as the first Idealist, opposed to pre-Socratic materialists as well as to the more "progressive" and empirically oriented Aristotle. In this view (which conveniently forgets that, in contrast to Aristotle's notion of the slave as a "talking tool," there is no place for slaves in Plato's Republic), Plato was the main ideologist of the class of slave owners . . .

4 – the existentialist anti-Platonism: Plato denies the uniqueness of singular existence and subordinates the singular to the universal. This anti-Platonism has a Christian version (Kierkegaard: Socrates versus Christ) and an atheist one (Sartre: "existence precedes essence").

5 – the Heideggerian anti-Platonism: Plato as the founding figure of "Western metaphysics," the key moment in the historical process of the « forgetting of Being,» the starting point of the process which culminates in today's technological nihilism ("from Plato to NATO . . .").

6 – the "democratic" anti-Platonism of political philosophy, from Popper to Arendt: Plato as the originator of "closed society," as the first thinker who elaborated in detail the project of totalitarianism. (For Arendt, at a more refined level, the original sin of Plato is to subordinate politics to Truth, not seeing that politics is a domain of phronesis, of judgments and decision made in unique unpredictable situations.)

"Plato" is thus the negative point of reference which unites otherwise irreconcilable enemies: Marxists and anti-Communist liberals, existentialists and analytic empiricists, Heideggerians and vitalists', in online International Journal of Žižek's Study, 7, 1, 2013, p. 2.

12 See Alain Badiou, *Wittgenstein's Antiphilosophy* with an excellent introduction by Bronu Bosteels. London and New York: Verso, 2011. I discuss Badiou's notion of antiphilosophy extensively in my essay in this collection. Here I just mention Slavoj Žižek who has recently complicated this notion of 'antiphilosophy' after Badiou. He writes: 'Who is antiphilosopher to whom? Badiou somewhere speculates that Heraclitus is the antiphilosopher to Parmenides, the sophists to Plato (although they temporarily and logically precede him), Pascal to Descartes, Hume to Leibniz, Kierkegaard (and Marx) to Hegel, and even Lacan to Heidegger. However, this picture has to be complicated: Is Hegel's thought – or even the entirety of German Idealism with its central motif, the primacy of practical over theoretical reason – not the antiphilosophy to classical metaphysics in its last great mode (of Spinoza and Leibniz)? Or is Sade – in the Lacanian reading – not the antiphilosopher to Kant, so that Lacan's "avec" means to read a philosopher through his antiphilosopher? And is Hegel's true antiphilosopher not already the late Schelling? Or, a step even further, is Hegel's uniqueness not that he is *his own antiphilosopher*?' in Slavoj Žižek, *Less than Nothing: Hegel and the Shadow of Dialectical Materialism*. London and New York: Verso, 2012.

13 This has been pointed out by Rolf Bothe in his 'Foreword' to *Nietzsche and 'An Architecture of Our Minds'*. The topic of this important collection was the subject of the symposium held in 1994 at Getty Research Institute for the History of Art and Humanities, Los Angeles. I rely on various fine essays in this collection to discuss

the influence of Nietzsche on modern architecture and the architects in the early twentieth century.

14   See Hanne Bergius, 'Architecture as the Dionysian-Appolonian Process of Dada', in *Nietzsche and 'An Architecture of Our Minds'*.

15   For this point see the singular volume, Theodor Adorno, Walter Benjamin, Ernst Bloch, Bertold Brecht and Georg Lukács, *Aesthetics and Politics*, With an Afterword by Fredric Jameson.

16   See 'Modern and Postmodern Architecture', reprinted in Michael Hays, *Architecture, Theory, Since 1968*. Cambridge, MA: MIT Press, 1998; also see his 'Modernity – An Incomplete Project', in *The Anti-Aesthetics*. Hal Foster (ed.). Port Townsend: Bay Press, 1983.

17   On this matter also see Gabriel Rockhill's contribution to the present volume.

18   Anthony Vidler in his 'Renaissance Modernism: Manfredo Tafuri' discusses Tafuri's seminal essay 'For a Critique of Architectural Ideology' written in 1969, and his preface to the second edition of *Theorie e storia*, cites Tafuri as having said: 'Any attempt to overthrow the institution [of architecture], the discipline, leading us into the most heightened negation or the most paradoxical ironies – as the case of Dada and surrealism teaches us – is destined to see itself overturned into a positive contribution, into a "constructive" avant-garde, into an ideology all the more positive because all the more dramatically critical and self-critical.' Vidler then makes his remarks: 'But in this passage we can understand architecture not simply as a case of the design of buildings or the planning of town, but rather as an institution. And as an institution, as a "discipline," subject to all the regulation of bourgeois society and capitalist state, "architecture" is a fundamentally modern phenomenon, one born with, and in support of, all the advanced institutions of developed capitalist societies. In this sense, "architecture" – the totality of structures, systems, ideas, practices that are bound up with buildings designed and built by architects – is an ideology', in Anthony Vidler, *Histories of the Immediate Present, Inventing Architectural Modernism*, 2008, p. 178.

19   Quoted by Irving Wohlfarth in his '"Construction Has the Role of the Subconscious": Phantasmagoria of Master Builder (with Constant Reference to Giedion, Weber, Nietzsche, Ibsen, and Benjamin)', in *Nietzsche and 'An Architecture of Our Minds'*, p. 142.

20   Wohlfarth, 'Construction Has the Role of the Subconscious', p. 144.

21   Wohlfarth refers to Sigfried Giedion's *Bauen in Frankreich*, written in 1928, translated as *Building in France, Building in Iron, Building in Ferroconcrete*, Sokratis Georgiadis (intro.), J. Duncan Berry (trans.). Santa Monica: The Getty Center for the History of Art and the Humanities, 1995, and to Walter Benjamin's prospectus in *Passagen-Werk*, 'Paris, Capital of the Nineteenth Century', written in 1935–9; see Walter Benjamin, *The Arcades Project*. Howard Eiland and Kevin McLaughlan (trans). Cambridge: Belknap Press of Harvard University Press, 1999.

22   In Walter Benjamin's *The Arcades Project*. The entire passage reads as: 'Just as Napoleon failed to understand the functional nature of the state as an instrument of domination by the bourgeois class, so the architects of his time failed to understand the functional nature of Iron, with which the constructive principle begins its domination of architecture. These architects design supports resembling Pompeian columns, and factories that imitates residential houses, just as later the first railroad stations will be molded on chalets', p. 4

23 Wohlfarth further adds: 'Here, too Weber's critique is of a piece with a large and divers avant-garde, political and aesthetic. What Weber calls the "disenchantment of the world," Baudelaire, Marx, and Benjamin described as the "loss of the halo" or the decline of aura. All form claimed that the failure to acknowledge this basic world historical fact is likely to result in a surrogate re-enchantment of the world. Benjamin describes such re-enchantment in terms of the manifold "phantasmagorias" of nineteenth-century bourgeois society, among them those of the "interior"' (1999, p. 146).

24 As Wohlfarth concludes his excellent reflections in his essay, 'There is no denying that Benjamin's theory and practice of historical construction belongs to a particular, dated, historical conjuncture. Its own historicity is indeed an integral part of the theory it proposes. Operating with a notion of construction that combines a particular version of historical materialism with a particular version of aesthetic Modernism, it configures Marx and Engels with Le Corbusier and Giedion, glass architecture with a "Copernican turn" in historiography. From Nietzsche and Ibsen to Benjamin, the scene has changed from the building of an ivory tower to the construction of an Eiffel Tower – one that is to provide a particular panoramic angle on the project of writing history from below. Needless to say, Benjamin's Marxist constructor cannot be said to have succeeded where Nietzsche's and Ibsen's (anti-) bourgeois Master Builders failed' (1999, p. 187).

25 Groys in his Introduction writes: 'The struggle against the power of ideology traditionally took the form of struggle against the power of the image. Anti-ideological, critical, enlightened thought has always tried to get rid of images, to destroy or, at least, to deconstruct them – with the goal of placing images with invisible, purely rational concepts. The announcement of Hegel that art is a thing of the past and that our epoch has become the epoch of Concept was a proclamation of victory of the iconoclastic Enlightenment over Christian iconophilia. Of course, Hegel was right at the time to make this diagnosis, but he overlooked the possibility of conceptual art. Modern art has demonstrated time and again its power by appropriating the iconoclastic gestures directed against it and by turning these gestures into new modes of art production' (2008, p. 9).

26 Giorgio Agamben, an astute interpreter of Benjamin's work, in a penetrating essay titled 'In Praise of Profanation' has brought up Benjamin's aforementioned essay in the context of his novel analysis of the notion of 'profanation', which directly relates to the issue I am discussing here, see Giorgio Agamben, *Profanations*. Jeff Fort (trans.). New York: Zone Books, 2007.

27 I owe this last statement to Karatani's interpretation of Marx's passage that he thinks is often misinterpreted. He points out that what Marx attempted to say is that 'it is impossible to dissolve any religion unless the "real suffering" upon which every religion is based is dissolved. There is reason to criticized religion theoretically, because it can only be dissolved practically' (Karatani, 1995, p. 187).

28 On this issue see the excellent analysis by Howard Caygill in his *Walter Benjamin, the Color of Experience*. London and New York: Routledge, 1998, see especially chapter 3.

29 See Theodor Adorno, 'Functionalism Today', published in *Oppositions*, 17 (1979), translated from 'Funktionalismus heute', in Adorno, *Gesammelle Schriften*, vol. 10, pt. 1. Frankfurt: Suhrkamp, 1977.

Bibliography

Adorno, T., Benjamin, W., Bloch, E., Brecht, B. and Lukács, G. (2007 [1977]), *Aesthetics and Politics*, with an Afterword by Fredric Jameson. London and New York: Verso.

Alliez, E. and Osborne, P. (2013), *Spheres of Action: Art and Politics*. London: Tate.

Badiou, B. (2010), *Five Lessons on Wagner*, with an Afterword by Slavoj Žižek. London and New York: Verso.

Benjamin, W. (1996), 'Capitalism as Religion', in *Walter Benjamin, Selected Writings, Volume 1, 1913–1926*. M. Bullock and M. W. Jennings (eds). Cambridge, MA: Belknap Press of Harvard University Press.

Bergius, H. (1999), 'Architecture as the Dionysian-Appolonian Process of Dada', in *Nietzsche and 'An Architecture of Our Minds'*.

Buddensieg, T. (1999), in 'Architecture as Empty Form: Nietzsche and the Art of Building', in *Nietzsche and 'An Architecture of Our Minds'*.

Groys, B. (2008), *Art Power*. Cambridge, MA: MIT Press.

Karatani, K. (1995), *Architecture as Metaphor: Language, Number, Money*. S. Kohso (trans.), M. Speaks (ed.). Cambridge, MA: MIT Press.

Kostka, A. and Wohlfarth, I. (eds) (1999), *Nietzsche and 'An Architecture of Our Minds'*. Getty Research Institute for the History of Arts and Humanities.

Lacoue-Labarthe, P. (1994), *Musica Ficta (Figures of Wagner)*. F. McCarren (trans.). Stanford: Stanford University Press.

Loos, A. (1982), 'Potemkin City', in *Spoken into the Void, Collected Essays 1897–1900*. J. O. Newman and J. H. Smith (trans), A. Rossi (intro.). Cambridge, MA: MIT Press.

Marx, K. (1994), *Selected Writings*. L. H. Simon (ed.). Indianapolis: Hackett.

Neumeyer, F. (1999), 'Nietzsche and Modern Architecture', in *Nietzsche and 'An Architecture of Our Minds'*.

Nietzsche, F. (1968), *Twilight of the Idol and the Anti-Christ*. New York: Penguin.

— (1984), *Human, All Too Human*. M. Faber (trans.), S. Lehmann (intro.). Lincoln: University of Nebraska Press.

Schrift, A. D. (1995), *Nietzsche's French Legacy*. New York and London: Routledge.

Vidler, A. (2008), *Histories of the Immediate Present, Inventing Architectural Modernism*. Cambridge, MA: MIT Press.

Wohlfarth, I. (1999), '"Construction Has the Role of the Subconscious": Phantasmagoria of Master Builder (with Constant Reference to Giedion, Weber, Nietzsche, Ibsen, and Benjamin)', in *Nietzsche and 'An Architecture of Our Minds'*.

Žižek, S. (2009), 'Foreword: Why Is Wagner Worth Saving', in Theodor Adorno, *In Search of Wagner*. London and New York: Verso.

— (2010), 'The Architectural Parallax', in *Living in the End Time*. London and New York: Verso, reprinted in N. Lahiji (ed.) (2012), *The Political Unconscious of Architecture: Re-Opening Jameson's Narrative*. Surrey: Ashgate.

1

The Forgotten Political Art *par Excellence*?: Architecture, Design and the Social Sculpting of the Body Politic

Gabriel Rockhill

Abandoned buildings

Through the course of the long twentieth century, an expansive and robust philosophical debate developed on the relationship between art and radical politics, ranging from the work of the Frankfurt School to post-war French Theory and contemporary discussions in the Anglophone world. Although there are a few important exceptions, this debate has evinced a decidedly disproportionate interest in the literary and visual arts at the expense of architecture and design. The theorists who have participated in it – including such prominent figures as Theodor Adorno, Max Horkheimer, Herbert Marcuse, Georg Lukács, Jean-Paul Sartre, Jean-François Lyotard, Jacques Rancière and many others – have primarily been concerned with the relationship between literature and the fine arts (occasionally music), on the one hand, and more or less radical forms of politics on the other. There are, of course, a few intermittent and partial reflections by these theorists and their major interlocutors on various types of public art and architecture, many of which have been meticulously collected by Neil Leach in *Rethinking Architecture: A Reader in Cultural Theory*.[1] However, these authors' voluminous writings on the literary and visual arts far outweigh the small handful of texts that have been collected in this anthology or elsewhere.

We must not confound this tendency with a general law or fall into simplistic schematizations that lose sight of the fine-grained nuances of historical dynamics. Let us insist at the outset, therefore, on the exceptions to this trend by briefly spotlighting some of the thinkers to have significantly engaged with the politics of architecture: Walter Benjamin, Michel Foucault, Henri Lefebvre and Paul Virilio in continental Europe, as well as David Harvey and Frederic Jameson in the Anglophone world.[2] As we will see with some specific examples below, architecture has clearly not been completely ignored. Nevertheless, it is still far from functioning as a lodestone in the dominant critical theory debates on art and radical politics in the long twentieth century, which have tended to gravitate around literature and the fine arts to the detriment of architecture, building, design, decorative art, public monuments, sculpture and urban planning.[3] Three of the more prominent and lengthy collections of essays on contemporary architectural theory appear to corroborate this observation, at least insofar as it concerns critical philosophic engagements with the art of building. In spite of the fact that they are all over 600 pages in length, they only include a handful of pieces by prominent philosophers, and some of them only approach the issue of architecture rather obliquely (see Nesbitt, 1996; Hays, 2000; Contandriopoulos and Mallgrave, 2008). This is likely one of the reasons why Hubert Tonka has forcibly proclaimed, in a recent interview that critically reflects on Jean Baudrillard's *Vérité ou radicalité de l'architecture?*: 'architecture is a domain that interests almost no one from a philosophic point of view. There are very few texts, especially contemporary texts, on contemporary architecture' (Tonka, 2013).

Architectural practice did not wait, of course, for its intellectual – and material – encounter with politics. Indeed, many of the political experiments of the long twentieth century cast their claims in concrete forms. The history of the modern world could, in fact, be written in terms of the battle of buildings, and the urban landscape is one of the privileged sites of ideological and social struggle. Kenneth Frampton provides an interesting account of these clashes in his now canonical work, *Modern Architecture: A Critical History*. In chapter 24, to take one poignant example, he revisits many of the central tensions of the period 1914–43 and recasts them in terms of the general opposition between the Modern Movement and the New Tradition. Analysing a number of the significant fronts in the architectural skirmishes of the period – from India and the Soviet Union to Italy, Germany and the United States – he charts out the shifting confrontations between monumental state powers and forces of change. The former ultimately triumphed, according to him, during the interwar period:

> That aspect of the New Tradition which took the form of a stripped Classical style emerged as the ruling taste in the 1930s, wherever power wished to represent itself in a positive and progressive light. [. . .] This taste for Neo-Classical monumentality was not restricted [. . .] to totalitarian states, but could be seen in Paris [. . .]. It also made itself manifest in the United States. (Frampton, 1992, p. 219)

> It was around the time of the Second World War that this tendency was reversed, he argues, and 'after the war the general ideological climate of the West was hostile to any kind of monumentality'. (Frampton, 1992, p. 222)

This is not to suggest that we can thereby isolate architecture and focus simply on the confrontation between individual edifices. To begin with, there is no essential or natural dividing line between architecture and the other arts. The concept and practice of architecture have a complex history, and it is only in the modern era that individual architects have come to be recognized as the responsible agents behind particular designs. The overwhelming majority of what is built today is still constructed without an architect per se. Moreover, the art of building is very often part of a larger constructed environment, and it frequently includes sculptural elements, as well as drawing, painting and aspects of scenography. Architects have sought, at times, to foreground and enhance this potential for architectural designs to function as *Gesamtkunstwerke*, or total works of art that integrate all or most of the other arts. Walter Gropius' 1927 Total Theatre project is a remarkable incorporation not only of the theatre with its biomechanical stage (based on the model of Meyerhold's October Theatre in Moscow) but also of film and the performing arts since it included a cinema screen and an aerial stage.

It is also important to note that many of the other arts have what could be heuristically referred to as architectural elements. This is readily apparent in a significant portion of contemporary installation art, as evidenced by the aesthetic ecosystems produced by artists such as Matthew Barney, Thomas Hirschhorne, Ugo Rondinone and many others. Public art in the form of happenings, graffiti, outside projections, public performances and so forth obviously also has an architectural and urban dimension. Alex Villar's project, 'Temporary Occupations', for instance, is an excellent example of the intertwining of performance art and architecture since he ignores city codes and the social regulations by occupying non-functional and unused spaces in the urban environment. Creators such as Leandro Erlich and Sophie Ernst weave together the art of building and the construction of art to such an extent that the borders between the two become porous, if not obsolete. It is also arguable, to take what might be considered a more extreme example, that there are prominent architectural elements in Victor Hugo's writings, both stylistically and in content, as well as in Charles Baudelaire's work. 'With Baudelaire', Walter Benjamin writes, 'Paris becomes for the first time the subject of lyric poetry. This poetry of place is the opposite of all poetry of the soil. The gaze which the allegorical genius turns on the city betrays, instead, a profound alienation' (Benjamin, 1999, p. 21). Architectural designs have also been reciprocally influenced by other arts, and Kenneth Frampton has suggested, for instance, that Albert Speer was so marked by Leni Riefenstahl's film, *Triumph des Willens*, that henceforth his 'designs for stadia at Nuremberg were determined as much by camera angles as by architectural criteria' (Frampton, 1992, p. 218).[4] For all of these reasons, and many more, we should avoid reifying architecture as a distinct entity with an identifiable nature and instead understand it as a negotiated social practice bound up in various and complex ways with other artistic – as well as social and political – practices.

With these important provisos in mind, it is now possible to nuance the structural frame of my argument. Rather than seeking to establish a massive historical generalization according to which philosophy missed its encounter with architecture in the twentieth century, my working hypothesis is much more specific: theoretical debates on the relationship between art and radical politics, particularly within the field of European critical theory broadly construed, have evinced a disproportionate interest in literature, the visual arts and sometimes music (which is also a special case) at the expense of what is commonly recognized as a distinct field of practices, namely those of architecture, building, design, urban planning and public art.

The social art *par excellence*?

As the practice of imagining and building a new world, architecture will always be political.

Kim Dovey and Scott Dickson

It is a question of building which is at the root of the social unrest of today; architecture or revolution.

Le Corbusier

The lack of gravitational pull exercised by architecture and design over core theoretical debates on art and politics in the contemporary era is particularly remarkable due to the patent ways in which the art of building is intimately interlaced with numerous social and political struggles. This is particularly apparent when we consider the social politicity of the built environment, meaning the various political aspects of its social life, including those operative in its design and production, its concrete materializations and its assorted appropriations.

Regarding design and production, to begin with, architecture and public art almost always take place, in our day and age, in a constructed milieu, or at the very least within the charted territories of traversed landscapes. They cannot, therefore, be easily isolated from their immediate inscription in a larger sociopolitical space, as the fetishization of individual buildings and architects is apt to do. National laws, local ordinances, building codes, zoning rules and urban planning influence the practices of architecture, as well as such things as non-codified regulations, building and design technologies, transportation routes, pressure from clients and investors, economic exigencies, media representations and cultural values.[5] The fact that built architecture tends overwhelmingly to be anchored in a functional setting brings with it a series of more or less immediate social and political concerns (see, for instance, Ghirardo, 1991, pp. 17–26).[6] Moreover, since production costs are often exorbitant, some authors have argued that 'architects are reliant on their clients' patronage in ways that other cultural producers are not' (Jones, 2009, p. 2521).[7] Whatever the case may be, it is clear that contemporary architectural design and production are very often the result of collective negotiations between multiple sources and types of agency. 'The actions of architects, and other agents involved in the production of the built environment', write Rob Imrie and Emma Street, 'are entwined in complex ways with a panoply of state, non-state and civil organizations, associations and relations' (Imrie and Street, 2009, p. 2508). It is in this force field of agencies that important sociopolitical battles are fought regarding what can be built, how it is constructed, what materials are used, where it is assembled, who erects it, how it interacts with its immediate environment, who has access to it and so forth. Louis Sullivan's brief summary of the emergence of the high-rise building points to some of these 'extra-architectural' pressures and sociopolitical struggles over production that led to a novel type of building: 'The tall commercial building arose from the pressure of land prices, the land prices from pressure of population, the pressure of population from external pressure' (Sullivan, 1924, p. 310).

Once they are built, the materialized products of architecture and design often stand as powerful and lasting symbols of cultural values and systems of meaning. This is quite obvious in the case of the five types of urban shrines identified by Maria Kaika and Korinna Thielen:

Pre-modern monuments—deference to state and church authority; public cathedrals of technology and money power – tributes to a new era of secularization and industrialization; private secular shrines – homage to individual achievement under capitalism; social housing projects – patially [*sic*] inscribed bold statements of the post-war welfare state; and private-public shrines – temptresses for global finance. (Kaika and Thielen, 2006, p. 67)

Above and beyond these forms of iconic symbolism, the built environment serves as the revealing agent of social structure, a powerful force of naturalization and a potential site of contestation. It demonstrates the fundamental values of a cultural world order, which materially manifests itself in such elements – depending on the location – as prominent financial districts, cheap structures propping up corporate signage, highly accessible tourist sites, the structural privileging of vehicles over pedestrians and public transportation, the destruction or sequestering of the natural environment, etc. The constructed milieu simultaneously naturalizes this cultural system as well as its dominant social relations by creating an ingrained sense of 'normal' relationships, as is the case not only with the examples just cited but also with such things as the ample use of individual as opposed to collective living units, or the isolation and ghettoization of certain social groups.[8] In all of these ways, architectural forms tend to both manifest and accentuate sociopolitical structures and norms, while at the same time being the site of ongoing struggles over the collective formation – and potential reconfiguration – of the social order.

Architecture and public arts also play a central role in sculpting the body politic by canalizing movement, structuring perception, forming social agents, conveying political imaginaries and codifying collective and individual behaviour in various ways. Walter Benjamin has cogently analysed, for instance, how the phantasmagorias of the marketplace took on architectural and urban forms in the transmogrification of the everyday aesthetics of modern Paris. From the world exhibitions and the proliferation of arcades to the rituals of fashion, the hypnotic meanderings of the *flâneur*, the development of private interiors and Haussmann's muscular rending of the urban fabric, the entire cityscape came to be saturated with 'the pomp and the splendor with which commodity-producing society surrounds itself, as well as its illusory sense of security' (Benjamin, 1999, p. 15). In addition to examining the various and sundry ways in which the city became an expansive and intricate shrine to commodity fetishism, he notoriously insisted on the direct political implications of Haussmann's project of slicing wide, long boulevards into the dense urban environment:

The true goal of Haussmann's projects was to secure the city against civil war. He wanted to make the erection of barricades in the streets of Paris impossible for all time. With the same end in mind, Louis Philippe had already introduced wooden paving. Nevertheless, barricades had played a considerable role in the February Revolution. Engels studied the tactics of barricade fighting. Haussmann seeks to forestall such combat in two ways. Widening the streets will make the erection of barricades impossible, and new streets will connect the barracks in straight lines with the workers' districts. Contemporaries christened the operation 'strategic embellishment'. (Benjamin, 1999, p. 23)[9]

This final expression appropriately summarizes one of Benjamin's chief concerns in his posthumously published *Arcades Project*: the ways in which the everyday aesthetic environment of the built world functions as a more or less discreet vehicle for sociopolitical and economic forces.

To take another example, Michel Foucault has poignantly argued that architecture plays an important role in the complex of power relations that shape and form subjects. In *Discipline and Punish*, he partially juxtaposed the classic schema of *le grand renfermement*, which erects strict boundaries between two spaces, with the modern model of disciplinary power, in which there are manifold divisions, individualizing distributions and multiple levels of surveillance. The emergence of disciplinary power produces, according to him, a specific set of architectural problems and concerns:

> A whole problematic then develops: that of an architecture that is no longer built simply to be seen (as with the ostentation of palaces), or to observe the external space (cf. the geometry of fortresses), but to permit an internal, articulated and detailed control – to render visible those who are inside it; in more general terms, an architecture that would operate to transform individuals: to act on those it shelters, to provide a hold on their conduct, to carry the effects of power right to them, to make it possible to know them, to alter them. Stones can make people docile and knowable. The old simple schema of confinement and enclosure – thick walls, a heavy gate that prevents entering or leaving – began to be replaced by the calculation of openings, of filled and empty spaces, passages and transparencies. (Foucault, 1977, p. 172)

Although the spatial orders of closure and disciplinary distribution are distinct, and Foucault identifies a partial sequential development from one to the other, they are by no means irreconcilable. In fact, he claims that disciplinary schemas are grafted onto exclusionary models in the nineteenth century:

> They are different projects, then, but not incompatible ones. We see them coming slowly together, and it is the peculiarity of the nineteenth century that it applied to the space of exclusion of which the leper was the symbolic inhabitant (beggars, vagabonds, madmen and the disorderly formed the real population) the technique of power proper to disciplinary partitioning. Treat 'lepers' as 'plague victims,' project the subtle segmentations of discipline onto the confused space of internment, combine it with the methods of analytical distribution proper to power, individualize the excluded, but use procedures of individualization to mark

exclusion – this is what was operated regularly by disciplinary power from the beginning of the nineteenth century in the psychiatric asylum, the penitentiary, the reformatory, the approved school and, to some extent, the hospital. (Foucault, 1977, p. 199)[10]

Furthermore, Foucault emphasizes the variable practical uses of spaces, as we will see below, and he rejects the idea that they simply have an inherent politics that is established at the moment of their creation. When Paul Rabinow asks him in an interview if certain architectural projects appear to represent forces of liberation or resistance, he retorts: 'I do not think that there is anything that is functionally – by its very nature – absolutely liberating. Liberty is a *practice*' (Foucault, 1984, p. 245).

The social politicity of public arts includes, in addition to the Byzantine struggles over their production and the diverse social effects of their materializations, their reception and appropriation by various agents. The proposed symbolism or signification of a building is not equivalent, of course, to its actual import or significance. As Paul Knox has argued, 'there is an important distinction between the *intended* meaning of specific groups or individuals and the *perceived* meaning of the built environment as seen by others. [. . .] Another important point is that the social meaning of the built environment is *not static*' (Knox, 1984, p. 112). The same is true for the projected purpose or use of a public construction, as poignantly emphasized by Louis Aragon in his significant ruminations on urban space in *Le paysan de Paris*: 'No one is suggesting that the architect foresaw the use that would be made of these fittings: could the engineer who drew up the plans for the Pont de Solférino have had an inkling of the debaucheries that his arches would one day shelter?' (Aragon, 1994, p. 57). Michel Foucault has similarly argued, using the example of Jean-Baptiste Godin's *Familistère* in Guise, that architectural spaces lend themselves to a myriad of possible appropriations rather than having a single political valence:

> Godin's architecture was clearly aimed at freedom. Here was something that manifested the power of ordinary workers to participate in the exercise of their trade. [. . .] Yet no one could enter or leave the *familistère* without being seen by everyone else – an aspect of the architecture that could be totally oppressive. But it could only be oppressive if people were prepared to use their own presence in order to watch over others. Let's imagine a community that might be established there, which would indulge in unlimited sexual practices. It would once again become a place of freedom. I think it is somewhat arbitrary to try to dissociate the effective practice of freedom, the practice of social relations, and spatial distributions. (Foucault, 1984, p. 246)[11]

There are various sociopolitical dimensions to the reception of public works of art as they take on a life of their own in the hands of their users. The re-appropriation of buildings or public spaces, for instance, can be an important part of political struggles, as the history of occupations clearly illustrates, as well as such catalyzing moments as the Paris Commune or the recent occupations of Tahrir Square in Cairo, the Pearl Roundabout in Manama, the Puerta del Sol in Madrid, Zuccotti Park in New York,

Taksim Square in Istanbul and so many other occupations elsewhere. Paul Virilio has argued, in this light, that the re-appropriation of functionalized spaces was key to the uprisings of May 1968 in France:

> The amazing phenomenon that abruptly emptied the streets and filled the monuments shattered the airtight compartments of our society. It revealed the alienation hidden beneath the most ordinary everyday habits. By forgetting prohibitions, for a time, and inhabiting the uninhabitable, the populace committed their very first adultery vis-à-vis the spatial appropriation that desocializes them, isolates them, and sequesters them. (Virilio, 2008, p. 31)

These types of communal struggles over the built environment and public spaces are a crucial aspect of the social politicity of architecture and urban planning.

Reflections on a missed encounter between theory and practice

Any etiological account of complex social phenomena requires a methodological framework that discards the structuralist assumption – which stretches well beyond structuralism in the strict sense of the term – that there is a single cause, a sole plane of determination or a unique underlying framework behind social circumstances. In the sociohistorical world, there are always multiple factors that are operative, and they form shifting constellations of pressure that change in each particular conjuncture. It is thereby necessary to eschew the search for single causes or determinants in favour of a multivariate analysis of dynamic complexes of force.

Without pretending to propose an exhaustive analysis, let us underscore some of the significant elements at work in the network of factors that has contributed to the largely missed encounter between radical politics and architecture in the broad critical theory tradition (with the exception of figures like Benjamin, Foucault and Virilio). To begin with, it is arguable that much of the contemporary debate on art and politics has grown out of the intellectual and cultural crucible of the late eighteenth and early nineteenth century. This is obviously not the place for a detailed investigation of this historical conjuncture, but it is worth highlighting the near simultaneous emergence of art in the modern sense of the term and revolutionary politics. Beginning with the former, we should note that the modern notion of fine art developed in part by distinguishing itself more stringently from crafts as well as from the work of the sciences, and it consolidated itself in new institutions such as the public museum. At the same time, the artist and the work of art were further individualized and more strongly affiliated with the creative powers of exceptional forms of imagination. The modern concept of literature also appeared at this time, and the term came to refer to a canonical group of writings that embody a specific experience of language (see Rancière, 2011). These changes did not occur, of course, as a swift sea change, and we must not imagine these complex and shifting reconfigurations in terms of the simple dropping and raising of a curtain allowing for a near instantaneous change in the set design of the historical stage. What happened in this gradual and intermittent alteration of social practices was that a relatively new problematic emerged, in certain foyers of transformation, in which a gulf appeared between the immediate functionalism of the manual arts and crafts, on the one hand, and the supposedly higher calling of the fine arts on the other. Multiple positions emerged on this issue, and there was no overwhelming consensus across society as a whole. In fact, one of the fundamental concerns that has continued to plague much of what is generically labelled modern art is precisely the overcoming of this divide, as evidenced by the Arts and Crafts movement, the Bauhaus, and so many other endeavours to unite hand and mind. This being said, the emergence of the modern institutions of art and literature, as well as of art history and literary history, has led to the development and sedimentation of parallel institutional worlds. At times, this has favoured an increasing separation between the manual arts, which are often affiliated with the lowly domain of crafts, and the lofty realm of art in the restricted sense of the term.

Revolutionary politics in the strict sense is also a modern phenomenon. As figures like Hannah Arendt, Félix Gilbert, Reinhardt Koselleck and Raymond Williams have argued, it is only in approximately the last third of the eighteenth century that the notion and practice of a social revolution appear. As in the case of the modern concept of art, fine methodological footwork would be necessary to avoid schematic accounts of the history of revolutionary practice. For our current concerns, let it suffice to say that there is ample evidence to suggest that radical social revolutions, which stretch beyond institutional and political changes in order to reconfigure the very structure of society, are relatively novel phenomena that began to appear around the end of the Enlightenment. It is not surprising, then, that one of the philosophical concerns that emerged at this point in time had to do with the relationship between the newly institutionalized fine arts, on the one hand, and the relatively recent appearance of revolutionary politics on the other. In fact, one of the unique features of much of the debate on art and politics in the modern world is that the question, 'what is the relationship between art and politics?', actually tends to mean: 'what is the relation between high art and revolutionary politics?'

One of the reasons for this, at least in the twentieth century, but perhaps earlier, is surely that many of the leading figures in German critical theory and contemporary French thought are members of the middle-class, white, male, intellectual elite. They are largely part of the *Bildungsbürgertum*, and they tend to incarnate the bourgeois liberal ideals of education. This means that they were usually well versed in the history of art, trained to appreciate the high arts, and inculcated to varying degrees to reproduce the social hierarchies inherent in the theoretical distinction between the lofty culture of the urbane elite and the lowly crafts and entertaining amusements of the uncouth masses. When they sought to break with the bourgeois tradition in order to engage in radical politics of various ilks, one of the pressing – but sometimes implicit – questions became: what is the relationship between the bourgeois art of our past and the political transformation that we aspire to in the future? Moreover, given the fact that many of these authors clearly continued to appreciate the high art on which they had been weaned, there was a general concern with how the art and literature of their bourgeois training could contribute to the revolutionary struggle that they hoped to instigate or support.

This preoccupation with the radical political implications of high art is particularly interesting given the number of architects in the long twentieth century who were dedicated to destroying the very opposition between high and low art. The Bauhaus could again be cited for its unique capacity to bring together architects, designers, painters, photographers, and so on in an effort to unify the spiritual and the material, the artistic and the technical, mind and hand. In fact, this concern cuts across many of the important architectural movements of the twentieth century, and it is perhaps Le Corbusier who provided the most concise summary of this agenda by defining architecture as the 'esthetics of the engineer', which unites the technical precision of building with the creative powers of art (Le Corbusier, 1995, p. xvii).

This corrective on the part of certain architects does not mean, of course, that the distinction between high and low art has dissipated, or that these hierarchies have stopped having social effects and implications. In fact, they continue to haunt the work of those architects and theorists who redeploy the very same hierarchy of high and low art within the built environment by juxtaposing true architecture (high art) to average building (low art). If we remain blind to such iterations of the distinction between high and low art, which is still obviously an important feature of much of the constructed milieu, then we run the risk of ignoring crucial sociopolitical aspects of the entire built environment. For this distinction creates, at least potentially, a social and often economic line of demarcation between the prestigious architect-designed buildings and the less than glamorous constructions of the everyday world. Diane Ghirardo has discerningly highlighted this problem in critical discussions of architecture:

> To the degree nonarchitect or builder designs enter into the architectural discussion, it is as the objects of thoroughgoing condemnation: from subdivisions, to mini-malls, to tract houses. In the current orthodoxy, such building production lacks the virtue of design [. . .] that is to say, the buildings lack the artistic qualities associated with architect-designed structures. Whereas fervent debate animates discussions about most architect-designed buildings [. . .] there is tacit and often explicit professional agreement that nonarchitect-designed buildings cannot be considered Architecture. Such a view refers back to a general belief that Architecture is an art, and that art in turn has a high moral purpose in the formation and transmission of culture. (Ghirardo, 1991, p. 11)

> It is with this in mind that she judiciously asserts that 'Whatever problems, flaws, or weaknesses one might discern in nonarchitectural building – or "low art" – ignoring them, dismissing them out of hand, or failing to analyze the relationship between high and low art in effect means that one is not engaging in the act of criticism, but rather acting to preserve a particular status quo.' (Ghirardo, 1991, p. 13)

Other important factors that have contributed to prescinding the built environment from major theoretical discussions of art and politics include the talisman complex and the social epoché, which have beleaguered a significant portion of contemporary debates.[12] Much of the current controversy tends to focus on individual works of high art and their ability or inability to directly produce political effects. This has the unfortunate consequence of reducing the politics of art to the talisman-like power of isolated aesthetic artefacts (talisman complex), which are largely sequestered from the various dimensions of their complex social existence (social epoché). Such an approach tends to lead, moreover, to an impasse insofar as the politics of art, far from being a force magically inherent – or not – in certain privileged objects, plays itself out in the ongoing social battles over the production, circulation and reception of collectively negotiated works. It is not surprising, given this isolation of aesthetic products and the general bracketing of the social world, that works of art strongly rooted in a functional environment of everyday social use have tended to be ignored.

Finally, we should note that architectural history does not fit well within many of the standard accounts of art history, and more specifically those that seek to establish certain political narratives. Consider, to begin with, the widespread description of artistic and literary history in terms of a classical age of mimesis, characterized in part by its conservative preservation of the status quo, which was supposedly followed by a modern era of anti-mimetic art and an iconoclastic assault on good form. Leaving aside the crucial question of the viability of such a schematization for the fine arts, it is far from obvious that classical architecture sought – at least in any straightforward sense – to imitate nature or that modern architecture merely repudiated such imitation. In fact, Gaudí's cavernous constructions, like the sinuous forms of Art Nouveau, could be considered closer to nature than many of the buildings of the seventeenth and eighteenth centuries. Furthermore, the other customary accounts of artistic modernism largely fail to capture what is commonly referred to as modern architecture. For instance, it is unclear how the supposed autonomization of art, the emergence of abstraction, the appearance of the 'aesthetics of the commonplace', or the development of what is called intransitive art and literature could help make sense of significant changes in building practices in the early part of the twentieth century. Many of these were bound up with the relatively new embedded technologies of concrete and steel (as well as novel uses of glass), but also with the social and economic pressures of the contemporary urban environment and capitalist expansion. These overlapped in many ways, moreover, with what is often called avant-garde architecture, which, once again, cannot be easily aligned with the now standard historical narratives regarding the development of avant-garde art and literature. Perhaps the most widespread thesis is still that of Peter Bürger, who vigorously argued that the historical avant-garde – understood above all as the avant-garde in the fine arts – ultimately failed in its sociopolitical aspirations because it was not able to truly link art with life. Yet, it could easily be claimed that this is precisely what avant-garde architecture and design accomplished. To begin with, most architecture, if it be identified as avant-garde or not, does not have to join art with life because its very existence presupposes just such a connection. Second, it might be argued that the architectural avant-garde succeeded in developing and spreading new forms of design that have now become more or less ubiquitous in the 'high modernism' of the contemporary urban landscape. Once again, we see that the case of architecture cannot be comfortably situated within the dominant historical schematizations of artistic and literary history, and more specifically within those that are premised on a certain political interpretation of historical developments (where modernism and avant-gardism are often linked to the iconoclastic rejection of established conventions). For these and other reasons, many theorists have conveniently sidelined or ignored architecture, public art and urban design.

This list of factors is surely not exhaustive, and the individual elements vary in intensity and form depending on the specific socio-historical intersection. However, it does provide us with at least partial indications regarding the conjuncture of factors that have contributed to the tendency to turn a blind eye to the social politicity of the built world in critical theories of art and politics.

Conclusion

The built environment forms and shapes our daily lives even if we do not go to museums or galleries, attend public performances, frequent the cinema or read books and periodicals. It delivers to us an implicit sense of our collective cosmos as a naturalized world, often inconspicuously enchanted with value and meaning. It is the art that sculpts our social existence and creates a physical field of possibility, punctuated by symbolic icons, as well as a structured realm of experience that forms us as social beings and codifies our behaviour and thought in multiple ways. 'Building is the art we live in', writes Robert Hughes, 'it is the social art *par excellence*, the carapace of political fantasy, the exoskeleton of one's economic dreams. It is also the one art nobody can escape' (Hughes, 1996, p. 164).

The social politicity of architecture and the built environment includes, in addition to the material forms that directly shape daily social interaction, the complicated battles and debates that go into the production of buildings. In the contemporary world, it would be naïve to separate architectural practice from its inscription in a larger sociopolitical space and a general struggle over a common world. This is not only because individual edifices are almost always part of a larger built milieu, or at the very least a charted territory, but also because the entire sphere of construction is bound up with the political stakes inherent in establishing and negotiating a material domain of shared existence.

A third aspect of the social politicity of public art is the way in which it is appropriated and used by the general population, which often includes significant clashes over the meaning and role of constructed spaces. Once a structure is erected, it takes on a social life of its own and becomes a site that can be appropriated and re-appropriated to various ends. The politics of constructed spaces does not end, therefore, with the erection of buildings. This is, one might say, only its beginning.

Ignoring or bracketing these assorted aspects of the social politicity of architectural practices has the unfortunate consequence of excluding from debates on art and politics what might be considered – at least from a certain point of view – the political art *par excellence*. Much of contemporary critical philosophy, marked by the inheritance of the historical problematic of the relationship between high art and revolutionary politics, has indeed turned a blind eye to architecture in favour of meditating on the potential for the grand art of the bourgeoisie – and particularly individual works of fine art and literature – to contribute to social and political transformation. It thereby runs the risk of reproducing, at least implicitly or to a certain degree, one of the very same social hierarchies that radical politics aims at overcoming and that many architects have sought to destroy, in part by creating buildings that cannot be easily inscribed within schematic historical narratives concerning the politics of art.

The overall objective of this analysis has, therefore, been threefold: to highlight a fundamental problem and limitation in critical theory debates on art and politics, to explore the conjuncture of factors that have contributed to this predicament, and to propose an alternative methodology that allows us to abandon a restricted understanding of the politics of art in favour of a broad-based analysis of the social politicity of aesthetic practices. The ultimate goal has thus been to open space for a renewed interrogation into the political stakes of the built environment and the diverse ways in which the collective elaboration of a shared material and symbolic world is also the forging – and potential re-forging – of a people.

Notes

1 Since Rancière has written a number of important works after the publication date of Leach's book, it is worth signalling at least two chapters that constitute a partial but minor exception to his tendency to accord a considerable privilege to the visual arts, and especially to literature. He reflects on the question of design in a text in *The Future of the Image* (2009, pp. 91–107), and he pursues certain aspects of this reflection in a chapter in *Aisthesis* that also discusses issues related to architecture (2013, pp. 133–53).

2 Ernst Bloch, Guy Debord, Jürgen Habermas and Siegfried Kracauer (who studied architecture and worked as an architect) have also written pieces on architecture and urban planning. There are surely other examples that could be cited, ranging from the important work of the Situationist International to the relatively short writings on architecture by thinkers like Antonio Negri and Slavoj Žižek, or the rather brief musings by philosophers who were less dedicated to critical social theory, such as Martin Heidegger and Jacques Derrida.

3 Dance, both as a performing art and as a social practice, could probably be added to this list.

4 In 'Reflections on the Autonomy of Architecture', Frampton discusses the dissolution of contemporary architecture into an endless proliferation of images, and he claims that 'this is a situation in which buildings tend to be increasingly designed for their photogenic effect rather than their experiential potential' (Ghirardo, 1991, p. 26).

5 On this topic, see the special issue of *Urban Studies* on the regulation of design: 46, 12, November 2009.

6 In a longer article, it would be interesting to explore the important role and status of theoretical designs, meaning the significant number of architectural plans that are never actually materialized in concrete forms. For reasons of concision, I am here concentrating on built architecture.

7 This is a statement by Paul Jones, summarizing the work of Magali Safuri Larson.

8 On the latter issue see, for instance, Michel Kokoreff's work.

9 Also see Frampton's discussion of Haussmann in *Modern Architecture* (1992, pp. 23–4).
10 The rest of the quote reads: 'Generally speaking, all the authorities exercising individual control function according to a double mode; that of binary division and branding (mad/sane; dangerous/harmless; normal/abnormal); and that of coercive assignment, of differential distribution (who he is; where he must be; how he is to be characterized; how he is to be recognized; how a constant surveillance is to be exercised over him in an individual way, etc.)'.
11 Translation slightly modified (see Foucault, 1994, pp. 276–7).
12 I develop both of these ideas in *Radical History and the Politics of Art*.

Bibliography

Aragon, L. (1994), *Paris Peasant*. S. W. Taylor (trans.). Boston: Exact Change.

Benjamin, W. (1999), *The Arcades Project*. H. Eiland and K. McLaughlin (trans). Cambridge, MA: Belknap Press of Harvard University Press.

Contandriopoulos, C. and Mallgrave, H. F. (eds) (2008), *Architectural Theory, Volume II, An Anthology from 1871–2005*. Malden, MA: Blackwell Publishing.

Foucault, M. (1977), *Discipline and Punish: The Birth of the Prison*. A. Sheridan (trans.). New York: Vintage Books.

— (1984), 'Space, Knowledge, and Power', in *The Foucault Reader*. ed. P. Rabinow. New York: Pantheon Books.

— (1994), *Dits et écrits 1954–1988, volume IV: 1980–1988*. Paris: Éditions Gallimard.

Frampton, K. (1992), *Modern Architecture: A Critical History*. London: Thames and Hudson Ltd.

Ghirardo, D. (ed.) (1991), *Out of Site: A Social Criticism of Architecture*. Seattle: Bay Press.

Hays, K. M. (ed.) (2000), *Architecture Theory since 1968*. Cambridge, MA: MIT Press.

Hughes, R. (1996), *The Shock of the New: The Hundred-Year History of Modern Art – Its Rise, Its Dazzling Achievement, Its Fall*. New York: Alfred A. Knopf.

Imrie, R. and Street, E. (2009), 'Regulating Design: The Practices of Architecture, Governance and Control', in *Urban Studies*, 46, 12, pp. 2555–76.

Jones, P. (2009), 'Putting Architecture in Its Social Place: A Cultural Political Economy of Architecture', in *Urban Studies*, 46, 12, pp. 2519–36.

Kaika, M. and Thielen, K. (2006), 'Form Follows Power: A Genealogy of Urban Shrines', in *City*, 10, 1, pp. 59–69.

Knox, P. L. (1984), 'Symbolism, Styles and Settings: The Built Environment and the Imperatives of Urbanized Capitalism', in *Architecture & Comportment*, 2, 2, pp. 107–22.

Leach, N. (ed.) (1997), *Rethinking Architecture: A Reader in Cultural Theory*. London and New York: Routledge.

Le Corbusier (1995), *Vers une architecture*. Paris: Flammarion.

Nesbitt, K. (ed.) (1996), *Theorizing a New Agenda for Architecture: An Anthology of Architectural Theory 1965–1995*. New York: Princeton Architectural Press.

Rancière, J. (2009), *Future of the Image*. G. Elliott (trans.). London: Verso.

— (2011), *Mute Speech*. J. Swenson (trans.), with an introduction by Gabriel Rockhill. New York: Columbia University Press.

— (2013), *Aisthesis: Scenes from the Aesthetic Regime of Art*. Z. Paul (trans.). London: Verso.

Rockhill, G. (2014), *Radical History and the Politics of Art*. New York: Columbia University Press.

Sullivan, L. H. (1924), *The Autobiography of an Idea*. New York: Press of the American Institute of Architects, Inc.

Tonka, H. (2013), '*Vérité ou radicalité de l'architecture?* de Jean Baudrillard'. *Le journal de la philosophie*, 7/18/2013. Available at: <http://www.franceculture.fr/emission-le-journal-de-la-philosophie-verite-ou-radicalite-de-l-architecture-de-jean-baudrillard-201>.

Virilio, P. (2008), 'Critical Space', in *Log*, 13–14, pp. 29–31.

2

Architecture and the Politics of Aesthetics: Autonomy, Heteronomy and the Philosophy of Art[1]

David Cunningham

In what is probably his best-known book, *Disagreement*, originally published in France in 1995, Jacques Rancière makes a bold assertion: 'There has never been any "aestheticisation" of politics in the modern age because politics is aesthetics in principle' (1999, p. 58). The critical reference is, of course, to Walter Benjamin, and to the closing paragraphs of the latter's 1936 essay, 'The Work of Art in the Age of Its Reproducibility', in which Benjamin famously counterposes the *'aestheticizing of politics, as practiced by fascism'* to the communist strategy of *'politicizing art'* (2002, p. 122). Rancière's objection to this formulation turns on his own essentially trans-historical understanding of politics itself. If politics is in its very 'principle' a matter of democratically 'reconfiguring the distribution of the sensible . . . to render visible what had not been, and to make heard as speakers those who had been perceived as mere noisy animals', there is an irreducible 'aesthetics of [all] politics' (2009, p. 25). 'Politics revolves around what is seen and what can be said about it, around who has the ability to see and the talent to speak' (Rancière, 2004, p. 13). Political *struggle* is thus always an aesthetic struggle: a fight for some new distribution or 'partition' of the sensible that would break up the existing representations of what Rancière terms the 'police order' in order to make perceptible that which such an order excludes (1999). How then could politics, already aesthetic through and through, be *aestheticized*?

As a reading of Benjamin's essay, Rancière's argument is, however, not without its own problems; not least because it fails to register the semantic complexity already internal to Benjamin's essay in its considerations of the *historical* relations between art, politics and aesthetics, as these are organized under conditions of social-technological modernity. As one of Benjamin's best readers, Susan Buck-Morss (1992), notes, the notion that communism *'replies'* to fascism by *'politicizing art'*, if taken at face value, seems a fairly paltry response to those 'forms of staging power and mass mobilization' (Rancière, 2004, p. 25) which are at the centre of Benjamin's analysis of fascism. Benjamin must surely 'mean more', as Buck-Morss remarks, 'than merely to make culture a vehicle for Communist propaganda' – first, because such a politicization of art would evidently result only in a renewed aestheticization of politics at another level: 'Once art is drawn into politics (Communist politics no less than Fascist politics), how could it help but put itself into its service, thus to render up to politics its own artistic powers, i.e., "aestheticize politics"?' (1992, p. 5). Patently, Benjamin must be 'demanding of art' a rather different 'task' than at first appears (5).

Exactly what this 'task' might be depends, I want to argue, upon the development of a set of complex relations concerning art, the arts, aesthetics and 'aestheticization', on the one hand, and social life and politics, on the other, that go back to philosophical debates (along with new institutional innovations) of the latter part of the eighteenth century; debates through which the modern concepts of 'art' and 'aesthetics' were themselves 'invented' (Shiner, 2001). It is as a contribution to a somewhat schematic genealogy of these relations, therefore, that the following essay should be read. To argue that it is, however, questions raised by *architecture*, specifically, which might provide some privileged way into understanding such relations is far from immediately obvious, and hence requires some detailed justification and explanation (it also constitutes one rationale for beginning with Benjamin's essay). Yet, if it is the case that architecture has played a relatively marginal role in the major developments of a philosophy of art since the end of the eighteenth century, 'radical' or otherwise, there is something to be said about this very marginality itself. For its legacy is crucial to the construction at certain historical moments of a *privileging* of architecture as offering the possibility of art's reconnection with collective social life, for which it is precisely the *ambiguity* of architecture's 'art' status, from the perspective of philosophical aesthetics, that is most politically significant. If this identifies a specific discourse about architecture with a wider 'political problematisation of the concept of aesthetics' *as well as* the simultaneous desire for a 'direct politicization of aesthetics' that characterizes both Benjamin's 1936 essay and various projects of the interwar 'historical avant-gardes' (Alliez and Osborne, 2013), it also indicates the ways in which debates around architecture's 'art' status have become exemplary of a peculiar situation in which, as Rancière himself puts it, 'the notion of "aesthetics" as a specific experience [can] lead *at once* to the idea of a pure world of art and of the self-suppression of art in life, to the tradition of avant-garde radicalism and to the aestheticization of common existence' (2002, p. 134; emphasis added).

An art based on politics

It is worth returning, then, to the precise socio-historical conditions set out by Benjamin in the 'Work of Art' essay, and thus of the 'task' he assigns to the communist politicization of art. Famously, an art 'based on politics' is defined for Benjamin, above all, by its 'uselessness for contemplative immersion' (one post-Kantian definition of the distinctive character of aesthetic experience itself), thus emancipating itself not only from its earlier 'ritual' functions but also from the 'auratic' character of art's modern 'bourgeois' 'exhibition value' and its dominant aesthetic apprehension since the late eighteenth century. If the privileged cultural form in this regard is cinema, which is accorded a revolutionary significance in anticipating the possibility of new forms of collective and technical intercourse in (a future communist) society as a whole, the 'new mode of participation' that it heralds is prefigured elsewhere. For it is at this point that Benjamin introduces a famous comparison. The activity of the 'distracted masses' that absorb the cinematic work of art 'into themselves', as opposed to the individual who is absorbed *by it* (as an auratic, 'aesthetic' object of contemplation), finds its 'prototype', he writes, 'with regard to buildings' (119):

> Buildings have accompanied human existence since primeval times. Many art forms have come into being and passed away. [...] But the human need for shelter is permanent. Architecture has never had fallow periods. Its history is longer than that of any other art, and its effect ought to be recognised in any attempt to account for the relationship of the masses to the work of art. (120)

Having thereby established this historical privilege, as older than 'any other art' – largely in accordance with Hegel's historicized hierarchy of the individual arts (of which I will have more to say below) – Benjamin comes then, *contra* Hegel, to what he argues is 'highly instructive' about the specific 'laws of architecture's reception' for what are precisely the most *modern* of technological forms (120):

> Buildings are received [or appropriated] in a twofold manner: by use and by perception. Or, better: tactilely and optically. Such reception cannot be understood in terms of the concentrated attention of a tourist before a famous building. On the tactile side, there is no counterpart to what contemplation is on the optical side. Tactile reception comes about not so much by way of attention as by way of habit. The latter largely determines even the optical reception of architecture, which spontaneously takes the form of casual noticing, rather than attentive observation. Under certain circumstances, this form of reception shaped by architecture acquires canonical value. *For the tasks which face the human apparatus of perception at historical turning points cannot be performed solely by optical means – that is, by way of contemplation. They are mastered gradually – taking their cue from tactile reception – through habit.* (120)

Now there are a number of issues one might raise here. In (de-)historicizing architecture as that which has 'accompanied human existence since primeval times', Benjamin might well be said to identify 'architecture' far too quickly with *building*, so eliding the former's specifically modern constitution as an autonomous discipline and institution (as well as an 'art') in a way that has, since the late eighteenth century, partly served to distance it from its own material practice (see Vidler, 2008, pp. 178–80; Cunningham, 2007). (The choice of the term *building* [*Bauen*] in much early modernist practice, *as opposed to architecture*, has, of course, a particular rhetorical impetus to it in this respect, upon which Benjamin may be drawing.) At any rate, one can already begin to see that Rancière's somewhat hasty account of Benjamin's argument risks considerably oversimplifying what is at stake in the historically shifting relations *between* architecture, art and the concept of the aesthetic (as well as 'building', which appears to belong to a quite different conceptual series) that the 'Work of Art' is concerned to trace.[2] It is here, as such, that Benjamin's emphasis on the specific socio-technological conditions of capitalist *modernity* remains of evident importance.

Although she pays no real attention to the pivotal role played by architecture in this account, Buck-Morss's commentary on the famous 'aestheticization of politics' and 'politicization of art' distinction is particularly perceptive. As she puts it:

> The problem of interpreting the closing section of Benjamin's text lies in the fact that, halfway through this final thought (aestheticised politics, politicised art), Benjamin changes the constellation in which his conceptual terms (politics, art, aesthetics) are deployed, and hence their meaning. If we were really to 'politicize art' in the radical way he is suggesting, art would cease to *be* art as we know it. Moreover, the key term 'aesthetics' would shift its meaning one hundred and eighty degrees. 'Aesthetics' would be transformed, indeed, redeemed, so that, ironically (or dialectically), *it* would describe the field in which the antidote to fascism is deployed as a political response. (Buck-Morss, 1992, p. 5)

Although Buck-Morss doesn't mention this, it is for this reason that Benjamin's apparent assertion of an *opposition* between the 'optical' and the 'tactile' in the 'Work of Art' essay's discussion of architecture is potentially misleading, if only because the mode of appropriation at stake in the latter is clearly not solely a question of 'touch', for Benjamin, but rather refers to a much broader form of (historically constituted) bodily and spatial experience, which would include the 'visual' but not be dominated by it. Far from new to the twentieth century, as a complaint about the specifically *artistic* 'reception' of architecture this in fact repeats what was already, for example, Goethe's concern at the very end of the eighteenth century regarding an emerging 'aesthetic' apprehension of architecture (an apprehension which found one 'social' manifestation in the eighteenth-century Grand Tour[3]): 'It may well be thought that, as a fine art, architecture works for the eye alone, but it ought primarily . . . to work for the sense of movement in the human body' (cited Forty, 2002, p. 262).

As against architecture *qua* fine art's specific 'aestheticization' in the 'pure' opticality of contemplative auratic reception – the focus of Benjamin's critique of *bourgeois* 'aesthetics' – the 'Work of Art' essay thus locates architecture's specifically *modern* 'value' precisely in its 'primeval' connection to a mode of reception that remains (unlike other art forms) far closer to aesthetics' *original* philosophical meaning. As Buck-Morss notes, it is thus

> helpful to recall the original etymological meaning of the word 'aesthetics' because it is precisely to this origin that, via Benjamin's revolution, we find ourselves returned. *Aisthitikos* is the ancient Greek word for that which is 'perceptive by feeling'. *Aisthisis* is the sensory experience of perception. The original field of aesthetics is not art but reality – corporeal, material nature. . . . It is a form of cognition, achieved through taste, touch, hearing, seeing, smell – the whole corporeal sensorium. (Buck-Morss, 1992, p. 6)

The real question is, then, Buck-Morss continues, 'how it happened that, within the course of the modern era, the term "aesthetics" underwent a reversal of meaning so that in Benjamin's time it was applied first and foremost to art'; a question that 'demands a critical, exoteric explanation of the socioeconomic and political context in which the discourse of the aesthetic was deployed' (1992, p. 7).[4]

Given this, what then does Benjamin *mean* exactly when he refers to the aestheticization of politics? Here is the famous section immediately preceding Benjamin's final opposition:

> *All efforts to aestheticize politics culminate in one point. That one point is war.* War, and only war, makes it possible to set a goal for mass movements on the grandest scale while preserving traditional property relations . . . 'Fiat ars – pereat mundus', says fascism, expecting from war . . . the artistic gratification of a sense perception altered by technology. This is evidently the consummation of *l'art pour l'art*. Humankind, which once, in Homer, was an object of contemplation for the Olympian gods, has now become one for itself. Its self-alienation has reached the point where it can experience its own annihilation as a supreme aesthetic pleasure. (Benjamin, 2002, pp. 121–2)

In this way, the role played by architecture in Benjamin's wider vision of a politicization of art might be said to turn on what he perceives precisely as its *resistance* to 'aesthetics' in a *l'art pour l'art* sense. Yet, if it resists this, it does so only so as to provide a kind of haven (and training ground) for a mode of reception that would be fully 'aesthetic' in another sense; that is, as a cognitive experience of 'the whole corporeal sensorium' rooted in individual and collective physiology. This would be the delicate dialectical reversal (or irony) by which 'aesthetics' would be transformed by communism so that, as against aesthetic*ization*, '*it* would describe the field in which the antidote to fascism is deployed as a political response' (Buck-Morss, 1992, p. 5). That is to say, the politicization of art would have to be *itself* 'aesthetic' in a crucial sense.[5]

Benjamin's implicit identification of 'aestheticization' with a hegemony of the 'optical' – reflected in 'the concentrated attention of a tourist before a famous building' – is in this sense something like a code word for what Guy Debord (1983) will later describe as an emergent society of the spectacle: that 'self-alienation' in which humanity becomes an object of contemplation for itself. The dominance of the visual signifies, in other words – not least in philosophical aesthetics' dominant account of architecture *as* art – the mode of reception characteristic of auratic experience as a form of *separation* or 'distance'. (This is surely part of what Goethe means, already, when he complains that architecture should not work 'for the eye alone', but 'for the sense of movement in the human body'.) In so far as this is an 'aestheticization', it is so in the form of what is actually a drastically restricted 'aesthetic' experience when understood from the perspective of its original philosophical meaning as an all-encompassing 'form of cognition'. If Žižek is therefore right to argue that one should resist the condemnation of any 'collective artistic' experience as somehow 'proto-Fascist' – though wrong, in my opinion, to attribute the insight to Rancière, whose concerns are considerably less historically specific – this claim has to be seen, in fact, as making a point that is already internal to the 'Work of Art' essay's central concerns (Žižek, 2004, pp. 77, 78). While there is thus some historical truth in Žižek's suggestion that, for example, 'not only are . . . mass performances not inherently Fascist . . . it was Nazism that stole them and appropriated them from the workers' movements, their original site of birth', this is not only a question of 'their specific articulation' (78). For such articulation is also a *transformation*, in which the new 'mode of participation' promised by modernity becomes instead (as it will continue to be under the post-war conditions of capitalist spectacle) a mode of *alienation*: the collectivity at the heart of political praxis, and the focus of the historical avant-garde's desire, rendered as an *auratic* object of contemplation. If this 'overcomes' the post-eighteenth-century separation of 'autonomous art' from political life it does so at the cost of the alienation of the forms of experience promised by each.

Architecture, art and the arts

I want to return to some of these questions raised by the 'Work of Art' essay in a moment. But, before doing so, it is not implausible at this point to juxtapose with Benjamin's 'art based on politics' a series of more recent issues that have been attendant upon discussions of architecture's relationship to both art and aesthetics. In his 2013 'philosophy of contemporary art', Peter Osborne cites from Jeff Wall's book on the artist Dan Graham a claim that he rightly takes to be applicable to a wide range of artistic practices over the last 50 years (p. 160). Writing in the early 1980s, in the wake of what Wall describes as conceptualism's 'feeble response to the clash of its political fantasies with the real economic conditions of the art world', and to the realization that minimalism and pop art had 'given rise only to a new, more complex and distressed version of the art-commodity', it was *architecture*, Wall states, which emerged 'as the determining or decisive art form' for a range of 'post-conceptualist' practices in Europe and America during the late 1960s and 1970s (Wall, 2007, pp. 37, 32, 34).[6] Architecture acquired, in the work of Graham, Lawrence Weiner, Daniel Buren, Michael Asher, Robert Matta-Clark and others, 'canonical value' for *art* – to use Benjamin's phrase – as 'the discourse of siting the effects of power generated by publicity, information and bureaucracy in the city' (p. 34). In this way, it hoped to 'construct a critique of formalist or "purely aesthetic" art and thereby to turn directly toward "reality" (identified with the city) "with a view to changing it"' (p. 19).[7]

At the same time, as Osborne's adoption suggests, if Wall's argument concerns, primarily, the immediate historical legacy of conceptualism during the 1960s and 1970s, it also has a considerable contemporary resonance. Thus, in a recent book, Hal Foster describes the way in which the encounter between 'architecture' and 'visual art' – '[s]ometimes a collaboration, sometimes a competition' – has become, today, 'a primary site of image-making and space-shaping in our cultural economy' (Foster, 2011, p. vii); albeit in ways that Matta-Clark or Smithson could scarcely have predicted. Similarly, if less critically than Foster, Jane Rendell in her 2006 *Art and Architecture: A Place Between* also notes a contemporary 'blurring' of 'traditional boundaries between art and architecture' apparent in, for instance, site-specific work, public art and a variety of 'urban interventions'; referencing, on the one hand, artists such as Anya Gallacio, Rachel Whiteread and Thomas Hirschhorn, and, on the other, architectural practices including Koolhaas's OMA, FAT, MUF and Diller and Scofidio. And it is certainly the case that such an 'art-architecture complex', as Foster defines it, would appear to play an increasingly unprecedented role in both contemporary art *and* architecture, as well as in the development of the contemporary art institution itself. Indeed, to observe such a tendency towards the architectural has become a commonplace in contemporary art criticism, just as it has to regard it (with further echoes of Benjamin) as having some potentially distinctive 'political' (as well as cultural-economic) dimension.[8]

Nonetheless, if what Osborne (2013) calls this pervasive 'architecturalization of art' is, in some respects, a distinctly post-1960s phenomenon[9] – in which, at its extreme, 'something like "architecture" became, if not the new name for art, then certainly, for many, its model' (p. 141) – it also has its own history. This is a history which belongs, most forcefully, to the twentieth-century history of the *avant-garde*, as Wall's book makes clear. But it belongs, too, to a rather longer history of the emergence of the very modern concept of *art* itself. Benjamin's emphasis on architecture (or building) as that which is thus older than 'any other art' – and the semantic slippage in the term 'art' as it is used here – has perhaps, as we will see, a particular significance in this regard.

Since Paul Kristeller's classic account in his essay 'The Modern System of the Arts', first published in 1951–2 over two issues of the *Journal of the History of Ideas*, it has become gradually accepted that the modern concept of art – '"Art" with a capital A' – dates back only as far as the latter part of the eighteenth century in Europe, consequent upon the breakup of an older 'functional' idea of the arts – derived from the Greek *techne* and Latin *ars*, which referred to *any* human 'skill' – into the separate categories of 'fine art' and 'craft' (or popular forms) (Kristeller, 1951, p. 498). As Kristeller shows, and as has been explored at much greater length by Larry Shiner in his 2001 book *The Invention of Art*, this conception of 'Art', in the singular, depended, in turn, on a reorganization of the 'arts', in the plural, into the particular or several *fine* arts (or beaux arts). The historical process through which these several arts came, by the beginning of the nineteenth century, to be codified as the system of the *five* arts of poetry, painting, sculpture, music and architecture is a fascinating one, though its full scope obviously exceeds the space I have available to elaborate this here. Nonetheless, it is worth noting one aspect of it – what appears to have been the particularly problematic status of architecture within the early elaboration of these 'five arts' themselves.

In fact, although Shiner suggests that the core set of five arts was stabilized around the 1740s (2001, p. 81), in actuality this was not quite the case.[10] It is true that the magic number 'five' was well established by this time, but architecture's place within it was far from immediately secure. In Charles Batteaux's 1746 *Les beaux arts réduit à un même principe*, for example, the five arts are named as poetry, painting, sculpture, music and *dance* (Shiner, 2001, p. 83). Similarly, and more famously, while Diderot and D'Alembert's 'Preliminary Discourse' in the *Encyclopédie* (written by D'Alembert) lists the conventional five 'beaux arts', the 1751 'tree of knowledge' includes *engraving*, not architecture, among the five arts of 'imagination' (under the general heading of 'poesie') (see Shiner, 2001, pp. 83–5).

Both Kristeller and Shiner narrate what is, then, part of a general shift: one in which, among the various principles put forward to produce a concept of fine art(s), including imagination, genius, taste, originality and so on – precisely those 'traditional concepts' that Benjamin in the 'Work of Art' essay makes a claim to 'neutralize' (2002, p. 101) – 'pleasure versus utility played a pivotal role'. As Shiner notes, prior to the eighteenth century, most often 'pleasure was seen as subordinate to the aim of instruction or utility' (2001, p. 82), and it is that that was, of course, in romanticism extended into an even more profound distinction between the 'freedom' or *autonomy* of the artist versus the 'dependence' or *heteronomy* of the artisan (and in which 'service' as opposed to freedom came to be associated with 'trade', and thus subservience to the market[11]). Yet, significantly, architecture remained particularly resistant in this regard – hence, no doubt, its relatively late fixing in place within the five arts.[12] The institutional (and ideological) condition of its own 'aestheticization' (or, rather, 'artification') was thus, of course, precisely a split *between* 'architecture' (as the concern of the professional architect) and 'building' (as the concern of the engineer, surveyor or master mason); precisely the division that Benjamin tends to displace in his own account of 'architecture' in the 'Work of Art' essay. In the drawings and writings of a figure such as Etienne-Louis Boullée, as Shiner notes, architecture thus had to become, at the end of the eighteenth century, 'a species of poetry, something to be looked at rather than lived or worked in', and the architect 'primarily an artist who creates images' (Shiner, 2001, p. 105; see also Rosenau, 1974).[13] The roots of Benjamin's own counter-distinction between the 'optical' object of contemplation and the 'tactile' space of 'habit' are evident here.[14] Similarly, and with equally obvious relevance to the 'Work of Art' essay's account of the 'aesthetic', as the literary critic M. H. Abrams noted of the eighteenth century's 'Copernican revolution', it is during this period that we find 'the construction model . . . replaced by the contemplation model [of art], which treated the products of all the fine arts as . . . objects of rapt attention' (cited in Shiner, 2001, p. 6). What Kant famously defines as the 'distinterestedness' demanded of the 'aesthetic' as a *distinctive* form of experience becomes itself, in this way, very much a question *of* 'interest', in the rather different sense of 'focused attention' (Shiner, 2001, p. 144).

As Kristeller rightly notes, it is against this backdrop, then, that the 'basic notion' that 'the five "major arts" constitute an area all by themselves, clearly separated by common characteristics from the crafts, the sciences and other human activities, has been taken for granted by most writers on aesthetics from Kant to the present day' (1951, p. 498). It is thus unsurprising that the philosophy of art, along with aesthetics (and the problematic relationship between these two, which is registered in Hegel's opening remarks to his lectures on aesthetics), was itself 'only invented in that comparatively recent period', as Kristeller observes (1951, p. 496). Indeed, the very rationale *of* 'aesthetics', one might say, became one of providing a systematic justification for the modern system of art as a whole. Among other things, it is from this that Hegel's *historicization* of a hierarchy of the five arts thus develops. And, significantly, it is *architecture* that for Hegel is necessarily positioned as the earliest (and hence most 'primitive') among the arts, succeeded, in turn, by sculpture, painting, music and poetry. The passage is worth citing at some length:

The *first* of the particular arts with which, according to their fundamental principle, we have to begin, is architecture considered as a fine art. Its task lies in so manipulating external inorganic nature that it becomes cognate to mind, as an artistic outer world. The material of architecture is matter itself in its immediate externality . . . In this material and in such forms, the ideal as concrete spirituality does not admit of being realised. Hence the reality which is represented in them remains contrasted with the Idea as something external which it has not penetrated, or has penetrated only to establish an abstract relation. For these reasons, the fundamental type of the fine art of building is the *symbolical* form of art . . . [Architecture] raises an enclosure round the assembly of those gathered together, as a defence against the threatening of the storm, against rain, the hurricane, and wild beasts, and reveals the will to assemble, although externally, yet in conformity with principles of art . . . So much, indeed, may architecture attempt in this respect as even to create an adequate artistic existence for such an import [*Bedeutung*: meaning, significance] in its shape and its material. But in such a case it has already overstepped its own boundary, and is leaning to sculpture, the phase above it. For the limit of architecture lies precisely in this point . . . (Hegel, 1993, pp. 90–1)

Hegel's dense argument, which has to be placed within the much broader context of his philosophy of art as a whole (and poetry's privileged place within it), deserves a much fuller commentary than can be given here. I cite it at such length though to make a fairly simple point. For it becomes apparent in this way that Benjamin's own *privileging* of architecture has to be read as the effective inversion of this Hegelian account. That is to say, it is precisely *because* architecture (or building) is the 'oldest' of arts that it, paradoxically, provides a 'prototype' for the possibilities offered by the very 'newest' (cinema) to 'redeem' a different, fuller conception of the aesthetic.

To put it crudely, then, architecture's increasingly 'canonical value' for the avant-garde, in the first decades of the twentieth century, would be, from this perspective, that it is never *quite* art, at least as conceived in its post-romantic, modern sense. Architecture would thus always harbour a certain non-identity to its art status; a non-identity which appears on the side of 'utility' as opposed to the 'contemplative' forms of 'pleasure'. If, in this sense, Benjamin would seem, in his references to architecture's ancient or primeval origins, to draw upon the classical German Idealist division of the arts, for which this is a question of architecture being somehow *less* than art – that is, not quite *yet* an art form in the true sense, as Hegel argues in the passage above – equally it relies upon a contemporaneous avant-garde positioning of architecture as effectively *more* than art: the site, that is, of (autonomous) art's possible future overcoming.

It is this that must be seen, in turn, as the backdrop to the more recent encounters of 'art' and 'architecture' mapped out in, for example, Jane Rendell's book. As the latter puts it:

Architecture's curiosity about contemporary art is in no small way connected with the perception of art as a potentially subversive activity relatively free from economic pressures and social demands; while art's current interest in architectural sites and processes may be related to architecture's so-called purposefulness, its cultural and functional role . . . Artists value architecture for its social function, whereas architects value art as an unfettered form of creativity. (Rendell, 2006, p. 15)

While 'art' may here then 'offer architecture a chance for critical reflection and action' by virtue of its 'greater degree of separation from economic and social concerns' (p. 192), as Rendell argues (writing largely from the side of architecture), more telling, perhaps, is precisely the precarious 'art' status of architecture itself in this scenario. For it is in this precariousness that what Benjamin calls its 'canonical value' *for* a certain artistic practice, and for a certain understanding of the 'aesthetic', most evidently lies.

Signifying the social

In his recent philosophy of contemporary art, Peter Osborne writes:

First and foremost, for Western art since the Second World War – locked in the prison of a restricted understanding of its autonomy – architecture has functioned as a *signifier of the social*, of the functionality or practicality of form: economically, technologically and politically . . . [As] a signifier of the social, via the urban, architecture offers a 'privileged access' to the contemporary via the technologies of social production. The architectural aspect of contemporary art is thus that of a socio-spatial *effectivity*. It represents art's social being-in-the-world. (2013, pp. 141–2)

Yet, crucially, this (post-)avant-gardist conception of architecture relates also to the difficult and distinctly modern question of architecture's own status as 'art' in more general terms. As Tafuri narrates it, for earlier avant-gardes like Constructivism

Art's suicide should, in fact, be carried out in successive steps. First of all should die painting, absorbed (after having performed to the end its role as carrier of avant-garde methodology) by architecture, as concrete existential space: but only temporarily, because architecture itself will have to dissolve in the city, in the *ordered* metropolis. (1980, p. 37)

Of course, it is precisely the possible *actuality* of this overcoming or sublation – and particularly of its final 'step' – that has come, for many, to seem an increasingly utopian fantasy (indeed Tafuri was among the first to insist upon this). Hence, as Buchloh puts it, from such a melancholic perspective:

As far as the historically significant preoccupation with architectural dimension is concerned, the present-day artist is in a position that bears no comparison with the circumstances that had surrounded the Russian Productivists or El Lissitsky who could optimistically discuss his Prouns in terms of a 'changeover from painting to architecture'. The political situation no longer justifies that sort of utopian impetus and what is more, the aesthetic producer, even if he were at all willing and able to analyse the world that surrounds him, has no way of becoming effective outside the narrow domain of art allotted to him. Any thought of creating a functional relationship with reality is instantly ruined by that reality. (1980, p. 40)

As Wall's critical engagement with Buchloh on this point suggests, the latter's position here is one that would, as such, appear to identify itself, less with Benjamin's relative 'optimism' of the 1930s, than with Adorno's 'radicalism of negation'; a 'radicalism' which is read by Wall against the historical backdrop of the failure and 'deformation of revolutionary subjectivity and potential in the working-class movement' over the course of the interwar years and beyond (Wall, 2007, p. 12).

It is not insignificant, then, that it is precisely the unfolding historical problematic of architecture's *art* status with which Adorno himself will struggle in his one essay devoted to architecture, first delivered as a paper to the German Werkbund in 1965 – a problematic in relation to which his claim that architecture is 'in fact *both* autonomous and purpose-oriented' may well appear as a merely rhetorical solution. 'Functionalism Today' starts out from a confrontation with Loos's separation of the purposeful from the purpose-free, manifested in the elimination of 'ornament' from 'useful objects', which would emphatically seem to sever architecture from the concerns of an *autonomous* art. Yet, as Adorno argues, if in 'autonomous art, the useless is contained within its limited and particular form' and is 'thus helplessly exposed to the criticism waged by its opposite, the useful', it is also the case that, '[c]onversely, in the useful, that which is now the case [or already exists] is closed off to its possibilities': 'Functionalism would like to break out of this entanglement; and yet it can only rattle its chains in vain as long as it remains trapped in an entangled society' (Adorno, 1997a, p. 17).

According to this argument, the very possibility of a genuine 'functionality' or 'use' comes, in a society 'bewitched' by exchange value (whereby 'new *needs*' are called forth 'according to the profit motive') to be paradoxically dependent upon a moment of autonomy. Rather than being opposed, as Loos could be taken to suggest, art and architecture may thus represent different ends of the same problematic under the conditions of capitalist culture. This is why their *dialectic* for Adorno – the continually reconstituted relations *between* art and architecture – both registers, and is mediated by, a historically variable dialectic of the autonomous and heteronomous more generally. ('The curse of exchange has overtaken autonomous art as well', as Adorno puts it, just as it 'defiles useful work' (1997a, p. 17).) A dialectic of form and function is in this way internal to the work, in *both* art and architecture, and mediates the dialectic *of* art and architecture, as well as of autonomy and heteronomy, without thereby simply identifying the two: 'In any given product, freedom from purpose and purposefulness can never be absolutely separated from one another' (1997a, p. 8).

What makes 'Functionalism Today' interesting in the general context of Adorno's own work is the extent to which architecture (understood, in exemplary modernist fashion, as the articulation of a 'sense of space') thus appears in this way as a point of disturbance, not so much for this dialectic of autonomy and heteronomy itself, than for Adorno's tendency only to *affirm*, as genuinely critical, that art which would appear to operate at the extreme end of autonomy in such a dialectic.[15] Unwilling simply to declare that the works of Loos or Corbusier are not, *in some sense*, 'art', Adorno is compelled to shift subtly the terms of his own account, in revealing ways.

Now this is not the place to restage (yet again) the Adorno–Benjamin debate, but clearly, as so often, Adorno's reflections here may well be read as a belated response to Benjamin's own invocation of an architectural 'use-value' in the 'Work of Art' essay as elsewhere. Yet, as Buchloh writes, echoing Adorno in this respect, if use-value may be viewed as (autonomous) 'art's most heteronomous counterpart', such 'value' is nonetheless determined by 'the specific conditions of a given historical situation'. The 'artist as constructivist engineer in revolutionary Russia' – a model upon which Benjamin could still confidently draw in the 1930s – 'fulfilled a functional and aesthetic necessity, whereas forty years later . . . constructivist engineering necessarily functions merely as aesthetic objects' (Buchloh, 2000, p. 198). If this sets out the parameters, as Buchloh claims, for both 'the development of architecture since constructivism and the Bauhaus' *and* for, say, minimalism's ultimately 'aestheticizing' neo-avant-garde reprisal of constructivist images of functionality, the work of Graham, Asher or Matta-Clark is marked, on this account, by a conscious attempt to retrieve 'use-value' as the performance of a 'programmatic *critique* of the work of art as exchange value', and as a means to 'induce dialectics within the reality of cultural history' (2000, p. 220; emphasis added). And it is in this context that architecture *re*-emerges, under new historical conditions, as 'the determining or decisive art form'; in doing so, having recourse, again, precisely to its troubling *utility* when viewed from the perspective of the modern concept of 'art' itself.

If the key historical term here is indeed, therefore, the one upon which Adorno rightly focuses – *function* – this concerns less the ideological opposition of function *to* form, which marks so many of the theories of architectural modernism itself, and which tended simply to equate form with a traditional 'aesthetic' per se, but rather the dialectical and dynamic conception of form *as* function which provides one horizon for the avant-gardiste image of an art projected into life. In fact, as Adrian Forty notes, until the end of the nineteenth century – with a few rare exceptions – '"function" was a term primarily relating to the tectonics of building', to the action of a building's own mechanical forces upon its form (Forty, 2000, p. 174). It is only in the first decades of the twentieth century that 'a new use of "function" became more widespread . . . in which buildings themselves were described as acting upon . . . social material' (p. 174). The problem of whether industrial *buildings* should, given their utilitarian purposes, be considered architecture is crucial to this second, developing sense. The American architect Albert Kahn, for example, made a clear distinction within his own practice between what he called the '*art* of architecture' and the '*business* of building', between his designs for schools, libraries or churches and his factory constructions for Ford and others (see Leatherbarrow and Mostavi, 2002, pp. 2–6). Yet it was precisely the latter – appropriated as functional *architecture*, and thus of artistic significance – that would make Kahn a pivotal figure for the Modern Movement. (In fact, George Nelson's 1939 monograph on Kahn *only* includes these types of buildings.) At the same time, for avant-gardists like the German G group in the 1920s, the concept of functionality, as Forty notes, served to disturb, far more radically, 'the whole previously existing conception of architectural aesthetics' derived from post-Kantian German philosophy:

'The interrelationship of architecture and use was now presented as the primary content of architecture, not just in opposition to the "aesthetic", but taking its place, to constitute a whole new meaning to that concept' (Forty, 2000, p. 183). Aesthetic space becomes 'living space', as Behne puts it in his influential 1926 book *The Modern Functional Building*, which is, in turn, conceived as both a return to, and an entirely *new* form of, architecture's embedding in the 'social sphere', in which, Behne writes, anticipating Benjamin, 'after all, must lie the *primeval* elements of the aesthetic' (cited in Forty, 2000, pp. 183, 185; emphasis added).

It is the supposed 'failure' of the political hopes embodied in this for avant-gardists like the G group or the Constructivists, as well as theorists such as Benjamin, that will, of course, then come to seem metonymic of the general failure of the avant-garde. Attempting to render its work 'political', the avant-garde finds itself instead, according to this narrative, simply returned to 'art' on a different level; reduced, with the corporate building's 'aestheticization' of functionalism itself, to what Tafuri calls 'sublime uselessness'. Led, by its desire to be more than *mere* art, to architecture, it finds that it can only produce architecture *as* art in a way that furthers the construction of that 'self-alienation' inherent to commercial spectacle; progressively limited to the specialized production of 'unique events', the individual building as auratic artwork, where, as Žižek puts it, 'aestheticization reaches its climax . . . [in] the gap between skin and structure' (2011, p. 275). Thus faced with an intractable contradiction, architecture is, as Tafuri puts it, apparently 'obliged to return to *pure architecture*, to form without utopia' (Tafuri, 1976, p. ix; emphasis added).

The artification of architecture

A further point must however be made. For what Tafuri describes as a return of architecture to art – to 'form without utopia' – is itself ambiguous, and its 'sublime uselessness' is only useless in one sense. First of all, because it is put to some pretty obvious *uses* within contemporary capitalism, in ways which mark a developing post-war functionalization *of* art's autonomy itself. As Peter Bürger rightly notes: 'Only an art that has become (relatively) autonomous can be harnessed. The autonomy of art is thus simultaneously the precondition for its later heteronomy. Commodity aesthetics presupposes an autonomous art' (1984, p. 113.) Or, in Adorno's words, in capitalist society 'usefulness has its own dialectic' (Adorno, 1997a, p. 9): 'If an advertisement were strictly functional, without ornamental surplus, it would no longer fulfil its purpose as advertisement' (1997a, p. 17). Indeed, this is, in some sense, the insurmountable dialectic of form and function as such, as it is socially constituted by the value form.

It is worth saying that it is this, then, that lies, invariably, in the background to recent discussions about architectural 'spectacle', for which, say, the extraordinary 'aestheticization of the "skin"' manifested in Gehry's Bilbao Guggenheim (1991–7) has become emblematic (Žižek, 2011, p. 276). As signs of 'artistic expression', Hal Foster argues, Gehry's recent work presents itself less as the production of some new form of social space and more as *sculpture*: such 'cultural centres' are – recalling the 'attentive concentration' of Benjamin's tourist's gaze – primarily optical 'sites of spectacular spectatorship, of touristic awe' (Foster, 2002, pp. 40, 37, 41). Yet, crucially, what is perceived in this regard as 'sculptural' cannot but be inscribed, therefore, within a history of architecture's relation to the category of 'art', which is perhaps more complex than Foster allows.[16] If for Hegel, for example, as we have already seen, architecture is still somehow *less* than art, its capacity to 'create an adequate artistic existence' for *Geist* is precisely dependent upon it 'overstepping' its 'own boundary', in historical terms, and 'leaning to sculpture, the phase above it' (Hegel, 1993, pp. 90–1). To the extent that the avant-garde conception of architecture inverts this schema, to conceive of architecture as autonomous art's historical overcoming – so as, in Benjamin's terms, to restore it to some new 'aesthetic' terrain in a more fundamental sense – Gehry might then be understood to invert this avant-garde narrative in turn. In this sense, to dismiss the work too quickly as *merely* sculpture (and therefore as 'art' pure and simple) is to miss the historical complexity of the dialectic of art and architecture, form and function, that is apparent in it, however seemingly acritical it may well be.

In his account of post-1960s art's movement from an ontology of the visual to that of the spatial in his book *Real Spaces*, David Summers, like Osborne, presents architecture as of 'canonical value' insofar as it is the 'art of social space' (Summers, 2003, p. 43). Yet this passes over certain intrinsic problems with such a straightforward conception. First, because the 'art' of architecture as an art of social space, as Summers invokes it, hesitates, necessarily, between a kind of general technics and a more specific, autonomous, post-eighteenth-century conception. This would be its intrinsic dialectic of form and function, of art and non-art, played out continuously in both contemporary architecture and post-conceptual art's architectural turn. Second, because the very idea of architecture as 'social space' is not a simple given – it has itself a history; one, as in Benjamin's 'Work of Art' essay, inextricably related to the question of the avant-garde, as well as to the very modern formation of the concept of art. In fact, a conception of architecture as the production of space (social or otherwise) scarcely exists before the last decade of the nineteenth century, and is, in some sense, born *from* the problems of its 'art' status. The relation of form to the social is, from this perspective, an ongoing *problem* in actual architectural production, not its simple starting point.

Of course this does not necessarily alter the fact that it is the ongoing and immanent *visibility* of social 'contradiction' in architecture that may well be the general condition of its 'canonical value' for other cultural practices today: that is, its embodiment of some 'underlying deadlock or antagonism' which it may 'enact' in a more or less 'directly palpable way' (Žižek, 2011, p. 255). Yet this is less a question of some political 'use-value' embodied within modern architecture understood simply *as* the 'art of social space', so much as it is a question of its positioning as the privileged site of social contradictions *of* space within the urban and cultural forms of capitalist development itself as mediated by the (exchange) value form. It hardly needs to be said that such contradictions are not (and cannot be) resolved either in architecture or art themselves. Rancière may well be right, in this sense, to argue that the 'entire question of the "politics of aesthetics"' rests on a certain 'experience' of an '*and*', of 'the same knot binding together autonomy and heteronomy' (though wrong to think that this wasn't what was *precisely* at stake in modern art for Adorno, as 'Functionalism Today' so clearly shows) (Rancière, 2002, p. 134). Yet, if this is a consequence of the late-eighteenth-century emergence of what

Rancière terms the 'aesthetic regime' – for which Schiller's conjunction of 'the art of the beautiful *and* of the art of living' is exemplary (p. 134) – it is also, in the end, a consequence, above all, of the overdetermining forces of a *capitalist* modernity, in which the very desire to escape 'art' in the direction of some new 'aesthetic' life cannot but confront art's 'outside' as a world currently dominated by the value form. The *communist* 'politicization of art' named, for the Constructivists as for Benjamin, the promise of a *different* social world in which some different experience of the 'aesthetic' might be redeemed. In its absence, a radical philosophy of architecture is less an 'aesthetics' in any significant sense, than it is a philosophy of the 'entanglement' of autonomy and heteronomy that is the mark of our 'entangled society' itself (Adorno, 1997, p. 17).

Notes

1   This essay revisits some material first published in a piece entitled 'A Seam with the Economic: Art, Architecture, Metropolis', in Marta Kuzma and Peter Osborne (eds), *ISMS: Constructing the Political in Contemporary Art*. Oslo: Office for Contemporary Art Norway, 2006, pp. 131–66. My thanks to the editors for permission to rework that material here.

2   In part, this is a result of Rancière's own mobilization of two different (if connected) meanings of 'aesthetics': one that is effectively trans-historical, since it is a feature of *all* politics in whatever era (as well as, presumably, of all 'building'), and one which is, as applied to 'art', specific to the *modern* 'aesthetic regime'. Yet, by virtue of his broader animus towards any form of sociological explanation, Rancière ultimately has little means of explaining *why* exactly such an aesthetic regime should emerge when and where it does, outside of a fairly loose set of connections to some post-1789 conjuncture, or undeveloped references to the impacts of industrialization and new media (see Cunningham, 2011).

3   As Larry Shiner observes, the Grand Tour was crucial to architecture's eighteenth-century incorporation within the emergent system of the 'fine arts', in so far as it 'encouraged the tendency to look at architecture, the most "utilitarian" of the fine arts, primarily in terms of beauty and style' (Shiner, 2001, p. 92).

4   In fact, the problems entailed by this 'reversal of meaning', as Buck-Morss calls it, have been noted throughout the history of the philosophy of art's identification with 'aesthetics'. As Friedrich Schlegel writes in 1798: 'In the sense in which it has been defined and used in Germany, aesthetic is a word which notoriously reveals an equally perfect ignorance of the thing and of the language' (1991, p. 5). A similar point is made in the opening remarks of Hegel's lectures on aesthetics: 'The name "Aesthetic" in its natural sense is not quite appropriate to this subject [that is, "Fine Art"]. "Aesthetic" means more precisely the science of sensation or feeling. . . . As a name . . . it may be retained. The proper expression, however, for our science is the "Philosophy of Art", or, more definitely, the "Philosophy of Fine Art"' (Hegel, 1993, p. 3).

5   It is worth noting that it is this that also links the 'canonical value' of architecture to its particular place, not so much within the visual arts alongside painting and sculpture (the customary post-Kantian terrain of its 'aesthetic' reception), as within a larger history of a 'kinaesthetic' sense of *space* – a conception of architecture as a

technics (or 'art') of space that has itself, following the terms of a theoretical account developed in the last decade of the nineteenth century by the likes of August Schmarsow and Theodor Lipps, a distinctly modern history. Most influentially, it is this that reaches a certain highpoint in Moholy-Nagy's *Von Material zu Archiketur* (1928), his effective textbook of Bauhaus pedagogy, which plots a well-known – and implicitly hierarchical – trajectory from painting (material) to sculpture (volume) to, finally, architecture (space), and upon which Benjamin may well have drawn.

6   Much of Wall's analysis is itself implicitly Benjaminian in some respects. Thus, for example, Lawrence Weiner's ruptural 'gestures' are interpreted as ones which 'interrupt the induced habits of the urban masses'. At the same time, however, its lengthy discussion in the 1981 'draft' version stresses the 'limits' of Benjamin's distinction between an aestheticization of politics and a politicization of art, in so far as Wall reads this, wrongly I think, as little more than a 'literary device' designed to 'veil' the defeats and betrayals of communism in the 1920s and early 1930s in the face of fascism (see Wall, 2007, pp. 12–14).

7   The quotes in this passage are taken from Buchloh, 1980, p. 43. From a slightly more formal perspective, it is worth mentioning that within art criticism and theory Rosalind Krauss' 1979 essay 'Sculpture in the Expanded Field', focused around the work of Robert Morris, Robert Smithson and others, also marks a key moment here in its analysis of the erosion of distinct borders between 'architecture' and 'landscape', although, in this case, such erosion was itself ultimately overcome via Krauss' delimitation of such an 'expanded' trans-medial field in terms of an enlargement of the specific 'fine art' of sculpture itself. See Krauss, 1986.

8   A special issue of the art magazine *Frieze* [May 2006] devoted to the subject would be exemplary in this respect; see, in particular, Higgie, 2006, on the work of Marjetica Potrc.

9   In this sense, the art-architecture complex can also partly be understood as a consequence of what in the 1960s Adorno began to describe as an advance of 'nominalism' across the arts: that is, an increasing emphasis on the *singularity* of the individual artwork in the face of the ongoing destruction of plausible 'aesthetic' norms, whether grounded in genre, medium or discipline. In so far as each artwork, according to this account, demands to be taken, *in theory*, 'on its own terms', it cannot be prejudged by any given criteria, including whether it 'belongs' to architecture or the visual arts (see Adorno, 1997b, pp. 199–201, 219–20).

10 An indication of the kinds of earlier taxonomies that preceded the system of the five arts is to be found in Ephraim Chambers's 1728 *Cyclopedia*, which puts Architecture in with 'Mechanics', as a derivation of 'Mixed Mathematics', along with Sculpture, Trades and Manufactures. In the *Cyclopedia*, Painting comes under Optics, while Poetry is included in a completely distinct set designated as 'Symbolic', with Grammar, Rhetoric and Heraldry (see Shiner, 2001, pp. 80–1).

11 Of course, as Shiner points out – and the argument is made very similarly by Adorno in *Aesthetic Theory* – this might more accurately be thought in terms of two different relations *to* the market: 'In the purest form of a market system, by contrast [to an older system of patronage], writers, painters, and composers produce in advance and then attempt to sell their work to an audience of more or less anonymous buyers, often using a dealer or an agent. The absence of a specific order or a prescribed context of use gives the impression that the artists are completely free to follow their own inclinations' (Shiner, 2001, pp. 126–7). Significantly, of course, this is only very

rarely true of architecture, which, to varying degrees, remains generally dependent on some relation to a specific client, if only a developer.

12 Tellingly, both the Ècole des Beaux-Arts *and* the Ècole Polytechnique, established at the end of the eighteenth century following the French Revolution, offered courses in architecture, 'a fact reflecting architecture's "mixed" status' (Shiner, 2001, p. 105).

13 Questions of *social* distinction were also crucial here, to the degree that this sought to rectify the relatively low status accorded to architecture (as opposed to poetry, particularly) since antiquity, which had only been partly altered during the Renaissance. See Kristeller, 1951, pp. 502–3.

14 This is not, of course, as already remarked in relation to Goethe, without its own resistances internal to the philosophy of art. Herder, for example, in his account of sculpture forcefully rejects a privileging of 'contemplation' over sensory touch. At the end of the nineteenth century, Alois Riegl, in his notorious account of the 'art drive', will historicize this very distinction itself, narrating art's development as one from the tactile to the 'redemptive' pleasures of the optical.

15 There is a certain shifting of terms in Adorno's essay whereby the *differend* between the purposeful (*zweckgebunden*) and the purpose-free (*zweckfrei*) comes, via Loos's arguments concerning 'ornamentation', to be translated into one between the 'necessary' and the 'superfluous'. This allows Adorno to construct what he describes as a more than 'journalistic' relation between Loos's 'functionalism' and Schoenberg's decomposition of romantic cliché, and to view both as engaging a problematic 'inherent' in the work which is 'not defined by the work's relationship – or lack of it – to something outside itself' (1997a, p. 7). Yet this involves a pretty clear sleight of hand. The problem of 'function' or 'purpose' in modern architecture and modern music evidently does not involve the 'same' issues, nor is the nature of the relation (or lack of it) to 'something outside' of the work simply equivalent.

16 The sculptor Richard Serra's critical account of current architecture, in conversation with Foster, is interesting in this respect: 'One of the problems I see in architecture now is the division between the structure, the more engineered part, and the skin, the more architected part. The architect becomes the person who focuses a little on the layout and a lot on the ornament, whether it's glass, titanium that bends, or scenographic surface, while the structure is handed over to the engineer' (Foster, 2011, p. 234). In this sense, Serra implies, the architect risks becoming more of an 'aesthetic' artist than the hands-on sculptor who needs to remain closer to the 'engineer' in dealing with construction.

Bibliography

Adorno, T. W. (1997a), 'Functionalism Today', in N. Leach (ed.), *Rethinking Architecture: A Reader in Cultural Theory*. London and New York: Routledge, pp. 6–19.

— (1997b), *Aesthetic Theory*. R. Hullot-Kentor (trans.). Minneapolis: University of Minnesota Press.

Alliez, E. and Osborne, P. (2013), *Spheres of Action: Art and Politics*. London: Tate.

Benjamin, W. (2002), 'The Work of Art in the Age of Its Reproducibility'. E. Jephcott and H. Zohn (trans), in *Selected Writings, Volume 3, 1935–1938*, ed. H. Eiland and M. W. Jennings. Cambridge, MA: Harvard University Press, pp. 101–33.

Buchloh, B. H. D. (1980), 'Context-Function-Use Value: Michael Asher's Re-Materialization of the Artwork', in *Michael Asher: Exhibitions in Europe, 1972–1977*. Eindhoven: Stedelijk Van Abbemuseum.

— (2000), *Neo-Avant-Garde and Culture Industry: Essays on European and American Art from 1955 to 1975*. Cambridge, MA: MIT Press.

Buck-Morss, S. (1992), 'Aesthetics and Anaesthetics: Walter Benjamin's Artwork Essay Reconsidered', *October*, 62, pp. 3–41.

Bürger, P. (1984), *Theory of the Avant-Garde*. M. Shaw (trans.). Minneapolis: University of Minnesota Press.

Cunningham, D. (2007), 'Architecture as Critical Knowledge', in M. Dorrian, M. Fraser, J. Hill and J. Rendell (eds), *Critical Architecture*. London and New York: Routledge, pp. 31–9.

— (2011), 'Flaubert's Parrot', *Radical Philosophy*, 170, pp. 46–50.

Debord, G. (1983), *The Society of the Spectacle*. Detroit: Black & Red.

Forty, A. (2000), *Words and Buildings: A Vocabulary of Modern Architecture*. London: Thames & Hudson.

Foster, H. (2002), *Design and Crime (and Other Diatribes)*. London and New York: Verso.

— (2011), *The Art-Architecture Complex*. London and New York: Verso.

Hegel, G. W. F. (1993), *Introductory Lectures on Aesthetics*. B. Bosanquet (trans.). London: Penguin.

Higgie, J. (2006), 'Form Follows Function', *Frieze*, 99, pp. 136–41.

Krauss, K. (1986), 'Sculpture in the Expanded Field', in *The Originality of the Avant-Garde and Other Modernist Myths*. Cambridge, MA: MIT Press, pp. 279–90.

Kristeller, P. O. (1951), 'The Modern System of the Arts: A Study in the History of Aesthetics Part I', *Journal of the History of Ideas*, 12, 4, pp. 496–527.

— (1952), 'The Modern System of the Arts: A Study in the History of Aesthetics (II)', *Journal of the History of Ideas*, 13, 1, pp. 17–46.

Leatherbarrow, D. and Mostavi, M. (2002), *Surface Architecture*. Cambridge, MA: MIT Press.

Osborne, P. (2013), *Anywhere or Not at All: Philosophy of Contemporary Art*. London and New York: Verso.

Rancière, J. (1999), *Disagreement: Politics and Philosophy*. J. Rose (trans.). Minneapolis: University of Minnesota Press.

— (2002), 'The Aesthetic Revolution and Its Outcomes: Emplotments of Autonomy and Heteronomy', *New Left Review*, 14, pp. 133–51.

— (2004), *The Politics of Aesthetics*. G. Rockhill (trans.). London and New York: Continuum.

— (2009), *Aesthetics and Its Discontents*. S. Corcoran (trans.). Cambridge: Polity.

Rendell, J. (2006), *Art and Architecture: A Place Between*. London: I.B. Tauris.

Rosenau, H. (1974), *Boullée and Visionary Architecture*. London: Academy.

Schlegel, F. (1991), *Philosophical Fragments*. P. Firchow (trans.). Minneapolis: University of Minnesota Press.

Shiner, L. (2001), *The Invention of Art: A Cultural History*. Chicago: University of Chicago Press.

Summers, D. (2003), *Real Spaces: World Art History and the Rise of Western Modernism*. London and New York: Phaidon.

Tafuri, M. (1976), *Architecture and Utopia: Design and Capitalist Development*. B. Luigia La Penta (trans.). Cambridge, MA: MIT Press.

— (1980), *Theories and History of Architecture*. G. Verrecchia (trans.). London: Granada.

Vidler, A. (2008), *Histories of the Immediate Present: Inventing Architectural Modernism*. Cambridge, MA: MIT Press.

Wall, J. (2007), *Selected Essays and Interviews*. New York: Museum of Modern Art.

Žižek, S. (2004), 'The Lesson of Rancière', in J. Rancière, *The Politics of Aesthetics*. G. Rockhill (trans.). London and New York: Continuum, pp. 69–79.

— (2011), 'The Architectural Parallax', in N. Lahiji (ed.), *The Political Unconscious of Architecture*. Farnham and Burlington, VE: Ashgate, pp. 253–95.

3

We Are Already Dwelling: Hegel and the Transcendence of Place

Todd McGowan

Material in a spiritual world

Of all the arts, Hegel has the least to say about architecture. The fact that he begins his discussion of the fine arts with architecture provides the leading clue concerning its relative value for him. As anyone conversant with even one of Hegel's philosophical works is aware, the starting point always has the least importance for him in relation to everything that follows. Hegel begins with abstraction and moves in the direction of concreteness. For example, pure being is the most abstract and empty form of thought, which is why it begins the *Science of Logic*, and the case is exactly the same with sense certainty in the *Phenomenology of Spirit*. He doesn't begin either work with the absolute, though it is clear that this is where his real allegiance lies. In Hegel's philosophy, the first is last, and the last is first. Hegel locates architecture first in his discussion of the various arts in the *Aesthetics* not in order to give it pride of place but in order to reveal its poverty in relation to the other arts.[1]

The poverty of architecture stems from its association with matter itself. While poetry, the greatest of the arts for Hegel, completely leaves behind the material world and inhabits language or the realm of the spiritual, architecture is unthinkable without its materiality. The muteness of the architectural work derives from the lingering materiality that poetry shakes off. Language lifts the subject out of its natural being, but materiality brings the subject back to the stupidity of its origin in nature. Nature is not an ideal for Hegel, but a barrier to freedom. This attitude towards the natural world leads directly to his unsympathetic treatment of architecture.

In the conclusion of the *Critique of Practical Reason*, Kant links the sublimity of nature to what is highest in humanity – the moral law – and he implicitly views both as surpassing the most beautiful work of art.[2] For Hegel, this claim by Kant about the lofty status of nature represents a grave philosophical error. Instead of privileging the sublimity of the natural world, we should see that spirit gives nature whatever sublimity it has and thus that spirit is infinitely more valuable. Hegel devalues architecture because he believes that 'the beauty of art is *higher* than nature' (1975a, p. 2). Not content with this reversal of the typical way of ranking the beauty of nature and art, Hegel goes on to add, 'considered formally [i.e. no matter what it says], even a useless notion that enters a man's head is higher than any product of nature, because in such a notion spirituality and freedom are always present' (1975a, p. 2). The most inane comment uttered by the most inane person surpasses, according to Hegel's way of thinking, even the most beautiful sunset or mountain landscape. For anyone who prefers beautiful sunsets to inane people, this is a difficult position to accept.[3] And there is a direct line from this dismissal of nature to the relegation of architecture to the position of the most abstract of the fine arts. Hegel's lack of interest in architecture stems from his denigration of the natural world.

In the natural world, beings have an attachment to place. They evolve and prosper in particular places, and the transformation of place typically has a deleterious effect of their chances for survival. Beings suffer extinction when an event displaces them or renders their place uninhabitable, which is precisely what occurred with the Javan Tiger in 1979. The intrusion of human population into the animal's place made its continued existence impossible. Human beings, at an earlier point in their existence, had a similar relation to place. But with the emergence of language, which, in Hegel's terms, spiritualizes the human animal, the animal becomes a speaking subject and loses its place. For the speaking being, displacement doesn't lead to extinction but defines the contours of its existence. Once the subject begins to speak, it breaks the bond that it has with place as it transcends its natural being. This alienation from natural being is at once the basis for the subject's freedom: there is no freedom without alienation.

Philosophy, as Hegel practises it, identifies how freedom manifests itself through alienation. In the light of philosophical interpretation, alienating events miraculously become visible as sites for the emergence of freedom. In the *Phenomenology of Spirit*, the absolute fear that the slave undergoes and the work that the master demands of the slave alienates the slave from itself. No one envies the slave in this state of total alienation, but this alienation, as Hegel's analysis shows, becomes the engine for the latter's freedom. The disruption of the slave's natural life makes possible a freedom that the master, who remains ironically enslaved to the natural world, cannot enjoy. Similarly, our removal from place is what enables us to recognize ourselves as free beings. Given its connection to place and the natural world, architecture would seem to be inherently unfree and thus inartistic. It would seem to develop a place for us rather than to alienate us from our place. In this sense, it would not be an art but just part of our natural being.

Nonetheless, architecture does qualify as an art for Hegel, and in his analysis of it, he identifies the chief task of architecture as the constitution of a privileged site through which the first transcendence of natural life occurs. Architecture's proximity to the natural world enables it to be the site of a clear break from this world. Originally, the need for shelter drove people into caves, but the need itself could not produce art. Need is natural rather than spiritual. Hegel dismisses the importance of the cave as a form of shelter because the cave dwellers accept what the natural world provides for them.[4] The cave offers an enclosure, but there is no freedom in the refuge of the cave, in contrast to the simplest hut built above ground.

The first great architectural advance occurs with the creation of tombs and mausoleums. When the Egyptians build structures for the dead, they enact through architecture the break from the natural world of life and death. In the pyramids and other sites, spirit becomes evident for the first time. Though he sees clearly the limits of this form of architecture devoted to creating a home for the dead, Hegel nonetheless expresses his appreciation for it in the *Aesthetics*.[5] The interruption of the natural world tears the subject out of its natural destiny. Even in death, the individual attains transcendence through the tomb.

There is an affirmation of individuality in the building for the dead. Hegel claims, 'in the case of the Egyptians the opposition between the living and the dead is strongly emphasized; the spiritual begins in itself to be separated from the non-spiritual. It is the rise of the individual concrete spirit which is beginning. The dead are therefore preserved as something individual and in this way are fortified and preserved against the idea of absorption into nature' (1975b, p. 650). By building a sacred home for the dead, the Egyptians asserted the freedom of the dead individual from its finitude. Architecture is the most abstract of the arts because it lacks language, which is the basis of the subject's concrete development. But as the most abstract art, it provides the initial impetus that frees the subject from its immersion in the monotony of the natural world. In the case of architecture, the break constituted by the starting point is more evident than the philosophical achievement of this art's conclusion. Unlike other objects of Hegel's philosophical speculation, architecture doesn't seem to lead so clearly towards an absolute form. Its abstractness functions as a direct obstacle to the absolute.

And yet, there is an absolute that architecture attains. When it does, the subjects who dwell in the architectural structures can experience a home in their displacement itself. The great achievement of architecture as an art is the alienated world that this art creates in which subjects can dwell while not having a natural place. This dwelling enables subjects to reconcile themselves to their unnatural being and thus experience how the infinite disrupts their finite being and renders them incapable of simply being finite.

The philosophical and political role of architecture consists in fostering the subject's recognition of its fundamental displacement. Architecture doesn't have the power to ameliorate this displacement, but it can change the way the subject relates to it. Rather than trying to overcome this displacement and find a place in the world, the task is to grasp the displacement as constitutive of subjectivity and to dwell within it. The chief danger of a constitutive displacement lies in our proclivity to seek a cure for it, in trying to root subjectivity in a place. The absolute form of architecture allows subjects to dwell in their displacement without envisioning the possibility of overcoming it.

An absolute architecture

In the construction of a philosophy, one must always arrive at the position of the absolute – the point where thought reconciles itself with its object. This is the motivating idea of Hegel's philosophical project. The drive to the absolute is not a function of Hegel's commitment to teleology but his recognition that we are always already at the end, that we think from the perspective of the end.[6] The absolute is unavoidable, though we oftentimes fail to recognize it. Each domain of thought has an absolute perspective from which we must think it if we are not to disfigure and misrepresent this domain. The history of philosophy must attain the absolute philosophy, the philosophy of religion must discover the absolute religion and the philosophy of aesthetics must find the absolute form of each art. The problem with the philosophical failure or refusal to achieve the absolute is that this gesture belies the actual situation of thought and thereby obscures the speculative identity of thought with its object.

As long as thought remains on this side of the absolute, the reconciliation of thought with its object appears as something yet to be accomplished and thus embodies a possible overcoming of contradiction. This is the shared weakness of Kant's moral philosophy and Derrida's deconstruction. In each case, the awaited future – either moral perfection or the *à venir* – marks a possibility that remains constantly on the horizon. But this refusal to reconcile thought with its object has the effect of hiding the contradictory status of thought itself. This is why, from the beginning of his philosophy to the end, Hegel criticizes any form of 'ought'. If philosophy tells us what ought to happen – that we ought to obey the moral law or that we ought to attend to the justice to come – this philosophy disguises its own limitations by including what hasn't been accomplished or thought within its system. A thought that doesn't reconcile itself with its object misrepresents its true relation to its object, which is inherently absolute. It is only by arriving at the absolute in thought that the necessity of contradiction or limit becomes evident.[7] At the moment thought achieves identity with its object, this object sustains its status as non-identical with thought.

The difficulty with architecture, as Hegel sees it, lies in its attachment to the natural world, an attachment that logic, for instance, doesn't have. One reaches the absolute in the *Science of Logic* with much more facility than one does in the architecture section of the *Aesthetics*. Poetry, the art most distant from architecture, has a clearer path to the absolute. The attachment to the natural world creates a philosophical obstacle for the thinker confronted with the architectural work of art. The problem lies in identifying the absolute architectural work – the work in which thought can find itself and, at the same time, its opposite. Because architecture bears the stamp of the natural world, it confronts thought with an otherness that appears to represent an external barrier. But the challenge of aesthetic philosophy lies in converting this external barrier into the internal limit of thought itself, so that the subject can find itself at home within its otherness. If architecture cannot avoid externality, it cannot attain the absolute.

At the conclusion of his discussion of architecture, Hegel identifies the absolute architectural structure of his epoch. Architecture reaches its zenith, as Hegel sees it, in the Gothic church, an edifice that completely separates subjects from the natural world. Even the natural light of the sun has no role to play in Gothic church. In contrast to previous architectural structures, the church establishes a self-sufficient internal world in which the opposition with nature no longer exists. According to Hegel, 'What people need here is not provided by the world of nature; on the contrary they need a world made by and for man alone, for his worship and the preoccupations of his inner life' (1975b, p. 686). The break from nature that begins with the Egyptian tombs for the dead reaches an endpoint in the Gothic church.

But the Gothic church does not just provide a home removed from the natural world. It also enables subjects to develop a speculative relation to absolute otherness through its structure. The radicality of this structure lies in its secularization of the infinite. Even though it is a sacred place, the Gothic church is a product of the death of God, the transmutation of God as an absolute otherness into an otherness that belongs to the people themselves. In the architecture of the Gothic church, God ceases to be external and becomes present within the structure itself. The Gothic church thus has an absolute status, as Hegel's description of the edifice reveals. He admires the pillars that rise far above the people and meet at the arches of the church. In these pillars, subjects can grasp the infinite as internal to the structure itself. By facilitating this recognition, the architectural work of art produces a site where subjects can dwell in their displacement.

The church doesn't point towards an infinite that exceeds it but includes this infinite within itself. In this way, it transforms an external barrier into an internal limit. As Sylviane Agacinski points out in her analysis of Hegel's theory of architecture, 'The edifice, in general, like the book, must interiorize its limits, deny every exterior, accidental, and natural limit, in order to appear as a totality' (1987, p. 148). By creating a total structure, the Gothic church allows the subject to exist with what transcends it and reconcile itself with this transcendence. This edifice represents, for Hegel, the architectural absolute, but this doesn't mean that it puts an end to architecture as such. At every point in history, we have the capacity for recognizing the absolute, for recognizing our speculative identity with absolute otherness. Our sense of place enacts a barrier to this recognition, which is why architecture's role involves not renewing our sense of place but making possible the awareness of a thorough displacement.

Obviously, the role of contemporary architecture cannot be one of building Gothic churches. But in Hegel's analysis of the Gothic church, we can see the possibility for a theoretical approach to architecture in the terms of the absolute. An absolute architecture allows for spirit's reconciliation with itself, but as Hegel explains whenever he discusses the absolute, this reconciliation includes an acknowledgement of spirit's own limit. The absolute in this form only becomes possible with modernity's extension of the break from place that begins with the emergence of language. Hegel's embrace of dwelling in displacement reveals his status as a thoroughly modern philosopher.

Subject to displacement

The effect of modernity is nowhere so self-evident as it is when we examine place. In the Aristotelian world of the Middle Ages, humanity had a definite place in the scheme of things, and at the same time, each subject had a place within humanity. Even if earth occupies the lowest position in the ontological spectrum, it nonetheless has a clearly defined place where it belongs. And the lowliest peasant shares this sense of belonging to an order no matter how poorly this order treats her or him. This is what the emergence of modernity completely disrupts.

The fundamental gesture of modernity – the break from traditional authority and the decision to stand apart on one's own – decouples the subject from its place. When Descartes begins his philosophy not with scholastic arguments but with his own act of thinking, he accepts the absence of a secure place that this entails.[8] As the inaugural figure of modern philosophy, it is significant that Descartes never had a real home. Just as he deprived the subject of its secure place within tradition, he himself abandoned any permanent dwelling. He lived less than half his life in his native France and died on a voyage visiting Queen Christina of Sweden. Though Galileo (the founding figure of modern science) lived a less itinerant life than Descartes, he created a similar break from tradition.

By accepting the Copernican system and endeavouring to provide empirical proof for its validity, Galileo unravelled the Aristotelian conception of space and set the stage for modern physics. As an ultimate consequence of Galileo's efforts, humanity lost not only its place in the physical world but also any sense of stable place whatsoever. His scientific effort did not only help to remove earth from its former place at the centre of the world but also began the scientific movement towards the rejection of place altogether. Place would become relative to other places, and no place would any longer be absolute.

The philosophical and scientific displacement ushered in by Descartes, Galileo and other modern thinkers has a parallel in the psychic displacement that the capitalist economy enacts. The development of capitalism requires the destruction of place. In order to expand their accumulation, capitalists must constantly seek out new sites for cheaper production and new markets for their goods. As Marx points out in the *Grundrisse*, capitalism necessitates the transcendence of the limits that constitute place. He claims, 'Capital by its nature drives beyond every spatial barrier. Thus the creation of the physical conditions of exchange – of the means of communication and transport – the annihilation of space by time – becomes an extraordinary necessity for it' (1993, p. 524).[9] If an individual capitalist decided to respect the uniqueness of place and refuse to move production or target new consumers, this capitalist would stand no chance of surviving in the face of others who obeyed the exigencies of the system. Individual capitalists don't destroy place; capitalism itself does.

Modern modes of communication and transport that capitalism develops eviscerate the uniqueness of place. Air travel renders even the most distant places on the planet accessible in a number of hours. News coverage produces live reports from wherever significant events occur, no matter how far away they might be. Cell phone networks enable people to communicate with other people across the world with relative ease. The distance of space constitutes the uniqueness of place, and capitalism's elimination of the former leads to the destruction of the latter.

But there is an even more direct way that capitalist modernity eliminates the sense of place. It causes each place to resemble every other place. The architecture of the strip mall or the suburban single-family house represents a case of universalized reproduction. And though this is not the mechanical reproduction that Walter Benjamin discusses in his celebrated essay on this phenomenon, it has the same effect. According to Benjamin, mechanical reproduction destroys the aura of the work of art that otherwise has a unique and singular existence.[10] The reproduction of the strip mall eliminates the aura of place by reproducing the same structure over and over again in different places. The architectural distinctiveness of one city disappears amid the construction of a uniform structure.

Though probably no strip mall developers have based their structures on a reading of Descartes or Galileo, there is nonetheless a parallel between the revolution that they have made in thought and the architectural revolution of the strip mall developer. In each case, place has no place. Both Descartes and Galileo advance the idea that we have no rooted place from which we see, and the real estate developer creates an objective correlative for this idea in the figure of the strip mall. Even the most conscientious observer can detect no difference in the strip mall located in Boston and the one located in Los Angeles. The same stores populate the same architectural structures, and this architecture is nothing but the index of the subject's alienation from place.

The cell phone and the strip mall bring to a head the crisis of place that modernity inaugurates. Homelessness comes to function as a transcendental structure of modernity, and what results is an inability to identify where we are. This inability is the result of the modern revolution and its capitalist uprooting of tradition. The modern disruption of place is thoroughgoing and unrelenting. But it has occasioned a notable philosophical response.

Building a future dwelling

The primary critics of capitalist modernity often make its destruction of place one of the chief grounds of their attack. This is certainly the case for Martin Heidegger, whose philosophy is in large part a call for the recovery of what modernity has eliminated through the technological development that it unleashed. Heidegger associates dwelling or being at home in a place with the form of being that mortals must take up. Our locatedness in a place attests to our finitude, which is why Heidegger values it.[11]

As Heidegger sees it, the role of architecture lies in its capacity for enabling us to dwell – that is, to facilitate a relation to place. No such dwelling exists naturally, but it requires the architectural act to bring it into existence. Through the act of building a structure like a farmhouse in the Black Forest, peasants enter into a relation with their world, and the building makes this relation evident to them. While living in their farmhouse, the peasants experience their connection to a specific place and the importance of this connection for their existence. Building must provide shelter, but it only leads to dwelling which enables those who live in the building to live in an authentic relation to their finite being.

Of all major philosophers, Heidegger has probably given the most attention to architecture. Unlike Hegel, who conceived it as the most abstract art and the furthest removed from poetry, Heidegger aligns the function of architecture with that of poetry. In the same way, he theorizes the role of the architect as proximate to that of the poet. While the poet creates a space for us to reside within language, the architecture performs the same act through the creation of a home in the natural world. In an essay entitled '. . . Poetically Man Dwells . . .', Heidegger associates poetry directly with our dwelling on the earth. He says, 'Poetry does not fly above and surmount the earth in order to escape it and hover over it. Poetry is what first brings man onto the earth, making him belong to it, and thus brings him into dwelling' (1971b, p. 218).[12] As speaking beings – and especially as modern speaking beings – we are displaced from the earth and fail to dwell at all. Poetry is one version of the corrective, and architecture is another. The two arts, as Heidegger views them, work in parallel to enable us to learn to dwell. That effort is our philosophical challenge.

For Heidegger, architecture allows us to dwell on the earth, and poetry allows us to dwell in language. In each case, the art makes a place in which humans can exist in relation to the natural world. Hegel sees in art the capacity for lifting subjects out of the natural world and its finitude, a task for which architecture is barely suited because of its reliance on natural material. These contrasting attitudes come to head in the encounter with modernity. Hegel celebrates the Gothic church for separating subjects from the natural world, and Heidegger criticizes modernity for its profound indifference to the surrounding natural world in which it builds.

As Heidegger sees it, the problem with modernity is that it has made such dwelling impossible. Modern buildings alienate us from out capacity to dwell. We live in them, but their homogeneity rules out any specificity of place. When one is in a modern house, one could be in Paris, Los Angeles or Lagos. This indifference to place leads those who live in these houses to forget place, and when they forget place, they fail to engage in being itself, which is, for Heidegger, indissociable from the problem of dwelling. In his compelling description of Heidegger's philosophical project, Jeff Malpas writes, 'dwelling is the mode of human being, so human being is essentially a being in place, just as it is also a being in the world' (2012, p. 63). Modernity doesn't simply threaten our sense of place. It also threatens the recognition of our being in the world that place allows us acknowledge.

Heidegger's anti-modernity is not straightforward and uncomplicated. He criticizes modernity not for creating an existential homelessness but for disguising the homelessness that it produces. As Heidegger sees it, in modernity everyone is homeless, not just those who are actually sleeping on the streets. In fact, the empirical problem of the homeless in the modern world obscures the destruction of place that occurs with modernity. We cannot return to the rootedness of the peasant farmhouse in the Black Forest, but we can take up the question of learning to dwell. Modern architecture, along with the rest of modernity, acts as a barrier to this questioning, which is why Heidegger attacks it and calls for a return to authentic dwelling.

In 'Building Dwelling Thinking', Heidegger insists on our inability to dwell, which is what architecture must work to remedy. He says, 'the *real plight of dwelling* does not lie merely in a lack of houses. The real plight of dwelling is indeed older than the world wars with their destruction, older than the increase of the earth's population and condition of the industrial workers. The real dwelling plight lies in this, that mortals ever search anew for the nature of dwelling, that they *must ever learn to dwell*' (1971a, p. 161). In the modern world, we no longer see learning to dwell as a problem for us. We give ourselves over to a nomadic life and even enjoy the absence of a home. Architecture's abandonment of place represents a barrier to dwelling, but this barrier is also, as Heidegger sees it, the site of a solution.[13]

There is no question of returning to the construction of peasant farmhouses, despite Heidegger's clear affection for them. Instead, architecture must commit itself to the creation of buildings that would call us to dwelling out of the homelessness of the modern world. Heidegger envisions an architecture that would allow us to remember the problem of dwelling, even though we are in the midst of forgetting it. The modern destruction of place requires a vigilant construction of sites that lead us to rediscover place and thereby learn how to dwell.

Staircases leading nowhere

Heidegger marks a radical response to the modern destruction of place, but his radicality is not political radicality. Heidegger's hostility to modernity is a wholly nostalgic hostility, not a revolutionary one. The politically radical response to the destruction of place doesn't call for its reassertion and the possibility of dwelling but rather an architecture that would bring awareness of the destruction of place to the fore so that we could transform the socioeconomic system that has destroyed it. According to this position, the task of architecture in the capitalist world is alienating the subject and highlighting the subject's displacement when it occupies a building. Architecture's failure to provide dwelling becomes, from this perspective, a virtue. Subjects become revolutionary – or at least politicized – when they confront the displacement that capitalist modernity imposes on them.

Throughout his intellectual trajectory, Fredric Jameson has identified the moments of utopian potential within works of art. Even though he recognizes in what he calls postmodern art an overarching abandonment of the utopian impulse and an acquiescence to universal reification, he nonetheless sees points of resistance within the artistic landscape. One of these points is the Frank Gehry's house in Santa Monica, which Jameson focuses on while discussing architecture in his *Postmodernism*. The contrast with the Gehry house is the Westin Bonaventure Hotel in downtown Los Angeles, a building that gives itself over completely to the loss of place.[14] In the Bonaventure Hotel, the alienation is so thorough that no one can ever perceive it as such, and visitors end up unable to map the dislocation that occurs.

The Bonaventure Hotel hides the absence of place. Through its isolation of the subject from any discordant externality, the hotel creates a space without any place. One is so displaced that one cannot even locate the shop that one wants to revisit, but this displacement remains obscure. The Gehry house, in contrast, enables the subject to experience the dislocation of the contemporary capitalist world. In Santa Monica, Gehry built a new structure around an existing house. The existing house has a traditional design, while the shell of corrugated metal with which Gehry surrounds it has the look of a modern work of art. This combination produces a visible disjunction that contrasts with the homogeneous space of the Bonaventure Hotel.

The redoubled structure of the Gehry house produces a dialectical tension that forces the inhabitant to live out the contradiction that makes dwelling impossible. One cannot dwell here, and the building brings the absence of dwelling to the subject's attention. As Jameson puts it, 'The problem, then, which the Gehry house tries to think is the relationship between that abstract knowledge and conviction or belief about the superstate and the existential daily life of people in their traditional rooms and tract houses' (1991, p. 128). The spatial contradiction of contemporary capitalism is that of the massive state apparatus that incorporates all space and the isolation of the subject in an individual house. The subject lives somewhere in the capitalist world but cannot find a place because every place disappears within the capitalist system. The Gehry house emphasizes this contradiction through its divided structure, a structure in which the space of the superstate and that of the individual house constantly confront each other.

In the Gehry house, one confronts all the time one's failure to dwell, a failure endemic to advanced capitalism. But the utopian promise of this structure lies in its highlighting of the failure and its capacity for rendering this failure visible. In this way, the building points towards a utopian future in which we will really have a place. Awareness of homelessness indicates the possibility of a future home. In contrast to the Bonaventure Hotel, the Gehry house thematizes contemporary alienation without simply allowing it free reign and thereby giving into the loss of place. This is why Jameson celebrates it. The architectural project of our time, as he conceives it, is one of producing utopian moments by showing us just how far from utopia – and how far from place – that we are. The architectural alienation from place points us in the direction of place.

Alain Badiou offers a contrasting position to Jameson, even though he belongs to a similar Marxist tradition. In his masterpiece *Theory of the Subject* (2009), Alain Badiou recognizes place not as a home to rediscover but as a trap to be avoided at all costs. What differentiates Badiou from fellow Marxist Fredric Jameson is that Badiou's thought includes no reference to an ultimate sense of place that one might discover with the onset of communist society. For Badiou, place represents a danger no matter when it becomes a point of reference. The problem with place is that it hides the displacement that always accompanies it as its ontological shadow. The political gesture for Badiou is the interruption of place rather than the indication of its absence, and this is the key to a more radical position than that of Jameson.

The problem with Jameson's position is akin to the problem with that of Heidegger. Both Heidegger and Jameson, despite their political differences, fail to see the absolute status of our dwelling. Alienation from place or displacement is not a barrier to our dwelling but the essence of it. The problem with these two positions is that both oppose place and alienation from place without grasping their interconnectedness. We dwell not when we solve the problem of displacement but when we recognize this problem as its own solution. Displacement makes dwelling possible, and dwelling exists only when we sever our connection to place.

A dwelling that is no place

Hegel's refusal of any nostalgia for place in the natural world separated him violently from his contemporaries. Even Schelling, the thinker closest to him philosophically despite their personal differences, saw nature as a model for subjectivity. In fact, Robert Pippin sees him as the only thinker of the Romantic era to hold this position. He states,

'Hegel is one of the very few philosophers or writers or artists of this period – I would guess the only one – for whom *the beauty of nature was of no significance whatsoever.* Nature's status as *ens creatum*, as a reflection of God, or natural beauty as an indication of purposiveness are of no importance to him, and he expresses this while evincing no gnostic antipathy to nature itself as fallen or evil' (2002, p. 9). Hegel could never view the natural world with any attitude other than indifference.

For Hegel, nature is place, and place is what the subject frees itself from. The escape from place is not an escape from evil. It is, in Christian terms, a fall into evil. But the evil of our displacement is a liberating evil for Hegel. It frees us from the monotonous existence of the natural world, in which the only break from total determination is the interruption of contingency.

Though architecture is the most abstract art, it is also the site of a liberating evil. It perpetuates our fall from the natural world when its structure ceases to serve the human animal's need for shelter. As long as it solely provides shelter, building sustains its connection with place, but architecture, which transcends shelter, displaces the subject who inhabits its structure. Architecture enables the subject to recognize that its homelessness functions for it as a home, that the fall into evil is a necessary condition of our subjectivity.

Hegel has a place for architecture and the dwelling that it provides because his conception of subjectivity is not a nomadic one. A nomadic existence refuses any dwelling and insists on wandering from place to place. This is, of course, the position that Deleuze and Guattari endorse in their joint works and one that has attracted many contemporary political philosophers.[15] Though Hegel's emphasis on a constitutive displacement of the subject seems to align him with nomadism, the distinction between the two positions is stark. For Deleuze and Guattari, any idea of home is a trap to be avoided. For Hegel, on the other hand, one can make a home in one's displacement. In fact, recognizing that one is at home in one's displacement has the status of a philosophical and political necessity. To fail to do so is to perpetuate the illusion that a genuine place exists for the subject, even if the nomad rejects that place.

Architecture's great accomplishment is the recognition of constitutive displacement that it facilitates. When it promises a place for the subject, architecture betrays this accomplishment. Whether this place exists as a lost past or as a utopian future, the postulate of place deceives the subject confronted by the architectural work of art. When art slides into nostalgia or utopia, it loses touch with the absolute and its capacity for enabling subjects to recognize their freedom. Freedom is inextricable from the artistic refusal of both nostalgia and utopia.

Heidegger and Jameson mark the two primary philosophical approaches to architecture in the twentieth century. One seeks in it the possibility of establishing a place where we can secure our dwelling within the rootlessness of modernity. The other looks for a utopian promise of a new form of place that alienated subjects have yet to achieve. Both of these positions give in to the temptation that the form of architecture renders omnipresent. Because buildings typically use natural materials and have a fixed location, we tend to believe that architecture has an intrinsic bond with place. But architecture becomes an art only at the moment when it severs this bond and evinces the subject's capacity to transcend its place. In the edifice of absolute architecture, the subject dwells in its displacement. It recognizes its identity with absolute otherness.

When we take Hegel's position on architecture as a foundation for thinking about its role in the contemporary world, we can see this possibility of identity with absolute otherness. Rather than alienating us from place or affirming our rootedness in a place, architecture can reveal how we inhabit and dwell in the transcendence of place even when we remain tied to a particular place. It can show us, in other words, how we are already experiencing the infinite while we are rooted in the finite. The task of critical thought, for Hegel, lies in seeing the infinite within the realm of the finite, in recognizing that which transcends place within a place.

Notes

1 Despite its status as the most abstract of the fine arts, architecture at least merits discussion as a major art form. Dance, in contrast, submits to a far worse fate in the *Aesthetics*. Not only does Hegel refuse to discuss dance, but his dismissal of it as unworthy of discussion associates it with the art of gardening.

2 Kant famously says, 'Two things fill the mind with ever new and increasing admiration and reverence, the more often and more steadily one reflects on them: *the starry heavens above me and the moral law within me*' (1996, p. 269).

3 Just to be clear, on this point I follow Hegel completely. I do not count myself among those who prefer beautiful sunsets to inane people.

4 The unfreedom of the cave manifests itself in the animated film *The Croods* (Kirk DeMicco and Chris Sanders, 2013). It is only when their cave is destroyed that the cave-dwelling family in the film finds freedom from a total enslavement to the exigencies of the natural world. In a completely Hegelian fashion, the film depicts catastrophe as the necessary vehicle for freedom.

5 Earlier in the *Aesthetics*, Hegel makes his well-known statement that the problem with the riddles of Egyptian art is not that they are riddles for the modern interpreter but that they were riddles for Egyptian society itself. Egyptian symbolic art manifests an absence of knowledge rather than the subject recognizing itself in its other. When art acknowledges its absence of knowledge in the work of art, it bespeaks its continued entrapment in the natural world, a world synonymous with opacity. As Hegel notes in his *Philosophy of World History*, the contrast between the natural world and spirit centres around the question of self-transparency. He points out, 'Those who reckon truth to be incomprehensible in every respect are directed to the natural domain; for spirit is transparent to itself, is free, and reveals itself to spirit; it has nothing alien within itself. Nature, however, is what is hidden. With their thought in bondage, the Egyptians have to wrestle with something incomprehensible, and they possess it in the naturalness of animal life' (2011, p. 350). As a result of the hiddenness it promulgates, the work of art attached to the natural world always suggests that there is more to be discovered, when in fact the absolute lies in the obscurity itself.

6 For a conception of Hegel as a teleological thinker of aesthetics, see Desmond, 1986.

7 This critique of the 'ought' first appears in Hegel's early *Difference between Fichte's and Schelling's System of Philosophy*. There, he attacks Fichte for positing the 'ought' as his philosophical endpoint. He writes, 'the highest synthesis revealed in the system is an

ought. Ego *equals* Ego turns into Ego *ought* to equal Ego. The result of the system does not return to its beginning' (1977, p. 132). The absence of a return to the beginning in Fichte's system forces one to anticipate a reconciliation to be accomplished, and in doing so, Fichte hides the reconciliation that already exists and the contradiction that it reveals.

8   In his biography of Descartes, Desmond Clarke makes a point of noting that Descartes, in contrast to our typical image of the philosopher, did not spend much time reading. For him, philosophy must emerge out of oneself and not out of engagement with the thought of others. Clarke writes, 'Throughout his life he read few books, and he consistently avoided as much as possible the company of those who were regarded as learned. There was a sense in which his intellectual project was uniquely personal and solitary' (2006, p. 68).

9   Though Marx's point about capitalism's destruction of space is undoubtedly correct, his idea that capitalism replaces space with time is much less certain. It seems, in contrast, that both space and time disappear under the weight of capitalist development. Capitalism constantly seeks to reduce the time of production, the time of distribution and the time of consumption to zero. And with the development of digital technology, time – or the necessity of waiting – loses its hold over the subject. For more on capitalism's relationship to time, see McGowan, 2011.

10   See Benjamin, 2003.

11   Though it is impossible to locate one component of Nazism that enabled it to appeal to a philosophy of Heidegger's stature, surely its apotheosis of place played a significant role. Nazism promised a cure for the rootlessness of modern life that Heidegger himself sought in his philosophy and that he continued to seek even after Nazism's defeat.

12   Heidegger's conception of poetry here contrasts completely with that of Hegel. For the latter, poetry's great achievement is that it liberates us from the finitude of the natural world, not that it anchors us in this world.

13   One constant in Heidegger's philosophy is his claim that the more dangerous a situation is, the more hope that there is for salvation from that situation. Alluding to Hölderlin, he famously ends his essay 'The Question Concerning Technology' with this idea. He writes, 'The closer we come to the danger, the more brightly do the ways into the saving power begin to shine and the more questioning we become. For questioning is the piety of thought' (1977, p. 35).

14   Jameson doesn't make this contrast explicit. He identifies the Bonaventure Hotel as an index of the postmodern condition and with total displacement owing to its creation of a self-contained world (almost on a par with Disneyland). In a separate discussion, he describe how the Gehry house fosters an awareness of displacement through the juxtaposition of two contrasting realities, a juxtaposition that could not exist within the space of the Bonaventure Hotel.

15   The most notable exponents of universalized nomadism as a political position are Michael Hardt and Antonio Negri. See especially Hardt and Negri, 2004.

Bibliography

Agacinski, S. (1987), '*Architecture et métaphysique dans L'Esthétique de Hegel*'. *Le Cahier* (*Collège International de philosophie*), 4, pp. 47–151.

Badiou, A. (2009), *Theory of the Subject*. B. Bosteels (trans.). London: Continuum.

Benjamin, W. (2003), 'The Work of Art in the Age of Its Technological Reproducibility',
    H. Zohn and E. Jephcott (trans), in H. Eiland and M. Jennings (eds), *Selected Writings,
    Volume 4: 1938–1940*. Cambridge: Harvard University Press, pp. 251–83.

Clarke, D. (2006), *Descartes: A Biography*. Cambridge: Cambridge University Press.

Desmond, W. (1986), *Art and the Absolute: A Study of Hegel's Aesthetics*. Albany: SUNY
    Press.

Hardt, M. and Negri, A. (2004), *Multitude: War and Democracy in the Age of Empire*. New
    York: Penguin.

Hegel, G. W. F. (1975a), *Aesthetics: Lectures on Fine Art*, vol. 1. T. M. Knox (trans.).
    Oxford: Clarendon Press.

— (1975b), *Aesthetics: Lectures on Fine Art*, vol. 2. T. M. Knox (trans.). Oxford: Clarendon
    Press.

— (1977a), *The Difference between Fichte's and Schelling's System of Philosophy*. H. S. Harris
    and W. Cerf (trans). Albany: SUNY Press.

— (1977b), *Phenomenology of Spirit*. A. V. Miller (trans.). Oxford: Oxford University Press.

— (2010), *Science of Logic*. G. di Giovanni (trans.). Cambridge: Cambridge University
    Press.

— (2011), *Lectures on the Philosophy of World History, Volume I: Manuscripts of the
    Introduction and Lectures of 1822–3*. R. Brown and P. Hodgson (trans). Oxford:
    Clarendon Press.

Heidegger, M. (1971a), 'Building Dwelling Thinking', in *Poetry, Language, Thought*.
    A. Hofstadter (trans.). New York: Harper and Row, pp. 143–61.

— (1971b), '. . . Poetically Man Dwells . . .', in *Poetry, Language, Thought*. A. Hofstadter
    (trans.). New York: Harper and Row, pp. 211–29.

— (1977), 'The Question Concerning Technology', in *The Question Concerning Technology
    and Other Essays*. W. Lovitt (trans.). New York: Harper and Row, pp. 3–35.

Jameson, F. (1991), *Postmodernism, or, the Cultural Logic of Late Capitalism*. Durham:
    Duke University Press.

Kant, I. (1996), *Critique of Practical Reason*. M. Gregor (trans.), in M. Gregor (ed.),
    Practical Philosophy. Cambridge: Cambridge University Press.

Malpas, J. (2012), *Heidegger and the Thinking of Place: Explorations in the Topology of
    Being*. Cambridge, MA: MIT Press.

Marx, K. (1993), *Grundrisse*. M. Nicolaus (trans.). New York: Penguin.

McGowan, T. (2011), *Out of Time: Desire in Atemporal Cinema*. Minneapolis: University of
    Minnesota Press.

Pippin, R. (2002), 'What Was Abstract Art? (From the Point of View of Hegel)', *Critical
    Inquiry*, 29, 1, pp. 1–24.

4

Kant, Modernity and the Absent Public

Mark Jarzombek

The word public has such strong colloquial usage that even philosophically we can forget that it 'has a history'. And if we then try to trace that history we usually find our discussion expanding into issues of politics, law, governance, economics and even journalism and art. What I want to do in this chapter is to focus not on what public is or can be or should be, but on what it is not, to argue that, from a philosophical perspective, the idea of the *modern* public is haunted by the devastating and purposeful negation of that concept by none other than Immanuel Kant, often heralded as one of the great fathers of modern liberalism.

In *Critique of Judgment*, Kant outlines the three maxims of how a society moves towards Enlightenment: (1) think for oneself; (2), think in the mindset of others; and (3), think consistently (Kant, 1914, pp. 169–73). The longer one considers these propositions, the stranger they sound. For example, if we take Maxim 2 seriously, we could become so busy connecting with others and, of course, they with us, that there is little room for that special someone, who presumably would get most of our empathetic energy. Friends, lovers, spouses and even relatives have no particular place in Kant's world. Hegel stated it perhaps all too bluntly; marriage for Kant 'is degraded to a bargain for mutual use' (Hegel, 2001, p. 140).

Now this might seem like a strange and much too casual way to begin a conversation about Kant, but one must remember that Jean-Jacques Rousseau made a big deal about the family and its importance both historically in mankind's development and symbolically in each of our lives. According to Rousseau, 'The most ancient of all societies, and the only one that is natural, is the family'.[1] Rousseau also dealt directly with issues of love, its passions and complexities in his novel *Julie*, a sensation when it first appeared in 1761.[2] Though Kant was always more resolutely intellectual than Rousseau, that does not itself explain his ambivalence to the topic of family and love. This is not to say that Kant is against 'the family'. He deals with the question in *The Metaphysics of Morals* (1797), where he spends a few pages discussing marriage, procreation and parental obligations. But there are no particular details and the tone is purposefully lawyeristic. The main issue for Kant hinges on when a young person who was 'brought without his consent into the world, and placed in it by the responsible free will of others', becomes 'in fact a Citizen of the world (Weltbürger)'.[3] In other words, Kant is less interested in the before as he is in the after, for it is only when a person strikes out as a independent *Weltbürger* can she/he then presumably engage in Kant's planned three-step plan for enlightenment.

Whereas Rousseau consciously tries to match his philosophy with a real world principle, Kant does not. For him, it is not our family that is the source of our 'naturalness', but rather an innate and placeless sense of 'sociability'. In Paragraph 41 of the *Critique of Judgment*, just a few sentences after outlining his famous maxims, Kant points out that 'sociability' is 'requisite for man as a being destined for society, and so as a characteristic (Eigenschaft) belonging to humanity' (Kant, 1914, p. 174). The actual phrase he uses for what gets translated as sociability is 'Trieb zur Gesellschaft', which is much stronger than the English word might imply. It is an innate drive or compulsion towards the social.

The astonishing thing about this Trieb is that it is not linear. In fact, for Kant, we (and that means me and all the other billions of 'I's the world over) are motivated by our independence as individuals. In a sense, the Trieb is an internal dialectic that makes us want to be both independent and yet connected. Imagine that you are not married, sitting on a beach talking to your friends on Facebook with your IPad. That would be a perfect Kantian situation. With that image in mind we can see that Kant's 'sociability' is fully modern. It would be better perhaps to say that Kant's modernity is markedly different from Rousseau's. One might even be tempted to say that he is more utopian than Rousseau, but that would be wrong. It is certainly obvious that we today might have greater difficultly envisioning what Kant might have wanted even in our modern era, and indeed the underlying tone of my chapter is to suggest that we can never be as fully modern as Kant would want even in the age of Facebook. Stated differently, though we like to generally think that we live in a modern age, Kant was in some respects more modern than we, if we take by the word modern a break from natural orders.

This break was not just when a young person becomes a world citizen, and it is not just when that person releases himself or herself to the driving dialectic of sociability. It is also a break *within* the discipline of philosophy. Whereas Rousseau discussed 'the public' in his *Social Contract*, differentiating the public person from the private individual and making the public person a key element in his republican ideal (a basic premise of much political thought even today) Kant shuns this distinction and, indeed, clearly tries to deconstruct that classic duality. The word that he proposes instead is *sensus communis,* a complicated term that he points out has a legal, Latin meaning and a more colloquial meaning as 'common sense'. *Sensus communis* is created not at the beginning of the three-step process, but at the end. Just as the Trieb is technically and initially split against itself between the I and the We in order to eventually be fused, *sensus communis* has a high and low, a legal and a colloquial, that in the end resolves itself into powerful commonalities.

Before I look more closely at the *sensus communis*, let me return to Maxim 2, where Kant asks us to 'think in the mindset of others'. The German phrase is *an der Stelle jedes anderen denken,* which means something a bit more like 'put yourself mentally in the shoes of others'. It involves almost a type of physical displacement of the mind. It is obvious that regardless of what this entails, it is *not* the same as engaging in a public discourse, nor is discourse even asked for. Kant seems to suggest that I am not just sitting down at a table and talking to the person, but, for a while at least, trying to 'be' that person, in my mind. It is a type of alternative ontology where I have to suppress my notion of self-hood and try to become someone else. The question then appears. How does one inform oneself deeply about this person's – any person's – life and activities? Kant does not say exactly how you and I should go about doing this. What does that person eat? Is he grumpy in the morning? How does he have friends? Etc. I would be expected, I presume, to do this with both men and women, since Kant nowhere – despite his culturally conditioned assumption that Man is a He – states that we should be careful to separate men from women.

Naturally, in the late eighteenth century, Kant would have imagined a restrained interest in each other's lives. Even so, his position is as scary as it is exciting and nowhere does he warn against 'going too far'. Nowhere does he imply that there are some things off limits to such a probe. Today we might use to word empathy to describe such a connection. But it is not exactly correct. When we think of empathy, a late-nineteenth-century concept, we associate it with emotional contact or with sympathy. It is a psychological attitude usually associated with a positive human value. But Maxim 2 is not about emotional contact. On the contrary! It is where Kant locates the empirical. The process is purely fact finding. It does *not* involve compassion or judgement. Its neutrality is key. Perhaps we can see the activity of Maxim 2 as performing a type of sociology or anthropology. We have to have a disinterested interest in the life of other people in order to successfully perform Maxim 2.[4]

Now Kant wants the person that I am having this exchange with to do the same with me. I am not just the instigator of such interest; I am the subject of the interest of others, *many* others in fact. And finally, we have to remember that he wants all of us to do this with everyone else over the extended period of our lives. That is the essence of Maxim 3, the cumulative result of which produces an allusive '*sensus communis*', the sense of the communality. This concept is sometimes discussed as if it were equivalent with 'the public'. It is sometimes also discussed in relationship to the now proverbial Public Sphere. In both cases this is a mistake, for if the *sensus communis* is a public, it is only because we have produced it inside out and that means, for Kant, that it has no external, potentially alienated Will separate from our personal lives. In *Beantwortung der Frage: Was ist Aufklärung?* (1784), Kant admits that the making of a *sensus communis* is a process that is easy to state theoretically, but is, in fact, 'difficult and slow to accomplish' in real life. '*Daher kann ein Publikum nur langsam zur Aufklärung gelangen*' (Kant, 1784, p. 483). A public can reach Enlightenment only very slowly. Kant's use of the word *das Publikum* in this context is not neutral. It is not quite a put-down, but nor is it particularly positive. The people who constitute a *Publikum* are people who have not achieved Enlightenment, namely who have not elevated themselves out of its limitations.

In replacing the concept 'the public', which importantly does not appear at all in *The Critique of Judgment*, with *sensus communis*, Kant changes the terms of the discussion, producing a whole new architecture of thought. If we want to coin a term it would be

Sphere of Sociability. In producing this communality, we are in essence deconstructing the classic duality of public/private.

What then does it take to have not a mere *Publikum*, but an enlightened *sensus communis*? It certainly does not require a vote. It does not necessarily require a democracy. Public spaces are not necessary either, nor even a parliament building. People do need the status of freedom, however, and spaces to meet and talk, but this could be served just as effectively on a public bus as in a private room. In this, Kant's philosophy is striking different from the conventions of what we might think when it comes to liberalism. The revolution in Egypt could be considered a good example of Kantian politics in the way that it unified Facebook with events in the street. But it is clearly not Kantian in other respects, since Kant would want the Egyptians to connect with the Israelis and vice versa and for the supporters of the Muslim Brotherhood to connect with the secularist, and this is most certainly not going to happen. Once again, Kant is imagining a modernity that was just as difficult in the eighteenth century as it is now.

My point here is to remind ourselves that the concept of 'the public' is hardly as stable as we might suppose, and in the case of Kant we have to deal with a difficult theoretical situation where there literally is no 'public'. We would have to draw up a footnote here, however, for just as Kant suggests that we are not by nature 'public' but 'social' so too are we not by nature 'private'. This complicates matters yet further, for all of us today would generally assume an interiority to our lives that would be impossible in the philosophy of Kant. Though his critique of 'the public' is quite conscious, his critique of 'the private' is, however, an accident of history, since 'privacy' as we understand it today is largely a construct of the nineteenth century. This means that in coming to terms with Kant we should not imply a 'private' where there is none; just as importantly, we should not sneak 'a public' back into his thought, a problem that vexes several contemporary interpretations of Kant.

Among the philosophers against whom Kant was arguing was, of course, John Locke, who gave us the first modern, theorized distinction between public and private, or more specifically between public good and private possession. Locke – like Kant for that matter – was not interested in private thoughts, private feelings or anything that we might include in the general discussion of 'personal privacy'. His primary concern was the relationship between you and what you own. It was a thoroughly mercantile perspective. Owning a sack of coffee beans, for example, requires a distinctive set of legal protections, such as a contract, that guarantees the legitimacy of that private ownership and that allows the beans to be sold or marketed without corruptions.

Kant gets rid of the issue of possessions in that standard sense. In fact, his entire perspective is mildly anti-capitalist if not outright anti-legalistic. What I 'possess' is not a thing, but my 'sociability'. But as we have seen, Kant also gets rid of 'the private', for a good Kantian would have to give up the boundary of privacy whenever a stranger walks up and wants to go fishing around in his or her ontology. So if it is not laws or contracts that hold us together, what is it? Basically it boils down to good behaviour. In *Groundwork of the Metaphysic of Morals*, Kant writes that the one thing in the world that is unambiguously good is the 'good will'. He opens the book with the following words: 'Nothing in the world – or *out of it*! – *can* possibly be conceived that could be called "good" without qualification except a "Good Will." ' In fact, so he continues, 'power, riches, honor, even health, and happiness' are for naught 'if there isn't a good will to correct their influence on the mind' (Kant, 2005, p. 5). Kant is in a sense challenging the emerging tradition of Enlightenment legalism the very one that was to become the foundation of a certain stream of modern thinking. He is fighting several fronts at the same time, whether it be legalism, which for him is too static, or the family, which limits the individual's right to free association.

And this brings us to the reason Kant's philosophy was so distasteful to so many philosophers in the nineteenth century. Kant argued that it was precisely because we are potentially so different from each other that we have to strip away the natural over-determinism of our ontology to engage the ontology of the Other. This *de*-ontological move is the most astonishing aspect of Kant's thought. We may be neighbours, but we are yet completely unknown to each other – and to *ourselves*! – until we begin the laborious, life-long process of interaction.

The splitting of the Self into a Self and a not-Self, which is the requirement of Maxim 2, is Kant's most radical proposition, and the one that Hegel would later most vehemently disparage since, for Hegel, it breaks the Self into incompatible and irreconcilable parts. For Hegel, philosophy, because it is philosophy and not social science, *must* talk about the Self as a unit, and for better or worse begin from that basic proposition. One cannot start philosophy, according to Hegel, with a Self split against itself. Ultimately, Hegel won the argument, since his views became the basic tenet not only of Romanticism and nationalism, but of existentialism and phenomenology with their long reaches into contemporary philosophy and politics.

Perhaps one can say that if Kant removed 'the public' from philosophical legitimacy and tried to replace it with an alternative concept, the *sensus communis*, it was really only the first effort that succeeded. Once 'the public' was removed as a philosophical project it was never really reinstated. Hegel, for example, does claim to put the public back into play, but he limits it by equating it with the nation-state. And the situation gets no better with Edmund Husserl. Husserl's idea of the Life-World, for example, is diametrically opposed to the idea that there is a metaphysics of 'the public' or even of 'the nation'. Needless to say the word does not appear in any of his major writings. In fact, Husserl is so anti-public that there is almost no glue holding society together. Kant at least believed in the significant power of moral teaching and the principle of duty, concepts that provided the 'glue' in the face of the absent public. These enlightenment abstractions are completely absent in Husserl.

According to Husserl, in a lecture he gave in 1935, 'to live as a person is to live in a social framework, wherein I and We live together in community and have the community as a horizon.' He then points out that by communities he means things such as 'family, nation, or international community', where it is expected that I participate in 'creating culture' within these continuities. Though this sounds not particularly controversial, remember that 'I' and the 'We' are first separate and, second, bound together into a cultural formation. As the lecture continues, he makes it clear that there are only two types of cultural formations, healthy and sick. The European nations he says 'are sick' this largely because of the false promises of science. So he asks his listeners to return to the 'birthplace' of Europe, namely to Greece, which developed 'a new kind of attitude of individuals toward their environing world'. It was 'a new type of spiritual structure, rapidly growing into a systematically rounded (geschlossen) cultural form that in its totality can be called philosophy' (Husserl, 1935).

The standard English translation 'systematically rounded' is not accurate since the term is actually *geschlossen*, which means 'closed', 'closed off' or even 'locked up', like a door. The 'We' in that sense is not particularly inclusive. If anything it resists newcomers and thus stands as the furthermost antithesis to Kant's system that, politically speaking, made no such injunction. The need for this closedness is, however, obvious in the philosophy of Husserl, since he needs to explain how the 'I' connects to the 'We' in a situation where there is no inbuilt requirement for social interaction.

The differences with Kant are obvious. Kant's command to put yourself in the place of others, even though he means this conceptually and not literally, will only yield a coherency over a long period of time. Initially, if anything it produces a purposeful destabilization of the ego. Husserl can accept no such shock to the system. A healthy community begins from a powerful 'I' that when multiplied along the line produces a closed reality, which in turn allows the 'I' and the 'We' to coexist, something which is not possible and not even wanted if the 'We' is sick.

To simplify a bit, one can say Hegel took away Maxim 2 and asked us to go from Maxim 1 to Maxim 3, which in his philosophy focuses on the nation-state. Husserl then took away the nation-state as just another metaphysical falsity, leaving, in a sense Maxim 1. And so the damage was done. As liberating as it is, Husserl's world is a potentially dangerous place to be. If the 'We' is sick, that liberates the 'I' from its social obligations. What then?

This foray into the twentieth century was only meant to raise the question, How did the 'public' as a philosophical project survive this assault against it? Why is that today we can talk of 'the public' with a sense of normalcy, against the grain of its spectral position within modern philosophical discourse?

The answer has a lot to do, ironically, with the rise of the nation-state in the nineteenth century. It was in the interest of the nation-state, after all, to have 'a public' that does not reflect on the philosophic impossibility of that term, much less return to Kant's positive negation of the word. Just as Romantic philosophy wants to produce a stable and active ego, it wants to produce the image of a stable and active public if only because the nation-state needs to stabilize its increasingly bureaucratic hold on life. The rise of the bourgeoisie, of global colonialism, and of professional societies in the Victorian era especially in the 1880s played a critical part in normalizing the idea of a public. But the 'public' was put back into the philosophical system really only with Karl Marx, who demanded the abolition of property in the name of some vaguely defined 'public purposes'. In other words, for Marx, 'the public' was the new super-structure that was bigger than the defunct bourgeois word, with its self-serving interests. And therein lies at least one of the sources of the modern confusion about the public as a type of enemy of the individualism. But that is a different story and takes me out of philosophy and into history and politics. I want to remain focused on the post-Kantian, philosophical resistance to 'the public', for I am not convinced that the return of 'the public' – often associated with a liberal rejection of self-interest – matches with the anti-public philosophy of liberal thinking.

Let me take as a small example the case of Richard Sennett who sees himself as a champion of what he calls the 'public realm'. According to him,

> The most important fact about the public realm is what happens in it. Gathering together strangers enables certain kinds of activities which cannot happen, or do not happen as well, in the intimate private realm. In public, people can access unfamiliar knowledge, expanding the horizons of their information. Markets depend on these expanding horizons of information. In public, people can discuss and debate with people who may not share the same assumptions or the same interests. Democratic government depends on such exchanges between strangers. The public realm offers people a chance to lighten the pressures for conformity, of fitting into a fixed role in the social order; anonymity and impersonality provide a milieu for more individual development. This promise of turning a fresh personal page among strangers has lured many migrants to cities. [This takes place in] squares, major streets, theatres, cafes, lecture hall, government assemblies, or stock exchanges.[5]

Strangers meeting, talking and sharing experiences in the real and metaphorical openness of the public space is very Kantian and is based on the core principles of Kant's liberalism. But Kant never says that this has to take place in a public space. This means that Sennett, by inserting 'public space' back into the system, winds up adopting an anti-public position. He claims, for example, that he is part of a 'performative school' of thinking, which, 'stripped of the jargon', means simply that we focus 'on how people express themselves to strangers'. It is an interesting ambition. Sennett does not say how this happens in real life and he most certainly does not say that people should go and live like these strangers for a while 'in thought and place'. Rather, I am expected to *express* myself and it is up to the stranger to try to figure it out. It demands an ethos of attentiveness, which, as admirable as that might be, is – remarkably – not required in Kant. We are not witnessing someone's studied performance, but engaging their ontology more directly (as impossible as that may in fact be). Kant, in other words, wants us to do much more than just 'express ourselves'. It is, in fact, precisely, because of the stresses in the expressive exchange that Sennett then needs the public space to be real, where it serves not as a 'public space', but as a space of temperance and surveillance. Kant's modernity needs no such space.

Sennett, of course, is being reasonable, for Kant's position is, in truth, almost nonsense. It is impossible to imagine a true Kantian modernity; but I am more interested in his nonsense than the liberalist repair job that tries to insert – all too quickly I argue – 'the public' back into the machine.

I close with a thought experiment. What would a Kantian city actually look like? First, it would be a city without houses. A house would be the symbolic locus of 'family' and there are no 'families', so no houses. It would probably be a city of apartments. One could envision any number of scenarios from linear cities to sprawling field cities to smaller more irregular towns. At regular frequencies in the city there would have to be meeting and seminar rooms, and places where people can visit and talk. A university as such would be too top heavy for Kant; there would be instead a loose infrastructure of exchange-and-learning centres and community colleges. The city would also have a good deal of glass, both transparent and reflective, for in Kantian world there is no mandate for private intimacy as it is conventionally understood today, namely as an area outside the jurisdictional gaze of the State. 'Private space' as it conventionally might be called would be needed, but only as places to get away and think about things. 'To think for yourself' – that is Maxim 1 – you have to go to a place where one can shut down the interfering voices of all the thousands of people one knows. But this could happen in any number of places.

So imagine a city of streets and no freestanding houses; then imagine that the street facades and many of the interior walls are made of glass. But like Swiss cheese, there are dark boxes of space where individuals can spend time alone, perhaps reading a book, listening to music, or at any rate, thinking for oneself. Some of these places may be 'owned' by individuals, but most would be open to anyone. Next, imagine Encounter Buses that drive around the city which allow one to meet with people for short exchanges. Perhaps there could be Exchange Pods, where such meetings could be stretched out for hours or even days.

There would also be no professions in the modern sense. And that means there would be no architect professionals. As to how the city would get built, the closest model today that might work for Kant would be 'design-build' where clients and architects work together to solve problems. But if everything were design-build, there would be no progress, no conceptual jump into a better world that is so critical to the Kantian Enlightenment project. We would just have a continual repetition of the same. The *genius*, or several of them, would be required, meaning that the city would have an occasional building by Frank Gehry or Le Corbusier. We would study these buildings and appreciate them just like the other great works of art that make up the history of civilization. The city would even have an assortment of memorial statues dedicated not to our politicians, but to these artistic geniuses as inspiration for those who think that they can be the next genius.

This Kantian city would be a relatively serious place. It is hard to imagine ballrooms or circuses in a Kantian city. There are no Foucaultian, heterotopic zones. Nor would there be major public buildings like courthouses and parliament buildings, since Kant wants us to work together to come up with our own laws, from the bottom up, so to speak, and not just swallow whatever comes down from above. Political parties would not exist, but there would be associations created by people who come together to define a particular common interest around a particular problem or concern. Courthouses would not be banned, of course, but they would only exist in a small scale and be distributed throughout the urban landscape as places that stabilize and reaffirm the thinking of the *sensus communis*. They would need to be 'blended in' and not freestanding edifices. In the Kantian city, there is no principle of citizenship, no police force, no army and even the sciences would be barely autonomous from the imprint of communal humanism. A place like MIT or Harvard? Impossible. The city would have to be networked across the landscape with other villages and cities and in no way cut off or isolated. There would have to be places where foreigners could come and meet and indeed, most inhabitants themselves would have travelled widely in the great coming and going of cultural exchange. In the Kantian town there would be a wide range of hostels and hotels, clustered around 'connection zones'. Residents would have to be accustomed to signs reading: 'Not currently in my office. Work will resume in two weeks.' Imagine the late nineteenth-century Victorian city with its city hall, post office and concert hall. Most definitely, not Kantian.

These quick and purposefully reductive ruminations on Kant are meant to show that despite Kant's wide influence in our thinking, we never created a fully Kantian world. Perhaps thankfully, and this means that if we can agree that we live in a world saturated with the presumption of its modernity, Kant's modernity, if we can call it that, never became realized as such, even though pieces of it infiltrated here and there into various disciplinary and political realities. Its most powerful impact, however, was to transform the philosophical understanding of the public into a dialectic, the negation of which became the dominant thematic in the philosophy of Hegel, Husserl and others. The modern idea of a public is not just a signifier of certain types of realities, but signified by its negation, which it carries with it like a scar despite the various attempts to maintain and normalize it as a signifier. What I, therefore, intended in this chapter was to bring us back to that particular moment in Kant's thought where we can see the beginning of this rupture and indeed the mechanism that put it in place. Kant had hoped that his deconstruction of the public would yield a new positive, but it did not play out that way. Instead it produced a powerful reactionary movement. This means that before we can write a history of the concept of the public, we have to recognize the productive strangeness of the Kantian premise and the fact that this strangeness, built around a strategy of calculated impossibility, wound up producing the unresolved equation of our modernity.

Notes

1 Jean Jacques Rousseau, 'Book I', *The Social Contract*. Available at: <http://www.constitution.org/jjr/socon_01.htm>.

2 For a good discussion of Rousseau see: Eileen Hunt Botting (2006), *Family Feuds Wollstonecraft, Burke, and Rousseau on the Transformation of the Family*. Albany, NY: State University of New York Press.

3 I. Kant (1797), *The Science of Right* (*Rechtslehre*) in *The Metaphysics of Morals (Die Metaphysik der Sitten)*. First Part, Par. 28. To this he adds

> All this training [by the parent] is to be continued till the Child reaches the period of Emancipation (emancipatio), as the age of practicable self-support. The Parents then virtually renounce the parental Right to command, as well as all claim to repayment for their previous care and trouble; for which care and trouble, after the process of Education is complete, they can only appeal to the Children by way of any claim, on the ground of the Obligation of Gratitude as a Duty of Virtue. [*The Science of Right*: First Part, Par. 29]

Available at: <http://oll.libertyfund.org/?option=com_staticxt&staticfile=show.php%3F title=359&chapter=55767&layout=html&Itemid=27>.

4 Some scholars had mistakenly argued that Kant was a type of empathy theorist. See for example: C. Calloway-Thomas (2010), *Empathy in the Global World: An Intercultural Perspective*. Thousand Oaks: Sage, p. 10; M. Moen (1997), 'Feminist Themes in

Unlikely Places: Re-reading Kant's Critique of Judgement', in *Feminist Interpretations of Immanuel Kant*. Robin May Schott (ed.). University Park: Pennsylvania State University, p. 221.
5   Available at: <http://www.richardsennett.com/site/SENN/Templates/General2. aspx?pageid=16>. [accessed June 12, 2012].

Bibliography

Hegel, G. W. F. (2001), *Philosophy of Right*. S. W. Dyde (trans.). Kitchener: Batoche Books.
Husserl, Edmund, H. (1935), *Philosophy and the Crisis of European Man*. (Lecture delivered by Edmund Husserl, Vienna, 10 May 1935.) Available at: <http://www.users. cloud9.net/~bradmcc/husserl_philcris.html>.
Kant, I. (1784), 'Beantwortung der Frage: Was ist Aufklärung?' in *Berlinische Monatsschrift*, December, 1784.
— (1914), *The Critique of Judgment*. J. H. Bernard (trans.). London: Macmillan.
— (2005), *Groundwork for the Metaphysic of Morals*. J. Bennett (trans.), p. 5. Available at: <http://www.earlymoderntexts.com/pdf/kantgrou.pdf (accessed 12 June 2012)>.

5

The New Phantasmagoria: Transcoding the Violence of Financial Capitalism

Douglas Spencer

Radical philosophy may thus far have missed a critical encounter with contemporary architecture, but architecture has, for some time, encountered theory as the instrument of its own disciplinary reinventions. Since the late 1960s, architecture has imported from theory, especially in its 'continental' variants, a range of concepts with which to freight its own discourse as radical, or as at least 'progressive'.

From the Situationist International and the *événements* of Paris May 68 Bernard Tschumi, at the Architectural Association in London in the early 1970s, derived his architecture of 'events', while Nigel Coates (also at the AA) borrowed from their 'psychogeography' to fabricate a narrative approach to architecture and urbanism. In the 1980s Tschumi, alongside others, most notably Peter Eisenman, then took the philosophy of deconstruction as the inspiration for the invention of a 'deconstructivist' architecture (Eisenman even working with Derrida on a design proposal for the Parc de la Villette in Paris).[1] By the early 1990s, following the movement of a broader Deleuzian turn in theory itself, it was to the thought of Gilles Deleuze and his writings with Félix Guattari that certain architects and architectural theorists began to express their allegiances.

This architectural 'Deleuzism'[2] initially centred on Deleuze's *The Fold: Leibniz and the Baroque*,[3] and the chapter '1440: The Smooth and the Striated', from *A Thousand Plateaus: Capitalism and Schizophrenia* (Deleuze and Guattari, 1992). A special edition of *Architectural Design*, titled *Folding in Architecture*, was published in 1993 featuring essays and projects by Peter Eisenman, Greg Lynn and Jeffrey Kipnis, among others (Lynn, 1993). Its contributors sought to correlate Deleuze's account of 'the fold' in the philosophy of Leibniz with the formal complexity of a 'new architecture' (Kipnis, 1993, p. 18).

Conceptually related to the fold, the schema of the smooth and the striated was originally elaborated in *A Thousand Plateaus* to articulate the relations between open and closed systems in technology, music, mathematics, geography, politics, art and physics. Smooth space was figured as topologically complex, in continuous variation and fluid. This was a space through which one drifted, nomadically. Striated space, by contrast, was defined by its rigid geometry, a territory carved into functional categories channelling the movements of its occupants along the pre-inscribed lines of a Cartesian grid. Striated space was standardized, disciplinary and imperial. Again, these concepts, particularly Deleuze and Guattari's implicit (though qualified) privileging of smooth space and continuous variation over static geometry, were found to resonate with architecture's engagement with complex topologies.[4] At the same time, they were used to imbue architecture's move to formal experimentation with philosophically radical implications. The virtues of Deleuzian 'smoothing' and the pursuit of 'continuous variation' were affirmed in the architectural writings of Lynn, Reiser and Umemoto, Zaha Hadid, Patrick Schumacher and Alejandro Zaera-Polo, among others, so as to suggest the philosophical substance of the complex formal modulations characteristic of their work.[5]

The usefulness of Deleuze and Guattari's philosophy to architecture was not confined, however, to servicing it with the formal tropes of folding and smoothing. Architecture's Deleuzian turn also offered the discipline an escape route from its prior entanglements in the linguistic and semiotic paradigms of postmodernism and deconstruction. The new Deleuzian orientation, wrote Kipnis, marked a turn from 'post-structural semiotics to a consideration of recent developments in geometry, science and the transformation of political space, a shift that is often marked as a move from a Derridean to a Deleuzean discourse' (Kipnis, 1993, p. 18).

What was decisive in this new theoretical orientation, however, was not just its switching from linguistically based paradigms to more 'properly' architectural concerns with space, form and geometry. The Deleuzian turn in architecture also marked the initial stages of its still ongoing mission to disengage itself entirely from the perceived dead end of theory's critical negations, and to forge a new alliance with the corporate and managerial agendas of neoliberalism.

Trouble in theory

The trouble with theory, especially of the type once so eagerly embraced by architecture, had been that the perspectives it opened up tended to be deeply destabilizing and unsettling, particularly for any host discipline aiming to selectively harness these to its own agenda. As François Cusset has observed, 'Sometime in the third quarter of the twentieth century, in France but not only there, theory joyfully *stopped* making sense, and began cracking all existing frames . . . theory used to be reasonable, more than strictly *rational*, and for some reason which remains to be fully explained theory turned *crazy*' (Cusset, 2011, p. 25). Unleashed from the *lieu propre* of Hegelian dialectics and freed from the confines of its disciplinary demarcations – by figures such as Althusser, Foucault and Derrida – theory began to produce 'a transdisciplinary open field, loose yet closely related to literature, politics and psychoanalysis' (Cusset, 2011, p. 25). Theory turned 'crazy', Cusset suggests, because its critical labour was endlessly multiplied and turned against itself with every encounter it staged between once discrete fields of knowledge. It lost its identity in the multiple displacements, doubts and suspicions arising from these encounters. Troubled and troubling, theory became a 'demon' that 'began to possess the Western intellectual body' (Cusset, 2011, p. 24).

Something of theory's demonic quality is also apparent in the description of its encounter with architecture given by K. Michael Hays in the introduction to his *Architecture Theory Since 1968*:

> From Marxism and semiotics to psychoanalysis and rhizomatics, architecture theory has freely and contentiously set about opening up architecture to what is thinkable and sayable in other codes, and, in turn, rewriting systems of thought assumed to be properly extrinsic or irrelevant into architecture's own idiolect. (Hays, 1998, p. xi)

Throughout the period from 1968 to 1993 with which Hays's anthology is concerned, theory may be conceived as a demonic, troubling presence within architecture – at the same time as an exhilarating one – since it forges all manner of unforeseen connections between architecture and language, the unconscious, capital, class and gender, and, locating these in the forms, practices and structures of architecture, shows them residing in the very places where the discipline might have thought itself able to locate its autonomy. Rather than finding itself straightforwardly enriched by such encounters, architecture, like theory itself, in its relentless work of translation, correlation and displacement, found its foundations unsettled and, according to some, its mission compromised. Michael Speaks, for example, writes that theory 'attached' itself to architecture and then drove it towards a 'resolutely negative' condition (Speaks, 2006, p. 103).

The Deleuzian turn was also related, in significant ways, to the subsequent emergence of a 'post-critical' architectural discourse. Marked by the publication of Robert Somol and Sarah Whiting's 'Notes Around the Doppler Effect and Other Moods of Modernism' in the journal *Perspecta* in 2002, the post-critical position argued that critique was extrinsic to the 'proper' concerns of architecture and served the discipline only as a counterproductive form of 'negativity' (Somol and Whiting, 2002). Alejandro Zaera-Polo (principal, with Farshid Moussavi, of the now defunct Foreign Office Architects), for instance, described the critical, in its negativity, as inadequate to deal with contemporary levels of social complexity. Deleuze, in contrast, offered insight into this condition and affirmed its productivity:

> [The] paradigm of the 'critical' is in my opinion part of the intellectual models that became operative in the early 20th century and presumed that in order to succeed we should take a kind of 'negative' view towards reality . . . today the critical individual practice that has characterized intellectual correctness for most of the 20th Century is no longer particularly adequate to deal with a culture determined by processes of transformation on a scale and complexity difficult to understand . . . you have to be fundamentally engaged in the processes and learn to manipulate them from the inside. You never get that far into the process as a critical individual. If we talk in terms of the construction of subjectivity, the critical belongs to Freud

a Lacan [*sic*], what I called 'productive', to Deleuze. (Zaera-Polo and van Toorn, 2008)

More bluntly, Kipnis described criticality as a 'disease' that he wanted to 'kill' 'once and for all' (Kipnis, 2004, p. 579). Today, the post-critical has become a new orthodoxy within certain tendencies in architecture, and its attacks on criticality are no less strident or (paradoxically) negative than those of Zaera-Polo or Kipnis. In his *The Sympathy of Things*, Lars Spuybroek describes the twentieth century as 'our true Dark Ages' (2011, p. 264). Among the horrors that define it as such for Spuybroek, including those of Auschwitz and nuclear weapons, he reserves special mention for the objects of post-criticality's censure: 'we even survived semiotics and deconstruction. And criticality too' (Spuybroek, 2011, p. 264).

The castigation of critical 'negativity' has been extended further (and from the same quarters), into arguments against thought, cognition and intellectual reflection as conditions of architectural and spatial experience. In their place affect, complexity, networked relations, new materialisms and new vitalisms are now privileged. Kipnis, for instance, has stated that now is the 'time of matter', not ideas. This principle, he argues, derives from the origins of the universe: 'There were no signs, no ideas, no concepts, no meanings, no disembodied spirits, no dematerialized abstractions whatsoever around during the first couple of seconds after the Big Bang, nor during the first million or billion years, or, for that matter, even these days' (Kipnis, 2004, p. 571).

For Spuybroek, 'meaning' is a 'horrible word that lets us believe that the mind can trade aesthetics for textual interpretation' (Spuybroek, 2011, p. 174). Ideas and intelligence are properties of the relations between life, matter and technique, rather than products of the mind. 'Matter' he writes, 'can think perfectly well for itself'. Humans have no special place or distinctive capacity within Spuybroek's world of 'things'; a world in which all relations are ones of 'sympathy', understood as 'the power of things at work, working between all things, and between us as things'. 'Humans', he says, 'are nothing but things among other things' (Spuybroek, 2011, p. 174). Reified in this fashion, human subjectivity is relieved of its interpretive, reflective and critical capacities and required, instead, only to give itself over to the immediacy of purely affective relations passing between things.

Alejandro Zaera-Polo, likewise affirming the primacy of affect over intellect and matter over meaning, has outlined the implications of this position for architecture. 'The primary depository of contemporary architectural expression' he writes, in his essay 'The Politics of the Envelope', 'is now invested in the production of affects, an uncoded, pre-linguistic form of identity that transcends the propositional logic of political rhetorics' (Zaera-Polo, 2008, p. 89). Pursuing a similar line of argumentation, Sylvia Lavin, in her *Kissing Architecture*, has proposed a 'kissing [intimately relational] architectural surface', which is not 'legible and demanding of focused attention', but that is 'affective and eidetic because it shapes experience through force rather than representation' (Lavin, 2011, p. 30).

From this position contemporary architecture is able to release itself from any obligation to articulate an intelligible relationship to the social. In place of this it proposes to produce a purely sensible and immediately experiential condition through the fabrication of 'atmospheres' and 'environments' through which subjects may be steered. In the second volume of Patrik Schumacher's *The Autopoiesis of Architecture*, for example, he tasks contemporary architecture with 'channelling bodies' and 'guiding subjects' through the design of such environments (Schumacher, 2012, p. 135). Questions and representations of the political, the social and the economic are to be excluded from consideration in the design of these environments, on the basis that we now inhabit some form of pre-linguistic or post-representational world, or that these concerns should be placed, as Schumacher has argued, beyond the purview of architecture,[6] or, according to Zaera-Polo (following Manuel De Landa in this), because it is probably best not to speak any longer of larger totalities such as capitalism or society.[7] Rather than to a capitalist axiomatic of growth and accumulation, it is to matter, now construed as productively complex, self-organizing, networked and creative, that power is ascribed. Architecture should, it follows, understand its practice as operating in accordance with this understanding. Its self-assigned task is to organize the relations between a reified subjectivity and a vitalized matter.

From its initial turn to Deleuze and Guattari, then, this architectural current has arrived at an argument accounting for architectural design and spatial experience as practices of pure immediacy. The question of mediation – of the relation of this architecture to the operation of power (other than as an immanently materialist one), on the one hand, or to the social subjects of its operation, on the other – has, it is supposed, been entirely superseded. Furthermore, architecture has extricated itself from the troubling nature of radical thought, either through ditching theory altogether, or through aligning itself with theorists who share its hatred of criticality, such as Bruno Latour,[8] or with figures such as Manuel De Landa, who have served them with a version of Deleuze and Guattari from which any Marxian residue has been wiped clean.[9] It is precisely at this juncture, and on these terms, however, that the prospect of a critical re-encounter between radical philosophy and the type of architecture discussed here emerges. The first task of this re-encounter would be to address the relations between architecture and the larger totalities that its discourse has suggested lie beyond its proper concerns, or refused even to countenance the existence of.

Becoming progressive

Architecture has not been alone in undertaking to refashion its identity and purpose according to vitalist and new materialist paradigms. The creative productivity imputed to networks, complexity, emergence and self-organization has, in fact, been embraced across a wide range of social, economic, political, institutional and commercial fields. Advocate of the 'digital economy', Don Tapscott, for instance, writes that 'The industrial hierarchy and economy are giving way to molecular organizations and economic structures' (Tapscott, 1996, p. 53). In their book, *It's Alive: The Coming Convergence of Information, Biology, and Business*, Christopher Meyer and Stan Davis observe:

> we will again have scientific management – but this time the underlying science will be 'general evolution'. The theories that drive biology will be adopted in the way

we use information, and the way we manage our enterprises. Biology, information, and business will converge on general evolution. (Meyer and Davis, 2003, p. 33)

Such developments in business management have been acknowledged by figures such as Schumacher and Zaera-Polo as significant for architecture's future orientation. Schumacher has argued that architecture should translate the 'new social tropes' of contemporary organizational models into new 'spatial tropes' (Schumacher, 2005, p. 76). Architecture, he suggests, not only becomes more relevant in servicing these organizational models, it also joins them in affirming what is described as an 'emancipatory' project of producing de-hierarchized, flexible and informal networks. There is, Schumacher writes, 'no better site for a progressive and forward-looking project than the most competitive contemporary business domains' (Schumacher, 2005, p. 79).

Zaera-Polo has similarly argued for the progressive and productive qualities inherent to de-hierarchized and complex 'material organizations', understood as now encompassing economics, politics, infrastructures, education and cultural production. Claiming that 'contemporary power structures operate as physical aggregates where behavior is created through the localized complex association of molecular components' (Zaera-Polo, 2008, 103), he suggests that architecture will become progressive through aligning itself with such 'emerging complex orders' (Zaera-Polo, 1994, p. 28).

Raw material

Architects have thus acknowledged the widespread turn to the organizational models referred to here, and the contribution of their own practice to these, but have mystified the historical conditions of their appearance. To the extent that the origins of these models are addressed at all, they are typically held to have themselves 'emerged', *zeitgeist*-like, in the natural – and 'progressive' – course of things. In the latter thought of Deleuze (largely, and for obvious reasons, ignored within architectural writing), however, a succinct account is offered of how the appearance of complex, laterally organized and 'open' organizational models, across a broad spectrum of fields and practices, were coming to constitute a new and ever more totalizing form of power operating through what he termed 'societies of control' (Deleuze, 1995b). In perhaps one of the philosopher's most infamous statements on power, he warns: 'Compared with the approaching forms of ceaseless control in open sites we may come to see the harshest confinement as part of a wonderful happy past' (Deleuze, 1995a, p. 175).

Deleuze's conception of a 'society of control' was, in part, developed from certain perspectives opened up in the earlier work of Foucault, whose *Discipline and Punish* first addresses the appearance of a post-disciplinary society of 'lateral controls' in which 'the massive, compact disciplines are broken down into flexible methods of control, which may be transferred and adapted' (Foucault, 1977, p. 211). In his subsequent analysis of neoliberalism, as a historically specific mode of governmentality, he described it operating as 'an environmental type of intervention instead of the internal subjugation of individuals' (Foucault, 2008, pp. 259–60).

Luc Boltanski and Eve Chiapello, in their *The New Spirit of Capitalism* (2007), have produced a critique of contemporary networked, self-organizing and anti-bureaucratic models of workplace management attending, in depth, to their historical conditions of emergence. Worker's demands for 'autonomy' and 'self-management', articulated in the wake of May 68, they argue, were strategically subverted by employers' subsequent demands that workers should indeed manage themselves, though not in the cause of liberation, but of increased productivity and efficiency. Self-motivation, flexibility and interpersonal skills, they argue, became the requisite attributes of a new organizational paradigm in which control was to be effectively internalized by the worker:

'Controlling the uncontrollable' is not something with an infinite number of solutions: in fact, the only solution is for people to control themselves, which involves transferring constraints from external organizational mechanisms to people's internal dispositions, and for the powers of control they exercise to be consistent with the firm's general project. (Boltanski and Chiapello, 2007, p. 80)

Such analyses of the historical conditions under which the new organizational models developed, and of how they have been instrumental to new modes of power, all centre to some extent upon questions of subjection. Theorists of Italian post-*operaismo* – Paolo Virno, Maurizio Lazzarato, Christian Marazzi, Antonio Negri[10] – have, in their accounts of 'general intellect' and 'immaterial labour', been especially concerned with the ways in which contemporary techniques in management and organization are now invested in the production of subjectivity, rather than, or at least alongside, those of commodity production. These organizational techniques are, they have argued, addressed to the subject's communicative, creative and affective potentials, and to the mobilization of these in the production of value. 'If production today is directly the production of a social relation', writes Maurizio Lazzarato, 'then the raw "material" of immaterial labor is subjectivity and the "ideological" environment in which this subjectivity lives and reproduces' (Lazzarato, 1997, p. 142).

While this current of radical thought has long been concerned with the ways in which, under post-Fordism and neoliberalism, subjectivity becomes the 'raw material' of valorization, it has also attended to the existential insecurities and 'precarities' that the subject is exposed to in the all-pervasive financialization of the economy. The 'violence of financial capitalism', as Marazzi has recently described it, stems precisely from the fact that financialization is not confined to a specific sector of the economy, or to a particular aspect of social practice, but is spread throughout its entirety. Furthermore, it is through networked and laterally connective conditions, ones that architects and the gurus of new managerial models alike have affirmed as progressive, that financialization, with its concomitant precarities and crises – especially evident in the wake of the financial crisis of 2007/8 – seeps into all the spaces and times of everyday life. This all-pervasive condition of financialization may, then, be understood as operating through the same 'open' systems as those that characterize Deleuze's 'societies of control'. Continuous modulation and lateral connectivity constitute both an apparatus of control and a medium of financialization. In fact, these two functions combine to form a particular mode of governmentality.

As Lazzarato has argued, in his *The Making of the Indebted Man*, the social and existential conditions produced through financialization are not the result of some merely temporary glitch in the system – as the term 'crisis' problematically implies – but serve as a technique for the production of a compliant subjectivity for that system. 'Governmentality', he writes, 'has produced a collective capitalist . . . which is not concentrated in finance, but operates throughout business, administration, service industries, political parties, the media and the university' (Lazzarato, 2012, pp. 107–8). Jonathan Crary similarly observes in *24/7: Late Capitalism and the Ends of Sleep*, that 'the elaboration, the modeling of one's personal and social identity, has been reorganized to conform to the uninterrupted operation of markets, information networks, and other systems' (Crary, 2013, p. 9). This relentless exposure of the subject to the logic of financial capital at all levels marks its violence; the violence of being compelled to be always at or available for work (paid or unpaid), to be always working upon oneself, in the acquisition of contacts, projects and connections, to produce in oneself the requisite mental dispositions and affective skills, and to make oneself mobile and flexible enough to survive the now normalized existential conditions of debt, precarity and crisis.

It is vital to the maintenance of this arrangement, of course, that these conditions are mediated, at the points where they are to work directly upon the production of subjectivity, in significantly more positive terms. Given the turn in architecture towards the accommodation of contemporary managerial paradigms, and its enthusiasms for the 'progressive' character of marketization, its contributions to this work of mediation ought to be addressed. Radical philosophy's re-encounter with architecture might concern itself, among other things, with how it is that an architecture identifying itself with a condition of uncoded and pure immediacy contributes, in fact, to the mediation, the affirmative 'transcoding', of financial capital (Hays, 1998). However seemingly anachronistic, it may be through the concept of the phantasmagoria, as employed first by Marx, and later by Walter Benjamin and Theodor Adorno, that some critical purchase on this concern may be gained.

The matter of mediation

Marx, in the first volume of *Capital*, invokes the concept of the phantasmagoria in his analysis of the fetishistic character of the commodity form:

> The mysterious character of the commodity-form consists therefore simply in the fact that the commodity reflects the social characteristics of men's own labour as objective characteristics of the products of labour themselves, as the socio-natural properties of these things . . . It is nothing but the definite social relation between men themselves which assumes here, for them, the fantastic ['*phantasmagorisch*' (phantasmagorical) in the original] form of a relation between things. (Marx, 1976, pp. 164–5)

Marx argues here that we do not, and in fact cannot, experience our social relations through face-to-face interaction, or directly through our labour, but only through the exchange of the things produced by our labour. The commodity-form of these things then takes on the fetishized quality through which our social relations are mediated: 'the labour of the private individual manifests itself as an element of the total labour of society only through the relations which the act of exchange establishes between the products, and through their mediation, between the producers' (Marx, 1976, p. 165). The phantasmagorical appearance of these relations – thing-like between people and social between things – conceals the actual conditions of labour in the fetish character of the commodity, but is not to be regarded simply as an optical illusion that might be removed by rational understanding. This phantasmagoria is, rather, the lived reality of the social relations Marx is describing, and through which these relations 'appear as what they are' (Marx, 1976, p. 165), that is, as necessarily mediated by things.

Without being entirely superseded, the conditions of labour, social relations and commodity production that Marx describes here have also been developed into the post-Fordist and neoliberal realms of immaterial labour with which the thought of Italian post-*operaismo* has been concerned. Now we also work upon ourselves, in and through the relational conditions that sustain the financialization of everyday life (and not simply, as before, so as to reproduce ourselves for work), so as to become, in effect, the exchangeable products of our own labour. It is our subjectivity that, through this productive labour, now itself becomes thing-like, a commodity defined by the exchange value of our knowledge, skills and affective dispositions, of our adaptability, availability and flexibility. Marx's characterization of relations under industrial capitalism, as thing-like between people and social between things, might then be reformulated, for financial capitalism, as ones in which the social is a thing-like relation between people treated as things.

If these relations can be described as also appearing in phantasmagorical form, it is because the conditions of labour they necessitate are similarly concealed. Only now these are not, or not only, the working conditions of the factory, but the conditions of working upon oneself, of making oneself subject to the precarities, extended hours and continuous training involved in fashioning the self for exchange, and of encountering others under conditions of what Virno has described as 'opportunism, cynicism and fear' (Virno, 1997, p. 33). The discursive work of the new phantasmagoria consists of expressing these conditions in the affirmative terms of actor-networks, assemblages, self-organizing systems and new materialisms. When Spuybroek claims that humans 'are nothing but things among other things', for example, and that we are relieved of the burden of critical reflection through this knowledge, the supposed immediacy of his materialism actually operates as a form of mediation: the reification of subjectivity is presented as returning us to an ontological truth we should aspire to conform to, rather than one determined by the conditions of financial capitalism.

Marx used the figure of the phantasmagoria to analyse social relations in the general sense of their 'appearance'. In the phantasmagorical critique subsequently developed by Benjamin and Adorno, however, the term is deployed as a means of analysing specific forms of cultural and spatial production such as Wagnerian opera, Art Noveau, the Parisian arcade and World Fairs. It is from Adorno's account of the Wagnerian phantasmagoria in particular, though, that the following comments regarding contemporary architectural practice are derived.

In his *In Search of Wagner*, Adorno writes that the 'occultation of production by means of the outward appearance of the product' is the 'formal law governing the works of Richard Wagner' (Adorno, 2005, p. 74). The production referred to by Adorno here as 'occulted' concerns Wagner's compositional practice – 'the primacy of chromaticism and the leading note' (Adorno, 2005, p. 74) – but it also refers to the staging and performance of his operas. As Susan Buck-Morss has elaborated: 'At Bayreuth the orchestra – the means of production of the musical effects – is hidden from the public by constructing the pit below the audience's line of vision' (Buck-Morss, 1992, p. 25). Similarly the labour and techniques through which the Rhine Maidens appear to float above the stage, in Wagner's *Der Ring des Nibelungen*, are obscured from view. Hence Adorno considers the composer's work as essentially phantasmagorical according to the criteria already established by Marx: their conditions of labour are concealed, but the products of these appear in the commodified form of a fetishized object of consumption.

Today's architectural phantasmagoria are similarly invested in the 'occultation of production'. The actual working conditions of architectural production – short-term contracts, unpaid internships, long hours – rarely resemble, in practice, the type of de-hierarchized and naturalized organizational models promoted within architectural discourse. These conditions, alongside the labour of the actual design processes and those of building construction, are rendered imperceptible in the smoothed forms and undulating surfaces that characterize the projects of practices such as Reiser + Umemoto, Spuybroek's NOX or Ali Rahim and Hina Jamelle's Contemporary Architecture Practice. Of course one would probably not want to dwell at length in any architecture premised, through a kind of Brechtian *verfremdungseffekt*, upon self-reflexively foregrounding its own means of construction and production. Nevertheless, contemporary architecture's fetishization of the continuous and biomorphic modelling of its surfaces and forms can be tellingly contrasted with other possibilities. In architectural Brutalism, for instance, labour and construction processes were revealed through the trace of the wooden shuttering indexed upon its concrete surfaces. Modernist architecture, more broadly, speaks of itself, in its shaping of form according to strict geometrical and/or functional principles, as at least implicitly resulting from the intellectual labour of a conscious design process. The contemporary architectural phantasmagoria, however, is made to appear as if it had produced itself, autogenetically emerging into the world independent of any practice of labour, design or construction.

Adorno identifies the purpose of this phantasmagoric mode of appearance in the work of Wagner. 'The product' he writes, 'presents itself as self-producing . . . In the absence of any glimpse of the underlying forces or conditions of its production, this outer appearance can lay claim to the status of being' (Adorno, 2005, p. 74). The architectural phantasmagoria may be said to operate in a similar fashion, but rather than to a transcendent conception of 'being', it lays claim to the immanence of a vitalized materialism and its immediate appearance as such. This immanence is expressed in a recurrent trope of contemporary architectural design where buildings, even entire urban systems and their infrastructural components, appear as having been collectively warped or deformed by an encounter with an abstract set of forces with which they are now aligned. Aedas/Aecom's West Kowloon Terminus, which is to connect Hong

Kong to cities in the Chinese Mainland by rail, for example, appears to register, in its fluid, undulating morphologies, the passing of some great wave through the terrain from which it emerges. The design of the terminus also suggests, in its alternating bands of generic 'green space' and pedestrian pathways, the idea of an unconflicted and elegantly achieved convergence of infrastructure, nature and mobility. Conditions of friction, conflict and contestation – the processing of subjects through the protocols of immigration and customs, the environmental impact of large-scale infrastructural projects – are mediated in the reassuringly naturalized and affirmative forms of an architectural phantasmagoria.

Work upon the acquisition of contacts, skills and information through continuous self-mobilization also constitute forms of labour 'occulted' by the architectural phantasmagoria. The compulsion to 'network', to move with the currents of a hegemonic connectivism, is facilitated by designs in which the ground is modelled as continuously ramped or wave-like. The ground planes of projects like Reiser + Umemoto's Foshan Sansui Urban Plan, or SANAA's Rolex Learning Center in Lausanne, remodel the relational imperatives of neoliberalism as artificial landscapes so as to imply an experience of freedom from the constraints of older, and more static spaces of containment. Likewise the trope of 'porosity' – exemplified in the openings that perforate the planes of both of these projects, or the envelope of Zaera-Polo/ Foreign Office Architects' Ravensbourne College, punctuated with a network of circular fenestration and internally 'landscaped' circulation – mediates, as liberating, the conditions in which subjects must continuously expose themselves to opportunities for refashioning their subjectivity. In the case of Ravensbourne, these conditions of mobilization and exposure are derived from new models of education – the 'learning landscape' for instance – through which students are to be 'released' from the traditional confinements of the 'ivory tower' and exposed to the entrepreneurial and business models through which their work will now be valorized. The Ravensbourne project, in common with the numerous 'hubs' and 'hives' with which older universities have now been retrofitted, is designed as the spatial complement to these models (Spencer, 2011).[11]

Adorno, in *In Search of Wagner*, criticized, as 'totalizing', the environments of the Wagnerian *Gesamtkunstwerk* in the following terms:

> [T]he task of [Wagner's] music is to warm up the alienated and reified relations of men and make them sound as if they were still human. This technological hostility to consciousness is the very foundation of the music drama. It combines the arts in order to produce an intoxicating brew. (Adorno, 2005, p. 89)

Much contemporary architecture is also aimed at the production of an 'intoxicating brew', and for related ends. Through an appeal to the sensuous realm of pure affectivity, architecture, now conceived as the production of environments and atmospheres, affirmatively mediates financialization's existential conditions as ones of smooth transitions, liberating flexibility and vitalized mobility. It does so through the production of a totalizing aesthetic in which the subject is fully immersed. Designed to present an unbroken perceptual field of sensory experience, any inconsistencies or interruptions that might break its affective spell are to be eliminated. The ribboned undulations of a project such as Thomas Heatherwick's Pacific Hall mall in Hong Kong, for example, not only define the aesthetic character of its large-scale elements, but are also to be found reproduced in the smallest of details, such as the elevator buttons, or the hinges of toilet doors specially designed so as to allow the designer to 'bend the wooden wall without any visible hinge or line'.[12] Likewise, in the architecture of Zaha Hadid detailing is used to produce what Buck-Morss, in her account of the phantasmagoria, has termed a 'total environment' (Buck-Morss, 1992, p. 22). In projects such as the BMW Central Building in Leipzig or the MAXXI Museum in Rome, the circulational diagrams of the building, with their fluid trajectories and precisely calculated intersections, are rendered sensual through the detailing of walls and ceilings with the parallel linear elements that snake through their spaces. Here, the goal would seem to be to induce a synaesthesia between the internal sense of one's bodily movements – 'proprioception' – and the perception of one's external environment – 'exteroception' – through which body and eye are seamlessly aligned with a movement sensualized as free-flowing and elegant.

The architecture of such environments offers its occupants no sensory relief from a totalizing aesthetic designed explicitly not to be read but to be felt, and affords no time or space, in its atmospheres, from which any distance from their affective work might be consciously reflected upon or interpreted. This is, therefore, an architecture that appears, or supposes itself, to have outmaneuvered critique.

However, the ideas through which this supposition is maintained and affirmed – those of the post-critical and the post-linguistic, of the new materialisms and vitalisms where biology, society and the market happily converge upon a benevolently de-hierarchized model of organization – should also be understood as a kind of phantasmagorical work. As a spurious form of historicism, through which contemporary conditions are affirmed as the herald of some fundamentally new paradigm that should now be adhered to, they conceal the longer historical continuities (even if ones of continuous change) within capitalism and power in which architecture, in this case, is, and has been for some time, implicated. As Crary has recently written, in a similar context:

> A logic of economic modernization in play today can be traced directly back to the mid nineteenth century. Marx was one of the first to understand the intrinsic incompatibility of capitalism with stable or durable social forms, and the history of the last 150 years is inseparable from the 'constant revolutionizing' of forms of production, circulation, communication, and image-making. (Crary, 2013, pp. 37–8)

Given that Crary also rightly identifies the most consistently used techniques over this period as those concerned with 'the management and control of human beings', we may say that the models through which these techniques have been critically engaged have no more been absolutely superseded than the conditions they addressed themselves to (Crary, 2013, p. 36). The critique of the phantasmagoria, then, though of course in need of rethinking in relation to the specific terms of financialization – as suggested in this essay's brief remarks on the subject – may serve as one useful point of contact in radical philosophy's re-encounter with architecture.

Notes

1   This collaboration between Eisenman and Derrida began in 1985. In 1989, however, Derrida published a letter to the architect in which he repudiated the latter's understanding of deconstruction and publicly severed his connection with architectural deconstructivism. Jacques Derrida 'A Letter to Peter Eisenman', trans. Hilary P. Hanel in *Assemblage*, no. 12, August, 1990, Cambridge, MA: MIT Press, pp. 6–13.

2   The author has written elsewhere, and at greater length, on this Deleuzian turn in architectural theory. See Douglas Spencer, 'Architectural Deleuzism: Neoliberal Space, Control and the "Univer-city"', in *Radical Philosophy*, 168, July/August, 2011, pp. 9–21, and also Douglas Spencer, 'Architectural Deleuzism II: The Possibility of Critique'. Available at: <http://terraincritical.wordpress.com/2012/03/24/architectural-deleuzism-ii-the-possibility-of-critique/>.

3   Gilles Deleuze, *The Fold: Leibniz and the Baroque*. Tom Conley (trans.). London: Athlone Press, 1993.

4   Deleuze and Guattari cautioned against any straightforward conception of smooth space as in itself liberatory or salvational in *A Thousand Plateaus*: 'Never believe that a smooth space will suffice to save us', p. 500.

5   See, for example, Jesse Reiser and Nanako Umemoto, *Atlas of Novel Tectonics*. New York: Princeton Architectural Press, 2006; Patrik Schumacher, 'Research Agenda', in Brett Steele (ed.), *Corporate Fields: New Environments by the AA DRL*. London: AA Publications, 2005; Patrik Schumacher, *Digital Hadid: Landscapes in Motion*. Basel: Birkhäuser, 2003; Alejandro Zaera-Polo and Roemer van Toorn, 'Educating the Architect', 2008. Available at: <http://www.xs4all.nl/~rvtoorn/alejandro.html>.

6   According to Schumacher, the bounds by which architecture is circumscribed, as an autopoietic system, foreclose the very possibility of its exercising any critical faculties or political agency. Schumacher insists that architecture's accommodation of the existing social order must now be absolute since 'it is not architecture's societal function to actively promote or initiate political agendas that are not already thriving in the political arena', Schumacher, 2003, p. 447.

7   Manuel De Landa's 'assemblage theory' models all modes of organizational processes as 'isomorphic' operations occurring at different scales across the biological, the geological and the social. This model, a kind of 'flat ontology', allows for causal agency between different 'singularities' but admits of no encompassing force directing them towards a preconceived end. See Manuel De Landa, *A New Philosophy of Society: Assemblage Theory and Social Complexity*. London and New York: Continuum, 2006. Zaera-Polo, following De Landa, argues in 'The Politics of the Envelope' that 'In fact, it may be good to stop speaking of power in general, or of the State, Capital, Globalization in general, and instead address specific power ecologies comprising a heterogeneous mixture of bureaucracies, markets, antimarkets, shopping malls, airport terminals, residential towers, office complexes etc.' Zaera-Polo, 2008, p. 101.

8   Bruno Latour's 'actor-network theory', conceived along similar lines to De Landa's 'assemblage theory', recognizes no hierarchies within any system, only agents – human and non-human – interacting amidst a network within which there are no privileged centres. Bruno Latour, a figure increasingly prominent within design and architectural discourse, has argued against the 'negativity' of critique, and suggested that it has, in any case, 'run out of steam', that 'Critical theory died away long ago.' See, Bruno Latour, 'Why Has Critique Run Out of Steam? From Matters of Fact to Matters of Concern', in *Critical Inquiry* – Special issue on the Future of Critique, 30, 2, p. 248.

9   Manuel De Landa has argued that Deleuze and Guattari's attachments to Marx represent their own Oedipus complex, from which his own philosophy liberates their thinking. See Manuel De Landa, John Protevi and Torkild Thanem, 'Deleuzian Interrogations: A Conversation with Manuel De Landa, John Protevi and Torkild Thanem', in *Tamara: Journal of Critical Postmodern Organization Science*, 3, 4, 2005. For a critique of De Landa's de-Marxification of Deleuze and Guattari see Eliot Albert, 'A Thousand Marxes', in *Mute*, Autumn 1998. Available at: <http://www.metamute.org/en/A-Thousand-Marxes>.

10 See, Paolo Virno, 'General Intellect', trans. Adrianna Bove, 2000. Available at: <http://www.generation-online.org/p/fpvirno10.htm>; Paolo Virno, *A Grammar of the Multitude*, trans. Isabella Bertoletti, James Cascaito and Andrea Casson. Los Angeles and New York: Semiotext(e), 2004; Maurizio Lazzarato, 'Immaterial Labour', in Hardt, Michael and Paolo Virno (eds), *Radical Thought in Italy: A Potential Politics*. Minneapolis and London: University of Minnesota Press, 1997; Christian Marazzi, *Capital and Affects: The Politics of the Language Economy*, trans. Giuseppina Mecchia, Los Angeles and New York: Semiotext(e), 2011; Antonio Negri, *Marx Beyond Marx: Lessons on the Grundrisse*, H. Cleaver, M. Ryan and M. Viano (trans), New York: Autonomedia, 1991.

11 See Spencer (2011), for a more extensive analysis of this project.

12 Thomas Heatherwick, 'Pacific Hall'. Available at: <http://www.heatherwick.com/pacific-place/>.

Bibliography

Adorno, T. (2005), *In Search of Wagner*. R. Livingstone (trans.). London and New York: Verso.

Albert, M. (1998), 'A Thousand Marxes', in *Mute*, Autumn 1998.

Boltanski, L. and Chiapello, E. (2007), *The New Spirit of Capitalism*. G. Elliot (trans.). London and New York: Verso.

Buck-Morss, S. (1992), 'Aesthetics and Anaesthetics: Walter Benjamin's Artwork Essay Reconsidered', in *October*, Volume 62. Cambridge, MA: MIT Press.

Crary, J. (2013), *24:7: Late Capitalism and the Ends of Sleep*. London and New York: Verso.

Cusset, F. (2011), 'Theory (Madness of)', in *Radical Philosophy*, 167, May/June.

De Landa, M., Protevi, J. and Thanem, T. (2005), 'Deleuzian Interrogations: A Conversation with Manuel De Landa, John Protevi and Torkild Thanem', in *Tamara: Journal of Critical Postmodern Organization Science*, 3, 4.

Deleuze, G. (1993), *The Fold: Leibniz and the Baroque*. T. Conley (trans.). London: Athlone Press.

— (1995a), 'Control and Becoming', in G. Deleuze, *Negotiations, 1972–1990*. M. Joughin (trans.). New York and Chichester: Columbia University Press.

— (1995b), 'Postscript on Control Societies', in *Negotiations, 1972–1990*. M. Joughin (trans.). New York and Chichester: Columbia University Press.

Deleuze, G. and Guattari, F. (1992), *A Thousand Plateaus: Capitalism and Schizophrenia*. B. Massumi (trans.). London and New York: Continuum.

Derrida, J. (1990), 'A Letter to Peter Eisenman', H. P. Hanel (trans.), *Assemblage*, 12, August. Cambridge, MA: MIT Press.

Foucault, M. (1977), *Discipline and Punish: The Birth of the Prison*. A. Sheridan (trans.). London: Penguin.

— (2008), *The Birth of Biopolitics: Lectures at the College De France, 1978–79.* M. Senellart (ed.), G. Burchell (trans.). Basingstoke and New York: Palgrave MacMillan.

Hays, K. M. (ed.) (1998), *Architecture Theory Since 1968.* Cambridge, MA: MIT Press.

Kipnis, J. (1993, reprinted 2004), 'Towards a New Architecture', in G. Lynn (ed.), *Folding in Architecture.* Chichester and Hoboken, NJ: Wiley-Academy.

— (2004), 'On the Wild Side', in F. Moussavi, A. Zaera-Polo and S. Kwinter (eds), *Phylogenesis: FOA's Ark.* Barcelona: Actar.

Latour, B. (2004), 'Why Has Critique Run Out of Steam? From Matters of Fact to Matters of Concern', in *Critical Inquiry* – Special issue on the Future of Critique, vol. 30, no. 2.

Lavin, S. (2011), *Kissing Architecture.* Princeton: Princeton University Press.

Lynn, G. (ed.) (1993, reprinted 2004), *Folding in Architecture.* Chichester and Hoboken, NJ: Wiley-Academy.

Lazzarato, M. (1997), 'Immaterial Labour', in M. Hardt and P. Virno (eds), *Radical Thought in Italy: A Potential Politics.* Minneapolis: University of Minnesota Press. [the year referenced for this publication should be changed from 1977 to 1997].

— (2012), *The Making of the Indebted Man.* J. D. Jordan (trans.). Cambridge, MA: MIT Press.

Manuel De Landa, M. (2006), *A New Philosophy of Society: Assemblage Theory and Social Complexity.* London and New York: Continuum.

Marx, K. (1976), *Capital: Volume 1.* B. Fowkes (trans.). London: Penguin.

Meyer, C. and Davis, S. (2003), *It's Alive: The Coming Convergence of Information, Biology, and Business.* New York: Crown Business.

Reiser, J. and Umemoto, N. (2006), *Atlas of Novel Tectonics.* New York: Princeton Architectural Press.

Schumacher, P. (2003), *Digital Hadid: Landscapes in Motion.* Basel: Birkhäuser.

— (2005), 'Research Agenda', in B. Steele (ed.), *Corporate Fields: New Environments by the AA DRL.* London: AA Publications.

— (2012), *The Autopoiesis of Architecture, Volume II: A New Agenda for Architecture.* Chichester: Wiley.

Somol, R. and Whiting, S. (2002), 'Notes Around the Doppler Effect and Other Moods of Modernism', *Perspecta 33: Mining Autonomy.*

Speaks, M. (2006), 'Intelligence After Theory', in *Perspecta 38: Architecture After All.* Cambridge, MA: MIT Press.

Spencer, D. (2011), 'Architectural Deleuzism: Neoliberal Space, Control and the "University"', *Radical Philosophy*, 168, July/August, 2011.

— (2012), 'Architectural Deleuzism II: The Possibility of Critique'. Available at: <http://terraincritical.wordpress.com/2012/03/24/architectural-deleuzism-ii-the-possibility-of-critique/>.

Spuybroek, S. (2011), *The Sympathy of Things: Ruskin and the Ecology of Design.* Rotterdam: V2_Publishing.

Tapscott, D. (1996), *The Digital Economy: Promise and Peril in the Age of Networked Intelligence.* New York: McGraw-Hill.

Virno, P. (1997), 'The Ambivalence of Disenchantment', in M. Hardt and P. Virno (eds), *Radical Thought in Italy: A Potential Politics.* Minneapolis: University of Minnesota Press.

Zaera-Polo, A. (1994), 'Order Out of Chaos: The Material Organization of Advanced Capitalism', in *Architectural Design Profile.*

— (2008), 'The Politics of the Envelope', *Volume* #17, Fall 2008.

Zaera-Polo, A. and van Toorn, R. (2008), 'Educating the Architect'. Available at: <http://www.xs4all.nl/~rvtoorn/alejandro.html>.

6

Imitating Critique, or the Problematic Legacy of the Venice School

Andrew Leach

Among those instances in which architectural culture attended to the invitations (and demands) of radical philosophy, few exceed in impact the translation enacted by Manfredo Tafuri of a Trontian *critica dell'ideologia* into the architectural domain. Famously couched in the critique of the Left modelled by Rossana Rosanda in *Il Manifesto* and pursued by Tafuri and the circle for whom Antonio Negri served as anchor in the pages of *Contropiano* (1969b, 1970, 1972), *Progetto e utopia* (1973; Engl. ed. 1976, *Architecture and Utopia*), *Socialismo, città, architettura* (1971), Tafuri's *critica dell'ideologia architettonica* served to position the modern architectural project as entirely complicit with the capitalist system. Within this critique, Tafuri isolated historical research as a form of work (and hence action) uniquely capable of demonstrating this same complicity: a proper site of resistance within architectural culture, where production and the architectural project had accommodated the pressures of capitalist development and aided its objectives by giving them expression and offering them programmatic resolution. Explicitly positioning himself as an historian of architecture, working in the mode of a critical historian concerned as much with ideas as with artefacts, Tafuri cast reflection and analysis as being outside a system that had become, as the opening words of *Progetto e utopia* suggest, one means by which bourgeois art might, as 'one of its principal ethical exigencies', 'ward off anguish by understanding and absorbing [the] causes' of the anxieties of the modern age (Tafuri, 1976, p. 1). By declaring, famously, the operating principle of the group he assembled at Venice as being the conflation of criticism and historiography – of critical action, the self-conscious production of historical representations and (although this would follow) the representation of historical research – Tafuri acted to shift the position of history and historical knowledge within architectural culture to assign it a radical character informed by the Trontian imperative.

As Tafuri would write much later in the opening pages of *Ricerca del rinascimento* (1992, Engl. ed. 2006, *Interpreting the Renaissance*), history was not the oil one poured upon rough waves to make order from chaos; it was instead an approximation of that very same chaos, being the past with which the historian obliged architecture to learn to live rather than to ignore. Positioned thus, Tafuri's version of history's tasks secured for the historian's practice a resistant role in a world otherwise given over to forces that treated architecture as their play thing, these forces being (in the schema tabled in *Progetto e utopia*) those of capitalist development (as a blunt target) and late capitalism (as an insidious structural force). Ideologically bound accounts of architecture's history served this entrenchment by justifying it historically, while Tafuri argued to bring new materials and new analytical perspectives to bear upon architecture's bad habits and corrupt alliances to demonstrate the choices being made by architecture as an institution in favour of capitalism. These targets, clear though they may have been in the late 1960s, were, however, far from static, demanding of the historian who assumes the position proposed by Tafuri a mobility in relation to both the tools and specific tasks governing his or her work – this thereby ensuring an ongoing yet equally mobile role for the historian in architectural culture not predicated on a single ideological problem demanding a stable critical toolkit.

That there is little diminished in this project over the subsequent two decades is demonstrated in the pages of *Ricerca del rinascimento*, which echo (if on different terms, as we shall see) the opening lines of his earlier book and their immediate and poignant diagnosis of the problem of a bourgeois art (as architecture is clearly construed) as being its capacity for internalizing and neutralizing the causes of modern anguish. Already by the end of the 1960s Tafuri had laid out an historical trajectory leading to that moment, furthermore showing how architecture had conceded its agency to capitalist development as it had become increasingly self-conscious and introspect over time. Like the *Contropiano* articles from which it was drawn, *Progetto e utopia* demanded of its readers a disruption in the false consciousness fostered by a near ubiquitous bourgeoisie: an intervention in the world using architecture's tools, but trading architecture's tasks for those of a critique of a capitalism that had authorized architecture's relegation to a service profession subservient to the needs of governments, institutions and development.

The writing of historical criticism and critical history – thus cast as vehicles for architecture's capacity for resistance – acted against architecture's embrace of a position of what Tafuri in his more cynical moments treated as its sublime indifference to the world around it, not least by recalling those moments in which the architect soundly rejected neutrality in favour of direct intervention in the world and its structures and in which architecture and architectural ideas were made to figure as a force for disruption. Tafuri's treatment of these themes within the frame of architectural history complemented numerous efforts by those of his circle to enervate architecture's critical capacities and to generate those conditions that would provoke architecture to assert its own agency in order to distinguish between the objectives (the projects) of architecture and capitalism.

In Venice, and beyond

On one hand and at the most mundane level, in formulating architectural history on these terms he was doing little more than coming to grips with the referents and motivations of the highly engaged group he found upon his arrival proper to Venice for the 1968–9 academic year: the group comprising largely of students who had followed Negri's courses at Padua, and which famously included the young philosopher Massimo Cacciari as well as the young architects Francesco Dal Co and Marco De Michelis. And yet he also recalibrated for Venice and led in a new direction a discussion that had already informed the premises underpinning his work as a critic, historian and protagonist. In one form or another this discussion dated to the earliest moments of his engagement in contemporary architectural culture and through his participation in this debate Tafuri arguably saw it shift from the radical fringes of architectural discourse to a position of clear prominence, from one angry young man's voice among a swarm of angry youth to an institutional position that gave structure to the determination that fed his polemic. Indeed, his idiosyncratic personalization of its main lines and premises and the institutional corollary for it that he built in Venice arguably lent this a profile and, in its reception, an international prominence unmatched by the expression it found with other writers and centres who had demonstrated a stronger grasp of the nuances of the lessons of Tronti and, in particular, readings of such figures as Walter Benjamin and the protagonists of the Frankfurt School that most directly shaped what would come next.

(A further, more speculative observation on the structural logic of Tafuri's position: his entry to the debate as a catalyst for its wider uptake in architectural culture is not entirely inconsistent with the discursive structure of *Contropiano* itself. *Contropiano* was a Roman journal, after all, for which some of the clearest voices emanated from the Veneto region. The presence of Asor Rosa in the *argomenti* Tafuri pursued from his arrival to Venice recalls a polarity (Rome vs Venice, complex centre vs resistant or reflective exterior) rather than a complicated insularity (Venice and the Veneto) of the discussion sustained in the pages of that journal – a polarity neither unfamiliar to Tafuri nor out of step with his own institutional ambitions to bring to Venice those Romans like Giorgio Ciucci and Mario Manieri-Elia who had since the early 1960s proven sympathetic to the polemical structures and imperatives that Tafuri evidently found important as a critic and as an historian.)

The most visible of those structures was what came to be widely called the Venice School of architectural history: an identification between Tafuri's institutional and private projects that eclipsed the earlier (and more generous) meaning of the Venice School as the legacy of Giuseppe Samonà's leadership of the Istituto Universitario di Architettura di Venezia (IUAV) across the twentieth century's middle decades and the architectural leadership of Carlo Aymonino, Vittorio Gregotti, Aldo Rossi and Carlo Scarpa. In the institute he inherited from Bruno Zevi following the senior historian's relocation to Rome in 1963, Tafuri recast its aims in light of a programme of heavily politicized historical research into those moments of the nineteenth and twentieth centuries in which the relation between ideological systems and their architecture – a term extending to the scale of the city – became openly available to problematization. Zevi had understood history as a filter through which the student of architecture could acquire an architectonic and spatial sensibility appropriate to the present, informed by a deep knowledge of architecture's traditions and a deep appreciation of the models offered to the architect by his or her exemplary forebears. Tafuri rejected this idea as predicated on an over-instrumentalized concept of history's impact on the present through which the historian had too much power in shaping the present by using historical authority to legitimize favoured strains of contemporary architectural practice.

The past was a battlefield on which power, technology and ideas were all at stake – both as a tussle between past and present and as a matter of legacy (for the past) and model (for the present). History should reflect this capacity for conflict, this lack of certain outcomes, this fragility of historical certainties. It should not take sides in denial of there having been any conflict at all. This, he argued, was one domain in which (the wrong kind of) architectural history acted to reinforce architectural ideologies and hence, in the modern era, to enable it to maintain the false consciousness of bourgeois art where anxiety might otherwise and properly productively reign.

He pitched the teaching and research agenda of his Istituto di Storia dell'Architettura against the idea of architectural history as architecture by other means to the extent of holding his group up as a moment of resistance to the theoretical premises and historical models claimed in legitimacy of architectural production. It was underpinned by a profoundly critical, contrarian attitude that all but withheld historical legitimacy for the actions of the architect operating in the present. The painting by Aldo Rossi (*L'architecture assassinée*, 1975) that famously adorns the English edition of *Progetto e utopia* expresses the sense that Tafuri had, in playing this agenda through, dismantled the foundations on which architecture had come to rest and through which the concept of architecture – architecture as an institution in and of itself – was defined across time. He had seemingly opened up what Reyner Banham (1990) much later called the 'black box' of architectural acculturation and initiation, removed history as a cohering component and refashioned it as a tool to act upon that same black box process, which now, consequently, had seen externalized one of its key elements while at the same moment being made subject to the most incisive of tools. *Progetto e utopia* decisively shifted the diagnosis of architecture's profound corruption in the maintenance of architecture as a vehicle for capitalist development on to the shoulders of a readership concerned with realizing works of architecture in the present for which he wrote. He expressed a capacity for resistance, feeding resistance with tools that were taken up, much like the burden he had himself assumed, by those students and young radicals (*I Radicals*, as they self-styled) who sought in alternate practices and forms of anti-architecture the path through the morass that Tafuri had so incisively described.

Tools and tasks

While all these positions shaped the ambitions and reception of *Progetto e utopia*, the premises of this book's role in architectural culture had been laid out in an earlier work in which the institutional framework of his group at Venice had, in a very meaningful sense, already been professed: *Teorie e storia dell'architettura* (1968, Engl. ed. 1980b, *Theories and History of Architecture*). Tafuri therein conceived of and laid the groundwork for institutionalizing architectural historiography (as a practice) as working within the institution of architecture as a form of conscience, laying bare the tension between the historical moment and the *longue durée* in order to undermine the authority of historical narrative and to radicalize an otherwise latent knowledge of the past. Over time, the programme of research, conferences and publications intended to address this function appeared to leave the proximity of the present and a patrimony that was both immediate and insistent in the work of the early 1970s, gravitating instead towards studies in the fifteenth and sixteenth centuries that had been in play since the 1960s in Tafuri's work. This trajectory culminated in *Ricerca del rinascimento*, being Tafuri's masterful return (after *Teorie e storia dell'architettura*) to the five-centuries-long arc from the (anachronistically cast) origins of architecture's relationship with capitalism to its capitulation to capitalism's forces. This capitulative arc describes both the increasingly clear operation of an ideological device lending architectural thought a sturdy defense from a reality that might otherwise hold it to account and the increasingly problematic role of that device in light of its necessity to the very concept of architecture as a trans-historical category subject to historicization as an institution, a body of knowledge and a practice. Various forms of check had been in play across this trajectory, and the contemporary historian inherited a role that architecture had once internalized through a sceptical and 'operative' approach to history's received models and lessons. This, at least, is how the story goes.

We will return to this trajectory below, but for the time being it is important to note that in its European and Anglo-American reception within the intertwined domains of architectural history and architectural theory, the Venice School was quickly and inextricably linked to the powerful efforts of Tafuri and his contemporaries to carve out an engaged and instrumental role for critical and historical knowledge in contemporary architectural culture. This role was directly informed both by a criticism of architecture's capacity to which they (but primarily Tafuri) arrived from within architecture and by a critical apparatus fostered in the discussions staged around *Contropiano* and those journals that shared its mission of radical cultural critique and complemented the radical strains of artistic and architectural practice of the 1960s and 1970s. From the moment that Tafuri began teaching at IUAV (from 1968), he sought out like-minded thinkers drawn from architecture, art history, philosophy, politics and aesthetics to problematize the place of architecture in the world and the place of historical knowledge in the field of architectural knowledge. Some of these thinkers were his students and then his assistants, while others joined the programme he had set in train from positions either of intellectual maturity or with a compatible formation secured elsewhere. The collaborations staged and then documented across the 1960s and 1970s attest to the repeated success, at least for a number of years, of an historiographical formula: addressing the intersections of architecture, construction and planning culture, politics and institutions in the historicized urban settings of the United States, Germany, Austria and the Soviet Union, the great Left to Centre-Right ideological systems of the twentieth century.

Not in the least cast as a unitary 'project' before that loaded term drifted across the threshold separating Tafuri's analysis of the long modern era from his disciplinary ambitions for architectural history, the Venice School as we now think of it rather caught the ebbs and flows of an aggressive, multivalent research programme intended to shed light on the structural problems of contemporary architecture and the crises it fostered and sustained and which lent form to the local manifestations of a broader, pan-European and North American generational change affecting intellectual work and its institutions. While for several years maintained at a local and national level, this discussion and its terms of reference resonated with the increased footholds found by architectural criticism and theory in various countries and language groups, translating a radical gesture with institutional ambitions into the institution it sought to be – not only in Venice, where Tafuri came to preside over what was then one of the world's most important departments of architectural history, but internationally, where Venice served as the touchstone for claims of criticality within architecture, its theory and its historiography.

The paths drawn between one and another element of Tafuri's European (and then international) uptake across the 1960s, 1970s and 1980s are by now so varied and heavily annotated by historical commentary as to sustain the most cursory of acknowledgements here en route to a more substantial point. This, namely, concerns the task assigned by Tafuri and his colleagues at Venice to architectural history (and to architectural theory as historiography by other means): their insistence on the reorientation of history from playing a patrimonial role, supplying contemporary architecture with models and legislation, to serving analytical and critical functions structurally (or at least rhetorically) disarticulated from the production of architecture. This was largely contingent on a peculiar intersection of institutional circumstances and intellectual motivations, all within what Pippo Ciorra recently called the '*critical hegemony*' of Giulio Carlo Argan' (2011, p. 54, my trans.) – which, fundamentally, had opened the history of art (and the history of architecture within it) to deployment of the kinds of critical tools Tafuri and his circle had found in semiology, information sciences, critical theory, Freudian psychoanalysis, sociology, anthropology and elsewhere. Yet the apparently monolithic result of this search, initially codified in *Progetto e utopia* and demonstrated in the book projects mentioned at the outset of this piece, undermines the process implied by the very premises of the Trontian *critica dell'ideologia* and its refusal to assume that the forms taken by the criticism of ideology – effective though they might be for any given moment – would themselves be immune to the criticism of ideology. Fundamental to their uptake of Tronti's ideas and clearly signalled in their reading of the architectural avant-garde (Tafuri, 1980a) was the premise that neither the subjects nor tools of historical criticism would (or should) remain static.

(That Tronti was not simply a source for these discussions but engaged in them to various degrees has been well documented in Aureli (2008). That this constituted a moment is beyond doubt, although less clear is the extent to which the 'encounter' between architecture and radical philosophy was missed or misrepresented rather than internalized is a matter subject to further discussion (compare, Brown, 2010).)

Just as the circle around *Contropiano* had tested and then demonstrated what a radical criticism of architecture might be for architecture in those brief years spanning the turn of the 1970s, those same actors were also demonstrating the fragility of the tools and positions they laid out in the face of both capitalist encroachment and critical ossification. (This was at the heart of the crisis of the Partito Comunista Italiana – the PCI – at the end of the 1960s as Rosanda's *Manifesto* opened to public scrutiny those reservations with and criticisms of the PCI that had hitherto been the proper domain of a closed democratic centralism.) Just as the tools and tasks of a political critique necessarily responded to the problems of the present – which included the natural yet nonetheless problematic tendency to lock down the tools and tasks of that same critique – by being open to adaptation and change, so too did Tafuri and the group anchored to Venice continue to shift their attentions and alter the nature of their analytical tools in response to the pressing needs of the field in which they were working and to their core ambition to function as architecture's live conscience.

The burden of the image

While the principle of mobility might have served them well at an operative methodological level, the group at Venice, and Tafuri above all, were nonetheless problematically tied to the image Rossi had crystallized on their behalf of a seismically disrupted city strewn with riven walls and decapitated columns: architecture assassinated by historians and critics who no longer shared the architectural project and advanced alongside its architects, but who took architecture and the city as targets and set about dismantling the historical authority and ideological foundations on which their relationship was premised. This not exactly undeserved image – and the polemical writing that had given rise to it – formed a monumental burden of its own with which later work of the group, and its legacy, would be obliged to contend.

Of the 'classic' Venice School of Samonà, Carlo Aymonino (1975, p. 8) once observed that it was less a 'scuola' than an 'elenco di problemi' – a directory of problematics that lent form to an otherwise dispersed group of interests that condensed and dispersed according to the exigencies of each moment. Likewise the Venice School of Tafuri, Dal Co, Cacciari, Ciucci and others: their own directory of problems of pressing import in the 1960s and 1970s responded immediately to institutional exigencies and possibilities and to the cultural and political concerns of that moment, all under the general ambition to free architecture to play a role in the world. Like a garage band forming and dispersing as opportunities came and went, the group's composition and ambitions were nothing if not fluid. As the state of disciplinary knowledge shifted and Italian architectural history obliged itself to respond to new problems both within the disciplinary field of architectural history and to a profoundly changed landscape of the Italian Left – to the extent that, as Jean-Louis Cohen has insisted (2008), politics remained inextricable from their disciplinary motivations – Tafuri's reputation as a critic of modernism and its legacies among readers of French, Spanish, Dutch and English demanded an attention to themes and issues that had been, to a greater or lesser extent, internalized and surpassed by the so-called Venice School as they moved on to other questions and subjects towards the end of the 1970s and into the 1980s.

None of this is to suggest that either Tafuri or his colleagues set aside their politics, moved to the Right, withdrew into the past, or ceased to find interest in the political theory and radical philosophy that had so fundamentally held their attention at the end of the 1960s. Rather, as the targets of their research and writing and teaching moved, it became necessary to change the tools to suit the problems then facing them. One could use Gramsci or Adorno to address the oeuvres of Giulio Romano or Francesco di Giorgio Martini, but their effectiveness as tools in positioning and processing these historical subjects is far from guaranteed and invites anachronisms, at the very least; as Tafuri ably demonstrated, one gets much further with devices more responsive to the problems these two figures present the twentieth-century historian (1989, 1992). Micro-historiography might likewise serve to break open a quandary around the relationship between Andrea Palladio and Jacopo Sansovino (Tafuri, 1983), or to enliven the methodological toolkit of the historian at a particular moment (1977). But this would not necessarily be the most pertinent approach for understanding the relative impacts of the *proto* and the architect in Renaissance Venice – a theme resonating with the status of the architect in capitalist development, but played out through an evidentiary body demanding a kind of close reading that proved, among readers at least, decidedly and appropriately foreign to the tone and imperatives of *Progetto e utopia*. Following the changes to which Tafuri's work was subject across the decades in which he wrote we learn that no tool, no approach, survives time, and those that would appear to do so rapidly shift into focus as the historian's proper target.

Criticism of criticism

Herein lies a key problem for the legacy of the 1960s engagement with radical philosophy by architecture: such books as *Progetto e utopia* and *La città americana* (also 1973, Engl. ed. 1983, *The American City*) had a lasting impact on the conceptualization of architecture's historical problems for writers, architects and students from this moment onwards, as well as on the role of the historian and the critic – the necessarily engaged figure of the intellectual – in contemporary architectural culture. Readers of a certain age know these books well and they form a key component of the reading context of several academic generations. Tafuri might now be filtered by Fredric Jameson, K. Michael Hays, Reinhold Martin or Pier Vittorio Aureli, but he is not without status in the current or recent uptake of the questions of the nature of architecture's critical and historiographical problems, their conceptualization, the insight they offer into the present – or, indeed, their apparent prescience. (Indeed, despite the so-called crisis of criticism in architecture that has left it unclear to whom the role of intellectual belongs, Tafuri remains persistently a touchstone, even if not universally so.)

Reduced attention to the arguments of architectural theory's hey-day since the mid-1990s has, however, undermined what was once a widespread imperative to read in the genre of 'difficult theory' to which Tafuri's work arguably belongs – and which surely includes those histories written in a 'theoretical' cast – and to assign to Tafuri the crucial role in architectural culture that he had previously enjoyed as a figure whose political imperative translated into an intellectual imperative, and who offered a model for the politicization of architectural debate. In simple terms, and despite the idiosyncrasies to which we must readily concede, Tafuri's theorization and criticism of modern architecture (alongside the production of the Venice School more broadly) no longer seems as transcendent of the circumstances of its production as it might have done 20 years ago. What are the stakes of this change when the matter is something larger than the question of the critical fortunes of Tafuri, Dal Co, Cacciari and their peers, when it exceeds, that is to say, the arguably introspect mission of writing architectural history's history? What is the status of this moment in the present day, in which intellectual, institutions and political manoeuvres informed by the radical thinking of the 1960s absorbed that moment's lessons and moved on while the rest of the world struggled with its legacy? Where, that is to say, do these disciplinary gains of nearly half a century ago leave us today?

One of the crucial matters for understanding the import of this moment for the present is the trajectory of Tafuri himself – a trajectory informed by aspects of his research and writing of the 1960s and 1970s which tended to return (not *turn*) with greater insistency to moments in the fifteenth and sixteenth centuries as subjects of study. While I have elsewhere argued how this fails to constitute the retreat by which it was characterized both at the time and in Tafuri's posthumous reception – although advent of an English translation of *Ricerca del rinascimento* has gone a very long way towards scuttling this characterization for Tafuri's Anglophone audiences – there remains a point to make concerning the extension of a principle of radicality into historical research. This is not readily reconciled with the writings that accrue to the historical image of a radical and engaged Tafuri, yet the broader ambitions of a critique of ideology must admit that the targets of this critique are historically, and hence critically, contingent, demanding vigilance and adaptability in addressing an artistic and intellectual landscape in which the tools and tasks of criticism can all too readily become its subjects.

For Tafuri, as he wrote in 1992, the matter of origins is fundamental to the historian's purchase in this system. What is, as he put it, the 'original sin' of which architectural culture 'demands exculpation'? In 1973 and the opening lines of *Progetto e utopia*, the critic's target was bourgeois art, which served the modern age through its internalization and neutralization of an anxiety that the avant-garde sought to embrace. Twenty years later, the target had shifted from bourgeois art itself to its criticism and historiography. 'Few critics', he writes, 'are able to examine the bad conscience that afflicts contemporary art . . . [All] too often the anxious search for a means to overcome the malaise of contemporary art and architecture ends in formulae that obscure the problem behind clouds of anesthetic smoke' (2006, p. xxvii). What had moved in the meantime? In short, the intervening decades had witnessed the normalization of the critical mode of history that Tafuri championed – and with normalization, the seeds of its ossification and the concomitant need to turn the critical imperative against criticism itself.

Tafuri was clearly aware of this problem in writing 'Il "progetto" storico' (1977), but this did not alter his ambitions to understand how architecture's intellectual independence – nominally commencing from the mediated reception and historical representation of antiquity in the fifteenth century – served as an original moment in what he positioned as its consistent withdrawal from conditions of architectural and urban production that came to be, without effective resistance from within, entirely shaped by forces external to architecture. (His classic example, from 1973, is the Manhattan skyscraper, which for occupying a block determined by a grid giving, in turn, the most direct expression of the movement of capital, can be anything at all, since the grid, rather than the building, is what ultimately matters.) Simply attending to the capacity of modern art and architecture within it to assuage the effects of modernity through acts of reassurance and absorption did not go far enough into the problem of architecture's stake in the entire system – its stake, that is, in the world beyond architecture, and its agency, therefore, in that world. The conditions addressed by Tafuri in his historical account of architecture's entanglements with a capitalism borne of reason that constitutes the first chapter of *Progetto e utopia* ('Le avventure della ragione', 'Reason's Adventures') do not explain the basic pre-conditions of architecture's quiet renunciation of what Tafuri construed to be its critical mandate. They do not, therefore, sustain the same tools, or present the same subjects. Tafuri demonstrates his awareness of this point in the extraordinary *L'architettura dell'umanesimo*, which appeared in the year after *Teorie e storia* and in the same year as 'Per una critica dell'ideologia architettonica' (1969b, Engl. ed. 1998, 'Towards a Critique of Architectural Ideology'). In its pages, 'ideology' serves as a cypher for all those intellectual systems that stand between the realm of architectural ideas and the world on which they seek to act – played out in the Renaissance and its humanist return to the forms and ideas of antiquity through the tense relationship between reason and nature that architecture sought to mediate and which come to a head in the eighteenth century.

In returning to this problem in *Ricerca del rinascimento* – in a chapter that had already been given life as an article in the 1980s – Tafuri drew attention to Leon Battista Alberti's own conflicted views on the relationship between order and chaos that structured, in turn, Tafuri's persistence in analysing those figures in architecture's history for whom this relationship was fundamental. In Tafuri's hands, therefore, Francesco Borromini and Giovanni Battista Piranesi expressed the fragility of the traditions in which they worked, tracking the relationship between the conflicting authorities of the past represented and the past of artefacts and historical fabric (Tafuri, 1978). So far as Alberti was concerned, Tafuri asserted (1984), Carroll William Westfall (1974) had it wrong on two counts: he overestimated Alberti's standing in the Nicolan court, and he failed to account for Alberti's own reservations over the kinds of legitimations offered by his treatises on painting, architecture and the city and what those in authority might do with them – reservations now famously expressed in *Momus* and brought to bear upon a monumental Albertian legacy by Tafuri's hand.

The unfounded certainty Tafuri saw in Westfall's account stands well for the architectural historian's moving targets, being those foundations for the notion of architecture and for the architect's contemporary authority in their field that are regarded as solid but which are inevitably destabilized through close analysis. Alberti did not legislate Renaissance architecture or the Renaissance city, goes Tafuri's point, so much as to describe both the ideal (*De re aedificatoria*) and that which lurks at its edges (*Momus*). In framing Tafuri's engagement with the Trontian *critica dell'ideologia*, we are obliged to take this point into account, to consider the core imperatives, targets, referents and literary expressions of 1969 and 'Per una critica dell'ideologia architettonica' and to appreciate where we need to look to find Tafuri's own *Momus* (or, perhaps better, as we will see, his own S. Giovanni dei Fiorentini). If Tafuri is to remain a touchstone for criticality in architectural history we need to more actively position in our reading those moments in which he tempers the certainty of criticism's tools and tasks. The undoubted importance of *Progetto e utopia* cannot be read naively as a source for our current imperatives in the field of architectural history and criticism without appreciating and figuring in the edges that Tafuri himself understood that work to have – nor without understanding the operation of the imperatives themselves underpinning *Progetto e utopia* in work that since completely set aside its form and subjects.

The presence of the past

While many readers, including architects, found in Tafuri's writing the targets and language of critique of an architectural ideology – of a politicized form of architectural criticism capable of undermining architecture's participation in the system – the deep analysis of the modern era through which he activated historiographical representation as an agent of ideological critique was nonetheless long read by that same readership as a retreat, on his part, into the problems of the past. As the core of an institute re-formulated to train architects with the historiographical skills necessary to foment an ideological critique within architecture, what was still widely called the Venice School was caught up in precisely this paradox in its increased attention to and enlarged research capacity to work in early modern topics – by turning to the origins of the modern epoch, scholars and students became accountable to the scholarship of that era, but within an historiographical mission still connected to the founding principles of Tafuri's Istituto di Storia dell'Architettura (as it remained until the 1980s). Rather than being understood to explicitly return the lessons of the Renaissance within a critique of contemporary architectural ideology, or indeed to position that work so as to confront the thought of a contemporary architectural culture, the work of the Venice School appeared to enact an unintentional retreat at odds with the principles of its formation. While this turned out to be the case – at an institutional level, at least, and especially since the end of the 1980s – it initially accommodated an important reassessment of the status of historical evidence for architecture in the field of architectural history within the search for origins and original sin cited above. The early work of that group had provoked a broad reassessment of the status of (extra-disciplinary, critical) theory for architectural debate (Cohen, 1984) – a reassessment that obliged architecture to reconsider the relationship of history, theory and criticism to architectural design, and to reposition theory as a critical rather than a projective force. In light of the increased attention to the subjects and sources of the early modern era, two key matters were thrown up through this reassessment that proved important for the way that the theme of criticality played out in the work pursued in what was, in the 1980s, restructured as a Dipartimento di Storia dell'Architettura of IUAV.

The first of these matters was disciplinary and concerned the professionalization of architectural history as what I have elsewhere called a conditionally autonomous field of study (2006). With various largely unsystematic exceptions, the twentieth-century historiography of architecture owed an enormous debt to *Kunstwissenschaft* and its command both of the disciplinary rigors of art history and of its documents. The positioning of architectural history among the liberal arts or its location as a vehicle for advancing architectural knowledge within architecture both tended to take objects and their measured documentation – especially when those objects had the attention of archaeology – as the proper object of study. It took much longer to appreciate the value of archives for architectural history. Although he stood for an entire working tradition, Wittkower had demonstrated how to close this gap (Vidler, 2008) and in Wittkower and others working in his mode Tafuri appreciated the importance of documents.

As I have elsewhere argued (2010), Tafuri had been on the fringes of an important shift in the practice of historical research within architecture that took place across the years in which he was both arming himself with the tools of a critique of ideology and with the techniques then proper to the history of art. (In the European historiography of architecture, and especially in Italy, the tercentenary commemorations of Francesco Borromini, staged in 1967, were an important marker of this change.) Architectural history written by architects was no longer simply a ciceronic guide to the best work of the past, nor an explanation of how the past had made its way to the present. It no longer simply presented the idea of architecture as demonstrated in history, nor served in defense of the traditions build up around that idea. Of course, architectural history did indeed continue to be these things in many quarters, just as in some hands this remains the case. Tafuri, though, was among the first – effectively – to do what art historians did to architecture, but within architecture, and with an effect on architecture in mind that was not, strictly speaking, instrumental with respect to the architect's practice into the future. Architectural history thus conceived was a department of neither cultural history nor art history, although it borrowed their disciplinary tools and sought to match their rigors. It offered a critical philology of architecture's past, and with it a check on the narratives through which that past had hitherto been portrayed and deployed in defense of the present and its ambitions.

The second matter concerns the balance of critical assessment and rigorous analysis. If the most crucial audience of Tafuri's architectural history was the architect, and if its rigors were held against the standards maintained in the field of art history, the question remained one of how to pursue those rigors in light of modern architectural problems. The close analysis of the modern movement from within the history of art lagged well behind a relative maturity boasted by early modern topics, but this alone does not explain Tafuri's close attention to artists and architects of the Renaissance. Neither does the regularization of the architect-historians' participation in the large commemorative events focusing on major historical figures go far enough in providing an institutional justification for the systematic engagement that Tafuri's 1980s conducts with the fifteenth and sixteenth centuries. In 'Il "progetto" storico', however, Tafuri provided a justification of this trajectory, arguing therein the necessity to subject all preconceptions governing architecture's historical authority to the close scrutiny afforded through acts of constant re-reading. As he put it in the version of the essay that introduced *La sfera e il labirinto* (1980a) (Engl. ed. 1987, *The Sphere and the Labyrinth*), this process was like constantly shuffling a deck of cards, and in this, as he said, the problems both documented in that volume and, by implication, that would be pursued in its wake, grew from the discussions maintained over the course of the prior decade at Venice (1980a, p. 30). While functioning as a polite acknowledgement, this sentiment also reminds us of the thread connecting one decade's work to the next, this being the process, once cast as a critique of ideology, of withholding the certainty of the past's authority through the acts (first) of writing critical history and (then) documenting historical research. Each shuffle of the cards, each figure crystallized from the jigsaw puzzle, suggested the next iteration in the task of assessing the past in the present.

Criticism's contingencies

The shuffling of the cards and the reconfiguration of the jigsaw pieces constituted, over time, a dismantling not only of the ideological scaffolding mediating the relationship of architectural production to the reality in which that production occurred but also of the tools deployed in the first iterations of a *critica dell'ideologia*, on the back of which the group at Venice became important to generations likewise searching for the tools to conduct a political critique of contemporary architecture. Equating architecture's problematic relationship with capitalism with an historical trajectory spanning from the eighteenth to the twentieth centuries, or seeing the most pressing moments of that relationship in the interaction of architecture and city planning with ideological systems served to open an entire field of historical research up for closer inspection. It allowed, too, politically engaged scholars to find in history and criticism the tools for fomenting moments of resistance in the institutional machines that had come to define architectural culture. More than this, though, it made architecture political in a sense that put the architect and his or her ideas into play in a world of debate that cut to the quick of a problem that was otherwise too casually perpetuated by the structures of the university, the profession or the discourse of architecture. To what extent, the architect was asked, is architectural knowledge tied to the historical circumstances of architectural production? What governs the shifts to which that knowledge is subject?

The tools of a Trontian critique of ideology had the problem so surrounded as to encourage the visual response tabled by Rossi: the interior forces risked too great a degree of insularity from the world; exterior forces too readily made architecture the plaything of institutions, and of capitalist development above all. The compelling coincidence of Tafuri's disciplinary ambitions and their politics with the ideological scaffolding of the institutions in which and through which architectural ideology and its relationship to capitalism was made to be subject to critique has, ultimately, proven to be a burden to those who most assiduously insist upon the import of this intersection. By unpacking in finer and finer details the politics of this perfect moment and their translation into architectural history, theory and criticism, the faithful fail to understand this moment as an image that, in turn, needed to be dismantled in order to press on with the larger task with which Tafuri and his colleagues charged themselves.

They saw in the demands of this perpetual criticism of criticism and all the various permutations available to the presence of history and historiography therein questions that demanded further attention – and which others, in their footsteps, set about posing of modern (and later postmodern) architecture in all its various manifestations. Of the group, though, Tafuri was most agile in stepping away from the immediate form of either the questions posed by a direct application of a Trontian critique and the answers it (naturally) provoked. The double-edged problem was of rescuing a modern architecture too strongly in the grasp of capitalist development and of preventing its withdrawal into an institutional state that could allow for a form of self-perpetuation through the enacting of criticality as if on a stage. Tafuri had identified (1980a) this as one historical warning of the avant-garde: that the critic whose audience comprises a community of critics is doing little more than talking into the wind. He understood the necessity to look through modern architecture as a clear manifestation of architecture's capitulation to capitalism to understand better the situation in which the structures that allowed this to play out in the twentieth century were put into play and then confirmed. This concerned the root structures that positioned architecture as an intellectually circumscribed art form for which history and historical representation lent authority, which was nonetheless susceptible to expressing and advancing the needs of ideological systems other than its own without a clear capacity for resistance. Tafuri understood that this complexity was intrinsic to architecture's structural identity, based, as he held it to be, on representation. Positioning ideology as perpetually resident in the conceptual space between representation and reality – whatever either of those categories might amount to – provides the historian with his or her perpetual target.

As they eventually come to reside in *Ricerca del rinascimento*, Tafuri's reflections on the evidence proffered by *Momus* of Alberti's own reservations concerning the ideality of *De re aedificatoria* (or indeed *De pictura*) offered a clear warning of the apparently natural authority on which historical representation might be seen to rest. Another essay likewise collated into this book describes a mechanism for the treatment of this authority as a sustained target from *within* architecture, acting against architectural ideology by means of architecture's tools. In his treatment of S. Giovanni dei Fiorentini, Tafuri positions the church, terminating the monumental via Giulia, as the terrestrial, profane corollary to its spiritually superior, rarefied correspondent across the Tibur. As architects across the sixteenth century worked between these two major projects, S. Giovanni, Tafuri argued (2006, pp. 117–45), served as an active counter-point in which the servitude of the architect and of his ideas to the demands of the Curia were cast in a critical light. Recalling the values and ambitions of the Florentine community in Leonine Rome and the deep and complex relationship between the compositional, mathematical, typological and symbolic elements of the classical tradition as being at once supremely Christian and definitively Pagan, as an historical authority cleansed of an historical meaning by which it remained haunted – all this, he suggests, is played out in the competition and realization of the Florentine church; and all this, he insists, in plain view of S. Pietro as the epitomic marriage of architecture's classical tradition and its Renaissance authority.

Curiously, yet convincingly, these images of a deeply and programmatically impure architecture holding the notion of purity to account, or of structured doubt being wed to certainties expressed elsewhere, emerge from the pages of *Ricerca del rinascimento* as a response to the criticism Tafuri tables at its outset. For imitating the overtly critical language and choice of subjects through which Tafuri's contribution to architectural debate had become important, but for failing to share his appreciation of the need to push further and further into the core of the matters that early work had identified it had become conceptually stagnant. One of the most difficult discussions of the last decades resolves around the ossification of those same critical tools that once served this function, but which now enact a kind of theatre to one side of the battleground on which architecture and its extraneous ideological forces tussle. Tafuri's suggestion that this work had become so much anaesthetic continues to hold water. Taken as a whole, his writing suggests a deep imperative for radicality in architecture, for architecture – moments of critical pause, we might say, through the activation of latent elements through which the entire institution of architecture is called to account both in the representation of the past and in the present. Rossi's judgement that this had served to pull the edifice down upon itself had some truth when such a book as *Progetto e utopia* was read in isolation. Read within a trajectory in which criticality and radicality served as sustained operating principles independent of subject choice and methodological form allows us, however, to paint an entirely different picture.

Wrestling with a legacy

If Tafuri's encounter with the trajectory of radical thinking is important, it is neither solely as an historical instant to be unpacked with the tools of institutional or intellectual history, nor as an unfulfilled legacy by which the imperative to make more and more present the politics of that historical moment can enliven the political consciousness of contemporary architecture. Or at least this would be too blunt an instrument to fashion from too complex a model. And it would demonstrate his encounter with radicality in the 1960s as a thoroughly missed opportunity. The importance of this moment for Tafuri's thinking about architectural history and its relation to the critic's and the historian's role and status in architectural culture doubtless drew in a meaningful way upon the clarity offered by the role of the resistant critic by Tronti and his contemporaries. Its centrality to Tafuri and to the work that he pursued even to the regret of the audience he acquired across the 1960s and 1970s is demonstrated precisely in the way that Tafuri rendered it inert as he moved forward into the new problems that his Trontian critique of both modern architecture and the origins of its crises had suggested. In this sense, architecture's missed encounter with radicality as played through Tafuri's reception amounts to something like a distaste for setting aside Walter Benjamin in favour of heading into the archives, a preference for the broad sweep over the fine brush that has been compounded by the reassertion by Aureli above all of the need to recall the politics of the 1960s and 1970s in the treatment of Tafuri's legacy *in toto*.

Curiously, Tafuri has been all but expunged from the institutional memory of Italian architectural culture. His department at Venice has been dismantled as a casualty of the restructuring of the entire Italian university system, and European regulations have closed the door on a new generation who might have made their *tesi di laurea* (or, now, master-level dissertations) in architecture in the field of architectural history rather than design. The tools that Tafuri regarded as best equipped to conduct the interior critique of architecture that architecture structurally required to be something in and of itself would seem to be endangered by historical circumstances that undermine the future role of the historian in contemporary architectural culture. What would provide, today, the critical clarity that readers valued in Tafuri's thinking of the 1960s and 1970s?

Not, somehow, the pursuit of historical knowledge without an historical project – and not the historical project through which we might either crystallize Tafuri's historical import or present him as a model for our times. Clearly these latter possibilities belong to an effort to hold on to the gains of the 1960s by preserving them whole that has, to put it mildly, reached its limits. The problem for architecture, history, criticism and theory is the problem of carrying forward the principle of disruption within a coherent concept of architecture – or indeed a coherent concept of architecture's incoherence, or, to go further, a coherent concept of criticality for architecture through which these relationships might be clarified and called to account. What is architecture for one to be against it from within? And what is (historical) criticism, that it continues to play a part in this question? These are matters that have a life beyond one specific moment in which their terms were thrown more than usually into relief.

Author's note

My assessment of Tafuri's import for the issue discussed herein has been sharpened recently by vigorous discussions with Alexandra Brown and Emre Oztesis over their dissertations at the University of Queensland and RMIT University respectively. It articulates early thinking through the conceptual premises of a project funded by the Australian Research Council as Future Fellowship FT120100883.

Bibliography

Alberti, L. B. (1988), *On the Art of Building in Ten Books*. J. Rykwert, N. Leach and R.
    Tavernor (trans), from *De re aedificatoria* (ca. 1452). Cambridge, MA: MIT Press.
— (2003), *Momus* (ca. 1450). S. Wright (trans.). Cambridge, MA: Harvard University
    Press.
Aureli, P. V. (2008), *The Project of Autonomy: Politics and Architecture Within and against
    Capitalism*. New York: Princeton Architectural Press.
— (2011), *The Possibility of an Absolute Architecture*. Cambridge, MA: MIT Press.
Aymonino, C. (1975), 'Il patrimonio di Giuseppe Samonà', in C. Aymonino, G. Ciucci,
    F. Dal Co. et al., *Giuseppe Samonà. 1923–1975. Cinquant'anni di architetture*. Rome:
    Officina.
Banham, R. (1990, 12 October), 'A Black Box', in *New Statesman and Society*, pp. 22–5.
Brown, A. (2010), '*Operaismo*, Architecture & Design in Ambasz's *New Domestic
    Landscape*: Issues of Redefinition and Refusal in 1960s Italy', in M. Chapman and M.
    Ostwald (eds), *Imagining: Proceedings of the 27th International SAHANZ Conference*,
    cd-rom. Newcastle, NSW: Society of Architectural Historians, Australia and New
    Zealand.
Ciorra, P. (2011), *Senza architettura. Le ragioni di una crisi*. Rome: Laterza.
Ciucci, G., Dal Co, F., Manieri-Elia, M. and Tafuri, M. (1973), *La città americana dalla
    Guerra civile al New Deal*. Rome: Laterza. Engl. ed. (1983), *The American City from the
    Civil War to the New Deal*. B. Luigi La Penta (trans.). Cambridge, MA: MIT Press.
Cohen, J.-L. (1984), 'The Italophiles at Work'. B. Holmes (trans.), in K. M. Hays (ed.),
    Architecture Theory Since 1968. Cambridge, MA: MIT Press, pp. 508–20.

— (2008), 'Scholarship or Politics? Architectural History and the Risks of Autonomy', in *Journal of the Society of Architectural Historians*, 67, 3, pp. 325–9.

Fiore, F. P. and Tafuri, M. (eds) (1993), *Francesco di Giorgio architetto*. Milan: Electa.

Foscari, A. and Tafuri, M. (1983), *L'armonia e i conflitti. La chiesa di S. Francesco della Vigna nella Venezia del '500*. Turin: Einaudi.

Hays, K. M. (2010), *Architecture's Desire: Reading the Late Avant-Garde*. Cambridge, MA: MIT Press.

Jameson, F. (1985), 'Architecture and the Critique of Ideology', in J. Ockman (ed.), *Architecture, Criticism, Ideology*. New York: Princeton Architectural Press, pp. 51–87.

Leach, A. (2006), 'The Conditional Autonomy of Tafuri's Historian' = 'De provisorische autonomie van de historicus bij Tafuri', in *Oase*, 69, pp. 14–29.

— (2007), *Manfredo Tafuri: Choosing History*. Ghent: A&S Books.

— (2010), '*Francesco Borromini and the Crisis of the Humanist Universe*, or the Baroque Origins of Modern Architecture', in *Journal of Architecture*, 10, 3, pp. 301–36.

Martin, L. (2011), 'Fredric Jameson and Critical Architecture', in N. Lahiji (ed.), *The Political Unconscious of Architecture: Re-Opening Jameson's Narrative*. Farnham, Surrey: Ashgate, pp. 171–210.

Martin, R. (2008), *Utopia's Ghost: Architecture and Postmodernism, Again*. Minneapolis: Minnesota University Press.

Oztesis, E. (2013), 'Re-Visiting the Political Framework of Manfredo Tafuri's "Toward a Critique of Architectural Ideology": "Having Corpses in Our Mouths"', MPhil diss., RMIT University.

Rosa, A., Cassetti, B. and Ciucci, G., Dal Co., F., De Michelis, M., Di Leo, R., Junghanns, K., Oorthuys, G., Prochézka, V., Schmidt, H. and Tafuri, M. (1971), *Socialismo, città, architettura. URSS 1917–1937. Il contributo degli architetti europei*. Rome: Officina Edizioni.

Rosanda, R. (2005), *La ragazza del secolo scorso*. Turin: Einaudi.

Tafuri, M. (1968a), *Teorie e storia dell'architettura*. Rome: Laterza.

— (1968b), 'Il mito naturalistico nell'architettura del '500', *L'arte*, 1, pp. 7–36.

— (1969a), *L'architettura dell'umanesimo*. Rome: Laterza.

— (1969b), 'Per una critica dell'ideologia archittonica', in *Contropiano. Materiali marxisti*, 1969, 1, pp. 31–79. Engl. ed. 'Towards a Critique of Architectural Ideology', S. Sartorelli (trans.), in K. M. Hays (ed.), *Architecture Theory Since 1968*. Cambridge, MA: MIT Press, 2000, pp. 6–35.

— (1970), 'Lavoro intelletuale e sviluppo capitalistico', in *Contropiano. Materiali marxisti*, 1970, 2, pp. 241–81.

— (1971), 'Austromarxismo e città. "Das Rote Wien"', in *Contropiano. Materiali marxisti*, 1971, 2, pp. 257–311.

— (1973), *Progetto e utopia. Architettura e sviluppo capitalistico*. Rome: Laterza.

— (1976), *Architecture and Utopia: Design and Capitalist Development*. B. Luigi La Penta (trans.). Cambridge, MA: MIT Press.

— (1977), 'Il "progetto" storico', in *Casabella*, pp. 429, 1–18.

— (1980a), *La sfera e il labirinto. Avanguardie e architettura da Piranesi agli anni '70*. Turin: Einaudi. Engl. ed. *The Sphere and the Labyrinth: Avant-gardes and Architecture from Piranesi to the 1970s (1987)*. Cambridge, MA: MIT Press.

— (1980b), *Theories and History of Architecture*. G. Verecchia (trans.), from the 4th Ital. ed. (1976). London: Granada.

— (1983), 'Borromini e Piranesi. La città come "ordine infranto"', in A. Bettagno (ed.), *Piranesi tra Venezia e l'Europa. Atti del convegno internazionale di studio promosso* dall'Istituto di storia dell'arte della Fondazione Giorgio Cini per il secondo centennario della morte di Giovan Battista Piranesi, Venezia, 13–15 ottobre 1978. Florence: Leo S. Olschki, pp. 89–101.

— (1984), "'Civis esse non licere'. La Roma di Nicolò V e Leon Battista Alberti. Elementi per una revisione storiografica', in C. W. Westfall, *L'invenszione della cita. La strategia urbana di Nicolò V e Alberti nella Roma del '400*. Rome: La nuova italia scientifica, pp. 13–39.

Tafuri, M. (ed.) (1989), *Giulio Romano*. Milan: Electa.

Tafuri, M. (1992), *Ricerca del Rinascimento: Principi, città, architettura*. Turin: Einaudi.

— (2006), *Interpreting the Renaissance: Princes, Cities, Architects*. D. Sherer (trans.). New Haven, CT: Yale University Press.

Vidler, A. (2008), *Histories of the Immediate Present: Inventing Architectural Modernism*. Cambridge, MA: MIT Press.

Westfall, C. W. (1974), *In This Most Perfect Paradise: Alberti, Nicholas V and the Invention of Conscious Urban Planning in Rome*. University Park: Pennsylvania State University Press.

7

Gentri-Fiction and Our (E)States of Reality: On the Fatigued Images of Architecture and the Exhaustion of the Image of Thought

Hélène Frichot

How do we make ourselves worthy of what happens to us? (Deleuze, 1990, p. 149).[1] This is a question that can be addressed from amidst our contemporary encounters with architecture, and the relations that ensue from these encounters as we attempt to grapple, often blindly, with our disciplinary formation and the ways it unfolds in our contemporary urban environments. How do we make ourselves worthy of the architectural event? This correlate question articulates an ethical imperative that as architectural thinkers-doers we find the means to address an immanent problematic field that is political, social, and inextricably ideological, in order to address those questions that are most urgent. Making ourselves worthy of the event assumes the priority of events, as that which simply happens to us, making us who we are, ever in the process of becoming. The event takes us up in its folds, only subsequently enabling us to establish our positions or points of view in a field such as architecture. It also suggests the paradoxical nature of our encounters, qualified here as contingent necessities: in expressing our situations as we do from constructed environments and existential territories we necessarily suffer and enjoy daily encounters, but the varied qualities of these encounters remain contingent, as is what we decide to do about them. Though we are sufficiently educated in the arena of probabilities, we do not in fact know what will happen next, but we do know something will confront us, and that confronting our vicissitudes we must make the best of things. We might even take pleasure in peoples, places, things and their relations and create more positive, hopeful compositions from the affective assemblages that emerge with our encounters. To make ourselves worthy, with an emphasis on making or constructing, can be understood as a capacity to respond, to act, to do something about the impending problems of an immanent world. To make ourselves worthy of the architectural event means that despite immanent constraints there is still some room to move, some play in the structures that might otherwise curtail us, some potential capacity that might enable us to reformulate our images of architecture for a near future, and thereby contribute to an affirmative image of thought. And yet, what do we do when faced with the fatigued images of architecture, and with the exhaustion of the image of thought as it pertains to architecture?

What is at stake in the relation between an affirmative architecture and a radical, creative approach to philosophy, is a battle that rages between competing images of thought. The challenge becomes how to sustain a productive relay between these disciplinary domains, without succumbing to proscriptive ways of thinking. On the one hand there is the affective pull of an iconophilia that can be identified in the viral production and dissemination of architectural imagery for consumption, and on the other hand, the politically motivated move to enact an iconoclastic event that challenges the hold of this imagery, that seeks to secure an optimistic image of thought. This battle to secure a hopeful image of thought concerns how we construct the status of the real as it pertains to architecture, what I will dramatize below as our collective (e)states of reality. Like so many of the movies of our media saturated and electronic age, I offer a disclaimer that while this essay is based on a true story, and locates its scenes of action in proximity to what can be called the 'real', or else in relation to a necessarily meta-stable empirical ground, the characters and incidents portrayed and the names herein are fictitious and any similarity to the name, character or history of any actual person living or dead is entirely coincidental and unintentional. I proceed by way of a ficto-critical methodology, through the use of 'factions' that mix fiction and fact (Gibbs, 2005; Frichot et al., 2012b),[2] telling (un)true stories of the tricks of our trade of architecture and how very easily our creative gestures and image-making practices are co-opted towards the neoliberal ends of market Capitalism, understood as a globally integrating force. At the same time, it must be stressed that the powers of fiction should not be underestimated, as fiction produces very real effects.

To relay the story of the exhaustion of the image of thought and the fatigued images of architecture, I will place an emphasis on the affective labour of images, and how they operate in a reciprocal, if disjunctive relation to the concepts and discursive statements architects enunciate, so producing a disciplinary image of thought. It is very important to understand that images do not stand by themselves in isolation, there is no such thing as a glossy architectural image that can be taken as a thing in itself, because images operate within animated networks or assemblages involving all manner of things and relations: 'The image is not an object but a "process"' (Deleuze, 1998, p. 159). Given time it would be possible to elaborate an open-ended catalogue of images that contribute to architecture and the different kinds of work they undertake, affective, diagrammatic, indexical, informational and so forth, but these images operate exactly by producing relations and making new worlds emerge. The risk I identify is how easily such images prescribe realities, foreclosing how future peoples and places might express themselves.

For the purposes of this essay I locate the fatigued images of architecture as components operating within a broader disciplinary assemblage that is circumscribed by an image of thought. This image of thought, within which the fatigued images of architecture circulate, is like a map or diagram that enables us to orientate ourselves in thought (Deleuze and Guattari, 1994, p. 37), as such it helps us to qualify what our discipline can do, and what tasks properly belong to it. Yet, as I will argue below, the image of thought is ambivalent; either it over-determines how we conceptualize the work of architecture, forcing us to *think that* architecture is de-limited in a conventional and exclusive way, or else, through an exhaustive labour dedicated to the productive exhaustion of the image of thought, we might have the chance to affirmatively revise and transform our discipline.

To critique the fatigued images of architecture and to find the means to progress instead towards the paradoxically productive exhaustion of the image of thought, I will present two scenes, the first set in the seeming shelter of the pedagogical encounter of the final examination or 'jury' event where becoming-architects find themselves on the threshold of entering their profession, of being accepted into the fold of subjectivation that is architecture. The second scene comes later, and is set within what I call the gentri-fiction of the contemporary inner city and its constructed (e)states of reality, for once the architect graduates, soon enough they discover that they are apt to contribute to their local gentri-fiction, for better or worse. The laying out of these scenes draws on certain ficto-critical liberties, on the necessity of telling stories, as I have alluded to above.

As for the image of thought, it is the means by which we bring consistency to our thinking-doing, but it is always at risk of creating a delimited paradigm. The image of thought can get stuck in the rut of what 'everyone knows', in that which is presupposed, offering the means by which thought establishes its right to think *that* . . . (Deleuze and Guattari, 1994). For instance, *to think that* architecture cannot be conceived beyond bricks, and mortar, form and material and space, and the virtuosity of the architect able to best distribute these as master image-maker. The image of thought tends to be tied to a conceptual persona who calls up the image and gives it expression and content (p. 81), and this conceptual persona can turn out to be generous or despotic. In architecture this function too often devolves into the repetitive refrain of the big name architect or signature project; the idol or the icon. On the other hand, the greatest affirmative power of the image of thought is where it plays a productively disruptive role, that is, if we gather enough energy to create a new image of thought, a very difficult task as it requires shaking up the habits, opinions and clichés with which we are so comfortable. In this way the image of thought can even manifest as an iconoclastic gesture, the role of which is to imagine the formation of a new, or at least a revised image of thought. It is an endeavour that always faces the risks of error, illusion and stupidity. Images of thought can confront us and constrain us, over-determining our relations in a world, but we also have the reciprocal capacity to alter them, and even to remake them: to make ourselves worthy of the encounter with an image of thought. This is the promise that can be held out to becoming-architects as they grapple with the threshold condition of their graduating projects, and how they then project themselves into practice: how might they become something more than mere functionaries to a ready-made image of thought? How do they overcome what I have called the fatigued images of architecture?

Disciplinary schooling or becoming-architect

In addressing the missed encounter architecture may or may not have had with radical philosophy, I cannot get around the formative scene of the pedagogical critique, which haunts our discipline and has the most significant impact on the becoming-architect. As I write, in the many studios that are arrayed across KTH Architecture, Stockholm, anxious graduating students prepare their final project presentations. It is at this moment that the becoming-architect is initiated into the profession, or else excluded as somehow deficient. True to all quasi-secret societies, the selection criteria (even when explicitly listed) remain implicit and mysteriously obscured (Cuff, 1992; Scott Brown, 1990, p. 260; Webster, 2005; Webster, 2007).[3] What proves to be at work instead is some elusive production of affect, or what can be called the perceived aptitude of the affective labour of the becoming-architect, and how far they are able to *move* the examination 'design jury' to believe in their speculative work. My claim is that despite the conceit of objectivity, the encounter here is based exactly on the affective labour of the becoming-architect redistributed as imagery. There persists the temptation to take the route towards architectural imagery expressed as compelling forms of iconophilia, the kinds of images we are becoming increasingly familiar with on our screens, and wherever life has come to be branded, and an experience economy privileged. The power of the production of affect that is enabled through sophisticated architectural imagery is further augmented by the specific assemblage or occasion these images answer to, this in turn demands an ethico-aesthetic awareness of what is at stake in the encounter between judge, defendant and specified architectural problem. This ritualistic and oft-repeated architectural encounter raises many of the same questions over and again: Where is the project? What is at stake? How do you perceive your agency as an architect? How does this project 'belong' within the boundaries of the discipline? This last question indicating most explicitly how these boundaries are carefully policed. And then there is the demand to name your ancestors, or identify your architectural precursors, in order to position yourself as architect. What all participants hope to avoid is the drying up of the flow of voices, because silence is that which most swiftly dismantles a project.

The competent jury member can be identified as the one who assesses a project based on the criteria and concerns that the student-defendant has articulated. The poor critic brings their own myopic agenda to the table, and over-performs their role in an attempt to secure the admiration of their fellow jury members rather than to enter into dialogue with the becoming-architect. The design jury event should be a profoundly ethical encounter, yet it is easily led astray into the performance of over-inflated archi-egos, which effectively demonstrate to the becoming-architect what kinds of discipline-securing performances are deemed appropriate. The teacher, or in this instance the critic or architectural 'jury member' habitually refers to taught concepts, the already known, the images that have given pleasure previously, all the while demanding the new (Deleuze and Guattari, 1994, p. 62).[4] Furthermore the risk of this encounter is not simply based on the affects of imagery, but the way statements work alongside composed imagery. Forms of content and forms of expression work alongside each other producing disjunctive syntheses, not to be confused with the relation between signified and signifier. Language is fundamentally political, and the situation of the critique is often performed by way of 'a power takeover by a dominant language that at times advances on a broad front, and at times swoops down on diverse centers simultaneously' (Deleuze and Guattari, 1987, p. 101); the dominant language or discourse tends to be coupled with a political enterprise, here qualified by maintaining the boundaries of what belongs within a discipline such as architecture, and how 'order-words' are imposed as imperatives upon apprentices (Deleuze and Guattari, 1987, pp. 75–6). Forms of iconophilia in this context are secured at the interchange between architectural visibilities and statements, between forms of content and expression, and what will be admitted into the discipline concerning these admixtures. The power relations that are expressed in the encounter are unavoidable and structurally over-determined as 'knowledge is policed by [architects] codifying cognitive canon law' (Haraway, 1991, p. 183).[5]

It's important to pause here and reflect on the crucial role that ideological disciplining takes in our domain of architectural world-making where we envision new environments and the means to alter old ones and how the role of the architect is performed here alongside a set of human and non-human actors. Ideological for the purposes of this argument circumscribes a logic of ideas and 'order-words' that define a disciplinary context amidst which a subject comes to be formed, for instance, the process of subjectivation that makes the apprentice an architect, and the conjoint process of signification that determines what kinds of images they produce towards this end. What emerges is a noopolitics of the image, whereby the distribution and affective power of images effectively shifts the collective cognitive biases of a disciplinary collective, in this instance architecture.

The education of the architect often revolves around securing aesthetic responses to ready-made problems with predetermined answers, and even where new architectural concepts emerge they tend to be profoundly ambivalent, that is to say, it's not possible to determine in advance what kinds of affective assemblages are likely to emerge. Affect does not follow form, but remains autonomous and 'emergent' or non-linear (Massumi, 2002, pp. 39–40).[6] Although we habitually name affect once it has settled into an identifiable affection, feeling or emotion, it is rather a pre-personal power that gives rise to the very possibility of the surging forth of processes of subjectivation intertwined with environmental encounters. It's a grave mistake made by many an architect, the assertion that an inhabitant will feel comforted, or awed, or silenced in their encounter with a designed architectural occasion, as though it were possible to determine such affects in advance (Thrift, 2008). Nevertheless, the images architects make do produce affects of one kind or another, and the management and distribution of these images is increasing in sophistication.

The critique or jury event as disciplinary threshold is a moment shared by all who have travelled through the discipline, it remains deeply under-theorized, and it is simply not possible to escape the uneven power relations that emerge whenever a architectural-defendant comes before a 'jury' to show their aesthetic evidence and perform their affective labour. A crucial non-human actor whose impact cannot be underestimated in the critique is the role of the 'money-shot' a history of which remains to be written. It is the privileged point of view on the potentialities of space, an any-space-whatever if you can pay the price for speculating on a future yet to come, that creates a link between the virtuosity of the becoming-architect and the milieu into which they will soon enough enter. All the same, it comes as some surprise that architecture for the most part is mundane, worldly labour, sexed-up with sophisticated renderings and *urimages,* explored adventurously by way of form-finding algorithms (for those with sufficient skills in computation). On the job it is about time-lines, economic constraints, standard details, or mixing bespoke with off-the-shelf products, budgetary requirements, the management of consultants, how to meet local planning requirements and appease your clients and stakeholders. Architecture is as much about elaborating systems of organization as it is about form-finding and material specification, and one can wonder whether there are any opportunities to be radical amidst the banality of building, and at which juncture it is possible to perform an iconoclastic gesture when it is difficult enough to create an image that makes some difference to our disciplinary image of thought.

What opportunities are available to the becoming-architect to perform an iconoclastic gesture so as to confront the compelling affects of iconophilia, especially when they are disciplined to be affective labourers? Following the exhaustive relay of the critical versus projective debate that dominated architectural discourse through the opening decade of the new millennium, revived forms of expanded spatial practice driven by sociopolitical concerns that have reinvented the acts and images that pertain to architecture have been emerging. The status of the architectural image in these endeavours remains important, because architecture needs to secure the means to critically and creatively produce affects and percepts that increase a power of acting such that affirmative changes to a material milieu can be achieved. It's important to stress that images are neither inherently good nor bad, and the affective power of images, and the capacity of images to set percepts into circulation, can make a real sociopolitical difference, helping becoming-architects to shake up habits of thought and stir up a positive noopolitics. The image can also positively contribute to the production of valuable precursors for becoming-architects, who need to be equipped with the tools to create an architectural event as 'iconoclash' by reinventing the work of their precursors as a means of answering to pressing contemporary problems (Latour, 2002).[7] That is to say, the becoming-architect as apprentice can develop the paradoxical means to both love and hate, to revere and destroy the images they collect as historical and contemporary influences; to affectively transform these images so as to make a real difference to both their discipline and to their local environment-world and all its complex multiplicitous relations. The image is a non-representational, cross-sectional cut that produces relations between emerging, even protean subjects (in this case figured as becoming-architects) and transforming milieus or environment-worlds.

Making the material matter, engaging in sociopolitical projects, practising forms of participatory mapping and dialogic exchange with local human and non-human actors, altering practices, inventing radical feminist practices, all this is difficult to make evident through image-making (Schalk et al., 2012; Petrescu, 2007; Brown, 2011; Lloyd Thomas, 2007).[8] Importantly, the image here extends beyond the local, close-vision of the privileged 'money-shot', for the image, as I have been elaborating, contributes to an expanded image of thought, more or less hegemonic or liberatory depending on how we continue to revise, alter, transform our disciplinary framework. It is extremely difficult to make an image (of thought) that can make a difference and reorganize our ways of thinking and acting together, and sometimes this only becomes possible once a point of exhaustion has been reached.

Gentri-fiction and our (e)states of reality

On Saturday mornings the mail slot swings open and a free newspaper arrives. It's an excerpt from the conservative Stockholm based *SvD Magisinet*, and because it is Saturday morning the content is all about lifestyle, human interest and real-estate. What the real-estate pages communicate are the reified interior images of our immanent existential territories, perfectly curated; 'Photoshopped' so that living rooms are slightly stretched to exaggerate a quality of spaciousness, and the image brightness pushed up the scale so as to produce effects of light that are especially important in these Northern regions. What I see across these pages is that desiring production has fixed on received notions of the designerly home, and don't forget the obligatory Eames dining chair, or the Isamu Noguchi coffee table, or the quintessentially Nordic Bruno Mathsson's Pernilla lounge. Every Saturday morning the same series of images are further reiterated; they all own a family resemblance and contribute in this way to securing a spatial imaginary of the any-space-whatever of inner-city life, over-determining how it should look and how it should operate, and how hegemonic forms of subjectivation place us squarely in this scene, which is nonetheless abstracted from specific states of affairs. Is it possible to remain immune from a sensation of swooning when confronted with the curated and framed fantasy images of real-estate, especially when in search of a new home? (Tonkiss, p. 92). Welcome to your local taste community, which I perform here through the concept of gentri-fiction and how it manufactures our (e)states of reality, more often than not with our willing co-operation.

Here is my situated knowledge formation (Haraway, 1991), captured by what I want to call a contemporary 'gentri-fiction', and although I want to be wary of writing with my memories, of my travels, loves, griefs and fantasies, I do want to frame a point of view upon a specific urban landscape assemblage (Deleuze, 1998, pp. 2–3).[9] I assert that the point of view operates in the reverse direction from what architectural convention determines, positioning the architect as omnipotent authority organizing a world from their privileged point of view. The point of view does not so much affirm or commence from the secure position of a self-same subject capturing a landscape of affects and percepts, instead, the human subject comes to be fleshed out in reciprocal exchange with a milieu that enfolds them; the subject comes to the point of view, they do not, per se, construct it (Deleuze, 1993, p. 19). Put simply, my point of view does not come first, and is not privileged in relation to the milieu, field, or landscape it surveys; I arrive at a point of view that is shaped and given contour by joyful and sad encounters, and then I can attempt to make the best possible account of what has happened as I aim to make the best of things. Assuming the differential relation or variation between point of view and environment-world, I only ever perform my situated subject position for the time being, and must reassert with each new encounter how knowledge is provisionally secured.

The story I now relay of this mobile point of view on a transforming field, concerns my recent relocation with my family from one privileged inner-city urban context to another, from one gentri-fictional construct to the next. I have relocated from Melbourne, Australia to Stockholm, Sweden, from the Southern to the Northern hemisphere (Frichot, 2012a), and although vast distances have been traversed, perhaps my point of view has not moved so very much. A recent OECD report lists Australia and Sweden at the top of the 'better-life index', which has come to be broadly interpreted by the media through the specific affect of happiness.[10] Here also we have to assume that what is increasingly emphasized is city living, this being framed as our dominant and privileged contemporary condition. Melbourne has also regularly topped the most-liveable city charts, like a much-loved song we can't help but play over and again.[11] Happiness and liveability, both operate according to the circulation of affect, made operational through an economical matrix that emphasizes growth.

Imagine, then, a relocation from the happiest to the second happiest nation-state, and how such a migration might be undertaken as a kind of line of flight in search of a more supportive intellectual environment. Architecture as a discipline and as a profession is a hotly contested field of action, and sometimes there is no choice but to find a means of escape from the toxic fixity of an architectural hegemony where power relations have all but calcified around a sovereign figure successfully organizing an oligarchical form. Denise Scott Brown calls this the phenomenon of the 'king-maker' in architecture; invariably male, the king-maker curates a select group, and 'his satisfaction comes from making history in his and their image' (Scott Brown, 1990, p. 262). What does the king-maker do? He produces a reified image of thought and the expectation is that all who surround him must comply with it . . . or else.

It's interesting to note parenthetically Deleuze's warning that societies of control also risk reintroducing the anachronistic figure of the sovereign or oligarch, or what we can call the 'king-maker', who slows the flow of discourse and over-determines relations of power (Deleuze, 1995, p. 182). As I have suggested above, architecture is a discipline where such power relations are dramatically performed, and where it is forbidden to call out that the emperor wears no clothes (Foucault and Deleuze, 1977).[12] In dialogue, Foucault and Deleuze suggest that one task of the critical intellectual may be to call out what they perceive to have run amok in a state of affairs, despite the risk of rejection and persecution. Such a cry could be described as a moment of iconoclasm that attempts to break apart a hegemonic and rigid image of thought that is holding too fast. As the parable of the Emperor demonstrates, it is either the innocence of children or else those unafraid of appearing stupid or unfit for their designated work who are so willing to cry out. If the image of thought that the emperor or king-maker manufactures produces an oppressive ecology of ideas, then the necessity of producing a crack in the image of thought, and a line of flight through it, becomes all the more urgent.

While I have discovered a supportive intellectual environment here in Stockholm, through my own flight or migration I can also observe how well forms of subjectivation in our contemporary societies of control continue to modulate my expectations with respect to the question of real-estate. My consumption of real-estate imagery reformulates my point of view, and places my subject position under forms of affective threat (Deleuze, 1995, pp. 177–82). Most Saturday mornings I pour over the pages of *SvD Magisinet* with a combination of wonder and repulsion, digesting the fantasies of real-estate imagery, and recognizing after the fact the demotivating affects, or sad passions that have been aroused in this encounter. These images, which contribute to the composition of what I call our collective gentri-fiction, are expressed as a kind of iconophilia, an intense love of images, a captivation by images. Nadir Lahiji, after Boris Groys, argues that the rise of iconophilia in architecture is present in our new idols and icons, which desublimate the libidinal economy of consumer Capitalism.[13] What's more, as Groys argues, even moments of iconoclasm risk transforming into expressions of iconophilia: as soon as we destroy one image, another rushes in to take its place, suggesting a perpetual mobility in a symbolic economy of images (Groys, 2008, p. 44). More importantly, it is not a question of the image in its representational capacity, though of course it operates in this way too, but the affective power of the image and how it manufactures a point of view, and effectively circumscribes the process of individuation of the subject. It is through real-estate imagery that this essay pursues one trajectory of this tendency, but always by keeping in mind that such material images operate in relation to an ideological, or rather noopolitical image of thought that threatens to curtail the possible, and close down on alternative futures.

The noopolitical as a concept can be associated with the better-known term biopolitics. If biopolitics organizes the life of a population, noopolitics is that structuring force by which a sociopolitical collective's capacity for thinking is organized, *nous* being the Greek term for mind or intellect (Wallenstein, 2010, p. 54; Lazzarato, 2006, p. 187; Hauptman and Neidlich, 2010). As Deborah Hauptman and Warren Neidlich argue, in a world ubiquitously populated by technologies of information and communication, a discussion of biopolitics needs to be extended into a discussion of noopolitics (Hauptman and Neidlich, 2010, p. 11). The ubiquity of social media and our image-saturated societies facilitate the work of noopolitics as an organization of minds, as well as the reinvention of an augmented imaginary. The images I want to draw attention to, between architecture and the production of real-estate, participate in transforming how we think, even influencing us to think according to certain conceptual matrices that offer a false promise of consistency to an image of thought.

The images that proliferate on Booli.se and www.hemnet.se, prime Swedish real-estate websites where the hunt for a home is most likely to commence in Stockholm, make vividly visible an image-based market place wherein the home undertakes an inexorable transformation: electronic communications producing (e)states of reality composed of consumable images, including the material pages of print media. The images I make reference to produce exhaustive series that offer up the deceptive promise of inexhaustibility and an explicit form of iconophilia. In serial formation these images begin to give rise to an insidious image of thought, qualified by a remarkable ubiquity of whiteness: a white sample of bleached timber floor, a bone white wall, a white Eames chair, a patch of white carpet, a mirror propped on the floor and casually inclined towards a wall so as to reflect further shades of white upon white. These images, I argue, share their visual tropes with the rendered images becoming-architects feel compelled to use in order to forward a convincing, graphically communicative architectural argument. Gentri-fiction and the way it manufactures our collective (e)states of reality operates in the milieu of ever-transforming built environments ubiquitously expressed by way of the framed real-estate images of designed interiors. It's the proverbial 'money shot' (White, 2004) produced to an extreme point of fatigued tedium and organized in an impoverished assemblage of relations.

To get at what I mean by gentri-fiction it's necessary to take a brief detour through an account of the urban phenomenon of gentrification, which I suggest is dependent on the circulation of images that are less about representation than the production of the kinds of affective relations that disempower us. Gentrification is a trans-historical process, evident where ever and whenever cities emerge through the ways in which value is perceived in land that is then captured and delimited by the overcoded concept of private property. Manual De Landa examines the 'intense flows of energy' and the 'monetary catalysts' that fuelled the relative autonomy of cities in medieval Europe organized in loose trade networks, as resources and property rights changed hands in the market place (De Landa, 2000, p. 30). He dramatizes these agglutinations as the 'mineralization of humanity', though he also draws a distinction between cities emerging as bureaucracies aiming to extract 'energy surplus' or quite simply taxes from a regional population, and those towns first developing as marketplaces where traders gathered out of necessity to exchange their wares (p. 30). Complementary economic needs soon enough extend to the relative value perceived in the properties that together compose an urban formation. Deleuze and Guattari, commencing with a somewhat more positive take on the Greek city, argue that the ancient polis operated according to a milieu of immanence, which necessarily led to contingent associations of pure sociality based on friendships, rivalries, and the simple power of gathering. At the same time, even the ancient polis 'adapts the territory to a geometrical extensiveness that can be continued in commercial circuits' (Deleuze and Guattari, 1994, pp. 86–7).

Now, with the rise of neoliberal market Capitalism speculation on property has been allowed to proceed almost unheeded, resulting in the globally recognized phenomenon of the relocation of economically vulnerable communities that is called gentrification. Gentrification flowers with what Deleuze and Guattari call integrated, or *integrating* world Capitalism, to lay the emphasis on the processual dynamics of Capitalism evident in the accelerated circulation of capital. This tireless process of integration is exemplified for the purposes of my argument in the speed of production and consumption of real-estate imagery whereby the home becomes a set of fatigued images available for exchange (Deleuze and Guattari, 1987, p. 492; Guattari, 2000, p. 31). Luc Boltanski and Ève Chiapello, after Max Weber, define Capitalism as an imperative towards unlimited accumulation of capital by peaceful means; it is the tireless, seemingly inexhaustible reintroduction of capital into an economic circuit with the single-minded aim of ever increasing capital, producing, as Deleuze and Guattari also stress, a 'dynamic' and 'transformative' system able to seamlessly recuperate and co-opt all forms of resistance. Boltanski and Chiapello call this virulent version of capitalism 'connexionist' capitalism, and identify it under the rubric of the third spirit of capitalism, which begins to sound very much like Deleuze's societies of control, where control is something we have mistaken for autonomy and security in more or less equal measure (Boltanski and Chiapello, 2005, pp. 4–5; Budgen, 2000; Deleuze, 1995). Since their time of writing some 14 years ago, there has also subsequently occurred the notable event of the global financial crisis from 2008, brought on by the sub-prime mortgage sector and how property came to be abstracted as toxic debt, placing a further emphasis on the role that real-estate plays in integrating world Capitalism.

The globalized, uneven unfolding of gentrification presents one of the greatest impasses to a rethinking of contemporary cities as anything other than embedded spatial value ready to be perpetually exchanged as commodity. We all know the story: A perceived slum area, or else a working class neighbourhood comes to be gradually populated by a middle-class tired of the monotony of the suburbs, and this demographic shift subsequently pushes the property values up, at the same time pushing the lower socio-demographic groups out. Gentrification concerns both willed and forced economic migration at the scale of the city, and paradoxically the lead in this process of transformation is often taken by the figure of the creative labourer, the artist, the intellectual, the architect, with the best of intentions (Tonkiss, 2005). By the 1980s to the 1990s gentrification had become a recognized, globalized force, what David Harvey identifies as 'accumulation by dispossession' (Tonkiss, p. 34). That is to say, it was the period during which lower socio-demographics, and even the middle-class themselves came to be priced out of their own neighbourhoods, and also a period during which public housing stock, previously available as rental properties, was increasingly sold out to private interests. Tonkiss describes the process as a contest for the contemporary inner-city (Tonkiss, p. 92), and what the contest has paradoxically achieved is unambiguous homogenization, advertised through desirable real-estate images of an inner-city 'lifestyle' manufactured for the purposes of consumption, and evident in the multiplying simulacra of the loft or post-industrial aesthetic. It's important to stress that it is not as though there is anything inherently better about the inner-city as distinct from the suburbs (which are also increasingly advertised based on their inner-city qualities), or the regional hinterlands, instead it is how well a gentri-fiction comes to be constructed in a given context composing consensus around an affective atmosphere that over-determines our (e)states of reality.

We embody our gentri-fictions not for the purpose of utility or even as status symbols (though this surely still plays a strong role), but as Slavov Žižek suggests 'we consume them so as to make our life pleasurable and meaningful',[14] as though to suggest that any outside of Capitalism would plunge us into a meaningless void. We could be forgiven for believing there is no outside of integrating global Capitalism. We triangulate our abodes in relation to vibrant experience economies, hip cafés, boutiques, organic food stores, and we curate our everyday lives accordingly (Pine and Gilmore, 2011). What's more, it seems like this is a one-way street down which we progress, as though global processes of gentrification are only ever uni-directional. Beyond the third spirit of Capitalism, confronting the seemingly inexhaustible productivities and recuperations of Capitalism, it is rather that we are immersed in Capitalism to the nth degree. And for the architect, if there is no outside, why not simply work within it and become a functionary of this dominant image of thought?

The gentri-fiction of which I speak also unfolds in relation to the surplus labour we dedicate to forms of individualized urban renewal such as home improvement and

DIY, supported by tele-visual prompts or reality-TV. Here leisure time itself becomes productive as it is dedicated to increasing the resale value of the spatially embedded commodity that is the home. We collectively stockpile the images of the collective hallucinatory affects of gentri-fictionalization. The scene of globalized gentri-fiction is that into which graduating architects enter, and to grapple with contemporary architectural concerns is to be confronted with how to act into and make yourself worthy of the contests taking place in a city produced by images. Architecture feels compelled to manufacture a brighter future, a better world, a 'walkable city',[15] street life and urban vibrancy. The oxymoronic formulation of 'sustainable development' and 'sustainable growth' still assumes we must move ever forward satisfying higher productivity and answering to economic interests. Even when news agencies across the world report of riots erupting across Stockholm, here in the safe ghetto of the gentri-fiction, the fabric of the everyday is left unruffled because the riots are happening elsewhere, just outside the compact, mixed urban setting of the traditional European city (Tunström and Bradley).[16] It is at moments such as these when civil unrest finally takes to the streets and uses built material as its weaponry that one's steadfast security seems all the more disturbing. Are we inside or outside the walls of our human zoo where we have gathered a community of the like-minded tamed in relation to a reassuring kind of image-making? (Sloterdijk, 2009).

What this represents more generally is our consumption of architectural imagery and the (e)states of reality that we readily manufacture as architects projecting a capacity to affect and be affected. To borrow an oft-cited formulation from Deleuze's revision of Spinoza's ethics: We do not yet know what a city can do, or what affects it is capable of producing (Deleuze, 1992, pp. 222–6).[17] This presents both a promising challenge, as well as a great responsibility. If we want to avoid fixed moral frameworks and judgements determined in advance of emerging occasions, then we have to be able to ethically cope by following the immanent upsurge of relations, and make the best of our encounters and passages of becoming. What can we do with our shared gentri-fiction, how might we recompose our images into a more hopeful image of thought?

Gentri-fiction may well be a repulsive concept, creating antipathetic relations between peoples, places and things amidst neighbourhoods of increasing stratification and homogenization, where access is granted by pass-keys and where there can be witnessed the disappearance of public space, or else what is left of public space is over-determined, saturated in programme, and only available for consumption (Deleuze and Guattari, 1994, pp. 63–5).[18] The exhaustion of the possible manifest in images of real-estate leads, paradoxically, not to an extenuation of the possible, but only to the over-production of ever more images of real-estate. This is where fatigue enters the image relation. Images are fatigued as they cycle through repetitive refrains, like dirty pictures passed too long from hand to hand, edges frayed. We recognize the family resemblance in images, but rather than desist in their consumption and production we demand more of the same, resigned to the acceptance of superficial differences that make no real difference. The challenge is to turn the gentri-fiction around so as to create more sympathetic concepts that enable the celebration of new kinds of relations with our local environment-worlds, but not simply through co-option or recuperation, and not by giving up forms of creative and affirmative criticism. With each encounter the architect must ask again, what can I do? How do I make the best composition in response to this encounter?

Exhaustion of the image of thought as a methodology

To follow now from the fatigued images of architecture I have attempted to describe above across two scenes, the one pertaining to the affective images produced by the becoming-architect who aims to secure a right of passage into the profession, and then the second scene, progressing onwards into the context of professional practice where the becoming-architect encounters the collective affects of a global gentri-fiction, I will now develop the philosophical framing of these images as they pertain to architecture and how we might rethink our disciplinary image of thought. To do this I have extracted a methodology of exhaustion from Deleuze's brief and dense essay, 'The Exhausted', thereby removing it from the specific application he has tested in his reading of Samuel Beckett's television plays (Deleuze, 1998). I propose that this is a legitimate way of revising, and even transforming concepts, such as the operational concept of exhaustion. Although Deleuze enumerates four ways of exhausting the possible, this list should not be taken as exhaustive, and the results of the methodology of exhaustion can proceed towards a more powerful composition of forces, as well as towards a decomposition of our local environment-worlds. Although in Deleuze's argument the methodology seems to progress from exhaustive series (of concepts, images, things) towards the dissipation of the power of an image of thought, it is more useful to see what happens when the methodology is followed in both directions. The four approaches to a methodology of exhaustion include: (1) the formation of exhaustive series (of concepts, images, things), such as explored above with respect to real-estate imagery; (2) the drying up or exhausting of the flow of voices, where I suggest the role of discourse operates, for instance, in the way the 'king-maker' exhausts the possibility of what we are permitted to collectively enunciate; (3) the extenuation of the potentialities of space by way of the any-space-whatever; (4) the dissipation of the power of the image of thought, which as an iconoclastic moment leads either to a new more positive image or else to a more despotic image. This methodology of exhaustion also leads to the breakdown of the organic or inorganic body, defined in the broadest sense to include, for instance, a human body, a body politic, a built environment-body, an ecological body and so forth.

   Exhaustivity *and* exhaustion together present us with urgent ecosophical questions such as the over-consumption of our environments performed above via gentri-fictionalization, global warming, population expansion, species extinction, post-peak oil and a long litany of contemporary plights. Depending on which direction is taken through the methodology of exhaustion, the point of departure either proceeds from the exhaustive combinatorial of concepts and things towards the dissipation of the image of thought, or else, the methodology commences from an encounter with an image of thought, and even the creation of those hopeful images that assist in the establishment of an affirmative image of thought, thence proceeding again towards concepts. This reversibility of the methodology of exhaustion as it pertains to the image of thought becomes most clear in Deleuze's books on the cinema where he explains (by way of Artaud) that the image has as its object the functioning of thought, and that the functioning of thought brings us back to images and their powerful organization as an image of thought (Deleuze, 1989, p. 165). The methodology of exhaustion can operate in both directions, but notable in Deleuze's presentation where he studies Beckett is the way the methodology results in the iconoclastic gesture of the dissolution of the power of the image (see also Hême de Lacotte, 2010).

Exhaustivity, as Deleuze explains, demands that one combine the variables of a situation, but by renouncing any preference (Deleuze, 1998, p. 153). A logical process of exhaustivity, and its production of relations of sense (or sense-making procedures), suggests a compositional method that resists hierarchization and even judgement: Any choice is as good as any other, though we need to make ourselves worthy of the choices we make, as Deleuze emphasizes in a stoic manner in *The Logic of Sense* (Deleuze, 1998, p. 149). A stabilized surety of signification, importantly, is also renounced, as an exhaustive series does not allow us to rest on a secured signifying relation. It is also worth mentioning that there is a mathematical and geometrical definition of a method of exhaustion that allows the area beneath a curve to be calculated by approaching the problem of exactly measuring curvature without, strictly speaking, arriving at anything more than a sufficient answer, creating what might be called a working method. To be exhaustive, in the sense of a search party, is to search an area as completely as possible, but there is always the suspicion that some thing still remains to be unearthed, or that we missed some crucial detail. And so the search may well be taken up at a later date.

Exhaustivity and exhaustion together present a working method that enables us to engage in what to do with concepts and images, how concepts can be constructed, and how we can struggle to *make* an image from time to time that could really transform us and our environment-worlds (Deleuze, 1997, p. 158). To make a novel image of thought, and not recite a ready-made one, is difficult work, and there is always the threat of failure, or else corporeal or material exhaustion including the body that is our built environment. An image of thought enables the capture (more or less fleeting) of sense and sensation, or the powers of affects, percepts and concepts, and this capture or composition either offers a glimmer of liberation or else reinforces repression. Contributing to the formulation of an image of thought is the construction of concepts, again leading us from one end of the methodology to the other, from concepts to images, and back again by passing through exhaustive series, the drying up of voices, the extenuation of space, the image of thought, which in its novel remaking is paradoxically iconoclastic.

Concepts, following Deleuze and Guattari's oft cited account in *What Is Philosophy?* are created or signed off by philosophers (or conceptual persona), and are arranged on what they call a plane of immanence somewhat like irregular paving stones or a dry stone wall. Concepts are good for nothing if they are not attached to contemporary problems. The central task of philosophy, for Deleuze and Guattari, is the creation of concepts, but never *ex nihilo*, instead, concepts always emerge from the midst of things, and are achieved through a form of ethical experimentation that follows the materials that compose our existential, political, social and environmental territories. We undertake our work with concepts, which, as Deleuze and Foucault have famously discussed, are like tools, and concept-tools are what offer us a little hope. Concept-tools enable a relay between theory and practice, they are dedicated to specific local problems, and as tools, concepts shift in their application as they are passed from hand to hand (Stengers, 2005, p. 185). Furthermore, concepts characterize the constraints that pertain to singular practices, articulating a practitioner's obligations and their requirements, which in turn serve to situate the thinker (Stengers, 2010, p. 59). At much the same time that a concept is revised or produced by a thinker, the concept reciprocally alters who the thinker is in the midst of becoming or how they might contribute to the process of their own subjectivation, as I have described above with respect to how the point of view shapes the subject, rather than vice versa.

It is not possible to speak of exhaustive series either of signifying terms, nor of things without also speaking of the existential and physiological comportment of exhaustion, which Deleuze describes as follows: 'One remains active, but for nothing. One was tired of something, but exhausted by nothing' (1998, p. 153). That is to say 'exhaustion (exhaustivity) does not occur without a certain physiological exhaustion' (p. 154): The material mixtures of the corporeal stuff of a body and the event of sense cannot be extricated, they are co-dependent, co-constitutive registers. It is always a question of 'The exhaustive *and* the exhausted' (p. 154), and how these work together, organizing the proliferation of events of sense *and* material mixtures of bodies as independent, yet co-constitutive series (again, according to a Stoic logic of sense). As Deleuze explains 'a keen sense or science of the possible, [is] joined, or rather disjoined, with a fantastic decomposition of the self.' Disjoined, as sense and the body or self, although reciprocally constituted, have a paradoxical relationship of inclusive disjunction (p. 154). The methodology of exhaustion, the exhaustive *and* the exhausted, is also supported by the well-known, even industrialized, conjunctive work of the 'and, and, and', producing a stuttering that manifests in the body as it practises its compositions of exhaustive series. Exhaustivity is an approach that produces a thinking with AND instead of thinking IS (Deleuze and Parnet, 2002, pp. 9–10, 57, 59).

One way to arrive at an image of thought in this system, is to proceed through what Deleuze has named an any-space-whatever, which is the extenuation of space (Deleuze, 1998, p. 160). Although space enables the demarcation and determination of localized places and their respective assemblages of singularities, 'a sample of the floor, a sample of the wall, a door without a knob, an opaque window, a pallet . . .' (p. 165), so supporting the taking place of some event (p. 168), 'To exhaust space is to extenuate its potentiality by making any encounter impossible' (p. 163). Except that the any-space-whatever finally leads to an encounter with the image of thought. Now the any-space-whatevers I have dramatized above in the first instance pertain to those architectural images produced by becoming-architects, deployed to speculate on near and far futures, and in the second instance, to those exhaustive combinatorials of images that populate real-estate advertising sites contributing to our global gentri-fiction. Both follow a methodology of exhaustion, but risk arriving at images of thought that merely re-capitulate what is already known, remaining both insufficiently abstract, and never material enough, and thus lacking any capacity to create a shift in an architectural state of affairs. Where the any-space-whatever and what it communicates leads to an image of thought, this does not produce a representation of an object, but a movement in the world of the mind (p. 169). Simultaneously, the mind and the body collude: as the mind exhausts its images the body remains curled up and immobile, returning us again to the exhaustive, or exhaustivity *and* exhaustion.

Sometimes the methodology of exhaustion appears to lead towards the image of thought, but the image of thought can also precede the methodology. There is an ambivalence in the image of thought, either it is that which over-determines what we think, participating in the encounter that forces thought to think *that*, or else the image bears a relationship to immanence, to the plane of immanence as seemingly inexhaustible resource of concept construction. The image, as Deleuze explains in his essay 'The Exhausted', is outside language, it is the vastitude of space, but it also connects to the ambivalence of the any-space-whatever, which risks recapitulating a tired refrain, as witnessed in the seething production of real-estate imagery.

Thing, concept, language, voice, space, image, designate modes in a methodology of exhaustion, and have the capacity to create mixtures and compositions, which not only pertain to the medium of film, theatre or literature, where Deleuze focuses his attention, but also to the manifold media of architecture. An image, a face might loom up out of the darkness, and this appearance produces a cry, the voice is heard, and then the mouth and throat collaborate in the formation of words. Others, those outside us, beyond the walls of our house, or our city, are possible worlds, and their objects and words, 'constitute "stories"' (p. 157). Deleuze is frequently heard to assert that 'there is no language that is other than the foreign' (p. 157), and the foreign amidst our own familiar languages is what enables their regeneration. And yet, exhaustion achieved through exhaustive series also reveals that a people are missing (Deleuze, 1989, p. 216), or else they have already been eradicated, their voices having run dry, and we appear to be left with the choice of extinction, obliteration, or reinventing new images of thought and new concept-tools that might just keep what is possible minimally open in our shared environment-worlds, our manifold milieu, our local urban landscapes.

What do we do when faced with the fatigued images of architecture, and with the more general exhaustion of the image of thought as it pertains to architecture? Perhaps 'any creative life is also a process of self-destruction with the theme of fatigue as a vital process' (Deleuze, 2006, p. 266). Deleuze, in his seminars on Spinoza, goes so far as to suggest that 'ethics tells us nothing, it does not know' (Deleuze, 1980). Instead, ethics is a question of what you *can* do, what you are capable of, and this we will never know in advance. The any-space-whatever is a space from which all co-ordinates and all extensive values have been evacuated. What's more, Deleuze relates the any-space-whatever explicitly to the pure power of immanence. Is it possible to launch a radical empiricism from this field that belongs to no one, this pre-individual, non-hylemorphic field, without being sure of what will happen next? And from this pre-personal field of immanence, might it be possible to return again to an actualization of material relations, to *follow* the material of a reconsidered architectural project along more radical, political and ethical lines? Amidst the existential territories of architecture, after Deleuze, we still need to ask: 'What can I do, what power can I claim and what resistances may I counter? What can I be, with what folds can I surround myself or how can I produce myself as a subject?' (Deleuze, 1988, p. 114). The architect sees, confronts, and lives, and needs to invent solutions that meet the very specific qualities of their encounters. It does not suffice to further prop up the gentri-fiction that over-determines our (e)states of reality as this only serves to foreclose on a thinking of the future, or else to miss a promising encounter with a radical image of thought. And yet a methodology of exhaustion is as likely to fail as to succeed, for the job of inventing a new image of thought can be really botched, or else it might not be recognized until it is nearly too late.

Notes

1 Gilles Deleuze asks what it means to will the event, a question that can be addressed directly to architectural events. This question is also a question of an immanent ethics, the ethical imperative being 'not to be unworthy of what happens to us'. Deleuze argues 'Nothing more can be said, and no more has ever been said: to become worthy of what happens to us, and thus to will and release the event, to become the offspring of one's own events . . .' The event carries both misfortune as well as splendour and brightness it can bifurcate in either direction.

2 As Anna Gibbs explains, fictocritical writing as research is performative and must be reinvented anew with every singular problem.

3 Denise Scott Brown associates the ill-defined and even undefinable criteria of what makes a 'good designer' in architecture with a fixation on the star system in our discipline, specifically how our peers feel compelled to elevate fellow architects to the status of stars. An explicit connection can be construed between how we pedagogically form the expectations of our graduating students in terms of their future professional life. We risk instilling in them the desire to become recognized as 'stars', as though this would represent the pinnacle of a career. What is worse, Scott Brown suggests, writing originally in the mid-1970s, and continuing to revise her text into the 1980s, is that 'the guru must be male . . . architectural prima donnas are all male'. The challenge, Scott Brown asserts, is located in our schools, where we need to make student architects aware of the full range of skills, beyond design, that are valuable in an office.

4 Deleuze and Guattari argue that the teacher refers to 'taught concepts', to what is already known. They distinguish this from the conceptual persona of the idiot who is a private thinker creating concepts with their own innate powers.

5 In the original text is her argument supporting situated knowledges, Donna Haraway describes the oppressive risk of knowledge formations that are 'policed by philosophers'.

6 Massumi has famously argued about the autonomy of affect, that affects and their resulting effects or identifications via an emotional nomenclature follow no strict causality.

7 Bruno Latour uses the term 'iconoclash' to draw attention to a paradoxical quality of images, working between a desire to destroy and preserve or revere them.

8 The pedagogical design studio Critical Studies at KTH Architecture, Stockholm, which developed from the collaborative work of FATALE, has made it their mandate to explore alternative approaches to architecture with an emphasis on sociopolitical relations and the collaborative and participatory asset mapping of human and non-human actors in given problematic fields.

9   The challenge remains, as Deleuze explains: 'to write is not to recount one's memories and travels, one's loves and griefs, one's dreams and fantasies'. Instead, to write is to discover beneath specific persons a power of the impersonal. Nevertheless, through the points of view of individuated characters visions are experienced that carry them off towards potentially transformative becomings.

10   OECD Better Life Index See http://www.oecdbetterlifeindex.org. For examples of where this index has been described in reference to the affect of happiness see http://www.australiantimes.co.uk/news/australia-world-news/australia-ranked-happiest-developed-nation-by-oecd.htm; http://www.thelocal.se/48194/20130529/.

11   For the Liveability Ranking See https://www.eiu.com/public/topical_report.aspx?campaignid=Liveability2012

12   In their dialogue 'Intellectuals and Power' Deleuze and Foucault discuss the relationship between intellectuals and power, as well as the necessity of maintaining a dynamic relay between theory and practice. It is the intellectual who calls out that the emperor wears no clothes, who sees before others see, but who also risks being expelled from their milieu.

13   Please see the 'Introduction' in this volume.

14   See Slavoj Žižek (2011), 'The Architectural Parallax', in Nadir Lahiji (ed.), *The Political Unconscious of Architecture*. Surray, Farnham: Ashgate, p. 256.

15   In 2010 the Stockholm City Council published a planning document dedicated to making Stockholm a 'walkable city', part of a larger city planning proposal called Vision 2030: A World-Class Stockholm. The aim is to promote Stockholm as an 'attractive, vibrant and safe urban environment' (p. 1). The document also uses the formulation of 'sustainable growth' (p. 4), 'positive development' (p. 83). References to walking itself, concern cutting traffic emissions (p. 30); creating a more attractive place for walking everyday (p. 44); but always at the service of developed urban environments and more urban traffic.

16   Tunström and Bradley argue that current visions for the European city suggest that 'A current strong ideal is to build or rebuild "the traditional city" in terms of compact, functionally mixed urban blocks with streets, sidewalks and small shops.'

17   Deleuze, after Spinoza asks: 'What can a body do? Well, we do not yet know what a body can do' (pp. 224–6), and the ever-receding horizon of this not knowing is what turns out to be productive. Deleuze explains that an existing mode, for instance, we could speak of an architectural-body here, is endowed with a kind of elasticity, which is 'a margin, a limit' between our capacity to be affected and our capacity to produce active affects (pp. 222–3).

18   In delivering their argument for the creative construction of concepts, Deleuze and Guattari explain that there are also 'repulsive concepts', for instance, those that Nietzsche described concerning *ressentiment* and 'bad conscience', though there are often great ambiguities between sympathetic and antipathetic concepts.

Bibliography

Boltanski, L. and Chiapello, E. (2005), *The New Spirit of Capitalism*. London: Verso.

Brown, L. (2011), *Feminist Practices: Interdisciplinary Approaches to Women in Architecture*. Farnham, Surrey: Ashgate.

Budgen, S. (2000), 'A "New Spirit of Capitalism"', in *New Left Review*, January–February 2000. Available at: <http://newleftreview.org/II/1/sebastian-budgen-a-new-spirit-of-capitalism>.

Cuff, D. (1992), *Architecture: The Story of Practice*. Cambridge, MA: MIT Press.

De Landa, M. (2000), *A Thousand Years of Nonlinear History*. New York: Swerve Editions.

Deleuze, G. (1980), *Spinoza Lectures*. Cours Vincennes 12/12/1980: 21. Available at: <http://www.webdeleuze.com>.

— (1988), *Foucault*. S. Hand (trans.). Minneapolis: University of Minnesota Press.

— (1989), *Cinema 2: The Time Image*. Minneapolis: University of Minnesota.

— (1990), *The Logic of Sense*. M. Lester (trans.). New York: Columbia University Press.

— (1992), *Expressionism in Philosophy: Spinoza*. M. Joughin (trans.). New York: Zone Books.

— (1993), *The Fold: Leibniz and the Baroque*. H. Tomlinson and R. Galeta (trans). London: Athlone Press.

— (1994), *Cinema 2: The Time Image*. T. Conley (trans.). London: Athlone Press.

— (1995), 'Societies of Control', in *Negotiations*. M. Joughin (trans.). New York: Columbia University Press, pp. 177–82.

— (1997), *Essays Critical and Clinical*. Minneapolis: University of Minnesota.

— (1998), *Essays Critical and Clinical*. D. W. Smith (trans.). London: Verso.

— (2006), *Two Regimes of Madness*. A. Hodges and M. Taormina (trans). New York: Semiotext(e).

Deleuze, G. and Guattari, F. (1987), *A Thousand Plateaus*. B. Massumi (trans.). Minneapolis: University of Minnesota Press.

— (1994), *What Is Philosophy?*. G. Burchell and H. Tomlinson (trans). London: Verso.

Deleuze, G. and Parnet, C. (2002), *Dialogues II*. H. Tomlinson and B. Habberjam (trans). New York: Columbia University Press.

Foucault, M. and Deleuze, G. (1977), 'Intellectuals and Power', in *Language, Memory, Counter-Practice*. Ithaca, NY: Cornell University Press.

Frichot, H. (2012a), 'The Stockholm Bubble: Material Assemblages and Ecologies of Affect', in *Nordic: Journal of Architecture*, 2, 3, Winter 2012, pp. 40–6.

Frichot, H., Preston, J., Spooner, M., Pickersgill, S., Kovar, Z., Hann, C. and Evans, M. (2012b), 'An Antipodean Imaginary for Architecture+Philosophy: Ficto-Critical Approaches to Design Practice Research', in *Footprint*, special issue, *Architecture Culture and the Question of Knowledge: Doctoral Research Today*, Issue 10/11, Spring 2012. Available at: <http://www.footprintjournal.org/issues/current>.

Gibbs, A. (2005), 'Fictocriticism, Affect, Mimesis: Engendering Differences', in *Text Journal*. April 2005. Available at: <http://www.textjournal.com.au/april05/gibbs.htm>. Unpaginated.

Groys, B. (2008), *Art Power*. Cambridge, MA: MIT Press.

Guattari, F. (2000), *The Three Ecologies*. I. Pindar and P. Sutton (trans). London: Athlone Press.

Haraway, D. (1991), 'Situated Knowledges: The Science Question in Feminism and the Privilege of Partial Perspective', in *Simians, Cyborgs, and Women: The Reinvention of Nature*. London: Free Association Books, pp. 183–201.

Harvey, D. (2008), 'The Right to the City', in *New Left Review*, 53, September–October, pp. 23–40.

Hauptman, D. and Neidlich, W. (eds) (2010), *Cognitive Architecture: From Biopolitics to Noopolitics. Architecture & Mind in the Age of Communication and Information*. Rotterdam: 010 Publishers.

Hême de Lacotte, S. (2010), 'Iconoclasm of Gilles Deleuze? Deleuze, the Image, the Cinema, the Image of Thought'. P.-G. Desjardins (trans.), in *Trahir*, December.

Latour, B. (2002), 'What Is Iconoclash? or Is There a World Beyond the Image Wars?', in
    B. Latour and P. Weibel (eds), *Iconoclash: Beyond the Image Wars in Science, Religion
    and Art.* Cambridge, MA: MIT Press.
Lazzarato, M. (2006), 'The Concepts of Life and the Living in Societies of Control',
    in *Deleuze and the Social.* M. Fuglsang and B. Meier Sorensen (eds). Edinburgh:
    Edinburgh University Press.
Lloyd Thomas, K. (ed.) (2007), *Material Matters: Architecture and Material Practice.*
    London: Routledge.
Massumi, B. (2002), *Parables of the Virtual: Movement, Affect, Sensation.* Durham and
    London: Duke University Press.
Petrescu, D. (ed.) (2007), *Altering Practices: Feminist Politics and Poetics of Space.* London:
    Routledge.
Pine, J. and Gilmore, James H. (2011), *The Experience Economy.* Boston: Harvard Business
    School Publishing.
Schalk, M., Burroughs, B., Grillner, K. and Bonnevier, K. (2012), 'FATALE: Critical Studies
    in Architecture', in *Nordic Journal of Architecture*, vol. 2, pp. 90–6.
Scott Brown, D. (1990), 'Room at the Top? Sexism and the Star System in Architecture',
    in J. Rendell, B. Penner and I. Borden (eds), *Gender Space Architecture: An
    Interdisciplinary Introduction.* London: Routledge.
Sloterdijk, P. (2009), 'Rules for the Human Zoo: A Response to the *Letter on Humanism*', in
    Environment and Planning D: Society and Space, vol. 27, pp. 12–28.
Smith, N. (1996), *The New Urban Frontier: Gentrification and the Revanchist City.* London:
    Routledge.
Stengers, I. (2005), 'An Ecology of Practices', in *Cultural Studies Review*, 11, 1, March 2005,
    pp. 183–96.
— (2010), *Cosmopolitics I.* R. Bononno (trans.). Minneapolis: University of Minnesota
    Press.
Thrift, N. (2008), *Non-Representational Theory: Space Politics Affect.* London: Routledge.
Tonkiss, F. (2005), *Space, the City and Social Theory: Social Relations and Urban Forms.*
    Cambridge: Polity Press.
Tunström, M. and Bradley, K. (forthcoming), 'Opposing the Postpolitical Swedish Urban
    Discourse', in J. Metzger, P. Allmendinger and S. Oosterlynck (eds), *Displacing the
    Political: Democratic Deficits in Contemporary European Territorial Governance.* New
    York: Routledge.
The Walkable City: Stockholm City Plan (2010), Stockholm: The City Planning
    Administration.
Wallenstein, S. O. (2010), 'Noopolitics, Life and Architecture', in D. Hauptman and W.
    Neidlich (eds), *Cognitive Architecture: From Biopolitics to Noopolitics, Architecture &
    Mind in the Age of Communication and Information.* Rotterdam: 010 Publishers.
Webster, H. (2005), 'The Architectural Review: A Study of Ritual, Acculturation and
    Reproduction in Architectural Education', in *Arts and Humanities in Higher Education*,
    vol. 4, pp. 265–82.
— (2007), 'The Analytics of Power: Re-presenting the Design Jury', *Journal of Architectural
    Education*, 2007, pp. 21–7.
White, M. (2004), 'The Money Shot', in *Mongrel and Subaud*, Melbourne.
Žižek, S. (2011), 'The Architectural Parallax', in N. Lahiji (ed.), *The Political Unconscious of
    Architecture.* Farnham, Surrey: Ashgate.

8

Radical Infrastructure? A New Realism and Materialism in Philosophy and Architecture

Joel McKim

One of the most notable developments in architectural thought over the past decade has been the ascendance of infrastructural concerns within the theory and practice of the discipline. Contemporary architecture has increasingly shifted its attention from the design of individual signature buildings towards the organization of complex, overlapping and often transnational systems of energy, transportation and natural ecology. Urban objects or networks such as airports, waterways and public parks now vie with national galleries and corporate headquarters for the position of most prestigious architectural commission. An attention to infrastructural concerns has led to a reshuffling of several disciplinary hierarchies, with landscape design shrugging off its status as a minor practice; the vector of horizontality competing with the formerly privileged one of verticality; and biological and geological matter joining the more expected building materials of concrete, steel and glass.

While the architect and theorist Keller Easterling argues that the current architectural focus on infrastructure is inspired by 'radical changes to the globalized world' (2010, p. 96), the movement has, somewhat surprisingly, demonstrated a rather marked aversion towards an engagement with critical theory and radical philosophy. Responding perhaps to an oversaturation of deconstructive and Deleuzean discourse within the field, the proponents of infrastructural architecture often call for a form of design pragmatism that reprioritizes the concrete or physical practices of the discipline, eschewing abstract theorization. Yet this missed encounter between philosophy and architecture is an especially curious one given the recent proliferation of philosophical writing that seeks to address quite specifically questions of realism, materiality and natural forces that would seemingly pertain directly to issues of infrastructure. Whether grouped under the heading 'speculative realism' or 'new materialism', these varied currents of thought are linked by a shared interest in moving away from textual or cultural analysis in order to conceptualize the realm of non-human objects, systems and processes.

This essay will attempt to outline a small selection of these recent discussions, focusing primarily on the vital materialism of Jane Bennett and the object-oriented philosophy of Graham Harman and Timothy Morton. My objective is to raise a number of related questions: What does it mean to speak of such a thing as a philosophy of infrastructure? What insights might these recent philosophical forays into questions of realism and materialism offer architects attempting to design tangible interactions between human and non-human systems? And could this philosophy of infrastructure possess a radical or critical politics to match its radically non-anthropocentric ontology?

I'll begin by introducing a view of the design currents that fall loosely under the banner of infrastructural architecture. These include: manifestos, such as Stan Allen's 1999 call for an infrastructural urbanism that would return architecture to the realm of political and social instrumentality; projects that are realized or in the process of realization, such as the Lifescape landscape urbanism plan that is currently transforming Staten Island's Fresh Kills landfill, once the largest garbage dump in the world, into a public park and wetlands conservation area; and speculative proposals and competitions, including the ecological visions of the Toronto-based firm Lateral Office and the WPA 2.0 design initiative organized by UCLA's cityLAB. After charting some of this recent history of infrastructural architecture, I'll switch focus to the philosophical terrain established by Bennett, Harman and Morton in an effort to find lines of affiliation, establish points of potential connection and suggest the beginnings, at least, of a possible encounter.

The turn to infrastructure in architecture has many triggers, not least of which is the widely recognized transition from an industrial to a post-industrial or post-Fordist economy, an epochal change that has significantly altered the organization of cities and their surrounding areas. In their study of Detroit (arguably the quintessential example of this shifting city structure) Patrik Schumacher and Christian Rogner attempt to take stock of the urban effects of globalized capital markets, shrinking state-regulation of the economy, eroding labour relations and the resultant 'liquefied' architecture of business organization. In their assessment, the 'strictly coded stereotypes and neat allocation of zones' characteristic of the modernist city become incapable of sustaining post-Fordist production paradigms that are 'increasingly organized around principles of decentralization, horizontality, transparency, fluidity, and rapid mutability' (2001). Cities that are incapable of adapting to these 'vital processes of networking and self-organization' may be doomed to suffer Detroit's fate, 'an image of a post-industrial ex-urban center annexed to its own suburbs' (2001). Compare this picture of Detroit, a semi-abandoned historical city of industry, with Rem Koolhaas's description of the post-Fordist agglomeration of Altanta, 'a sparse, thin carpet of habitation' in which the 'strongest contextual givens are vegetal and infrastructural: forest and roads' (1998, p. 835).

The research work of landscape architect Alan Berger assumes the task of systematically documenting these forms of urban change, visualizing and analysing the 'in-between' spaces and transitional landscapes of a contemporary America where the population density of urban centres has declined by more than 50 per cent in the last 50 years and the majority of development is occurring at the peripheries of metropolitan areas (2006, p. 18). This is an urbanity stretched out across the surface of the country, reliant on an ever more strained network of highways, electrical grids, water supply, etc. Berger offers the designation 'drosscape' to encompass the combination of 'waste landscapes' (areas containing solid waste, sewage, etc.), 'wasted spaces' (abandoned or contaminated sites) and 'wasteful places' (large parking lots and retail malls) that are the problematic leftovers of the joint tendencies of de-industrialization and sprawl (2006, p. 45). In Kenneth Frampton's estimation, landscape design is becoming the 'remedial art par excellence' (2004, p. 12), charged with the task of rehabilitating the neglected and damaged regions produced by this lack of long-term sustainable planning. Yet these patterns of urbanization are by no means confined to the American geography. The German architect and urban planner Thomas Sieverts has gone so far as to suggest that the concept of 'city' may be an antiquated one as an increasing expanse of Europe, Germany's Ruhr area for example, is taken up by what he terms the *Zwischendstadt*, a kind of 'urbanized landscape' in which the distinction between rural and urban has effectively dissolved (2003, p. 2).

The problems of an under-resourced, hyper-extended urban landscape throw forward issues of infrastructure as a social and political imperative that the discipline of architecture simply cannot ignore. Dana Cuff, the director of UCLA's cityLAB, highlights the warnings of the American Society of Civil Engineers that the nation's infrastructure has been so poorly maintained, and for so long, that it would require a $2.2 trillion investment to ensure its safety (2010, p. 18). In response to this situation and partly inspired by the lack of architect and designer involvement in the 2009 post-crisis infrastructure-oriented American Recovery and Reinvestment Act, cityLAB initiated their WPA 2.0 design competition (submissions can be viewed at wpa2.aud. ucla.edu/info/). This reboot of the New Deal 1930s Works Progress Administration, which produced some of the country's most iconic public works, encourages architects and designers to imagine contemporary infrastructural projects capable of revitalizing communities and lending spatial coherence to a fragmented urban environment. With public investment, and therefore the public realm, in a prolonged state of contraction, Cuff suggests that necessary urban infrastructure projects must be envisioned as playing 'double duty' for the public – storm water channels serving simultaneously as bicycle lanes, for example (2010, p. 22).

The Toronto-based studio Lateral Office, one of the WPA 2.0 finalists, have specialized in the design of such speculative hybrid infrastructure projects as the leisure retro-fitting of oil rigs otherwise doomed to obsolescence, the construction of a high-speed rail link/artic eco-park in the Bering Strait and the production of a salt farm/recreational retreat at the site of a saline terminal lake in California. Through envisioning these future ecologies of nature and industry, Lateral Office promote what they describe as 'an architecture that responds to opportunities of contingency . . . Performing in a manner similar to infrastructures, these spatial formats support energies, flows, resources, and matter, yielding an emergent multivalent public realm' (2011, p. 8).

While attempting to respond to the specific political and environmental conditions of the contemporary urban situation, many of the participants in this developing wave of infrastructural architecture position their design and practice as a distinctly pragmatic, rather than theoretical, engagement. Architecture's turn towards infrastructure, in other words, is also a conscious turn away from philosophy. There are certainly intellectual links between infrastructural architecture and the, by now, infamous 'post-critical' moment in architectural theory, sparked by R. E. Somol and Sarah Whiting's provocative call for a projective architecture that emphasizes the discipline's instrumentality, its ability to produce effects and interactions among multiple economic, social and ecological systems, rather than its ability to represent, critique or signify (2002, p. 77). One of the design current's founding texts is Stan Allen's 1999 appeal for an 'infrastructural urbanism' that would return architecture to the questions of function and implementation that had been sidelined by postmodernism's semiotic turn. According to Allen, an architecture obsessed with self-critique and decorative localism had lost its ability to influence the economic and social infrastructure of the city. He petitions for a design practice that once again seeks to intervene in these processes; an approach that 'understands architecture as *material* practice – as an activity that works in and among the world of things, and not exclusively with meaning and image' (1999, p. 52, italics are his). Like Somol and Whiting, Allen claims that architecture must own up to its powers of instrumentality that set it apart from other representational media (architecture is importantly *not* the same as film or literature). Architecture, according to Allen, must once again engage with the question of infrastructure, becoming less concerned with the form and style of individual buildings and more concerned with the fields that dictate what it is possible to construct.

Infrastructural architecture attempts to distance itself from postmodernism's stylistic flights of fancy, but also from architecture's sustained philosophical engagements of the past several decades – both the Derrida-inspired works of deconstructive architecture and the Deleuze-inspired designs of digital computation. Cuff describes the current moment as one in which architecture must get its hands dirty again by allowing itself 'to be contaminated by the world outside our borders with all its messy problems' (2010, p. 18). The 'fast-forward urbanism' she and Roger Sherman currently promote is one in which architectural intervention is viewed 'in terms of temporal, opportunistic, and strategic transformations' (2011, p. 11) rather than slow and deliberate philosophical contemplation. Here application is privileged over theory, and political and economic contingency rather than intellectual commitment provides the ground for action.

I'd like to conclude this brief exploration of infrastructural concerns in contemporary architecture by highlighting the sub-movement that has most often answered this call for pragmatic application by successfully bringing proposed projects to fruition. 'Landscape urbanism' is also the infrastructure-oriented practice that my own research has approached most directly in the form of the 'Lifescape' project, the large-scale regeneration of Staten Island's Fresh Kills landfill. The landscape architect Charles Waldheim coined the term landscape urbanism and suggests that the movement's design strength lies in 'the conflation, integration, and fluid exchange between (natural) environmental and (engineered) infrastructural systems' (2006, p. 43). Proponents of landscape urbanism argue that the conceptual scope of landscape design, the discipline's 'natural' inclination to think in terms of networks, relations, temporal change and complex interactions, make it an ideal basis for the re-formulation of urban planning more generally. Waldheim argues that landscape has usurped the building to become the primary element of urban design (2002, p. 15). By expanding the traditional role of landscape design to include the integration of urban ecological systems with infrastructural networks, landscape urbanism claims to address the challenges of connecting the dispersed and continuous urban field that now exists between major cities, and recovering and reconditioning the brownfield and obsolete industrial sites that persist within the older city centres.

The most prominent example of realized landscape urbanism projects has been the transformation of disused or contaminated urban geographies into major city parks and nature reserves[1] (Seattle's Olympic Sculpture Park designed by Weiss/Manfredi architects and built on the former site of the Unocal oil and gas company being one heralded example). Perhaps the most ambitious of all these projects is entering into the fifth year of what will be a 30-year process of rehabilitation, reseeding and reprogramming. While in operation the Fresh Kills landfill, which occupies a 2,200 acre site on Staten Island, was the largest garbage dump in the world, receiving at its peak 29,000 tons of the city's waste daily (New York City Department of Planning, 2001). Closed in March of 2001 after over 50 years of service, the landfill was temporarily re-opened in September as the containment and processing site for the World Trade Center debris. By the time the landfill had assumed this final grisly task, plans to transform the site into a public park and wetlands conservation area had already commenced. In early 2003, a plan titled Lifescape put forward by the Field Operations landscape design practice was selected and the process of sealing over the landfills four mounds of garbage (reaching elevations as high as 225 feet) began. The firm, led by James Corner (one of the most articulate proponents of the landscape urbanism movement), describes the plan in the following holistic and biological (rather than philosophical) terms:

> Ecological reflection, passive recreation, active sports and exercise, creativity, performance and cultural events, community development, economic enhancement and neighborhood revitalization all take their place alongside the micro-macroscopic processes of lifescape. It is fully integrative. Lifescape is not a loose metaphor or representation – it is a functioning reality, an autopoietic agent. (Field Operations, 2002, p. 24)

The completed park will cover a territory almost three times the size of Central Park and apart from producing new leisure spaces for the city, it will also contribute to its energy reserves by harnessing and processing the methane gas emitted by the decomposing garbage that makes up the site's shifting topography.

The project is a marvel of design and engineering, making – as if by magic – the largest repository of human garbage effectively disappear, but the ecology of waste in which it continues to participate is a complicated one. With the termination of Fresh Kills, the city of New York no longer has any landfills or incinerators within any of its five boroughs. The closure has mobilized a dispersed and increasingly privatized organization of waste disposal that exports the city's garbage to poorer states willing to take on the ecological burden. The majority of New York's garbage now ends up in Pennsylvania, but these landfills are reaching the point of exhaustion and the more distant states of Virginia and South Carolina are now being increasingly relied upon (Ascher and Marech, 2005, pp. 190–1). A transportation network of semitrailer trucks, transfer stations and a dedicated railway line facilitate the removal of New York's garbage from the city's sightlines. While in many ways living up to the theoretical and instrumental claims of both the landscape urbanism and the wider infrastructural architecture movements – the project undoubtedly initiates and interweaves an impressive array of biological, cultural and industrial ecologies – the Fresh Kills redevelopment also highlights the political, environmental and ethical complexities involved in any such large-scale reorganization of the built environment. Architecture's ability to effectuate urban change while simultaneously thinking through these implications seems hampered by its recent extradition of philosophy from its borders. It's an expulsion that continues to haunt the infrastructural design debate, just as the exportation and interment of waste remains a problematic exclusion that may eventually come back to disrupt the city of New York.

The lack of engagement between infrastructural architecture and philosophy is especially curious and somewhat frustrating given the current set of terms, concepts and referents circulating within philosophical circles: matter, objects, ecology, energy, the non-human ... This is a dynamic intellectual moment in which few master voices dominate and thought feels very much to be in a state of formation. It would be unfortunate if the most exciting discussions within architecture failed to connect with their philosophical counterparts, particularly given that there appear to be so many shared objects of concern between them. I've chosen to look at three contemporary thinkers in this essay (there are many other potential candidates), selected in part because of their prominent position within their respective philosophical camps, in part because I happen to find their writing particularly engaging and relevant to architectural topics, and in part because a productive dialogue has already emerged between all three (in the form of book reviews, critical responses and colloquia). While Jane Bennett is most often identified as a 'new materialist', Graham Harman and Timothy Morton are two of the leading figures within the increasingly influential 'object-oriented' strand of philosophy. The projects of all three share a concern with questions of ontology, the primary conditions of existence, over those of epistemology. More specifically they have all, to various degrees, been associated with the 'speculative realism' movement in contemporary philosophy. They are all preoccupied with a speculation, 'about the nature of reality independently of thought and of humanity more generally', to use a description offered by Levi Bryant, Nick Srnicek and Harman (2011, p. 3). The human subject, in other words, does not reside at the centre of these ontologies and the philosophical systems they construct attempt to give (at least) equal weighting to the electrical currents, rabbits, hammers, Styrofoam cups and black holes that exist in the world or universe along with us. Yet there are important differences between the 'new materialist' and 'object-oriented' viewpoints and I will try to also pay heed to some of these points of divergence.

Bennett's overall project of thought is expressed quite directly and succinctly in her contribution to the recent *New Materialisms* collection, in which she questions: 'What would happen to our thinking about politics if we took more seriously the idea that technological and natural materialities were themselves actors alongside and within us – were vitalities, trajectories, and powers irreducible to the meanings, intentions, or symbolic values humans invest in them?' (2010a, p. 47). Bennett's horizontal flattening out of the tradition hierarchies of potential political agency also seeks to dismantle or disrupt the ontological dualisms of life and matter, human and non-human, and organic and inorganic. The full implications and possible applications of her philosophy of 'vital materialism' are most forcefully articulated in her book *Vibrant Matter: A Political Ecology of Things*. Here she outlines her conception of 'thing-power', an effort to acknowledge the independence of things from the human world and their capacity to affect and be affected by other bodies. Bennett's philosophical touchstones may by now be apparent: the thought of Spinoza, Bergson and Deleuze often underpins her discussions of vitalism, conatus and matter. Her notions of vibrancy are more uniquely her own and she vividly describes an encounter with a collection of detritus accumulated in a Baltimore storm drain, suggesting that the glove, pollen, dead rat, cap and stick she found there, 'shimmied back and forth between debris and thing' – between dead stuff no longer useful to human attention and live presence that 'commanded attention in its own right, as existents in excess of their association with human meanings, habits, or projects' (2010b, p. 4). It is the way that things vibrate back and forth between the human world and a radically non-human one, to which they ultimately belong, which interests Bennett. But a material sensibility for Bennett would also entail an awareness of the human body's own participation within these vital currents, similarly composed as it is from compounds of vibrant matter. Her ethical aim then is to promote recognition of the 'shared materiality of all things' (2010b, p. 13) and a 'strange and incomplete commonality with the out-side' domain of 'animals, plants, earth, even artifacts and commodities' (2010b, pp. 17–18).

Bennett makes the task of transposing her philosophical thought onto the architectural terrain discussed above a relatively easy one by devoting the second chapter of her book to an examination of infrastructure, in the most traditional sense of the term. Bringing the thought of Bruno Latour into the theoretical mix, Bennett attempts to describe the 2003 power blackout, which affected much of the American Northeast and parts of Canada, in terms of an assemblage of human and non-human things with agency. To consider these events as purely a breakdown of human systems, a political failing or a product of human error is clearly to minimize the causal power of the non-organic within this disrupted network of relations. She explains, 'To the vital materialist, the electrical gird is better understood as a volatile mix of coal, seat, electromagnetic fields, computer programs, electron streams, profit motives, heat, lifestyles, nuclear fuel, plastic, fantasies of mastery, static, legislation, water, economic theory, wire, and wood – to name just some of the actants' (2010b, p. 25). The political legislation that enabled cross-state trading of energy commodities was clearly a determining factor in these events, but so too was the 'behaviour' of the electricity itself.[2] Bennett thus provides us with a necessary introduction to the basic properties of alternating electrical current, explaining the distinction between the active power that supplies energy to our household devices and the reactive power that carries no wattage, yet supports the transfer of active power by maintaining the voltage of the electrical grid. In the case of the 2003 blackout, the production of necessary reactive power was ignored among the enthusiastic commodity exchange of active power across state lines, an oversight that helped lead to the grid's eventual collapse.

Bennett uses the term efficacy to describe the capacity to bring about change or to cause something new to appear (2010b, p. 31). Her claim is that a complex assemblage of actants such as this demands a theory of distributed agency and emergent causality; rather than a single root source of efficacy, we are confronted with 'a swarm of vitalities at play' (2010b, p. 32). The political implications of this recognition of distributed agency are equally complex and preclude our assigning of blame, however tempting this might be, to an irresponsible corporate power, a lazy or corrupt government body, an over-taxed engineering department, or any other easily locatable causal agent. We are no longer in the terrain of clear-cut moral judgements, but are instead compelled to consider political action in response to human and non-human assemblages that may indicate productive or destructive trajectories, tendencies or propensities. In one of the more controversial statements in the book, Bennett insists, 'a theory of vibrant matter presents individuals as simply incapable of bearing *full* responsibility for their effects' (2010b, p. 37, italics are hers). Situations and events of consequence are never that simple, Bennett maintains, and it would be unproductive to delude ourselves in this way. Yet such a position does not let any of us as individuals off the political hook and Bennett maintains that the distribution of potentially harmful effects and destructive resonances does not alleviate the preventative need to seek them out. Nor does it entirely dismiss the responsibility associated with our individual efficacy or causality. She concludes the chapter with the suggestion:

> Perhaps the ethical responsibility of an individual human now resides in one's response to the assemblages in which one finds oneself participating: Do I attempt to extricate myself from assemblages whose trajectory is likely to harm? Do I enter into the proximity of assemblages whose conglomerate effectivity tends towards the enactment of nobler ends? (2010b, pp. 37–8)

On an individual basis, the difficulties of extricating oneself from infrastructural assemblages or influencing their trajectories are, it must be said, quite overwhelming. Bennett's ontological propositions are far from being politically programmatic, but given the complexity of their objects, it would be problematic if they were.

Yet Bennett's promotion of an enhanced material sensitivity opens up relevant and important philosophical territory for designers seeking to intervene in the realm of infrastructure. And the concepts and reference points she gathers will be relatively familiar ones for architects already engaged in these discussions of ecological and material urbanism. The process-oriented, relational and vitalist traditions she mobilizes still provide the intellectual foundation for much of the discourse that surrounds or accompanies infrastructural design proposals. The thought and language of Deleuze, Bergson, Whitehead and others have been subsumed within many contemporary currents of architectural theory, even if direct references to these thinkers no longer carry the same intellectual currency as they once did in design circles. Apart from reinforcing the importance of considering the vibrancy of matter across human and non-human or organic and non-organic divides (a viewpoint that is strongly maintained within movements like landscape urbanism), Bennett's thought presents a refusal to simplify the ethical dynamics associated with our contemporary political assemblages.

In the case of the Fresh Kills redevelopment, for example, Bennett's ethics of assemblages would require an acknowledgement of the larger ecology of matter within which the Lifescape project is inevitably embroiled. A material ecology that must include not only the artificial/natural composite of the park itself, but also the dispersed network of causality and efficacy that now extends beyond the borders of Staten Island to Pennsylvania, Virginia and beyond – involving a greater number of human and non-human actants as it spreads outwards. The claims for a 'fully integrated' or 'autopoietic' design plan are immediately placed under scrutiny by Bennett's expansive materialism. There is a similar sense of inclusiveness in Corner's description of the landscape urbanism movement's ultimate potential: 'the development of a space-time ecology that treats all forces and agents working in the urban field and considers them as continuous networks of inter-relationships' (2006, p. 30). Rather than a radical shift in perspective, Bennett's thinking provides the opportunity for a political and ethical gut check, an occasion for infrastructural architecture to evaluate its capacity to live up to this self-declared promise.

The object-oriented philosophers I'd like to turn to next share many commitments and preoccupations with Bennett's vibrant materialism. Like Bennett, the philosophical stance of both Harman and Morton is staunchly non-anthropocentric. Things or objects are provided full-agency, independent of any interactions they may have with humans. There is a life of objects here that need not, and often doesn't, involve us at all. An object-oriented philosophy, like Bennett's brand of materialism, seeks to develop an ontology that preserves no special status for the *being* particular to humans. But it would be wrong to ignore the distinct differences between these philosophical views. Such existent cleavages are driven home by Harman's claim that his position amounts to '*realism without materialism*' (2011a, p. 40, italics are his). Indeed, many of the concepts currently taken as accepted starting points for contemporary thought – including those of materialism, process and relation – are rejected by object-oriented philosophy, making the movement productively out of step with current assumptions of both philosophy and design. The world of objects that Harman and Morton introduce is a decidedly strange one (both philosophers often use the adjective 'weird' to describe their particular genre of speculative realism) and it potentially invites an even more dramatic rethinking of some of the presumptions of infrastructural architecture.

Given the title of this volume, it seems necessary to begin by first acknowledging that Harman also sets his object-oriented viewpoint apart from prevailing 'radical philosophies', by which he means those that 'are trying to identify a single *radix*, the root of reality as a whole' (2009, p. 154). Here we find an explanation for Harman's aversion to materialism, a philosophical perspective he views as relying on the radical reduction of the objects of the world to a single substance – a common substrate of matter. In his assessment of Bennett's work, for example, Harman identifies the danger that, 'objects are liberated from slavery to the human gaze only to fall into a new slavery to a single "matter-energy" that allows for no strife between autonomous individual things' (2011b, p. 130). Somewhat unfashionably then, Harman advances such non-univocal propositions as the maintenance of a split between object and relations, the preservation of a distinction between object and subject, and the insistence that an objet is fundamentally different from both its qualities and its compositional pieces (2009, p. 154).

While promoting the agency of things or objects, new materialism, according to both Harman and Morton, does not go far enough in preserving their autonomy. According to Harman, the compulsion to dismiss, dispel or dissolve the object – to deny the existence of things-in-themselves – is in fact one of the most consistent moves within philosophy. The materialist version of this common tendency is what Harman describes as an attempt to 'undermine' the object by, 'explaining their existence in terms of a deeper material basis: whether it be God, physical elements, drives, or the preindividual' (Bryant, Srnicek and Harman, 2011, p. 9). In undermining philosophies the speculation of some underlying vital or dynamic force is required in order to prevent the object from being a lifeless or static lump of matter. One of the problems with this viewpoint, according to Morton, is that it treats some things (like processes or matter) as 'more real than other things' (2012, p. 210). Object-oriented philosophy, as we shall explore in greater detail in a moment, claims to require no such supplementary force of change or hierarchy of things.

The opposite, but Harman claims equally problematic, tendency of philosophy is to 'overmine' the object by interpreting it as essentially a fiction, 'a set of relations, qualities, or parts' requiring a higher-level entity for the construction of their apparent coherence or meaning (2011a, p. 38). This 'overmining' tendency is at work in claims that what we call an object is really just a bundle of qualities or appearances made whole within consciousness (such as Hume's assertion that an apple is just the bundling of experiential qualities like redness or sweetness), or in claims that an object can only be explained by its activity within a larger system of relations (such as the common claim that an object's meaning is conditioned by its position within a particular social, economic or ecological system). While hailing Bruno Latour as one of the heroes of object-oriented philosophy due to his bestowal of full agential powers to all manner of things, Harman also recognizes the 'overmining' tendencies in his work, his commitment to 'relationizing objects in a manner that leaves them with nothing but their effects on others' (2009, p. 228). Thus not only is Harman's object-oriented philosophy non-material, it is also adamantly non-relational.

So what would it mean then to remain at the level of the object, and neither dissolve it into its constitutive parts or processes through an 'undermining' tendency or dismiss it as a fabricated unity through an 'overmining' tendency? And what precisely do Harman and Morton mean when they defend the absolute autonomy of objects? The genesis of Harman's ontological convictions lies in his quite particular reading of Heidegger. More specifically, it stems from his belief that all of Heidegger's philosophy is ultimately contained in his discussions of equipment and his concept of 'readiness-to-hand', what Harman refers to as 'tool-being' (2002, p. 4). The essential revelation of tool-being, according to Harman, is that objects *withdraw* from any appearance or any use: their tool-being remains veiled, concealed or hidden. The object is, therefore, never exhausted by its relations and the being of any object is always deeper than its appearance. Using Heidegger's famous example of the broken hammer that suggests its tool-being only in its broken state, Harman writes, 'Heidegger's hammer is always *more* than what it seems – a rumbling underground reality that can never become present without distortion' (2009, p. 185, italics are his). So the reality of the hammer, or any other object, is never available to us directly, no matter how many different views we take of it or how many different uses we make of it. We may form relations with the hammer, experience its qualities, or even destroy it, but this interaction never entails contact with the object's essential being, which remains withdrawn from us.

Heidegger's primary error, according to Harman, was his failure to recognize that his tool-analysis was applicable to all entities, independent of human activity. Non-human objects withdraw from each other, in precisely the same way as they withdraw from human objects. Fire, for example, does not exhaust the 'tool-being' of cotton by its ability to burn it. This duality of every object, the rift between its presentness as appearance or relation and its simultaneous withdrawal or inaccessibility, simply cannot be explained away. This leads Morton to make, with conviction, such peculiar utterances as: 'Things are here, but they are not here' and: 'The qualities of objects are not the object. Objects then are both themselves and not themselves' (2013). According to him, there is no dispelling the mystery and contradiction that are inherent to any object. All things are, he insists, 'dialetheic' by nature (2013).

In his book, *Realist Magic: Object, Ontology, Causality*, Morton attempts to tease out the implications of some of these strange contradictory characteristics of objects through an appropriately architectural example, that of a cinder block. Here Morton, quite literally, attempts to concretize his philosophical assertions. He asks us to imagine a serious of interactions with a mundane cinder block: a butterfly landing upon it, a hand running across it, an architect making a cross-section diagram of it. Morton emphatically declares, 'But a cross section of a cinder block is not a cinder block. A finger's impression of a cinder block is not a cinder block. A butterfly's touch on a cinder block is not a cinder block' (2013). He runs through a number of thought experiments of how we might attempt to know the block completely: by cataloging the process of its creation, by documenting its changes over time, by somehow being able to account for every particle of its composition . . . Yet these would still be insufficient, not because any unified whole beyond this accumulation of perspectival views would be a construction or a fiction, but rather precisely because the block *has* an essential reality. The block, in other words, is more real than we can ever know. The being of an object is simply not available to us, Morton insists, even though we may be capable of affecting that object or experiencing many of its qualities. Withdrawn, he maintains, does not refer to a state of temporary hiddenness or resistance to knowledge, it means beyond all forms of access.

As is partly demonstrated in Morton's example of the cinder block, one of the strengths of object-oriented philosophy is its seeming ability to think persistence and change concurrently. It places in check the 'radicalism' of philosophical views that reduce individual objects to the chaotic swirl of vital matter, while also avoiding the conservative tendency of fixing objects in a static or eternal state. Put simply, it asks the question: how can we account for the fact that an object is in a perpetual state of change, and yet we continue to recognize it as the same object? We could agree, for example, that a tree is never precisely the same from moment to moment (it is growing and decaying slightly, the sunlight is illuminating its branches differently as the angle of light shifts, its meaning for me changes according to my altering mood . . .), but we don't mistake it for another object. As Harman explains, 'Objects may change rapidly; they may be perceived differently by different observers; they remain opaque to all efforts of knowledge to master them. But the very condition of all change, perspectivism, and opacity is that objects have a *definite character* that can change, be perceived, and resist' (2012, p. 195, italics are his). There is consistency within things, despite our inability to know them completely. Objects, we might say, are always becoming different from themselves, but in a manner that is specific to themselves. Or as Morton puts it, 'objects are ontologically prior to their relations' (2012, p. 205), including their relations to themselves.

This object-oriented viewpoint is not entirely opposed to the theory of assemblage put forward by Bennett. According to this philosophy, objects may come together and form larger unities accordingly, but in doing so they create another object (Harman explains that each relation has the potential to create a new object) and the same situation of appearance and withdrawal would be manifested at the level of the new object. Morton refers to an infinite possible 'progress' of objects involved within larger or more complex objects (a tree object is part of a forest object, which is part of an eco-system object . . .), as well as an infinite 'regress' of smaller objects within that object (the tree object is composed of branch objects, which are composed of molecule objects . . .) (2012, pp. 208–9). One of the significant repercussions of this infinite progress and regress, is that the philosophy of Harman and Morton conceives of a world consisting of objects and nothing else, each with the same intrinsic rift between their withdrawn reality and their relations.

But given this process of infinite regress and progress, how can we possibly know if we are confronted with a discrete or autonomous object? And is this not a way to smuggle overmining and undermining tendencies in through the back door? If every relation has the potential of creating a new object, rather than referring to an individual tree would it not be more accurate to speak successively of an illuminated tree object, a shaded tree object, a tree being rustled by a slight wind object, a man leaning on tree object, etc.? Harman suggests that there are criteria we may turn to which enable us to recognize conditions for the existence of emergent entities in the world. He borrows a list from Manuel De Landa and uses the example of the Paris Metro to illustrate it (2009, pp. 161–2). First, emergent entities must exhibit 'emergent properties' – they must have features that are not discernible in any of their constituent parts (so the Paris Metro has effects that are not generated by its wheels, its turnstiles, etc.). Second, emergent entities possess 'redundant causality' – they can lose or replace a part without necessarily changing as a whole (the colour of the cars could change and we would still recognize the Paris Metro). Third, emergent entities act retroactively on their parts (the bumpiness of the track impacts the digestion of the passengers in a contextually specific manner). And finally, many parts of the emergent entity do not pre-exist it, but are actually generated by it (in-car advertising or fare dodgers become possible objects due to the existence of the Metro). Harman insists, 'Real emergence cannot be merely functional/relational, but must amount to the generation of new autonomous things with new autonomous qualities *whether [they relate] to anything else or not*' (2009, p. 163, italics are his). This is a reiteration of Harman's claim that an object is never exhausted by its relations – the Paris Metro continues to exist even when the workers are on strike and the doors are shut. It also retains the capacity to surprise us and resist us by continuing to reveal new and unexpected features.

With object-oriented philosophy we are faced with a somewhat bewildering sphere of activity in which relations and effects do occur (and frequently), yet without direct access to the reality of the things involved. Morton names the region 'out in front' of objects in which causality and sensual relations happen the 'aesthetic dimension' (2013). Put another way, 'every entity throws shadows of itself into the *interobjective* space, the sensual space that consists of relations between objects' (2013, italics are his). But his use of these spatial metaphors is somewhat misleading, for Morton insists that there is no such thing as a space or medium independent of objects. Nor is there such thing as object-independent time. Morton claims instead that 'space and time emanate from objects' (2013), in other words, that objects are always in a process of 'spacing' and 'timing' in a manner particular to them (2012, p. 216). His conviction that all qualities, processes and effects emanate from specific objects themselves allows him to envision an ecological thought without recourse to a neutral field of containment, such as an environment or nature. Ecologies, according to Morton, are strictly made up of objects, all existing in the dual and contradictory condition of being separate, autonomous and distinct, yet in 'aesthetic' relation with other objects.

So how then might we begin to connect the image of the world that Harman and Morton present us with – a weird world consisting of object upon object, and nothing more – with the discussions of infrastructural architecture outlined earlier? One of the fundamental perspectives encouraged by object-oriented philosophy is a distinct humbleness in the face of the things that surround us, what Bennett refers to as an ethics of 'theoretical modesty' (2012, p. 230). We may relate to objects (including infrastructural resource flows), interpret them, combine with them to form larger objects, but we will never master them. Object-oriented philosophy's adamant reminder of the excessive quality of objects, the reservoir of being that they always withdraw from us, places in check the infrastructural desire to bring natural, cultural and industrial ecologies together into seamlessly productive assemblages. Harman and Morton ask us to be attuned to the manner in which objects often resist our attempts at manipulation and refuse to participate in our systems of relations. From an object-oriented perspective, the breakdown of the Paris Metro is an expression of autonomy. In its enthusiasm to return to the realm of instrumentality the discourse of infrastructural architecture seldom acknowledges these elements of malfunction, systems failure and lack of control, which are endemic to all objects, and certainly infrastructural ones. It is, after all, when the highway bridge collapses or when the water supply runs dry that these otherwise invisible infrastructures come to our attention. Bennett's electrical grid, which 'by blacking out, lit up quite a lot' (2010b, p. 36), testifies to this actuality.

This is not to suggest, however, that object-oriented philosophy is an inherently defeatist or nihilistic position. The reality is that we do relate to and communicate with objects all the time. In fact, Harman's objects, despite their state of being withdrawn, have the capacity to beckon to us and compel us to engage with them at a deeper level. One of his most intriguing concepts is the notion of 'allure', a term he uses to describe the manner in which objects hint at the 'inscrutable reality' that lies behind their 'accessible theoretical, practical, or perceptual qualities' (2012, p. 187). And far from being a meaningless grasping towards what can never be attained, both Harman and Morton, defend the crucial role of the arts vis-à-vis the object. Since reality is only accessible indirectly or obliquely (within a sensual or 'aesthetic' dimension), practices that are comfortable operating within the realm of metaphor and allusion are particularly appropriate strategies for engagement. Like literature and visual art, architecture has the potential to work through this method of askance revelation and object-oriented philosophy may well inspire new forms of architectural or infrastructural poetics.

In reaction to some of their critiques of materialism, Bennett wonders if process/ systems-oriented and object-oriented philosophy aren't closer in thought than Harman and Morton care to admit. Could there be an element of iconoclastic pleasure in their claims of ontological incompatibility? Bennett attempts to bridge the divide by suggesting:

> perhaps there is no need to choose between objects or their relations . . . why not aim for a theory that toggles between both kinds or magnitudes of 'unit'? One would then understand 'objects' to be those swirls of matter, energy, and incipience that hold themselves together long enough to view with the strivings of other objects, including the indeterminate momentum of the throbbing whole. (2012, p. 227)

Although Bennett's appeal for conciliation is well taken and there are clearly many lines of affiliation between the two philosophical positions, the significantly different viewpoints that object-oriented philosophy tends to invoke should also not be discounted. For one, although there are some common reference points, such as Latour and De Landa, object-oriented thinkers bring some very different figures to the philosophical table. Heidegger and Husserl are both palpably present in Harman's writing and Morton has referred to his object-oriented approach as post-Derridean. The inclusion, or perhaps re-inclusion, of these philosophers and the diminished role of thinkers such as Deleuze, Bergson and Whitehead creates a genuinely different atmosphere of thought. Harman and Morton also tend to gravitate towards different kinds of objects and relations than their new materialist counterparts. While relational thinkers are drawn to rapidly changing objects and networks in a state of dynamic flux, object-oriented philosophers often linger on stubbornly enduring things. New materialists emphasize our similarities and potential commune with matter in general, while object-orientated philosophers highlight the radical otherness of the objects that surround us.

I would argue that these shifts in perspective bring into view a number of objects that are particularly relevant to infrastructural concerns. Morton, for example, makes frequent reference to what he terms 'hyperobjects': objects that are, relative to humans, especially large or long lasting. He points to the example of global warming, an entity that could continue to impact the earth for another hundred thousand years. 'It's almost inconceivable', he writes, 'Yet we see the effects of global warming all around us: we see charts form NASA that plot temperature rises; we feel rain on our heads at strange times of the year; we witness drought. None of these experiences are directly global warming:

they are its aesthetic effects' (2013). An object like global warming is ontologically and temporally beyond us, yet it is still one we are obligated to contend with, relate to, and mitigate. Our survival depends on it. Object-oriented philosophy occupies rather than shies away from this inherently aporetic political terrain. And, as Morton notes, it is precisely the things we ourselves produce, from Styrofoam to plutonium, that produce these ethical and political quagmires. As Morton notes, 'Humans have manufactured materials that are already beyond the normal scope of our comprehension' (2010, p. 130). The human-made materials residing within the mounds of Fresh Kills are precisely these kinds of contradictory 'hyper-objects', made invisible by a marvellous act of design and engineering, yet still there beneath the surface of Lifescape. Despite their confinement, they continue to reveal their presence – through the leachate and methane gas they gradually release or by their involvement in an expanding network of waste management. And many of these objects will certainly outlast us; they are our enduring legacy. This fact does seem to require a greater degree of intellectual and design modesty than we have thus far exhibited. Perhaps infrastructural architecture must come to find these radically resistant objects as alluring as the more 'productive' flows and processes with which it currently engages.

This essay is an appeal for an encounter to occur between some of the most promising debates within architectural theory and practice and some of the most exciting developments in contemporary philosophy. The common ground they share is quite evident. Like new materialism and object-oriented philosophy, infrastructural architecture is firmly committed to ecological perspectives, considerations of the non-human, and cultivating sensitivity towards the 'thingness' of the world. Thankfully, the beginnings of a more sustained encounter between these streams of design and philosophy are already beginning to emerge. Relational, process and systems-oriented thought have underpinned infrastructural architecture and landscape urbanism from the outset and materialist thinkers such as Manuel De Landa and Keller Easterling have informed the discipline from within. Hopefully the current prohibition on philosophy will ease and new materialists from outside the domain of architecture, like Jane Bennett, will be welcomed into the discussion. Despite, or perhaps because of, its more acute alterity and unfamiliarity this process of architectural inclusion has already begun for object-oriented philosophy. Harman has been particular active in forging this encounter, appearing in recent events in London organized by The Bartlett School of Architecture and The Architecture Exchange. In the latter, architectural theorists and historians such as Peg Rawes, Jonathan Hale and Adam Sharr engaged in direct discussion with object-oriented philosophy and Harman himself, enquiring 'Is There an Object-Oriented Architecture?' The most recent publication of TARP, the journal of the Graduate Architecture and Urban Design programme at Pratt Institute takes on a similar question. For the moment, the responses tend towards the sceptical rather than speculative. In both his TARP submission and his response to Harman's Bartlett talk, for example, Patrik Schumacher expresses doubt as to whether object-oriented philosophy will be as instrumental to architecture as the systems-theory he espouses (2012). But as this essay suggests, pragmatism is not the only possible mode of exchange between philosophy and design. New materialism and object-oriented approaches may provoke a different form of encounter, one based on rethinking rather than instrumentalizing infrastructural assumptions.

Notes

1   Stan Allen, once a co-principal of the Field Operations landscape architecture firm, has recently suggested that landscape urbanism has not entirely lived up to its urban and infrastructural promise and has been too relegated to park planning, however ambitious these designs may be. He now puts forward the notion of the 'landform building', inspired by geology as much as biology, as a way to bring architectural structure back into the design mix. The architectural megaform of the 'artificial mountain' is the inspirational model of the design current. He writes, 'Landform building learns from the recent experiments of Landscape Urbanism and landscape ecology at the same time as it recuperates the specificity of architectural expertise in an expanded field' (2011, p. 34).

2   Rather than censor the kind of anthropomorphic language I've used here, Bennett finds it to be a potential useful method of facilitating our ability to bridge the apparent divisions between the human and non-human realms.

Bibliography

Allen, S. (1999), *Points and Lines: Diagrams and Projects for the City*. New York: Princeton Architectural Press.

— (2011), 'From the Biological to the Geological', in S. Allen and M. McQuade (eds), *Landform Building: Architecture's New Terrain*. Baden, Switzerland: Lars Müller Publishers, pp. 20–37.

Ascher, K. and Marech, W. (2005), *The Works: Anatomy of a City*. New York: Penguin.

Bennett, J. (2010a), 'A Vitalist Stopover on the Way to a New Materialism', in D. Coole and S. Frost (eds), *New Materialisms: Ontology, Agency, and Politics*. Durham: Duke University Press, pp. 47–69.

— (2010b), *Vibrant Matter: A Political Ecology of Things*. Durham: Duke University Press.

— (2012), 'Systems and Things: A Response to Graham Harman and Timothy Morton', *New Literary History*, 43, 2, pp. 225–33.

Berger, A. (2006), *Drosscape: Wasting Land in Urban America*. New York: Princeton Architectural Press.

Bryant, L., Srnicek, N. and Harman, G. (2011), 'Towards a Speculative Philosophy', in L. Bryant, N. Srnicek and G. Harman (eds), *The Speculative Turn: Continental Materialism and Realism*. Melbourne: re.press, pp. 1–18.

Corner, J. (2006), 'Terra Fluxus', in C. Waldheim (ed.), *The Landscape Urbanism Reader*. New York: Princeton Architectural Press, pp. 21–34.

Cuff, D. (2010), 'Architecture as Public Work', in K. Stoll and S. Lloyd (eds), *Infrastructure As Architecture: Designing Composite Networks*. Berlin: Jovis, pp. 18–25.

Cuff, D. and Sherman, R. (2011), 'Introduction', in D. Cuff and R. Sherman (eds), *Fast-Forward Urbanism*. New York: Princeton Architectural Press.

Easterling, K. (2010), 'Disposition and Active Form', in K. Stoll and S. Lloyd (eds), *Infrastructure As Architecture: Designing Composite Networks*. Berlin: Jovis, pp. 96–9.

Field Operations (2002), 'Lifescape', *Praxis*, 4, pp. 20–8.

Frampton, K. (2004), 'Stocktaking 2004: Nine Questions About the Present and Future of Design', *Harvard Design Magazine*, 20, Spring–Summer, pp. 4–52.

Fresh Kills: Landfill to Landscape – International Design Competition (2001). Available at: <www.nyc.gov/html/dcp/pdf/fkl/about_fkl.pdf>.

Harman, G. (2002), *Tool-Being: Heidegger and the Metaphysics of Objects*. Chicago: Open Court Publishing.

— (2009), *Prince of Networks: Bruno Latour and Metaphysic*. Melbourne: re.press.

— (2011a), 'On the Undermining of Objects: Grant, Bruno, and Radical Philosophy', in L. Bryant, N. Srnicek and G. Harman (eds), *The Speculative Turn: Continental Materialism and Realism*. Melbourne: re.press, pp. 21–40.

— (2011b), 'Autonomous Objects', *New Formations*, 71, pp. 125–30.

— (2012), 'The Well-wrought Broken Hammer', *New Literary History*, 43, 2, pp. 183–203.

Koolhaas, R. (1998), *S, M, L, XL: Small, Medium, Large, Extra Large*. New York: Monacelli Press.

Lateral Office (2011), *Pamphlet Architecture 30: Coupling: Strategies for Infrastructural Opportunism*. New York: Princeton Architectural Press.

Morton, T. (2010), *The Ecological Thought*. Cambridge: Harvard University Press.

— (2012), 'An Object-oriented Defense of Poetry', *New Literary History*, 43, 2, pp. 205–24.

— (2013), *Realist Magic: Objects, Ontology, Causality*. [online] Open Humanities Press. Available at: <http://quod.lib.umich.edu/o/ohp/13106496.0001.001> [accessed 20 July 2013].

New York City Department of Planning (2001), 'Fresh Kills: Landfill to Landscape – International Design Competition'. [online] New York City Gov. Available at: <http://www.nyc.gov/html/dcp/html/fkl/fkl2.shtml> [accessed 20 July 2013].

Schumacher, P. (2012), 'Architecture's Next Ontological Innovation'. [online] Patrik Schumacher. Available at: <http://www.patrikschumacher.com/Texts/Tarp.htm> [accessed 20 July 2013].

Schumacher, P. and Rogner, C. (2001), 'After Ford'. [online] Patrik Schumacher. Available at: <http://www.patrikschumacher.com/Texts/AfterFord.htm> [accessed 20 July 2013].

Sieverts, T. (2003), *Cities without Cities: An Interpretation of the Zwischenstadt*. New York: Spon Press.

Somol, R. E. and Whiting, S. (2002), 'Notes Around the Doppler Effect and Other Moods of Modernism', *Perspecta*, 33, pp. 72–7.

Waldheim, C. (2002), 'Landscape Urbanism: A Genealogy', *Praxis*, 4, pp. 10–17.

— (2006), 'Landscape as Urbanism', in C. Waldheim (ed.), *The Landscape Urbanism Reader*. New York: Princeton Architectural Press, pp. 35–54.

9

Casa Come Me: Rocks, Ruins and Shells in Kracauer and Chatwin

Graeme Gilloch

'Moi aussi'

It begins in the bedroom. The husband, Paul Javal (Michel Picoli), leans under the covers. His wife, Camille (Brigitte Bardot), lies naked face-down on top of the bed. She begins a coquettish little game: 'Do you love my feet?' she asks. 'Oui', he replies. Camille continues, working her way up her own body, naming each part in turn – ankles, thighs, buttocks, breasts, nipples, shoulders, face – asking the same question, and each time receiving the affirmative answer: 'Oui'. Later in the day there will be another, far less playful amorous interrogation: Camille, now 'acting strangely', exudes an irritation and indifference that perplexes Paul and her answers, now evasive, now ambivalent, provide him with no reassurance of her love. In a series of long takes lasting cumulatively just under 30 minutes of screen time, they prowl around the rooms of their still unfinished suburban apartment, walking through door frames awaiting glass panels, sprawling on a vivid red sofa, bypassing a room where a stepladder and assorted pots of paint indicate decoration in progress, typing away at an unfinished story. Perhaps Camille's ill-temper has something to do with Paul's earlier flirtation with Francesca (Giorgi Moll), assistant, interpreter and general gopher to the brash American film producer Prokosch (Jack Palance). Paul has spent the day at the crumbling Cinecitta studios in Rome, where the producer has invited him to rewrite the screenplay for a film version of the *Odyssey* currently being shot on location by none other than Fritz Lang (played by himself). The work will enable Paul to buy the apartment outright: he and Camille will realize their dream of having a home of their own. After meeting the celebrated director and reviewing the meagre film footage so far, Prokosch invites them all to his rambling house out of town, driving the reluctant Camille in his scarlet sports car while Paul is left to take a taxi and Francesca peddles there on her bike. But perhaps Camille's mood has nothing to do with Francesca. Maybe the lecherous Prokosch has made unwanted advances. His attentions and intentions are certainly obvious to everyone, everyone that is except Paul who remains strangely, blithely, unconcerned throughout. Camille is certainly reluctant to accept the invitation to join Paul at the producer's stunning modernist villa perched high on a cliff-top promontory, the Capo Masullo, on the island of Capri, where the script is to be reworked as filming continues. But notwithstanding her objections, Paul will still accept both the commission and the invitation to Capri; Camille will accompany him there. The action now shifts to the island where this quintet of eccentric figures will continue their erudite conversations and ruminations on film, money, writing and love. The relationship between Camille and Paul continues to disintegrate and, finally, she leaves husband and villa with Prokosch at the wheel. A fatal car crash awaits them. Paul, blasé to the end, decides against the rewrite and leaves Lang filming Odysseus's first sight of home on the flat roof top of the villa. All this callousness and calamity, all this contempt, still lie ahead of our on–off lovers but the signs are already unmistakable. Back in the bedroom, with Camille's little game at an end, Paul says: 'I love you totally, tenderly, tragically'; she replies: 'Moi aussi, Paul'.

Dreamers and dreamhouses

All undergirded by contempt, all set to a lush orchestral score by Georges Delarue, narcissism, film, architecture, the body, sexuality, mythology and home-coming are the principal themes of Jean Luc Godard's *Le Mépris* (1963), a film celebrating its 50th anniversary this year. Speculation has it that the opening bedroom scene was a questionable and gratuitous late addition to the film in an attempt to boost audiences. But for me, this perfect moment of self-obsession and self-adoration is wholly in keeping with the motifs and mood of the film. And it is another connection to my own interest here: not Camille's self-love of her own beautiful body, but another physical manifestation of narcissism, architectural rather than corporeal. My concern is with the extraordinary edifice that, with its flat roof terrace, sweeping steps, peeling red paint, and panoramic sea-view windows, Godard chose as the setting for the film's 20 minutes on Capri: Prokosch's villa is the Casa Malaparte. This in turn is one of the three remarkable residences built by eccentric visitors to the island described by the English writer Bruce Chatwin in his 1984 essay '(Self-Love) Among the Ruins' published in *Vanity Fair*. Coincidentally, the film was based on the novel *Il Disprezzo* (translated under the suggestive title *A Ghost at Noon*) by the Italian writer Alberto Moravia (1907–90),[1] who in 1930 started working with the Turin-based *La Stampa* newspaper,[2] under the editorship of one Curzio Malaparte (born Kurt Erich Suckert, 1898–1957), erstwhile Fascist, post-war Communist, a man described by Antonio Gramsci as 'an unrestrained social climber, excessively vain, and a chameleon-like snob', who 'For the sake of success . . . was capable of any villainy' (Gramsci, 2012, p. 318).

In this chapter I will not deal with the other two of Chatwin's triumvirate of 'dreamhouses' (1996, p. 151) on Capri, the Villa Lysis built by the Baron Jacques Adelswärd-Fersen, and Axel Munthe's 'pretentious museum-sanctuary, the Villa San Michele' (Munthe, 1994, p. 156)[3] but instead explore some correspondences between Malaparte's *casamatta* – a blockhouse or a madhouse, depending on which way you read that word in Italian – and another quasi-Futurist fantasy close by on the Amalfi coast: Gilbert Clavel's renovations of, and then troglodytic excavations beneath a so-called Saracen tower near the village of Positano, the bizarre subject of Siegfried Kracauer's 1925 essay 'Rock Mania in Positano' [*Felsenwahn in Positano*]. My concern with Kracauer's feuilleton piece, one of many reports from 'elsewhere' that he penned for the *FZ* and which he later selected for inclusion in his *Strassen in Berlin und Anderswo* collection from 1964, is two-fold: as part of an ongoing exploration of the encounter between Critical Theory and the cities of the Mediterranean;[4] and, partly also as an examination of the very notion of *anderswo* itself as a spatial motif in Kracauer's work and as a corollary of other categories such as 'distraction' (*Zerstreuung*).

Indeed, it is this notion of the 'elsewhere' that is the key inspiration for this essay for, in bringing together Chatwin and Kracauer, we find ourselves in the presence not only of two of the most sublime essayists of the twentieth century, but also, significantly, two of the least 'homely', that is to say, ones for whom settled homes and domesticity were themselves *terra incognita*. Having identified and lamented the existential condition of the modern metropolitan individual as one of 'spiritually shelterless' [*geistig obdachlos*],[5] a term highly indebted to Georg Lukács's famous invocation of the 'transcendental homelessness' expressed in the novel form,[6] Kracauer himself also comes to speak of his own prolonged experience of exile, first in France and then in the United States, as definitive of an 'extraterritorial' life,[7] and indeed he comes to extol the possibilities, indeed the necessities, of contemporary intellectual 'vagabondage' and estrangement.[8] And the ever itinerant Chatwin, who first made his literary name as a travel writer with his account of his impromptu expedition to Patagonia in 1974,[9] repeatedly asserts the virtues of peripatetic pedestrian journeys and, indeed, of nomadism as the true human condition.[10] 'The best thing', he writes, 'is to walk' (Chatwin, 1996, p. 103). Significantly, both of these writers lived lives *unterwegs* and *anderswo*.

My interest in these two extraordinary and enigmatic structures, the Torre Clavel and the Casa Malaparte, is threefold: (i) as architectural follies and fantasies, they constitute a pair of 'dreamhouses' (*Traumhäuser*) which combine in different ways elements of the most modern and the most archaic as part of a revitalized mythology;[11] (ii) each constitutes a 'home like me' and, as such, they form 'shells' bearing every detail and trace of their outré former occupants. These structures now remain as remnants or ruins from which the living organic body has long since departed; (iii) they both incorporate and invoke a particular and peculiar kind of 'homesickness' [*Heimweh*]. My argument, then, is that the notion of a *casa come me* involves a complex and curious synthesis of narcissism and nostalgia.

Into the labyrinth

From the outset of his article, Kracauer looks to invoke the mythical atmosphere of the Amalfi coast on which the little town of Positano stands – 'elemental powers dominate the place'[12] he notes before adding 'magic sweeps over the place. It is the enclave of lost forces which have found refuge in the landscape of antiquity and now appear incarnate' (Kracauer, 1987, p. 44).[13] But in writing these lines, Kracauer's tongue is firmly planted in his cheek. Having set such an elevated tone, his own arrival on board some old, creaking steamship is scarcely that of the returning hero: 'The steamer is a floating antiquity; it once served Odysseus on his wanderings. The wax has long since melted away, only the mast to which he had himself bound is still on show in the Naples museum' (Kracauer, 1987, p. 44).[14]

Gilbert Clavel (1883–1927), whose chronic ill-health as a child had resulted in spinal curvature and a weak constitution, had arrived years earlier in the hope that the warm climate would prove beneficial. He was to stay and transform the sixteenth-century watchtower on a promontory outside the town into the most eccentric of residences, not by building upwards and outwards, but by blasting and boring inwards and downwards into the very cliffs themselves. Kracauer observes:

> Clavel had not come to stay – he stayed on and blasted. The whispering in the kettle must have lured and held him. He blasted incessantly for seventeen years; it still isn't at an end. Something snapped in him, it drove him into the elements into which he doggedly cramped himself. Possessed by the powers of Positano he became an architect, an engineer. He constructed in the service of the inconstructible, soberly devised intricate passages. (Kracauer, 1987, p. 45)[15]

Part castle, part cave,[16] and all acquired for the princely sum of just 180 lire, Clavel's renovations and excavations, all his mechanical mine-workings, resulted in a curious subterranean cellular structure, a warren of interconnected intrusions and incursions into the rock: spiralling steps, chambers, galleries, tunnels and passageways, columns and arches. The erstwhile architect, Dr Ingenieur Kracauer beholds this mineralogical honeycomb with a mixture of astonishment and not a little wry amusement. 'Gilbert Clavel's rock site has nothing in common with human architecture' he claims,[17] adding: 'That it is inhabited is the only homely thing about these innards which burrow their way with no sense of direction, no beginning or end into the crusts. The bowels of the earth slip back indistinguishable in height and depth' (Kracauer, 1987, p. 43).[18]

For Kracauer, this most unhomely of dreamhouses and its mole-like owner are suggestive of the mythological in a number of complex ways. First, just as Freud famously uses the city of Rome as a metaphor for the unconscious and presents the reader with a veritable cityscape of memory in his *Civilisation and Its Discontents*,[19] so one might envisage Clavel's digging and dynamiting as a descent into ever-deeper and more archaic levels of the human psyche and instinctual structures. It is a drilling down into one's very own being, into the manifold layers and levels of one's 'inner life'. This interplay of the 'inner life' of the (extraordinary) individual and its expression in the work of art (here: the work of architecture) is a constant motif in Kracauer's writings and owes its origins to his reading of Simmel and his penchant for *Lebensphilosophie*. Clavel's life is made manifest not by means of 'surface level phenomena' (Kracauer, 1995b, p. 75) but rather by his underground exertions. It is as if he has taken not just seriously but literally Walter Benjamin's injunction in his 1932 'Berlin Chronicle' that whoever seeks to remember should conduct himself like a man digging in what amounts to a kind of archaeological excavation of the self.[20] And like Benjamin's tireless spade-worker, it is not the inventory of discoveries that is most significant, but rather the very act of digging itself that comes to constitute its own passionate pleasure, its own 'dark joy' (Benjamin, 1999b, p. 611).

Clavel's subterranean strivings are doubly irrational. On the one hand, they provide an image of the penetration of archaic levels of the self. Kracauer writes:

'Everything perishes in Positano' – the quotation comes from Clavel. He is familiar with the mythological Horde. It is easy for it to wreck the weak unity of civilised humankind. Amassed the elemental figures trample the consciousness, playfully cast aside the understanding, which is not their equal in birth. Through the corroded layers of the interior, they summon the depths, the dark. Formless instincts, nameless desires, drift to the surface, vent themselves with abandon, awoken by the shadow forces whose wings conceal the light. (Kracauer, 1987, p. 48)[21]

And, on the other, they are bereft of any logical purpose or ostensible goal, empty acts of emptying. Clavel is no Orpheus, venturing into the darkness to bring his beloved Eurydice back into the world of the living above. No: this is an endless blasting and burrowing undertaken seemingly and simply for its own sake. Like Sisyphus, this is a labour of 'Felsenwahn' – only it is not a punishment for some terrible transgression and there are no vengeful gods to demand and enforce it. It is as if the 'senseless urge to eat ever more into the rock' (Kracauer, 1987, p. 49)[22] were some kind of a primal compulsion emanating from the very depths into which Clavel descends, yet one coupled with the 'grandiose technical outlay' (Kracauer, 1987, p. 49)[23] underwriting present-day engineering and mining. Clavel's warren of tunnels is without destination:

His spatial effusions are of gigantic absurdity, a flight before the catastrophe which threatens the soul. Since the depths know of no conclusion, they are entangled in the infinite; and since there are no longer gods, they run dry. No Minotaur sits in Clavel's labyrinth, indeed it is no labyrinth but a chaos – mythology in terms of form, but without mythological content. (Kracauer, 1987, p. 49)[24]

No minotaur; no Ariadne; a manic maze with a vacant centre, not even Clavel himself. What Kracauer encounters on the cliffs outside Positano is a shell, a mineral structure that remains and bears the vestiges of a life that has now departed, an intact exoskeleton which now echoes only to the sound of the sea.

Clavel's modern mythological architectural fantasy – not a crystal palace redolent of the fairy-tale, but a Palaeolithic palace under the sway of primordial powers – calls to mind two rather different moments in Benjamin's work. The first is a passage in Convolute R ('Mirrors') of Benjamin's *Arcades Project*, when the now-ruinous interiorized shopping streets of Paris appear to him as ancient caverns festooned with fossils:

As the rocks of the Miocene or Eocene in places bear the imprint of monstrous creatures from those ages, so today arcades dot the metropolitan landscape like caves containing the fossil remains of a banished monster: the consumer of the pre-imperial era of capitalism, the last dinosaur of Europe. On the walls of these caverns their immemorial flora, the commodity, luxuriates and enters, like cancerous tissue, into the most irregular combinations. (Benjamin, 1999a, p. 540)

Like the now derelict and soon to be demolished arcade, Clavel's underground dreamhouse is precisely such a ruinous site of petrified existence, the afterlife of the extinct. The second concerns the story of a wondrous Chinese painter, Wu Daozi of the Tang Dynasty, mentioned in Benjamin's famous 1936 'Work of Art' essay, a great master of landscape who, one day when his picture was finally completed and his friends had gathered around to admire it, took his leave of the assembled host and vanished into the very image he had produced.[25] For Clavel, too, is seemingly engaged in such a dialectics of disappearance, of de-materialization, removing rock so as to remove himself, a solitary creature ultimately absorbed in and by his own outlandish creation. Indeed, his death in his native Basel in 1927, two years after Kracauer's visit to Positano, seems at the same time the very completion of this lifework, the finishing touch of his extraordinary, elemental *Gesamtkunstwerk*. And one is tempted to say a little more here. For the lung infection which had been, from his early childhood days, ceaselessly eating away at him, eroding him from within, corresponds to his own relentless etching and carving in the interior of the rock at Positano. Hollowed out, hollowing out – Clavel's own physical sufferings and suffocations found enduring expression in the Torre Clavel: as a dreamhouse of consumption it was not, as Benjamin imagines, a locus of cancerous cellular proliferation but rather an idiosyncratic architecture of evacuation and evisceration. The more he worked on his senseless scheme, the less it became, so to speak. And as such, his mine-like house was indeed a veritable *casa come me*.

Memento mori, memento mare

Just as Clavel's 'Felsenwahn' bemused Kracauer, so Chatwin struggles to find the right words for the Villa Malaparte, 'one of the strangest habitations in the Western world' (Chatwin, 1996, p. 162). Built between 1938 and 1941, this alien edifice defies simple description:

> A Homeric ship gone aground? A modern altar to Poseidon? A house of the future – or of the prehistoric past? A surrealist house? A Fascist house? . . . What we do know is that Malaparte asked his architect, Adalberto Libera,[26] to build him a *'casa come me'* – 'a house like me' – which would be *'triste, dura, sever,'* as 'sad, hard and severe' as he hoped himself to be. (Chatwin, 1996, p. 162)

Like Clavel's tunnellings into the earth, the Casa Malaparte is also a monument to the narcissism and mythomania of its occupant. Clavel's work is an intraterrestrial, existential contest with fate: feverishly tearing away at the innards of the earth as nature gradually consumes his own insides, excavating a secret but grandiose burial chamber fit for a pagan hero. At first sight, such hidden labours seem the very antithesis of the Villa Malaparte. This modernist 'monastery bunker' (Chatwin, 1996, p. 166), an accretion stuck on the side of the cliff top, makes no attempt to blend into the landscape, to be consumed by it, but rather to stamp the distinctive and unmistakable mark of the human upon it: orthogonal in design, mathematical in its exactitude, it proclaims the triumph of pure forms over Nature's imperfections and approximations. Far from vanishing below the surface, the architect here transforms Nature into mere spectacle to be enjoyed from the villa's panoramic windows. But here, too, one finds a resonance with mythic forms and fantasies. As Chatwin observes, Malaparte himself envisaged some kind of synthesis, a fusion indeed of classical antiquity and mechanized futurity:

> a house of the machine age that would nevertheless preserve the most ancient values of the Mediterranean. And unlike the 'Apollonian' temples of classical Greece, with their forests of columns and 'roofs set down from above', this building was to rise, like a Minoan sanctuary from the sea itself.

> The walls were the colour of bull's blood, the windows were like the windows of a liner, and there was a wedge-shaped ramp of steps which slanted, like a sacred way, up to the terrace roof. Here, every morning, Malaparte would perform a ritual of gymnastics, alone, while the women who were in love with him would watch from the cliffs above. (Chatwin, 1996, p. 166)

While Clavel retreats into his dreamhouse, hiding away his sickly body, Malaparte arranges his as a platform, a stage, on which to exhibit his own athletic prowess to admiring onlookers. Indeed, conceived as extension of his beloved self, the *casa come me* is, of course, the most perfect example of both narcissism and shell.

It is the French philosopher Gaston Bachelard who provides us with the most charming stories and dialectics of the shell in *The Poetics of Space*, his famous phenomenology of human and non-human habitations first published in 1958. Like Malaparte's monument, the shell is also a triumph of perfect 'transcendental geometry' (Bachelard, 1998, p. 105) which can come to form a house that 'turns out to be so beautiful, that it would be a sacrilege even to dream of living in it' (Bachelard, 1998, p. 107).[27] Bachelard notes how the shell not only constitutes 'an entire branch of dream houses' (Bachelard, 1998, p. 120), but also, as a 'primal image' (Bachelard, 1998, p. 121), prompts a myriad of fantasies: 'if we were to allow ourselves to indulge in all the daydreams of inhabited stone there would be no end to it' (Bachelard, 1998, p. 115).

This notion of 'inhabited stone' returns us momentarily to Clavel, a man for whom 'life's principal effort' became to make himself a shell, a man we see 'alive in the dialectics of what is hidden and what is manifest' (Bachelard, 1998, p. 111) as Bachelard puts it, a man indeed whose home, 'a synthesis of house, shell and cave', corresponds precisely to Bernard Palissey's daydream of a whole fortified mineral city built within and out of the rocks of the earth.[28]

In shells there is, Bachelard observes, another dialectic at work too: 'the dialectics of creatures that are free and others that are in fetters: and what can we not expect from those that are unfettered!' (Bachelard, 1998, p. 110). Beauty and narcissism, love and the wish to escape the unhomely home, to break free of one's bonds – all this brings us back to *Le Mépris*. Godard's film is one in which the main characters spend much of their time circling in and around two homes: the apartment Paul and Camille hope to buy – an unremarkable collection of box rooms in an ordinary box of a building, a banal dwelling that forms a potential future 'home like them'; and, Prokosch's remarkable cliff-top villa, both utterly spectacular and utterly soulless, showy and shallow, a veritable home like him. It is, of course, no coincidence that the film being made is the story of Odysseus, for this is the great mythological tale of incessant journeying and final homecoming. It is a story of 'nostalgia' understood here in its literal sense: pain / sickness [*algia*] for home [*nostos*]. This notion of homesickness is precisely the subject of the conversation on Capri between Paul and Fritz Lang as they wander down the steps to the Casa Malaparte. In this, Paul challenges the conventional reading of the story: is this really the tale of a man who longs to return home but whose journeys are endlessly prolonged by a jealous God (Poseidon), such that the ever-faithful Penelope must engage in her own cunning strategy of weaving and unpicking to ward off her ill-fated suitors? Why did Odysseus leave in the first place? Paul asks. It is not homesickness that brings Odysseus home after so many years, rather, it was homesickness – sick of being at home in the first place – that set him on his expedition to the walls of Troy and then across the seas on his myriad adventures. The Casa Malaparte and Clavel's constructions are precisely such sickly homes, meaningless and moribund, from which one wishes to depart. On the roof of the Villa Malaparte, Lang films Odysseus looking into the distance, supposedly spying his homeland for the first time in all those long years. It is a home *seen from the casa come me*. For such itinerants, home is always *elsewhere*. Here we have, then, not the 'transcendental homelessness' of the modern novel form perhaps, but rather the 'transcendental homesickness' of the film.

A contempt for home and the homely: is this not what fatefully prompts Camille to leave Paul? And what is left for him at the end. Seemingly unmoved by Camille's death, he is readily reconciled to his shell and willingly embraces his final isolation:

> We know perfectly well that to inhabit a shell we must be alone. By living this image, one knows that one has accepted solitude.

> To live alone: there's a great dream! The most lifeless, the most physically absurd image, such as that of living in a shell, can serve as the origin of such a dream. For it is a dream that, in life's moments of great sadness is shared by everybody, both weak and strong, in revolt against the injustices of men and fate. (Bachelard, 1998, p. 123)

Paul will no doubt return to the little dream apartment where it all began and make himself as at home there, as comfortable there, as timely as a 'ghost at noon'.

Notes

1   In an even stranger coincidence, Moravia wrote a 'full-page "rave" review' of Chatwin's final novel, *Utz* (1998a) following its publication in 1988. When Chatwin learned of this on 15 January 1989, he reportedly smiled and said: 'Better than the

Booker' (Chatwin and Shakespeare (eds), 2012, p. 525). Chatwin, who was at the time being nursed in the final stages of AIDS, lost consciousness the next day and was transferred from his home in Seillans to a hospital in nearby Nice where he died on 18 January aged just 48.

2 Moravia also later published in Malaparte's 'cultural review' *Prospettive* (see AR, p. 165).

3 First published in 1929, Munthe's own self-aggrandizing account of the building, *The Story of San Michele* was to become a best-seller.

4 Especially Kracauer and Walter Benjamin in southern France and Italy.

5 See Kracauer, 1998, p. 88.

6 See Lukács, 1978.

7 Reflecting on his own experiences of dislocation and invoking Georg Simmel's figure of the stranger, Kracauer writes in his unfinished, posthumously published study of history and historiography: 'I am thinking of the exile who as an adult person has been forced to leave his country or else has left it of his own free will. As he settles elsewhere, all those loyalties, expectations, and aspirations that comprise so large a part of his being are automatically cut off from their roots. His life history is disrupted, his "natural" self relegated to the background of his mind. To be sure, his inevitable efforts to meet the challenge of an alien environment will affect his outlook, his whole mental make-up. But since the self he was continues to smolder beneath the person he is about to become, his identity is bound to be in a state of flux; and the odds are that he will never fully belong to the community to which he now in a way belongs. (Nor will its members readily think of him as one of theirs.) In fact, he has ceased to "belong." Where then does he live? In the near vacuum of extraterritoriality . . . The exile's true mode of existence is that of a stranger' (1995a, pp. 83–4).

8 Kracauer notes: 'It is only in this state of self-effacement, or homelessness, that the historian can commune with the material of his concern. . . . A stranger to world evoked by the sources, he is faced with the task – the exile's task – of penetrating its outward appearances, so that he may learn to understand that world from within' (1995).

9 First published in 1977. See Chatwin (1998b).

10 In the essay 'It's a Nomad Nomad World' Chatwin writes: 'Evolution intended us to be travellers. Settlement for any length of time, in cave or castle, has at best been a sporadic condition in the history of man. Prolonged settlement has a vertical axis of some ten thousand years, a drop in the ocean of evolutionary time. We are travellers from birth. Our mad obsession with technological progress is a response to barriers in the way of our geographical progress' (1996 p. 102).

11 In coining this notion of 'dreamhouses' ['*Traumhäuser*'] in *The Arcades Project*, Benjamin's focus was, of course, on the 'Dream houses of the collective: arcades, winter gardens, panoramas, factories, wax museums, casinos, railway stations' (Benjamin, 1999a p. 404), that is to say, on *public* buildings and spaces constituting the modern cityscape. The dreamhouses discussed in this chapter are, by contrast, private dwellings far removed from urban life.

12 'Die elementarischen Mächte beherrschen den Ort' (Kracauer, 1987, p. 44).

13 'Zauberei fegt über den Ort. Er ist die Enklave verschollener Gewalten, die in der antikischen Landschaft ein Refugium gewonnen haben und nun leibhaft erscheinen' (Kracauer, 1987, p. 44).

14 'Das Dampfschiff ist ein schwimmendes Altertum, es hat dem Odysseus einst zu m seinen Irrfahrten gedient. Längst ist das Wachs geschmolzen, nur der Mast noch,

an den er sich festbinden liess, wird im Museum zu Neapel gezeigt' (Kracauer, 1987, p. 44).

15   'Clavel war nicht gekommen um zu bleiben – er blieb und sprengte. Das Geraun in dem Kessel mochte ihn locken und halten. Er sprengte unablässig, sprengete siebzehn Jahre hindurch, noch ist das Ende nicht da. Etwas war aufgebrochen in ihm, es jagte ihn unter die Elemente, in die er zäh sich verkrampfte. Besessen von den positanischen Kräften ward er zum Architekten, zum Ingenieur. Er konstriuierte im Dienste des Unkonstruierbaren, erdachte nüchtern verworrene Führungen' (Kracauer, 1987, p. 45).

16   Kracauer captures this upward projection and downward introjection with a dental metaphor. Comparing the Saracen tower itself to a 'broken tooth', Kracauer writes: 'Clavel has drilled down to the very root and clapped a crown on top [Clavel hat ihn bis zum Wurzelende ausgebohrt und eine Krone ihm aufgestülpt]' (Kracauer, 1987, p. 46)

17   'Gilbert Clavel's Felsenstaette hat mit menschlicher Architektur nichts gemein' (Kracauer, 1987, p. 43).

18   'Das es bewohnt wird, ist das einzige Haushafte an diesem Gekröse, das richtungslos, ohne Beginn und Abschluss, in die Krusten sich wülht. Ununterschiedbar nach Höhe und Tiefe gleiten das Erdinnere zurück' (Kracauer, 1987, p. 43).

19   See Freud, 2004.

20   See Benjamin, 1999b, p. 611.

21   '"Alles geht in Positano zugrunde" – das Wort stammt von Clavel. Er kennt die mythologische Horde. Die schwache Einheit des zivilisierten Menschen zu zertrümmern, ist ihr ein leichtes. Gesammelt überrumplen die Elementargestalten das Bewusstsein, schieben die ihnen nicht ebenbürtige Verständigkeit spielend beiseite. Durch die zersetzen Schichten des Innern hinduch rufen sie das Untere. Dunkle herauf. Ungeformte Instinkte, Begierden ohne Namen treiben an die Oberfläche, hemmungslos entladen sie sich, erweckt durch die Schattengewalten, deren Flügel die Helle verdecken' (Kracauer,1987, p. 48).

22   'sinnlosen Drang immer weiter einzufressen in die Felsen' (Kracauer, 1987, p. 49).

23   'pompösen technischen Aufwand' (Kracauer, 1987, p. 49).

24   'Seine Raumergüsse sind denn auch von gigantischer Absurdität, eine Flucht vor dem Verhängnis, das die Seele bedroht. Da das Untere einen Abschluss von sich aus nicht kennt, verstricken sie sich in Endlose; da es Götter nicht mehr gibt, laufen sie leer. Kein Minotaurus sitzt in dem Labyrinth Clavels, es ist auch kein Labyrinth, sondern ein Chaos – Mythologie seiner Form nach, ohne mythologischen Gehalt' (Kracauer, 1987, p. 49).

25   See Benjamin, 2002, pp. 119 and 393.

26   Adalberto Libera (1903–63).

27   Bachelard reminds us that 'Aphrodite was born in these conditions' (1998, p. 108): the shell then is an exquisite natural beauty and an origin of love.

28   See Bachelard, 1998, pp. 131–2.

Bibliography

Bachelard, G. (1998), *The Poetics of Space*. Boston, MA: Beacon Press.

Benjamin, W. (1999a), *The Arcades Project*. Cambridge, MA: Harvard University Press.

— (1999b), *Selected Writings Volume 2*. Cambridge, MA: Harvard University Press.

— (2002), *Selected Writings Volume 3*. Cambridge, MA: Harvard University Press.

Chatwin, B. (1996), *Anatomy of Restlessness. Uncollected Writings*. London: Picador.

— (1998a), *Utz*. London: Vintage Classics.

— (1998b), *In Patagonia*. London: Vintage Classics.

Chatwin, E. and Shakespeare, N. (eds) (2012), *Under the Sun. The Letter of Bruce Chatwin*. London: Jonathan Cape.

Freud, S. (2004), *Civilisation and Its Discontents*. Harmondsworth: Penguin.

Gramsci, A. (2012), *Selections from Cultural Writings*. Chicago: Haymarket Books.

Kracauer, S. (1987), *Strassen in Berlin und Anderswo*. Berlin: Das Arsenal.

— (1995a), *History. The Last Things Before the Last*. Princeton, NJ: Markus Wiener Publishers.

— (1995b), *The Mass Ornament. Weimar Writings*. Cambridge MA: Harvard University Press.

— (1998), *The Salaried Masses. Duty and Distraction in Weimar Germany*. London: Verso.

Lukács, G. (1978), *Theory of the Novel*. London: Merlin.

Munthe, A. ([1929] 2004), *The Story of San Michele*. London: John Murray.

— (1994), *The Story of San Michele*. Forgotten Books.

10

Habit, Distraction, Absorption: Reconsidering Walter Benjamin and the Relation of Architecture to Film

Richard Charles Strong

While it is true that many critical theorists and radical philosophers of the twentieth century engaged seriously with art and its relation to politics, it is also true that many focused perhaps too narrowly on literature, or film, or music and perhaps neglected architecture. Of course, many exceptions to this general trend are to be found. Among those who did encounter and engage with architecture we find Walter Benjamin. One Benjamin text, among others, which dealt seriously with architecture, one that is canonical and cliché, one that has probably been reproduced and read more than any other of his writings, is *The Work of Art in the Age of Its Technological Reproducibility*. It is the *Artwork* essay with which I will here primarily focus my attention. In the course of this essay I will attempt to show that Benjamin didn't miss an encounter with architecture, but that his encounter with architecture in the *Artwork* essay may have missed the mark. And yet, I also want to submit the hypothesis that we might be able to think as our present technological, aesthetic, and architectural milieu with a critical reading of the *Artwork* essay, paired with a recuperation and reorganization of certain key Benjaminian concepts.

In his *Artwork* essay, Walter Benjamin claims that perhaps the best way to understand the relation between film and the film-going masses is by looking at the way the masses relate to architecture. This relation between the masses and architecture is opposed to the way in which a single individual might visually contemplate a painting or similar art form (Benjamin, 2006a, p. 268). The analogy that Benjamin puts forward is thus that the masses relate to film like the masses relate to architecture; in a state of distraction and in a manner of habitual tactile appropriation. Today one finds more and more frequently that film or rather filmic images are not restricted to the cinema house or even to our private spaces. One finds that filmic images have made their way to our everyday public spaces and more specifically into the surfaces of our structures. Though it is by no means a foregone conclusion that such technologies and filmic applications will continue to proliferate. And yet, in a limited number of concrete cases, what were once wooden walls are now moving images. Benjamin's account remains apropos because it foregrounds the affects of the technical structure of the filmic medium at a time when that medium is increasingly encountered in new contexts. More specifically, Benjamin's account foregrounds the notions of distraction and tactility at a time when many theories in the field of media and technology dwell on attention and manifest visual content without taking into account the ways in which that content is conditioned by tactility or perhaps the way in which the technical structure of a given medium affects its reception.[1] Moreover, Benjamin's account remains timely and ought to be in-part recuperated because of the similarities he draws between film and architecture at a time when, as it will be shown, this relation has shifted, in some instances, from a possible analogy to certain mereology.

In the course of this essay I will argue that Benjamin's insight, namely, that the relation of the masses to film is best understood by an analogy with architecture, never held, or at least no longer holds. Further, I will show that the failure of Benjamin's analogy is, in part, because new building materials such as high definition screens qua walls and ceilings collapse Benjamin's analogy between film and architecture. Filmic images and surfaces are now elements of architecture. Additionally, I will show that despite Benjamin's analogical failure, his analyses of film and architecture can provide helpful inroads for thinking, theorizing, and reflecting upon the related technological and social changes in our built environment today. In particular, building on the premise that filmic images are possibly becoming a more ubiquitous part of our built environment and everyday life, I will show that this gives inherent 'shock effects' to some buildings, that the habituations and absorption that already occur within our built environment are made more robust, elaborate and varied, and that unlike film in a traditional context, architectural instances of filmic images are often site specific. These conclusions will be guided by the position that Benjamin's concepts of shock effects, distracted absorption and tactility qua filmic images remain viable and potent when the context is shifted from the traditional filmic milieu to applications in new fields such as architecture. More and more, so it seems, one is confronted with filmic images. This is not because we choose to go to the movies more often but because these moving images have come to us without our solicitation.

I will begin by giving an account of Benjamin's original sense of tactility, absorption, distraction, and shock effects and how they relate to the masses, film, and architecture in the *Artwork* essay. I will then show how and why the analogy between architecture and film no longer holds qua analogy and how it is the case that, with modifications, Benjamin's account of film and its relation to architecture can still provide potent theoretical ways for thinking about film and architecture today.

Original context and content, or; what's past is not merely prologue

Benjamin's *Artwork* essay written between 1936 and 1939 was published posthumously in 1955. The essay was composed in response to, or in light of, a number of historical conjunctures. Among these were the fall of the Weimer republic, the rise of National

Socialism, the invention of photography which begat film (art forms in which technical reproducibility is inherent), the supposed decline or shift of the auratic in art, the supposed shift in the function of art away from ritual towards politics, and the increase of leisure time that demanded new and accessible forms of entertainment among the working class.[2] The themes that are broached and addressed in the essay are therefore complicated, interwoven, dialectal and above all else fecund loci for many and varied investigations. However, for present purposes, I will limit the scope of my analysis primarily to section XV of the essay wherein Benjamin gives his account of architecture, tactile appropriation, distraction, and habit as a means for thinking about the emergence of the new mediums of photography and film and their relation to the masses.

Section XV of the *Artwork* essay is the final section of the essay notwithstanding the epilogue. It is preceded by a section claiming that the Dadaist attempts to shock the spectator morally promoted the medium of film which equally shocks the spectator physically or tactilely 'by means of its technological structure' (Benjamin, 2006a, p. 266; Armstrong, 2000, p. 66). Whereas the Dadaist artists might put together a collection of seemingly unrelated objects and images via collage, photomontage, or assemblage in order to attempt to create a shock effect, film, on the other hand, shocks the viewer not only by moving through frames on the reel one image after the next but more markedly in the editing cuts whereby disparate images, shots and perspectives are made contiguous. The 'shock effect' of film, in contradistinction to that of the Dadaist objects, should not be understood as something particularly jarring or even conspicuous. Indeed, the movement of the images themselves itself is all that is required. The shock effect of film, due to its being bound up with film's technical structure, means that any and every film has the quality of producing a shock effect regardless of any intention to do so. Thus a mild film for children shocks the spectator, as does a more experimental collection of intentionally disparate images, such as one might see in the opening sequence of Ingmar Bergman's *Persona*. In other words, shock effects are inherent in the medium of film regardless of content. Therefore, by 'shock' or 'shock effect' Benjamin has in mind the spectator or rather the mass spectators' collective perception of images being constantly interrupted by change or movement which then precludes, in most instances, something like thoughtful attention or contemplation. Or, as Georges Duhamel puts it in the first person, whom Benjamin quotes, 'I can no longer think what I want to think. My thoughts have been replaced by moving images' (Benjamin, 2006a, p. 267; Duhamel, 1930, p. 52). This highlights the extent to which the movement of the images is enough to create a shock effect. Jarring or unforeseen jump cuts are common but not necessary. Though this shock effect seems to overwhelmingly preclude contemplation, it includes the inscription of a memory trace not immediately or explicitly present to consciousness, according to Benjamin.

The relation of the shock effect to memory is essential to understanding Benjamin's account and thus to modify its scope in order to understand the ways in which I will expand the domain of the filmic shock effect in order to think changes in architecture and film today. In order to give more substance to the way in which shock effects relate to memory it is necessary to examine its fullest elaboration in Benjamin's essay

On Some Motifs in Baudelaire, written in 1939 and published in January of 1940 (Benjamin, 2006b, p. 343).[3] In *On Some Motifs in Baudelaire* Benjamin contends that exposure to shock causes consciousness to screen stimuli as a sort of defense or protection (Benjamin, 2006b, p. 317). That which gets screened, being incompatible with consciousness, is registered as a memory trace (Benjamin, 2006b, pp. 317, 319). This formulation can be understood in the following quotation in which Benjamin, not afraid of using many sources in a short span of writing, partially cites Freud from *Beyond the Pleasure Principle* in addition to supplementing Freud with his own words, couched in Proustian terms. He writes:

> The basic formula of this hypothesis is that 'becoming conscious and leaving behind a memory trace are incompatible with each other within one and the same system'. Rather, vestiges of memory are 'often most powerful and most enduring when the incident which left them behind was one that never entered consciousness'. Put in Proustian terms, this means that only what has not been experienced explicitly and consciously, what has not happened to the subject as an experience [*Erlebnis*], can become a component of the *mémoire involontaire*. (Benjamin, 2006b, p. 319; Freud, 2011, p. 156)

What this brings to the fore is that when we take the shock effect and its relation to memory and then apply it to film one can then say that the masses, under the influences of multiple shock effects inherent in the technical structure of film are not explicitly experiencing that which they absorb as memory traces or fragments because memory traces and consciousness are 'incompatible with each other within one and the same system' (Freud, 2011, p. 156). Though not experienced by consciousness, these memory traces can, couched in Proustian terminology, emerge explicitly in involuntary remembrance, which is to say, they do not necessarily remain latent forever. Moreover, it is likely that these memory traces inform the subject on a supra-, pre-, or subconscious level.

With respect to film, the specific difference is that these shock effects and subsequently produced memory traces are not operating at the unit of one individual, but quasi-simultaneously for the film-going masses. It is as if, to extend the Proustian theme, it is not only the individual named Marcel for whom all of Combray, for example, can be made present by the madeleine, it is the collective masses for whom these quasi-homogeneous memories, not present to consciousness, have been absorbed or inscribed as a memory trace. Moreover, according to Tim Armstrong, these non-traumatic 'shocks are written into the texture of modern life' with its crowds, incessant advertising, alienated labour, constant news cycles, and so on (Armstrong, 2000, p. 66). Armstrong is right in foregrounding the fact that these shocks are non-traumatic and common. It is beyond Armstrong's historical intent to try to think about how and where shock effects might confront us in the present. In addition, Armstrong seems to omit the fact that film was, due to its mode of quasi-simultaneous reception, imbuing *the masses* with seemingly *the same* memory traces. I say 'seemingly the same' in so far as the same images could of course be absorbed and 'understood' differently, as well as the fact that different images could be viewed or imbued with meaning that is similar.[4] Much of the possible difference in the non-deliberative interpretation of the images will be contingent upon the habitudes of thought and vision operative in given populations. This behavioural and epistemological haziness with respect to absorption foregrounds the extent to which our grasp on the relation between habit, memory, body, and learning was and is a problem.

Thus we have seen that inherent in the structure of film are non-traumatic shock effects which produce memory traces in order to protect consciousness from the onslaught of stimuli. These memory traces can emerge as involuntary remembrances or remain supra-, pre-, or subconscious. While film is not the only phenomenon to produce such effects it is differentiated by the fact that the spectators of a film are experiencing the same shocks and registering similar memory traces.

Returning now to the *Artwork* essay, we can see the stress Benjamin places on the key difference between the shock effects of film and its mass and quasi-simultaneous audiences versus other shock-producing phenomena or modes of experience. Thus, section XV begins by Benjamin stating:

> The masses are a matrix from which all customary behavior toward works of art is today emerging newborn. Quantity has been transformed into quality: *The greatly increased mass of participants has produced a different kind of participation.* (Benjamin, 2006a, p. 267)

First we find textual evidence that it is the masses and their relation to art and not merely the new medium of film that has brought about a change. Again, it is not the individual or film per se which bring about his 'change in behaviour towards art' it is both the new medium and its mode of presentation, working together, which bring about this change. Second, and furthermore, this quantitative shift in the relation of masses to art has brought about a qualitative change in the way people participate with the then new medium of film. What Benjamin means by quantity being transformed into quantity is that participation with many previous art forms in thoughtful attentive concentration and reflection by the few, gives way to participation that is marked by distraction, no longer by the few, but by the many, by the masses. In other words, the quantity of those experiencing the art object, at the same time nonetheless, changes the quality or mode of participation from individual concentration to collective or mass distraction.

Shock effects that break concentration and force the apparatus of perception to screen itself from overstimulation which produce memory traces are related to participation in a mode of distraction by intensity, not causality. That is to say, shock effects and participation in a mode of distraction can both stand on their own, they are not mutually implied and it is not the case that one is the condition for the other. However, given shock effects there is an intensification or guarantee of distraction because shock effects actively disrupt and largely preclude the contrary of distraction, concentration.

Distraction in its full elaboration is another essential concept for the sake of understanding the then new medium of film and its effects on concentration because it is the polar opposite of the previous mode of participation with many art works, namely concentration. Additionally Benjamin's assertions regarding distracted participation reveal a change whereby people are no longer absorbed into a work, rather, they absorb the work into themselves. The language of absorption may seem hermetic but Benjamin makes it clearer in the following passage from section XV of the *Artwork* essay. Here we see the relation of concentration and distraction to absorption. Benjamin writes:

> Distraction and concentration form an antithesis, which may be formulated as follows. A person who concentrates before a work of art is absorbed by it; he enters into the work, just as, according to legend, a Chinese painter entered his completed painting while beholding it. By contrast, the distracted masses absorb the work of art into themselves. (Benjamin, 2006a, p. 268)

The opposition between distraction and concentration is further explained in terms of the direction of the 'absorption' of the work of art. In front of a painting a contemplative individual is absorbed *into* the work of art, so to speak. The distracted mass, rather than being absorbed into the work, themselves absorb the work presumably as a memory trace due to the shock effects of film itself. Thus the direction of absorption is reversed when comparing painting or any other contemplative art object to film. Admittedly, the language of absorption is still somewhat vague. Echoing Kracauer on the subject of film, I think this notion of the masses absorbing the work (rather than being absorbed by or into the work) is best understood in terms of the production and reinforcement of the status quo or as Kracauer said, 'films are the mirror of the prevailing society' (Kracauer, 1995, pp. 291–304).[5] That is to say, what gets absorbed or 'internalized' are a whole host of values, givens, framings, comportments, roles and possibilities including, but not limited to, objects of desire, gender, class, race, labour, institutions, morality and rationality. This absorption is a matter of inconspicuous and habitual learning. These absorptions need not be present or manifest to the thetic consciousness of the subject spectator. Benjamin's notion of distracted absorption whereby the masses soak up what they have seen has the virtue of being sufficiently vague enough to allow for it to be understood beyond its original scope while at the same time providing a contrast to the absorption 'into' art objects by the attentive viewer confronting a painting, for example. Of course, film is not the only medium that begets absorption we might face today, but it was certainly a novel locus at the time. And yet, despite this mode of reception being new in cinema, one can, according to Benjamin, find antecedent works of art that function similarly.

According to Benjamin, such absorption or reception of values and understandings by the distracted masses has a prototype by which we can understand film, architecture. He writes:

> This [distracted absorption by the masses] is most obvious with regard to buildings. Architecture has always offered the prototype of an artwork that is received in a state of distraction and through the collective. The laws of architecture's reception are highly instructive. (Benjamin, 2006a, p. 268)

He writes further that,

> Architecture has never had fallow periods. Its history is longer than that of any other art, and its effect ought to be recognized in any attempt to account for the relationship of the masses to the work of art. Buildings are received in a twofold manner: by use and by perception. Or, better: tactilely and optically. Such reception cannot be understood in terms of the concentrated attention of a traveler before a famous building. On the tactile side, there is no counterpart to what contemplation is on the optical side. Tactile reception comes about not so much by way of attention as by way of habit. The latter largely determines even the optical reception of architecture, which spontaneously takes the form of casual noticing, rather than attentive observation. Under certain circumstances, this form of reception shaped by architecture acquires canonical value. *For the tasks which face the human apparatus of perception at historical turning points cannot be performed solely by optical means – that is, by way of contemplation. They are mastered gradually – taking their cue from tactile reception – through habit.* (Benjamin, 2006a, p. 268)

Thus, Architecture or the built environment is the paragon of art that can serve as an analogy for understanding the relationship of the masses to film, or collectively experienced art objects. Let me reiterate that this analogy does not hold for all arts or media, it only obtains for Benjamin in those cases where the scale of the relation is between the masses and art, not an individual before a painting, not a small group in a salon hearing and discussing a sonata.

Constructed environments, such as buildings, parks, town squares, or city streets are appropriated or absorbed in a twofold manner by touch (use understood as sensually unified and quotidian 'taking their cue from tactile reception') and by sight (privileged visual perception suggesting contemplation). A key claim for Benjamin is that it is touch or use that is primary and that the visual or sight is secondary and informed by the tactile. Tactile appropriation is not accomplished by attention or conspicuous awareness but by habit and in the case of architecture and film, at the unit of the masses or collective. For example, one can understand tactile appropriation in the following way; think of your own home or apartment and your knowledge of the light switches there. Turning them on or off is 'second-nature' and the appropriation of the placement of those light switches and their corresponding lamps and bulbs is not acquired primarily by visual attention but by tactile habituation or absorption. When one walks into a dark room for the first time and fumbles for the switches in what must look like a humorous flapping and flailing of arms, visual attention is not even an option as the room is unlit. Upon second and third attempts at entering the same unlit room one has already absorbed or appropriated the location of the switch. Now imagine, by analogy, that the light switch is the role of labour in society, or the concept of justice, and the room is film.

The tourist gawking at the *Unité d'Habitation* in Marseilles or the Comcast Center in Philadelphia is different in kind from those who live or work in those buildings, respectively. That is because in a derivative mode of privileged visual intuition the process of distracted habitual absorption through quotidian use is overlooked. It is the average everyday comportment with the built environment that Benjamin has in mind. To say that 'habit determines to a large extent even optical reception' means that one is habituated or inculcated to look up when one enters a lobby, for example, or to look for stairs that lead down if one is in a Parisian café and needs to find a toilet, or even the tacit awareness that the hierarchy of bureaucratic power is mirrored by the floors of an office building. These examples are habituated absorptions that certainly pertain to the visual, yet are principally informed by the tactile and habitual dealings we have with the grammar and content of our built environment. So too with film, the Benjaminian analogy contends, there are certain expectations to which the masses become habituated and expect unknowingly. For example, if one works hard they will be rewarded, or that given situation X one should feel the emotional response Y. The difference between the two is that with architecture the habituations are often inherently more limited in scope. While in the case of filmic habituations fewer technical limitations obtain. There is of course some liminal overlap of the architectural habit and filmic habit, which would be, for example, the learning or anticipating of certain actions of bodies in the built environment after having seen them on the screen or *vice versa*.

With this notion of tactile appropriation in mind, Benjamin goes on to make the even more substantial claim that 'the tasks which face the human apparatus of perception at the turning points of history cannot be solved by optical means, that is, by contemplation, alone. They are mastered gradually by habit, under the guidance of tactile appropriation' (Benjamin, 2006a, pp. 268–9). Benjamin's contention here is that we don't learn of the affects of pivotal new elements and media by examining the visual manifest content, or perhaps aural in the case of radio. We experience and absorb these changes without being ourselves aware. However, by looking at the new habituations of the masses in their use or tactile appropriation of new media we can take distance and thus give a functional account of the changes in habit and tactile perception which ground or inform other changes. It is only then, once an understanding of the reorganizations and modifications of tactile habit, and the other perceptions that they inform, that our 'tasks', be they positive potentials in the emergent media and elements or negative pitfalls to avoid, have even the possibility of coming to the fore.[6]

To be sure, these are imbricated and large-scale (yet perhaps slow) shifts of perception that cannot be isolated in terms of only a single new medium. That is to say, the developments and specific qualities of film that Benjamin outlines, namely, its shock effects, its tactile appropriation, and its distracted inculcation, also confronted the nineteenth-century person as they walked home on the crowded streets as recounted by Baudelaire and Poe and reflected upon by Benjamin (Benjamin, 2006b, pp. 329–30). And yet the example of crowds does not seem to bring with it the same level of homogeneity as one gets with film. By which I mean that when examining the shock effects of crowds, it is hard to say what might get absorbed in a manner that is sufficient to make general remarks about its possible affects. Moreover, shock effects and habituated appropriation are found in the process and practices of industrialization and alienation driven by Capital whereby the workers' task is repeated without completion, without contemplation, more by habit and use then by circumspect vision and attention on the assembly line. But again it is far more difficult to say what exactly might be absorbed in this way other that the memory trace of the habituated action which would vary greatly from person to person (Benjamin, 2006b, p. 329).[7] Filmic shock effects are a special case because of the seeming homogeneity of that which gets absorbed.

What we get from Benjamin's account of film and architecture is as follows. First, film has within its technical structure the property of producing shock effects in the viewer. These shock effects cause consciousness to protect itself from overstimulation by screening off content which then gets recorded as memory traces. This shocking, so to speak, technical structure of film is then coupled with the fact that the same films are viewed quasi-simultaneously by the masses as opposed to the careful attentive contemplation of an individual art aficionado. The mode of participation of these masses is one of distraction, not concentration. Moreover, Benjamin asserts that when the masses participate with film, or any other art, in a state of distraction they unknowingly absorb the content of the work of art. Given that film has within its formal structure shock effects which beget memory traces not manifest to consciousness, aided by a mode of participation that is one of distraction, the masses then absorb much of the content of films without being contemplatively aware of either the absorption or much of the content itself. Any art that is absorbed in a state of distraction does so primarily by means of tactile as opposed to optical means. The tactile is primary and largely informs the optical reception which takes the form of distracted casual noticing and not attentive contemplation. Benjamin then contends that this tactile absorption that one finds in film is best understood in terms of an analogy with architecture and that its mode of reception by the distracted masses serves as a paradigmatic example and helpful analogy for understanding the distracted masses and how they participate with film.

Problems with Benjamin's account

The first problem is the possibly specious nature of the analogy between architecture and film, the second, related to the first, is the lack of any inherent or formally constituted shock effect in architecture, and the third is the fact that Benjamin's analysis does not hold qua analogy in the present given the state of architecture vis-à-vis the filmic image. I will first bring these issues to light in order to show that they can be resolved by revising and updating Benjamin's own account.

Many commentators do in fact question whether or not the analogy between film and architecture is a good one. Joan Ockman, for example, does so on the grounds that film is often narratival whereas buildings are not (Ockman, 2000, p. 171). We also find that in their introduction and commentary to letters exchanged between Adorno and Benjamin found in *Aesthetics and Politics*, Livingstone, Anderson and Mulhern unequivocally claim that the analogy between film and architecture, as Benjamin presents it, is a spurious or specious generalization (Anderson et al., 2007, p. 115). They write:

His [Benjamin's] theory of the positive significance of distraction was based on a specious generalization from architecture, whose forms are always directly used as practical objects and hence necessarily command a distinct type of attention from those of drama, cinema, poetry or painting. (Anderson et al., 2007, p. 115)

While Livingstone, Anderson and Mulhern are more concerned with the larger issue of Adorno's dismissal of the positive value of distraction, that fact does not so much concern us here (Anderson et al., 2007, p. 115). What does concern us is the claim that architecture is 'always' practical and thus commands a distinct type of 'attention' that differs in kind from the 'attention' paid to entertainment or diversions such as those named (cinema, drama and so on) (Anderson et al., 2007, p. 115). Clearly, Livingstone, Anderson, and Mulhern are not adhering to Benjamin's own vocabulary of attention and distraction. However, their contention is that our relation to architecture and our relation to film are not enough alike such that one could best be understood by analogy with the other and therefore that Benjamin's analogy is a false one.

The claim that the attention paid to a building or built environment 'always' commands a different type of practical 'attention' than does the 'attention' required by film does have some credence because often one has an ulterior aim in mind when dealing practically with a public building, for example.[8] The building is often a better or worse means to an end in terms of our engagement with it. Contrariwise, one views a film in order to be entertained – the traditional cinema house therefore is not often a means to an end.[9] Again, to use the word 'attention' in this case is of course to misuse or miss the point of Benjamin's account which rests on the polar opposite of attention, namely distraction, but nevertheless the spirit of the criticism is a good and forceful one. When the masses have dealings with shared built environments or public buildings it is often for the sake of some other ultimate aim.[10] This is not 'always' as Livingstone, Anderson and Mulhern claim, but it is often or usually the case. For the cinema-going masses the distracted tactile appropriation occurs while pursuing an end in itself which is different from practical dealings in terms of its necessity and frequency. For example, the masses have daily dealings with subway station *in order to* catch a train to go to work. The masses file into shopping malls *in order to* purchase things. The masses enter religious meeting places *in order to* come together for worship. In contradistinction, the masses go to the movies in order to go to the movies. The former examples are instrumental while the example of going to the movies is terminal and therefore at least possibly indicates a different type of engagement. Surely, in the given examples of 'means to an end' dealings there is a process of tactile and distracted appropriation of the built environment by the masses but it is different from the tactile and distracted appropriation of the masses in the cinema in so far as with the case of the cinema house there is no practical necessity or ultimate aim motivating the behaviour or engagement save entertainment. Does this 'means to an end' versus 'end in itself' distinction render Benjamin's comparison of architecture to film a 'specious generalization?' Probably not 'specious', but it is at least suspect or questionable in light of the distinction between the necessary 'means to an end' engagement with most buildings and the contingent 'end in itself' of going to the movies.

The second fault that could be brought to bear on Benjamin's account is an extension of the point already made about the suspect generalization between architecture and film, but in different terms. One could just as easily claim that perhaps the shock effect which is part of film 'by means of its technical structure' is not to be found inherently in architecture, making a more robust case against comparing film to architecture because the shock effects of film are such a key notion for Benjamin's account.

Shock effects in film prevent contemplation, which precludes attention thus fostering incognizant absorption in a mode of distraction. Of course, making one's way through a busy shopping mall, or metro station, or boulevard with its crowds and sounds does indeed produce a shock effect (Benjamin, 2006b, pp. 329–30). However, are these cases not different in kind in so far as that which might get absorbed is more obtuse, less pointed, less homogenous? Is it not also true that not all built environments are always or even often crowded and noisy and that the crowds and noises are different from the built spaces themselves? Buildings have traditionally had no *inherent* shock effects.[11] Therefore, one can conclude that the shock effect is not necessarily to be found in architecture *in the same way* it is found in film. This is problematic for the analogy between film and architecture but not entirely damning unless one maintains a strict and clear etiology with respect to shock effects with their memory traces and distraction with its absorption. On the contrary, I maintain that the relation between the two is that the shock effects can intensify absorption, but that distracted absorption can occur without shock effects. Thus shock effects and distracted absorption are related, but not causally. This lack of inherent shock effects in buildings is a problem with Benjamin's analogy but not one that forces us to jettison his considerations *in toto*.

The two criticisms raised above, the problematic generalization that Benjamin makes between architecture and film qua use and qua shock effects are serious problems with Benjamin's claim that one can and should look to architecture and its distracted tactile absorption by the masses in order to better understand film. Or better, these *were* serious problems. Today, the more salient problem facing Benjamin's account is that his comparison no longer holds because the terms of the analogy have collapsed, that in certain instances, insipient yet concrete, film (or rather the filmic image) is an element of architecture. The fluid filmic surface is a material at the disposal of the architect and builder. This is true in so far as the filmic image is now a building surface material in essence no different from plaster, brick, drywall, marble façade or *béton brut* (perhaps not load-bearing, but certainly loaded).

In light of the fact that the filmic is now a building material which can be employed as the surface of walls, ceilings or other architectural elements, the problems of use (means to an end vs end in itself) and the shock effects must also be seen from a new perspective; a perspective in which these formerly problematic differences between film and architecture cease to be oppositions and come to form one single amalgam.

These problems with Benjamin's account demand that one revisit and see in a new perspective Benjamin's claim that laws of the reception of architecture are most instructive in understanding shifts in perception, and apperception, that occur with the advent of film. The question now becomes one of what sorts of changes take place when film becomes part of architecture? The collapse of Benjamin's analogy allows us to rescue and resuscitate some of Benjamin's keenest insights and to think about architecture's appropriation of filmic images using the guiding concepts of the masses, shock effects, distracted absorption and tactile habituation in a different context.

The present state of affairs (coming soon to a built environment near you)

[. . .] In a [political] state which is desirous of being saved from the greatest of all plagues-not faction, but rather distraction [. . .]

Plato, *Laws* V.5

If it is kept in mind that the filmic or the moving image is now part of architecture or the built environment, in some instances, much can be gained in terms of our understanding by rescuing elements of Benjamin's analysis of film and architecture in light of this change. Presently, many of the discussions surrounding emergent technologies and pedagogy announce a crisis of attention and then go on to study attention spans, streams, and styles, without concentrating on distraction, so to speak.[12] In this section I will provide a sketch of what these technological changes might mean for film and architecture thought together, and the way in which learning or ideology formation takes place unaided by attention. The changes I wish to highlight with respect to the rise of filmic images in our built environment are not opposed to discussions of information networks, computational architecture, or the rise of ubiquitous computing, but instead form part of the larger set of questions concerning how architecture is situated within the present technological and aesthetic milieu and what is at stake.[13]

The seamless integration of the filmic image into architecture is not currently a terribly common phenomenon, by and large. But it is to be found, and one of the best examples is located in Philadelphia, Pennsylvania in the lobby of the Comcast Center.[14] This is a paradigmatic example because the LED screens upon which the images play are quite different from a television mounted on the wall, a far more common and conspicuous phenomenon. The screens at the Comcast Center are seamlessly integrated into the lobby walls, or rather, they form the surface of the lobby walls. Their resolution is so high that if the screen produces an image similar to the wood panels around them one cannot easily distinguish them from the actual wood. However, the screens are usually presenting various moving images, be they scenes from the city of Philadelphia, depictions of the solar system, or even scenes of green pastures replete with butterflies fluttering by and so forth. The images often move between idyllic, bucolic and patriotic. It is notable that the content which gets displayed at the Comcast Center is specific to this location as opposed to using stock footage or merely replaying television or traditional film programming. The lobby wall is considered to be an art installation called *The Comcast Experience*.

Another example or case study one could look at in order to understand the more general shift in the relation of film to architecture is an outdoor walkway and focal point of a shopping and business centre in Beijing, China eerily called The Place. This example differs from the Comcast Experience in that it is outside, the filmic images are the surface of the ceiling of a large walkway, not walls, and it is more directly in the service of selling goods and services. The aim of selling goods and services is achieved in a straightforward manner by being host to advertisements and indirectly by drawing people to the shopping centre itself.

The lead designer of the centre walkway at The Place is an American by the name of Jeremy Railton (Railton, 2007). Railton also led the design and implementation of the Freemont Street Experience in Las Vegas Nevada, which is another notable example of the extension of the domain of the filmic (Railton, 2007). The walkway at The Place is 80 feet high (24.35 metres), 88 feet wide (26.82 metres) and 2,296 feet long (699.82 metres) (Railton, 2007). Like the Comcast Center, the filmic images are displayed using LED screens.

The content, or that which gets displayed at The Place, it is in keeping with traditional Chinese values. Or, as the designer puts it:

> Not only is The Place spectacular, but in the generous Chinese tradition, it offers a free theatre-like experience. For me, this inclusive atmosphere made the project more exciting and more challenging because the content of the shows must appeal to a wide range of interests by being new, while still calling on venerated Chinese traditions and values. (Railton, 2007)

He then goes on to describe more specifically the first moving images the installation displayed, writing:

> The premier show, The Blessing, begins with the flight of the red and yellow dragons of Fortune and Power, and then progresses through scenes such as updateable performances of Olympic hopefuls, Chinese hip hop, Kung Fu, fireworks, and the largest image ever created of The Great Wall. People on the street below experience the four seasons, from the peach blossoms of spring gently falling to the lightning strikes and thunderstorms of winter. My favorite line is, 'No matter what the weather is like in Beijing, The Place can always change it'. (Railton, 2007)

Importantly there is a veneration and production of a sense of Chinese identity, pride, tradition and values.

Railton himself was fully aware of the shock effects that the use of the filmic medium in the built environment will produce in the masses as they experience it. He writes that:

> The formula and techniques for these large screens are very different from the usual filmmaking techniques, and it has been hard to get the filmmakers to believe me. Flash cuts, zooms, and normal-speed objects make you feel like you are in an earthquake or that the sky is falling. (Railton, 2007)

What this quotation highlights is the extent to which Benjamin's remarks on the shock effects inherent in the technical structure of film, while perhaps forgotten when one has in mind traditional film in traditional settings, are again exposed. One finds verification of Benjamin's filmic shock effects to the extent that even the engineers of the new filmic built environments cannot help but run up against the shock effects of film. While Railton attempts to avoid these shock effects by omitting certain tropes and grammars of traditional filmmaking, such as jump cuts, he only mitigates these shock effects to the point at which the masses do not feel like they are in an earthquake. This only makes the shock effects less conspicuous and more pleasant.

Echoing Rancière, what the lobby of the Comcast Center and The Place show are crystalline examples of how moving images and architecture are no longer disparate genres of art.[15] Not only is there a mixing of genres of art but also an incorporation of technologies of communication and information into the technologies of construction, a crossover that is obviously not limited to filmic images (Virilio et al., 2001, pp. 32–53). As such, the filmic image has been infused into our built environment in a new way. The relation of the masses to architecture is not *like* that of film, it, in some instances, it *is* that of film. Thus, in the present, we should not look to architecture to understand film, but we should look to film theory to understand some of the changes taking place in architecture. With this reversal, come new consequences and demands for thinking about tactile distracted appropriation and the way in which the tactile grounds or informs the visual. In this respect Benjamin's notions of absorption and shock effect can act as a guide to thinking these changes. Again, to invoke the language of Rancière, the relation that obtains between architecture and film that I have tried to bring in to relief is not only an example of the aesthetic regime of art, but also educational, and therefore participating in the ethical regime of images as well.

Given this new or modified aesthetic arrangement one might ask what the relation between politics and aesthetics might be in these cases and other like them. While Benjamin famously stated the in the *Artwork* essay that the aestheticizing of politics as practised by fascism solicits the reply by communism to politicize art, I want to here suggest that we hold that suggested relation between art and politics in abeyance and focus on the concept of habit (and the production and reinforcement of habit), very broadly conceived, and aesthetics *vis-à-vis* politics *à la* the work of Butler, Bourdieu, Foucault, and Rancière, for example. I want to gesture, therefore, that this novel relation between architecture and film perhaps presents something like an increased sophistication when it comes to the production and reinforcement of dispositions in certain architectural spaces.

As was previously noted, Benjamin finds this shock effect to be part of the technical structure of film. Functionally, the shock effect largely precludes contemplation and promotes or causes distraction. Engagement with objects of art in a mode of distraction, according to Benjamin, has as its concomitant the inconspicuous absorption of the work by those who participate with it. Shock effects, like those found in film, in turn intensify distraction and absorption. Again this occurs with film by dint of the constantly changing or moving – often disparate – images. Distraction is here understood as the polar opposite of concentration or attention. Attention implies contemplation while there is no intellectual counterpart to distraction (Benjamin, 2006a, p. 268).[16] Certainly it was already claimed by Benjamin that the masses absorb architecture in a state of distraction and habit. However, as I previously highlighted, architecture was inherently more limited in terms of content for absorption than film. That is no longer necessarily the case with the implementation of the filmic image into repertoire of construction materials. That is to say that the content which gets absorbed in architecture can go beyond the abstract coding of power and gender or the more concrete habituation to placement and movements to incorporate the more robust and elaborate, yet tacit, ideologies one finds in film, as Benjamin understood it. Further, this means that not only are the masses going about constructed environments in a merely distracted manner and becoming inculcated and habituated to the buildings they, the masses, are also tactilely appropriating that which appears on the filmic walls or other filmic architectural components.

For Benjamin it was important to note that the quantitative shift in the reception of art, from the individual to the masses, resulted in a qualitative change. This aspect was important, among other reasons, because it highlighted the fact that most people were seeing and absorbing the same content, their sensibilities were being produced and reinforced quasi-uniformly. This was possible because the medium of film is made to be copied and disseminated – there is no authentic or meaningful 'original'. Those at the cinema in Berlin were watching the same film at the same time as those at the cinema in Paris, London, New York, and every other place where there was a cinema house. When the filmic image extends its presence into the walls, floors and ceilings of our built environment this widespread exposure that marked traditional film falls away. One has to enter specific places in order to experience these new filmic images, thus this new use of filmic images is topologically fettered. This means that, in contradistinction to traditional cinema, the images that are presented and that which then get absorbed will not of necessity be the same from place to place. However, there is still a collective absorption but it is not one that is similar for all places. Film is, in the architectural paradigm, site specific. It still informs or educates a collective mass but on a smaller scale, in a specific location, and with more tailor-made content.

In the previous section, I highlighted possible difference in kind between the way people relate to film and the way they relate to architecture. As it stands the two cannot be rigorously held apart because filmic images have entered the space of architecture outside of the traditional cinema house. Specifically, I highlighted the way in which it was not the case that buildings or built environments produced any shock effects, and if they did, it was not due to their technical or, one can say, formal structure. Buildings that use the medium of the filmic as the surface of its constituent parts – wall, ceilings and floors – *do* have this shock effect built-in. In other words, one can conclude that distraction, tactile appropriation, and absorption of a building are intensified and extended with the insertion of the filmic into the surfaces of our buildings.

In his original characterization of architecture, Benjamin highlighted the way in which a tourist staring at a building is a derivative mode of engagement that does not allow one to gain an adequate or proper understanding of the way in which use, habit and tactile appropriation take hold of the masses. With the introduction of filmic images into the basic elements of architecture it comes to be that even in this derivative mode of gawking at a structure there is, via filmic images, a shock effect which produces in the tourist certain memory traces or absorptions.

These changes may prove to provide positive potentials for architecture or they could be deleterious; it is too soon to make such a judgement.[17]

Conclusion

Thus, I have shown the original context in which Benjamin made his analogy between film and architecture. Further I have tried to show the way in which that analogy no longer holds and that this is the case because, most importantly, the filmic image has become incorporated into the walls of our built environment. Additionally, I have shown that Benjamin's analyses of film can form part of a broader analysis of not only changes in architecture and our built environment but also broader shifts in perception today. I highlighted the fact that architecture that integrates filmic images into its surfaces inherently produces shock effects. Moreover, these shock effects then promote distraction and absorption. This new architectural absorption, aided by the content of the filmic elements is notable because of the more robust and elaborate habituations and inculcations it is able to produce in a more targeted audience. In making my case I brought to the fore that perhaps distraction, rather than or in addition to attention, should form part of conceptual vocabulary that gets employed in trying to make sense of the interrelated aesthetic, artistic, perceptual and technological changes we face today.[18]

In light of my arguments advocating for a collapsing of the terms architecture and film in some cases, the question of the engagement between radical philosophy and architecture thus seems to be poorly framed in so far as the question assumes some real or perceived distinction between different genres or types of art. Whereas, today, I think it is the case that to ask questions of architecture or engage critically with architecture – which is a crucial task – means at the same time to incorporate other types of art, aesthetics, and social practices into the analysis and to abstain from meretriciously restricting the terms of the discourse to categories that are themselves not beyond scrutiny and critique. Rigidly isolating architecture can be illusory and misleading. Yet not engaging with architecture at all would be blind and ruinous.

Notes

1   See, for example, Hayles, Lomas, Haynes and Duttlinger (Hayles, 2007, pp. 187–99; Lomas, 2008, pp. 163–72; Haynes et al., 1998, pp. 187–93; Duttlinger, 2007, pp. 33–54). Duttlinger also notes the way in which there has been a 'flurry' of discussion of new media which focus on attention while omitting the Benjaminian notion of distraction from the discourse.

2   Benjamin's account of art history is not without condign criticism that is beyond the scope of the present essay.

3   Benjamin wrote *The Work of Art in the Age of Its Technological Reproducibility* from 1936–9, it having undergone many revisions before he allowed it to be copied by Greta Adorno. It was not published until 1955. Given the proximity of dates between the two essay it stands to reason that shock effects were, among other things, in the foreground of Benjamin's thinking at the time.

4   I have in mind here the work of Thomas S. Kuhn on the subject of 'givens'. The pithiest account of this is when Kuhn writes, 'The duck-rabbit shows that two men with the same retinal impressions can see different things; the inverting lenses show that two men with different retinal impressions can see the same thing' (Kuhn, 1996, pp. 125–30).

5   One could call this vague absorption by the name ideology or superstructure following Marx, or following Bourdieu, habitus, or following Castoriadis, the imaginary, or following Gramsci, cultural hegemony. Cf. (Marx, 1993; Bourdieu, 1977; Castoriadis, 1998; Gramsci, 2010).

6 Benjamin here clearly anticipates the work of Marshall McLuhan with his famous notion that the 'medium is the message' and also that media are never neutral (McLuhan, 1994).

7 As Benjamin puts it, 'the shock experience which the passer-by has in the crowd corresponds to what the worker "experiences" at his machine' (Benjamin, 2006b, p. 329).

8 Obviously there are counterexamples to such a claim and the binary opposition is heuristically employed for the sake of a generous reading of Livingstone, Anderson and Mulhern.

9 Yet it could be a means to an end it certain situations. For example, think of a training film or a public service announcement. What remains important are general trends, not hard and fast universality applicable laws.

10 A notable exception would be the wanderings of the *flâneur* or the similar Situationist practice of *dérive*.

11 The exception here is the funhouse.

12 See, for example, the work of Hayles, Lomas, Haynes and others (Hayles, 2007, pp. 187–9; Haynes, et al., 1998, pp. 187–93; Lomas, 2008, pp. 163–72).

13 See the work of Felicity D. Scott. Scott's essay draws a similar conclusion in her presentation and analyses surrounding a similar constellation of questions raised in the 1930s by Meyer Schapiro (Scott, 2002, pp. 44–65).

14 Other notable examples include Fremont Street in Las Vegas, Nevada, Harrah's Casino Façade in Atlantic City New Jersey, and myriad video installation pieces which forego the previous medium of traditional television sets or large screens in favour of large projections or LED presentations of moving images which often take up one or more walls of a gallery space, see the work of Kosuke Fujitaka, Mark Luyten or just pick up any given copy of *Artforum* published in the last 10 years.

15 This echoes Jacques Rancière's notion of the 'aesthetic regime of art' wherein genres, high versus low forms of art, and the ethical use of images are no longer necessarily at play. Rancière makes the case that his concept of the 'aesthetic regime of art' is more helpful than the nebulous notion of 'modernity' (Rancière, 2004, pp. 20–30). See also the work of K. Michael Hays. Hays is very good at elaborating this point with special attention paid architecture, Hays, 1995, p. 45.

16 Albeit in different terms, it might be helpful here to compare Benjamin's conceptualization of attention, distraction and absorption with the Merleau-Pontian phenomenological concepts of operative intentionality and sedimentation (Merleau-Ponty, 2012).

17 While the case could be made that Benjamin views the shifts in perception brought about by film as negative rather than simply functional, if one followed the gestures of the Situationist International it could be claimed that the thorough incorporation of film into architecture could serve to create situations or give a much higher degree of affective plasticity and dynamism to our build environment. Moreover, a plasticity and dynamism of which we (one is?) are in control (ed. McDonough, 2009).

18 These analyses are, of course, only the tip of the iceberg, so to speak, of the changes which confront the field of perception in the present milieu. The sea-changes in our built environment and networks in conjunction with how these changes affect the formation of subjects, habits, and affects is without a doubt a very large and difficult question or series of questions. Moreover, the analyses and cases I have provided are geographically and socially tied to places and people where there are enough resources to apply the filmic image quite literally into the very walls of our shared

spaces and brick and mortar (and filmic) institutions. Therefore one would do well to pay special attention to changes in media and perception without losing sight of specific differences in concrete cases.

Bibliography

Anderson, P., Livingstone, R. and Mulhern, F. (2007), Introduction to 'Presentation III' in P. Anderson, R. Livingstone and F. Mulhern (eds), *Aesthetics and Politics*. Adorno, T., Benjamin, W., Bloch, E., Brecht, B. and Lukács, G. London: Verso, pp. 106–17.

Armstrong, T. (2000), 'Two Types of Shock in Modernity', *Critical Quarterly*, 42, 1, pp. 60–73.

Benjamin, W. (2006a), 'The Work of Art in the Age of Its Technological Reproducibility', in H. Eiland and M. W. Jennings (eds), H. Zohn (trans.), *Walter Benjamin: Selected Writings, Volume 4, 1938–1940*. Cambridge, MA and London: Belknap Press of Harvard University Press, pp. 251–3.

— (2006b), 'On Some Motifs in Baudelaire', in H. Eiland and M. W. Jennings (eds), H. Zohn (trans.), *Walter Benjamin: Selected Writings, Volume 4, 1938–1940*. Cambridge, MA and London: Belknap Press of Harvard University Press, pp. 313–55.

Bourdieu, P. (1977), *Outline of a Theory of Practice*. R. Nice (trans.). Cambridge: Cambridge University Press.

Castoriadis, C. (1998), *The Imaginary Institution of Society*. B. Kathleen (trans.). Cambridge, MA: MIT Press.

Duhamel, G. (1930), *Scenes de la Vie Future*. Paris: Mercure de France.

Duttlinger, C. (2007), 'Between Contemplation and Distraction: Configurations of Attention in Walter Benjamin', *German Studies Review*, 30, 1, pp. 33–54.

Freud, S. (2011), *Beyond the Pleasure Principle*. T. Dufresne (ed.), G. C. Richter (trans.). Ontario: Broadview Press.

Gramsci, A. (2010), *Selections from the Prison Notebooks*. Q. Hoare and G. N. Smith (eds) and (trans). New York: International Publishers.

Hayles, N. K. (2007), 'Hyper and Deep Attention: The Generational Divide in Cognitive Modes', *Profession*, pp. 187–99.

Haynes, D., Mandel, M. and Robillard, R. (1998), 'Curriculum Revolution: The Infusion and Diffusion of New Media', *Leonardo*, 31, 3, pp. 187–93.

Hays, M. K. (1995), 'Architecture Theory, Media, and the Question of Audience', *Assemblage*, 27, pp. 41–6.

Kracauer, S. (1995), 'The Little Shopgirls Go to the Movies', in T. Y. Levin (ed.) and (trans.), *The Mass Ornament: Weimar Essays*. Cambridge, MA: Harvard University Press, pp. 291–304.

Kuhn, T. A. (1996), *The Structure of Scientific Revolutions*. Chicago: University of Chicago Press, pp. 125–30.

Lomas, D. (2008), 'Attentional Capital and the Ecology of Online Social Networks', in M. Tovey (ed.), *Collective Intelligence: Creating a Prosperous World at Peace*. Oakton, VA: Earth Intelligence Network, pp. 163–72.

Marx, K. (1993), *Grundrisse: Foundations of the Critique of Political Economy*. M. Nicolaus (trans.). New York: Penguin Books.

McDonough, T. (ed.) (2009), *The Situationists and the City: A Reader*. New York: Verso.

McLuhan, M. (1994), *Understanding Media: The Extensions of Man*. Cambridge, MA: MIT Press.

Merleau-Ponty, M. (2012), *The Phenomenology of Perception*. D. A. Landes (trans.). New York: Routledge.

Ockman, J. (2000), 'Architecture in a Mode of Distraction: Eight Takes on Jacques Tati's *Playtime*', in M. Lamster (ed.), *Architecture and Film*. New York: Princeton Architectural Press, pp. 171–96.

Railton, J. (2007), 'How I Did That: The Great Screen of China', *Live Design*. Available at: <http://livedesignonline.com/architainment/great_screen_china/>.

Rancière, J. (2004), 'Artistic Regimes and the Shortcomings of the Notion of Modernity', in G. Rockhill (ed.) and (trans.), *The Politics of Aesthetics*. New York: Continuum, pp. 20–30.

Scott, F. D. (2002), 'On Architecture Under Capitalism', *Grey Room*, 6, pp. 44–65.

Virilio, P., Lotringer, S. and Taormina, M. (2001), 'After Architecture: A Conversation', *Grey Room*, 3, pp. 32–53.

11

Hetero-Architecture: The Style of 'Whatever' in Art, Architecture and Fashion

Rex Butler

Introduction

Charles Jencks was already well-known as an architectural theorist when he came to write *Heteropolis: Los Angeles, The Riots and the Strange Beauty of Hetero-Architecture* in 1993. As early as 1977 he had written *The Language of Post-Modern Architecture*, which theorizes not only the architectural but also the wider cultural phenomenon of postmodernism. The book was a major success, and if today we have the sense that postmodernism appeared as early, if not earlier, in architecture as in any other field it is not only any actual building but also Jencks' own book we have to thank. Certainly, Fredric Jameson used Jencks in his ground-breaking (and also early) essay 'Theories of the Post-Modern', originally published in 1984. And, more specifically, in his celebrated analysis of the then-recently built Westin Bonaventure Hotel and the way its glass skin 'repels the city outside' in 'Post-Modernism and Consumer Society' (Jameson, 1984, p. 82), he repeats aspects of Jencks' own earlier treatment of the building in *The Language of Post-Modern Architecture* and his description of its exteriors there as an 'absolute geometrical image, parts of which in mirrorplate reflect like overblown jewels' (Jencks, 1978, p. 34).

For its part, *The Language of Post-Modern Architecture* seeks to identify a general style or language of the postmodern that lies behind any of its particular instances. Jencks had previously written a series of well-regarded books on major modernist architects – Alvar Aalto in 1967 and Le Corbusier in 1973 – and so was well attuned to the fact that something new had appeared to be happening in architecture from the early 1960s on. In postmodernism, there is a collapse of the distinctions between univalence and polyvalence, formalism and symbolism and newness and historicism that had defined modernism. Postmodernism, therefore, is characterized by a 'hybridity' (Jencks, 1978, p. 87), in that what was previously separated is now brought together. And Jencks sees this collapse of opposites in a whole series of buildings that might at first appear different. Thus in Robert Venturi's *Headquarters Building* in Pennsylvania (1960), we have the historical use of ornament. In Kisho Kurokawa's *National Children's Land Lodge* (1964–5), we have a traditional Japanese roof combined with a modernist lack of surface detail. And in Darbourne and Dark's *Pimlico Housing* (1961–8), we have heavy bricks coming out into space used as surface decoration. Postmodernism for Jencks is essentially a form of populism, in that the technical distinctions that formerly excluded outsiders in architectural discourse no longer apply and this discourse is now available to a much wider public. This for Jencks has an undoubted 'political' meaning and consequence – and he broadly associates postmodern architecture with a strengthening of democracy and the increased accessibility of people to their own culture and transparency of political representation.

Heteropolis, written some 15 years after the *Language of Post-Modern Architecture*, is a very different book. It is at once an extension of *Language* and an argument against it. Certainly, the book was not such a success as *Language* – it has virtually been ignored by both critics and general readers – and it is interesting to consider why. Obviously, *Heteropolis* comes at the end and not the beginning of that 'postmodernism' with which Jencks has been so closely associated. It does not therefore have the sense of discovery that *Language* had, but by contrast an air almost of retrospective summation. In fact, *Heteropolis* goes further than *Language*. It pushes the arguments first put in that book to their limit. But it finds there a kind of impasse, in which what Jencks is saying starts to suggest conclusions with which he does not agree. It is at this point that we can see Jencks retreating, not fully accepting what he discovers. *Heteropolis*, in other words, unlike *Language*, is something of a divided work. It is not as straightforward as *Language*, but is more interesting. In a sense – and this is perhaps the true 'hetero-morphosis' (Jencks, 1993, p. 33) the book theorizes – *Heteropolis* argues against itself, pulls back from consequences that it denies itself from reaching, but that are nevertheless to be read between its lines.

Heteropolis: Los Angeles

Heteropolis, like much of *Language*, revolves around the architecture of Los Angeles, which for Jencks is the place of postmodernism par excellence. Indeed, there is always a certain play in his work on that great American myth, in which the West is where the laws and social conventions of the East Coast no longer apply. It is where 'Europe' runs out and America at last becomes itself. In Los Angeles, there are no longer spatial hierarchies within the city – the book has a section titled 'Periphery as Center' (Jencks, 1993, p. 32) – and no longer distinctions between cultures – Jencks traces the mixture in Los Angeles of Japanese, Korean, Spanish and black cultures. In a way, that is, in the first of the methodological paradoxes of the book, Los Angeles architecture is not amenable to the usual climatic, geographical or even environmental explanations. Not only within Los Angeles are there no longer the usual spatial distinctions, but also between Los Angeles and what is outside of it the usual discriminations can no longer be drawn. In Los Angeles, in the words of one of its chapters, as opposed to 'E pluribus unum', 'Et unum et plura' (Jencks, 1993, p. 100). The city takes on its singular identity through being a combination or 'kaleidoscope' (Jencks, 1993, p. 104), but not simply a fusion or unity, made up of all other identities.

In *Heteropolis* Jencks attempts to sketch a 'history' of this situation, beginning with the 'informality' of the late '60s and early '70s, moving through the representational 'hetero-architecture' of the '70s and early '80s, and concluding with the final 'en-formality' of an identifiable LA Style of the '80s and '90s (Jencks, 1993, pp. 37–65). Here too, as in *Language*, Jencks outlines his arguments through a number of specific examples or case studies. Thus, for that first moment of Los Angeles informality, he looks at Charles Moore's *Sea Ranch* (1965), which mixes the industrial and the vernacular. For its representational 'hetero-architecture', he looks at Frank Gehry's *Santa Monica Place* (1979–81), in which one building piggybacks on top of another. And for its achieved 'en-formality', he looks at Morphosis' *Angeli's Restaurant* (1985), which mixes the industrial and the rustic with its support-beams that look like left-over scaffolding. But, again, in a paradox for Jencks' methodology, no real history of what he is speaking about is possible, nor even any real examples. There is not the usual stylistic progression or development towards the situation Jencks describes, nor can any building evidence the 'aesthetic' he argues for more than any other. Rather, it is notable that at the physical and methodological centre of the book is an image of the citizens of South Central LA walking past the both pre-historical and post-historical 'ruins' of a bombed-out building and rubble of bricks left behind after the Rodney King riots of 1992. In a sense, this image represents the absolute collapse of distinctions, the non-site and non-architecture that *is* the heteropolis Jencks is speaking about. And, in fact, the real logic driving the narrative of Jencks' book is not geography, history or architectural style but the movement between this heteropolis and its refusal or rejection. In the second half of the chapter 'What Caused the Justice Riots?', Jencks describes the efforts of concerned citizens to 'wall up' or otherwise 'dissimulate' spaces, to re-erect or reintroduce hierarchies and class distinctions that have otherwise been torn down, in what he calls 'defensible architecture' or 'riot realism' (Jencks, 1993, p. 89).

And again, following – and extending – the argument of *Language*, Jencks seeks to think the political meaning or consequences of this 'heterotopic' architecture. In the final chapter of the book, 'Towards a Post-Modern Liberalism', Jencks draws a distinction between the 'cosmopolis' and the 'heteropolis' (Jencks, 1993, p. 112). For Jencks, the cosmopolis – for all of its inclusiveness and associations with the ideal of cosmopolitanism – still remains rooted in its origins in Ancient Greece, whose traditional spaces and residual hierarchies are inadequate to the contemporary experience of Los Angeles. By contrast, Jencks puts forward the competing notion of 'heteropolis', which much more completely removes the barriers between the governed and those who govern and does away with the distinctions that have excluded or otherwise stereotyped individuals, a political form that is both the equivalent of the architecture of Los Angeles and seeks to bring out the liberatory potential of that architecture. In a heteropolis as opposed to a cosmopolis, there are no supervening categories that have the effect of putting some citizens above others. Rather, the inalienable difference between them is sought to be preserved for as long as possible, in a gesture that is at once the essence of democratic space and a certain exceeding of that space.

However, it is just at this point, towards the end of his text, when Jencks has time to pause and take a breath, that he turns back and looks at what he has done. And it is here that a certain qualification might be seen to enter into an otherwise unqualified and almost ecstatic text. For at moments Jencks can be said to be aware – almost between the lines – of the difficulties of his own position. The situation he describes in fact goes against any attempt to describe or account for it. As he himself admits, it cannot be explained by the usual tools of architectural analysis and does not even constitute a proper or identifiable style (or politics). Here is where *Heteropolis* goes beyond *Language*. In that book – and the very success of its terminology played a part in this – if postmodernism witnessed a collapse of the long-standing and often bitterly defended oppositions that marked modernist architecture, this is recouped precisely as postmodern pastiche, appropriation and plurality. There is a levelling or making-equivalent of parts that forms a new unified style. As Jencks writes in *Language*: 'Because metaphor and symbolism were suppressed by the modern movement their re-emergence now at a time of unsettled metaphysics is bound to be over-emphatic; but post-modernists are nonetheless committed to exploring this level of meaning' (Jencks, 1978, pp. 114–15). This is why, indeed, we might be able to speak today of a 'revival' of postmodernism, a recycling of it, certainly in music and fashion but also in architecture, because it can now be seen to constitute an identifiable style or expression of its own.

There is not quite this option available in *Heteropolis*. If the notion of 'hetero-architecture' stands for anything, it is the fact that it lies beyond the identifiable eclecticism of postmodernism. Although postmodernism is still the guiding 'stylistic' thread or trait throughout the book, Jencks proposes that it is to be seen in Los Angeles in its 'raw' or 'uncooked' state. This is the true 'Wild West' aspect of Los Angeles: the fact that its defining architecture is not describable, either stylistically or semiotically. Thus, as Jencks writes of Gehry's *Gehry House* (1978–9), 'one can see features from former styles, but the striking aspect of the design is its unclassifiability' (Jencks, 1993, p. 59). Or as he writes of Eric Owen Moss' *708 House* (1981), 'a strong idea is set up to be partially interrupted and refuted, a bold form is presented to be unceremoniously challenged by something completely different' (Jencks, 1993, p. 63). But it is also at this point that Jencks can be seen to be retreating, aware not only of the critical difficulty of trying to describe something that by definition can have no identity, but more importantly of the implications of this 'the one *and* the many' (Jencks, 1993, p. 104) for the possibility of political liberation, let alone any actual resistance to capitalism. This is ultimately Jameson's point, of course, that the cultural logic of postmodernism not only arises out of but is effectively complicit with the making-equal of capitalism, and his solution is to call for a 'resistance to the concept of totality' (Jameson, 1991, p. 330). This is Jencks' solution as well to the potential 'weak eclecticism' (Jencks, 1993, p. 116) he discerns, and he argues for a renewed taxonomy and another, more 'inventive' (Jencks, 1993, p. 104) democracy, which can through a certain 'double coding' (Jencks, 1993, p. 117) withstand the forces of homogenization for as long as possible.

In this essay we want to hold on to – undoubtedly, in an impossible, almost 'utopian' way – this original impulse of Jencks' book. We want to suggest that what Jencks identified there – exactly at the end of the period of postmodernism – is a new stylistic principle coming after postmodernism. We want to contend that Jencks was indeed prescient in identifying a new 'aesthetic' that is everywhere today, seen not only in architecture but also in the visual arts and fashion, in which the various parts of the same object are in fact *indifferent* to each other. It is an aesthetic of what we will call 'whatever', and it involves the difficult game of trying to put things together without producing any resulting style or meaning. It is a form of pastiche or bricolage, but without any quotational aspect, and thus no 'second degree'. It is rather just things 'in themselves', outside of any protective discourse. There is no criticality, no 'aboutness', no irony. Just a straightforward 'brutality of fact'. There is thus no metaphor, allegory, dialectic, nor any of the other ways of expressing how things are put together that have been used throughout the twentieth century: montage, collage, assemblage. Just a kind of neutrality or indifference. An indifference – and here another distinction from Jencks' position – that can have no direct political meaning or consequences. We simply cannot say what this artistic act is equivalent to. In this regard, what we are speaking of is resistant to all critical description and analysis – and if we nevertheless attempt to describe and analyse it here, it is with an absolute sense of the necessary self-contradiction involved.

Visual art and fashion

Let us begin by taking some examples from the visual arts and fashion. In the run-down suburb of Filipinotown on the outskirts of Los Angeles, Californian-born artist Jason Rhoades in 2005 put on a series of installations-cum-performances called *Black Pussy Soirée Cabaret Macramé*. At the lit centre of a darkened warehouse, hundreds of guests mingled, as overhead twinkled no fewer than 427 neon signs, each spelling out a different name for women's genitals in various African, Caribbean, Creole and gangsta rap vernaculars. Elsewhere throughout the cavernous spaces of the warehouse, looking more like a storage facility than anything resembling a conventional art gallery, Rhoades had arranged some 556 Native American Dreamcatchers, a seized consignment of hookah pipes, assorted Middle Eastern bric-à-brac, a set of Chinese contemplative Gongshi stones, 799 ceramic donkeys done in faux-Mexican style, 232 small brass Egyptian pyramids and a machine that periodically blew smoke into the air, which allowed the 180 beaver-skin cowboy hats Rhoades had distributed around the space to be moulded into either vulva-shaped dents or penis-shaped lumps (Danilowicz, 2007, pp. 34–44).

Rhoades himself, when not sprawled on a large bed in the corner of the space, alternately sprayed his guests with a mixture of hot wax and scented fragrance from his so-called *spukaki*-gun or enjoined them to come up with other pussy words in a 'black' language, so that they could be turned into a neon sign for the next iteration of the performance. The guests themselves, apart from being able to drink at one of the several bars scattered around the space, could avail themselves of vegan icecreams, although they had to eat them out of their shoes. Besides art-world guests – artists and dealers had their own Johnny Cash Bar – Rhoades also invited Mexican workers from nearby factories, both to fill out the crowd and to take the event beyond the usual art-world audience. For his part, the reviewer for the *Guardian*, who saw the show when it was later installed at the prestigious Hauser & Wirth Gallery in Piccadilly in London, went looking for the 10 'white virgins' mentioned in one of Rhoades' checklists, but regretfully informed readers that he could not find them among the hundreds of shelves and storage racks that made up the show, leading him to wonder whether they might perhaps be buried beneath the 896 glass vegetables also mentioned in one of the artist's subinventories (Searle, 2005).

Example two: in December 2007 the New Museum, recently relocated to the Bowery in New York, staged for its opening show *Unmonumental: The Object in the 21st Century*, curated by Richard Flood, Laura Hoptman and Massimiliano Gioni. The exhibition featured works by some 30 artists, some well known, like Sam Durant and Isa Genzken, and others not so well known, like Carol Bove and Rachel Harrison. The work in the show, which was specifically intended as sculpture and not the more prevalent form of installation, was variously described as 'intimate', 'small scale' and 'anti-heroic', which made it, according to the catalogue for the exhibition, ideal for our anti-utopian early twenty-first century (Flood et al., 2007, pp. 67–8). Thus Gioni, making a distinction between these works and previous forms of art, insisted that, if the work was 'unmonumental', it was not so much 'anti-monumental', which implied the still destructive and transgressive task of tearing what has already been built down, as 'non-monumental', in the more passive sense of simply not wanting to build anything up (Flood et al., 2007, pp. 64–5).

Thus in the show we had John Bock's *N.Y.* (2006), in which the arms of a stuffed sweater are sewn to two laser discs, which then lead us through a series of pipes to a metal table, on top of which a small casserole dish is balanced. On the other side of the room, a refrigerator, around which masking tape has been affixed, leans on a trolley against the wall, and next to that three taped-together bricks, an upside-down plastic cup and a golf club either rest on or are inserted through a collapsed spiral staircase. We had Isa Genzken's *Elefant* (2006), in which a series of corrugated plastic tubes, bound together with wallpaper and bubble-wrap, lean backwards over a rickety-looking cardboard plinth. Disassembled strips of white vertical blinds also hang over the plinth, and out of the middle of the wallpaper and bubble-wrap holding the tubes together silver and black plastic flowers thrust into the air. We had Rachel Harrison's *Huffy Howler* (2004), in which a child's BMX bike is held up in the middle by what looks like a glued-together selection of purple painted rocks. From the handlebars of the bike dangle a number of handbags, filled with stones and gravel, while off the back of the bike, suspended from a long pole, flap a fake sheepskin coat and a publicity still of Mel Gibson in the role of William Wallace in the film *Braveheart*.

Example three: we would start with the fashion designers Yohji Yamamoto and Rei Kawakubo, founders of the (mistakenly named) aesthetic of Minimalism in fashion. In 1981 for his debut show in Paris Yamamoto made asymmetrical dresses out of distressed fabrics with holes irregularly punched in them. In 1985 he put out a collection of men's jackets, in which, as well as his trademark exposed stitching, unexplained flaps and mismatched buttons, the waist is not tapered and all interior padding has been stripped out. Along the same lines, in the early 1980s Kawakubo made jumpers in which the wearer could decide which hole to put their head and arms through, thus making the outline of the garment arbitrary. In the early '90s she brought out her famous 'Bump' collection, in which the curve of the clothes did not match the profile of the body beneath but deliberately broke with it. And, extending this, in the late '90s she brought out a collection of bright red stretch gingham skirts, which were also padded with assorted bumps.

And there is now a younger generation of designers following Yamamoto and Kawakubo, who are not obviously 'Minimalist' (which proves that it is not a style that is in question here). We might think of the Belgium-based Martin Margiela, who pushes ever further their aesthetic of the unfinished and poverty-stricken, making clothes with uneven seams and frayed threads, often employing up to three unrelated materials (e.g. rose prints, gauze and fabric on which mould has been allowed to grow) for the same surface or disassembling one piece of clothing (e.g. a black leather jacket or a tulle ballgown) to make another, and either ripping off sleeves or adding extra ones in making suits. And, for all of his apparent excess, we can see something similar with Alexander McQueen. In his defining 1985 *Highland Rape* collection, he hung bodices off the models' skirts and combined tartan with taffeta. In 2009 he produced his extraordinary black and white houndstooth and stripe dress with Sydney Opera House hat, and in 2001 just after leaving the fashion house Givenchy he put on the show *Voss*, which featured models in gasmasks, dresses made of white varnished razor-clam shells and ballgowns made of red dyed ostrich feathers teamed with painted medical slides.

An aesthetic of 'whatever'

Is there really anything we can identify in common to Rhoades, the artists of *Unmonumental*, Yamamoto, Kawakubo, Margiela and McQueen? And how in turn do they all bear some relation to that 'hetero-architecture' Jencks points to in his book? Of course, in each case – just as in *Heteropolis* – there is a whole effort to impute meaning of some kind to their objects. In the wake of Rhoades' death in 2006, there has been a concerted biographical reading of his work and attempt to see it as the expression of a particular time and place. In an obituary for the *LA Times*, 'He Left One Puzzle Behind', Diane Haithman suggests that, given Rhoades' overloaded and over-stimulated art, it is somehow appropriate that he died of a combination of 'arterioschlerotic heart disease' and an 'accidental overdose' of pharmaceuticals and heroin (Haithman, 2006). The curators of *Unmonumental* lay out a detailed genealogy for the work, recalling Duchamp's readymade and Rauschenberg's assemblages, and go on to speak of the work's social relevance and significance. As curator Flood writes (admittedly, a little obscurely) in his catalogue essay: 'Works that appear hurled into uncomfortable, anxious relationships run parallel to life. Objects with knots of nerve endings reaching out to find a brain mirror the fugue states of everyday consciousness' (Flood et al., 2007, p. 12). And, of course, there is an entire industry devoted to giving clothes a style and fashion, a pedigree and justification (Yamamoto and Kawakubo as inheritors of Issey Miyaki's distressed fabrics and deconstructed kimonos, Margiela and McQueen as coming after Vivienne Westwood and her safety-pinned stitched-together kilts).

But we want to suggest that in each case there is also something resisting this, a deliberate attempt to defeat the mechanisms of meaning and relevance and achieving a state of what we might call indifference, an 'anti-aesthetic' with no meaning. In Rhoades, this would proceed by an 'excess' designed to outstrip all propriety and taxonomy. And perhaps the 'tragedy' of the work – although it is not biographical – is that Rhoades discovers no limit, no rules to transgress, no parties (women, Muslims) to insult. In *Unmonumental*, the sculptors proceed in the opposite direction: not by addition, as with Rhoades, but via a kind of subtraction. There would be in their work the slow withdrawal of all aesthetic properties, the gradual attenuation of all sense, meaning, art-historical genealogy, the work's status as art and any criteria by which to judge it. And with our designers, although there still remains a fashion and beauty (anti-fashion being, after all, only another form of fashion, indeed, it could be argued, what all fashion originally begins as), there is also something else: the attempt to prevent for as long as possible this turning-into-fashion, a muteness (no matter how loud or apparently bold the gesture), a 'fashion degree zero'. Tartan with taffeta or gauze, rose prints and mould: nothing happens. There is no resolution, no sudden affinity, merely a brute juxtaposition that leaves each material untransformed. And therefore no 'fashion', no identifiable style, for others to copy or emulate.

All of this is undoubtedly utopian, fugitive, no sooner remarked than done away with, necessarily betrayed by its commentators, curators and critics. And it is, of course, a form of postmodern pastiche, eclecticism, appropriation. Only next year's style or fashion, contemporary as opposed to postmodern, unwinding in a seamless and linear continuity. But at the same time the objects we have looked at are not within but somehow outside of the sign, are not second-hand but original. With regard to them we are involved in a confrontation with the raw materiality of the object outside of any sublimation, either discursive or aesthetic (this is perhaps what we mean by describing it as indifferent). Similarly, what we are describing is not a style or fashion but something 'before' this. The 'Minimalism' of Japanese fashion is precisely a word for this non-style, this non-fashion. Its essential 'unchangingness' or 'unfashionability' does not even rise to the level of 'resistance' or anti-fashion, as with punk, but is more like the refusal or fashion altogether, a certain 'I prefer not to'. It is not anything as heroic as anti-style, but more like the principle of always one more, as in the case of Rhoades, so that eventually any imagined unity that the various elements are said to have in common is exposed to a certain 'nothing in common', or an always one less, as with the case of *Unmonumental*, so that for any perceived aesthetic commonality, there will always be an exception, one that fails to fulfil the criterion.

Architecture

There is always, as we say, the impossibility of 'applying' Jencks' analysis to architecture beyond Los Angeles. It is not merely that we cannot turn it into a unified style, but it does not even belong to Los Angeles, is only to invoke a certain disaggregation of Los Angeles. Nevertheless, we conclude here by looking in some detail at a number of architectural instances of this style of 'whatever'. We do attempt to put our finger on what is happening now and happening worldwide. But it is not so much a style as a logic, a logic that, if in a way is always singular, is also to be found everywhere, insofar as it points to the possibility of an object having any style whatsoever. We are tempted to call it (despite everything we have said) the moment of the *contemporary* in architecture, which comes after postmodernism. It would be an extension of the making-equivalent of postmodernism, but without any final meaning, any final 'unity' of its differences, any point outside of it from which to remark upon it. Criticism would, therefore, remain as much as possible on the level of the object itself, unable to unify what it describes even as the style of pluralism, appropriation or postmodernism.

Our first example is the architectural practice of the London-based FAT (Sean Griffiths, Charles Holland and Sam Jacob). The practice is broadly known for its revival of postmodernism – indeed, in 2011 it co-edited with Jencks a special issue of *Architectural Design* on the topic. For the members of FAT, postmodernism is cutting-edge exactly because it is so unfashionable. In an essay for the special issue, 'Post-Modernism: An Incomplete Project', they quote artist Dan Graham suggesting that the most radical thing to do at any particular juncture is 'that which was most recently fashionable' (Jencks et al., 2011, p. 18). By this, what they really mean – for, in fact, their use of the term remains 'tactical' – is that they are opposed to what they see as the revival of a certain 'neo-formalism' or 'neo-modernism' after the 'end' of postmodernism (Jencks et al., 2011, p. 18). For FAT, postmodernism is associated with such qualities as decoration, figuration and ornamentation, and more particularly – this is a constant emphasis in their writing – a way of working against a 'central narrative' and 'hollow abstraction' (Jencks et al., 2011, p. 21). As opposed to this, they are aiming for a tone – and this is seen by their best critics – that is 'cool', 'objective', 'non-judgemental', almost like an autopsy (Jencks et al., 2011, p. 70). Indeed, they acknowledge the influence of the Pop Art of Warhol and Ed Ruscha on their work, in which repetition produces difference and the lack of obvious emotion paradoxically heightens it. FAT's signature architectural device – which it mobilizes in full awareness of how it cuts against current architectural orthodoxy – is the 'facade' or the 'figural section' (Jencks et al., 2011, p. 68). It is to be found in a wide variety of their buildings, from their early *Blue House*, Hackney (2002), in which an entire under-scale house motif is used as a cut-out billboard, through their *Islington Square* (2006), Manchester, in which residents' DIY interior renovations are used for exterior brick surfaces, to their more recent *De Grote Koppel*, Amersfoort, Holland (2010), in which over-scaled classical window surrounds have grown to become the entire exterior wall. It is a facadism that is not just vertical and seen at the front, but horizontal and takes place at the top. In 1998 FAT renovated a writer's house in Clapham in London, in the course of which they added a two-storey external library, which is now visible through backlit windows from inside the main house, producing an effect described as a 'grand Palladian house' squeezed into a small, Victorian terrace (Jencks et al., 2011, p. 81). Here, however, we want to consider for a moment the recent commission by FAT for the BBC drama production studios in Cardiff, which was undertaken with the firm Holder Mathias. Holder Mathias built the multi-purpose studios in which television shows for the Corporation were to be shot and staged, and across the front of these nondescript and factory-like buildings FAT have added a 300-metre long clip-on and cartoonish facade made of wood that does not completely cover the surface to which it is attached.

The radical point here is that there is deliberately no connection between the front of the building and what lies behind it. Sean Griffiths of FAT describes the incoherent planning process behind the building, insofar as the municipal authority had to complete the project by a certain date and effectively the two firms had to undertake two separate commissions without time to work together (Olcayto, 2011, pp. 26–7). However, the facade works here not, as is usually the case, to provide a coherent surface image to what might otherwise appear disparate, but on the contrary to bring out a gap not just between the front and the back of the building, but between the different elements of Holder Mathias' production facilities themselves. As Chris Patten, the BBC Trust Chairman, put it, the resulting combination is like 'Ikea crossed with the Doge's Palace' (Olcayto, 2011, p. 32). And this internal and not merely external disjunction can be seen in other aspects of FAT's practice, such as sudden jumps in scale between doors in the same room (*The Blue House*) or the insertion of a suburban living room inside a nightclub (*The Brunel Rooms*, Swindon, 1995).

There are any number of contemporary architects in whose work we can see this 'facadism': sudden discontinuities between front and back, interior volume and exterior surface and different and unmatched materials (Sou Fujimoto, Valerio Olgiati, Hild und K Architekten). But here, to conclude, we just want to look at a 'homegrown' (for us) instance of this 'hetero-architecture': the Melbourne-based Lyons Architects. Lyons, in fact, has a considerable institutional practice, particularly in hospitals and tertiary education institutes, so the radicality of their buildings is even more difficult to achieve than it might at first appear. The practice has a thoroughly worked-out philosophy, in which there is support for 'postmodernism' and the 'putting of oddly contrary ideas together' (Lyons, 2012, p. 2). And even more importantly for our purposes, when they speak of their practice as 'ugly', they insist that this is not simply an oppositional gesture but what they call 'agnostic' (Lyons, 2012, p. 343). In a sense, they aim for an uncompromised complexity or what they call 'synthesis without editing' (Lyons, 2012, p. 2). More technically, what we see in their work is a split between the interior function of their buildings (hospital, university campus, business centre) and its exterior form. But this is not, as even their more sympathetic critics see it, a mere dissembling of their buildings' underlying function (Lyons, 2012, p. 270). Rather, Lyons' more profound point is that this exterior introduces a split into the building's *interior* purpose.

A classic instance of this is their hospital for old people (*Sunshine Hospital*, Melbourne, 2001), where a polychrome wall of glazed bricks both references Monet's haystacks and offers an image of patients staring out of the windows for drivers on the nearby highway. Of course, this is a much remarked-upon break with the usual institutional grey of such facilities, but Lyons' point is that this façade changes what is within or even more exactly introduces a split into what lies within. Now the hospital is not just a place to rest and recover but also a kind of holiday resort. Two other examples of this split between exterior form and interior function can be seen in their *Nelson Campus Refurbishment* (1998), which features a foyer formed by two irregularly nested spheres, and the *IT Business Centre* for the University of Ballarat (2004), in which an asymmetrical central courtyard is formed by tracing the shadows cast by the sun at various times of the day. It is also to be seen in a series of buildings in which the supporting corners are apparently missing, as though something has bitten through them (*School of Medicine*, University of Tasmania, 2009; *North Richmond Community Health Centre*, Melbourne, 2012). But undoubtedly this logic reaches its high point in a number of buildings Lyons has done for university medical and biotech research centres (*School of Medicine*, University of Western Sydney, 2008; *Kenneth Myer Building*, University of Melbourne, 2011). Precisely their point here is that at the deepest level of life there is no match between the visual appearance of DNA and what forms it will produce. Instead, they want to capture the essential *epigenesis* of life, in which different outcomes can arises from the same original set of conditions. This is why so many of their buildings are conceived – like FAT's – as 'cross-sections' (Lyons, 2012, p. 377), in which what we see is only a sample of the available information that could be presented another way. As Lyons writes in its brief for the job: 'The precast "skull bones" that contain the research space are conceived of as part anamorphic and part architectural . . . Throughout the interior optical illusions draw one back to the strange workings of the brain. Can I believe what I see?' (Lyons, 2012, p. 379). Here architectural form is understood as *its own difference from itself*. In their *Kenneth Myer Building*, for example, there is an implicit relationship between how the different elements of the building connect with each other and the neuronal connections that take place in the brain. If thought takes place across bridges in the brain, so the 'ideas' in their buildings are understood as occurring across the perceived differences between the various forms and materials that make it up. Here is the equivalence between architectural thinking and its materials that Lyons is searching for. It does not occur within its materials, but only between them, in a kind of endless parataxis or opening up of things to the outside. As architectural critic John Macarthur writes in the essay 'Ugliness and Romanticism in the Work of Lyons':

> The practice speaks of 'turning up the dial of metaphor' towards literalism, punning and visual illusion, but at the same time this preference for 'reading' over 'experiencing' a building means turning down the dial of experience or rather the significance of experience. This is itself an aesthetic of a certain kind of experience, where one's phenomenal encounter seems incidental to the building's other concerns. What interests me most in the work of Lyons is this sense that the building knows and possesses itself independently of an observer. We often fantasise that buildings are actualised by the experience of the beholder, whereas they are objects indifferent to us. (Lyons, 2012, p. 270)

The 'missed' encounter

What would be, to conclude, the relationship between the work we have been discussing and any kind of 'radical' philosophy? And, moreover, how could this relationship be thought in terms of the long-running artistic and political problem of 'idolatry'? Obviously, the point we have been trying to make with regard to all of our works of art – architecture, the visual arts, fashion – is that they seek above all to break with the 'image'. That 'heterogeneity' they manifest is not amenable to any unity: visual, conceptual, critical, philosophical. They attempt – and this is the paradoxical task of all images today – not to form an image, to defeat iconolatry, to be in effect iconoclastic. And to this extent, they do not adhere to any political programme, progressive or otherwise. This is the challenge Jencks sees in *Heteropolis* and ultimately shrinks from: that the architecture he speaks of does not finally come from any recognizable politics, does not make up any kind of 'democratic' image. But it is also perhaps to say – contra Jameson and his attempt to see similar buildings as examples of a generalized 'cultural logic of postmodernism' – that they are also not 'illustrative' of capitalism. They attempt to resist – this is our admittedly self-contradictory project here – all attempts to symptomatize them like this, to make them stand in for anything. This is, if anything, what we have sought to do here: to understand these works of art in their own terms. It is only in this always 'missed' encounter that any kind of radical philosophy can think them: they *are* their missed encounter with philosophy. This is both how any so-called radical philosophy must think them and how they constitute themselves a form of radical philosophy.

As a final example of this missed encounter in action, and how it allows a certain 'symptomal' reading of philosophy, let us look at Slavoj Žižek's most recent book *Less than Nothing*. In the chapter 'Where There is Nothing, Read That I Love You', Žižek attempts to explain – perhaps in a slightly self-justificatory way – the meaning of an apparent mistake or self-contradiction in one of his earlier books, *The Fright of Real Tears*. In that book, Žižek begins by recounting an anecdote – almost in a Sokal hoax-like manner – in which, at a Cultural Studies conference, having nothing to say about a particular work of art, he came up with the concept of 'between-the-two-frames', which deliberately meant nothing, but that he was horrified to see his fellow delegates take seriously. However, later in the same book, as critics have pointed out, Žižek uses himself the same concept non-ironically and intending for it to be taken seriously. In explanation of this, Žižek writes in *Less than Nothing*: 'Even when a subject mocks a certain belief, this in no way undermines the belief's symbolic efficacy' (Žižek, 2012, p. 87). But, in fact, evidence for this 'seriousness' was already to be seen in the book before *Less than Nothing*, *Living in the End Times*, where in the chapter 'The Architectural Parallax' Žižek speaks of what he calls the 'architectural spandrel', in which there are always two 'frames', and these 'two frames by definition never overlap – there is an invisible gap separating them' (Žižek, 2010, p. 275). In other words, with regards to this between-the-two-frames or architectural spandrel, Žižek is even more serious than he realizes, or in fact more subject to its logic than he is conscious of. And the crucial thing about this spandrel is that it is not literal, but transcendental. It is not so much a simple physical space as a 'parallax' that allows the very perception of space. For even though Žižek begins by characterizing it as a gap in buildings between the inside and the outside – an 'interstitial space opened up by the disconnection between skin and structure' (Žižek, 2010, p. 276) – his real point is that there is a 'spandrel' even when there is no such gap between inside and outside. It is a distance that exists even between touching or contiguous surfaces, like the front and back of a window or in buildings in which there is no hollow space between the walls. In a sense, everything we have tried to speak of here has been this 'spandrel' or 'parallax', although as with

Žižek it has already been speaking of us before we opened our mouths. It has been the 'transcendental' condition of everything we have had to say here – or, to put this another way, like Žižek, we have done nothing but miss it.

Rex Butler

References

Danilowicz, N. (2007), 'The Occidental Death of Jason Rhoades', *ArtUS*, 18, pp. 34–44.

Flood, R., Hoptman, L., Gioni, M. and Smith, T. (2007), *Unmonumental: The Object in the 21st Century*. London: Phaidon.

Haithman, D. (2006), 'He Left Behind One Last Puzzle', *LA Times*, 18 August. Available at: <http://articles.latimes.com/2006/aug/18/entertainment/et-rhoades18>.

Jameson, F. (1984), 'Postmodernism: The Cultural Logic of Late Capitalism', *New Left Review*, no. 146, 53–92.

— (1991), *Postmodernism, or, The Cultural Logic of Late Capitalism*. Durham: Duke University Press.

Jencks, C. (1978), *The Language of Post-Modern Architecture* (2nd edition). London: Academy Editions.

— (1993), *Heteropolis: Los Angeles, The Riots and the Strange Beauty of Hetero-Architecture*. London: Academy Editions.

Jencks, C. and FAT (2011), 'Special Issue: Radical Post-modernism', *Architectural Design*, 81, 5.

Lyons Architects (2012), *More: The Architecture of Lyons 1996–2011*. Fishermans Bend, VIC: Thames & Hudson.

Olcayto, R. (2011), 'FAT Boyo Slim', *The Architect's Journal*, 24 November, pp. 24–32.

Searle, A. (2005), 'Sex Gods', *The Guardian*, 20 September. Available at: <http://www.theguardian.com/culture/2005/sep/20/2>.

Žižek, S. (2010), *Living in the End Times*. London: Verso.

— (2012), *Less than Nothing*. London: Verso.

12

Architecture and Antiphilosophy

Nadir Lahiji

When Alain Badiou, at the beginning of his *Manifesto for Philosophy* cites Jean-Francoise Lyotard as having said, 'Philosophy as architecture is ruined', it is only to immediately challenge it: 'Is it however possible to imagine a philosophy that is not the least architectonic?' (Badiou, 1999, p. 28).[1] Much later, on another occasion, Badiou made a significant remark that may be related to his statement in his *Manifesto*. He said: 'The architecture of a philosophical idea exists in itself; it has its autonomy. In this sense too, I am a Platonist' (Badiou with Tarby, 2013, p. 88).

Lyotard is, of course, one among the 'new' modern sophists on Badiou's list whom he takes to task in his *Manifesto*. In his rejoinder, Badiou might at first glance appear to resemble Kant – the philosopher whom he does not have so much sympathy for – who in the *Critique of Pure Reason* said that 'human reason is by nature architectonic' (Kant, 1998). Kant in his first *Critique* maintained that *architectonics* is the 'art of system' on which the philosophical knowledge is built.[2] He called 'the system that renders knowledge architectonic' by the name 'philosophy' (Lacour, 1999, p. 23). For both philosophers, Badiou and Kant, architectonics is more than just a 'metaphor of architecture', which is a recurring metaphor in philosophy from Plato onward. But one major difference, at least, would separate Badiou from Kant, which is the difference over the problematic of the relationship of architectonic to the concept of mathematics. Kojin Karatani in his impressive book *Architecture as Metaphor*, on which I will dwell extensively for my argument, claims that in times of crisis Western philosophy attempts to renew itself by reiterating the *will to architecture* (Karatani, 1995, p. 5).[3] Illuminating the role of metaphor of architecture in Plato, and in those who came after him namely, Descartes, Kant, and Hegel, Karatani perspicaciously writes:

> Even though, like architecture, mathematics is semi-becoming, philosophers since Plato have turned to mathematics because it ostensibly offers the ideal ground to architectonic on which something genuinely new can be established. Philosophy, in fact is another name for this *will to architecture*. Architecture as a metaphor dominated mathematics and even architecture itself until 1931, when Kurt

Gödel's incompleteness theorem invalidated mathematics as the ground for the architectonic. (Karatani, *Architecture as Metaphor*, 1995, p. xxxii)

For Kant mathematics is 'an priori synthetic judgement' as opposed to logic, which is 'an analytic judgement', because of the fact that mathematics 'requires sensuous intuition and thus cannot be logically grounded'.[4] For Badiou, who bases his mathematics firmly on Godel's incompleteness theorem and set theory – which as Karatani says 'invalidated mathematics as the ground for architectonic' – the *will to architecture* reaches its *limits*. The metaphor of architecture is evacuated from his philosophical system as he establishes mathematics as ontology, as it is well-known.[5] In the same way that Kant instituted a break with tradition in his time, so does Badiou in our time. He inaugurates a break with the metaphor of architecture, as he is not among the philosophers who used the metaphor of architecture 'as a way of grounding and stabilizing their otherwise unstable philosophical system' (Karatani, p. 5). In his case, architectonic is based on the idea of the Platonic 'dialogue'. Karatani himself engages in Kantian 'transcendental critique' as a firm conceptual tool to intervene into the discourse of 'architecture as metaphor' that nevertheless cannot be wished away by denial. He remarks: 'Although at first glance Kant appears to incline toward the Platonic use of architecture as metaphor, the opposite is true' (Karatani, p. xlii). This is even truer in the case of Badiou who goes back to Plato to renew philosophy in our time. Kant's critiques, Karatani crucially points out, were not intended to 'construct a system' but rather 'to reveal that any system "inevitably bring[s] with it the ruin of all" in as much as it is upheld under the aegis of the "arrogation of reason"' (Karatani, 1995, p. xliv).[6] More importantly: '*What is crucial to note is that architectonic as metaphor is indispensible to the critique of architecture as metaphor*' (Karatani, p. xliv) [emphasis mine]. This crucial but paradoxical distinction would be instructive and useful to attribute an architectonics role to Badiou's philosophical system, minimally necessary to understand his challenge to what he has named as *antiphilosophy*. Badiou's return to Plato and his invocation of architectonic as the art of building 'solid foundation', must be qualified, therefore, not as a return to the 'metaphor of architecture' but rather a critique of it in the line of Kantian critique. This critique must be granted its proper place in the notion of antiphilosophy. Badiou goes against the adversaries of philosophy, so-called modern-day sophists, or the 'new' postmodern sophists – whose stand would overlap with antiphilosophy in certain cases – in the same way Kant faced the empiricists like David Hume in his own time. Slavoj Žižek's commentary in his *Tarrying with Negative* in this regard is very illuminating:

> According to Alain Badiou, we live today in the age of the 'new sophist.' The two crucial breaks in the history of philosophy, Plato's and Kant's, occurred as reaction to new relativistic attitudes which threatened to demolish the traditional corpus of knowledge: in Plato's case, the logical argumentation of the sophists undermined the mythical foundations of the traditional mores; in Kant's case, empiricists (such as Hume) undermined the foundations of the Leibnizean-Wolfian rationalist metaphysics. In both cases, the solution offered is not a return to the traditional attitude but a new founding gesture which 'beats the sophists at their own game,'

i.e., which surmounts the relativism of the sophists by way of its own radicalization (Plato *accepts* the argumentative procedure of the sophists; Kant *accepts* Hume's burial of the traditional metaphysics). (Žižek, 1993, p. 4)

What makes Badiou's renewal of philosophy distinct is his paradoxical adherence to the 'antiphilosopher' Jacques Lacan, whom he called his 'master'.[7] It was first Lacan who coined the term antiphilosophy.[8] Badiou in *Manifesto for Philosophy* declared that 'the anti-philosopher Lacan is a condition of the renaissance of philosophy. A philosophy is possible today, only if it is compossible with Lacan' (Badiou, 1999, p. 84). In explaining Lacan's declaration, '*I rise up in revolt,* so to speak, against philosophy' ['Je m'insurge contre la philosophie'], Žižek further points out that it is 'post-Hegelian philosophy in its three main branches namely, analytical philosophy, phenomenology and Marxism that are conceived as "antiphilosophy" that Lacan is opposing.' Žižek in his defense of Lacan in the same *Tarrying with Native* says:

> In his *German Ideology,* Marx mockingly observes that philosophy relates to 'actual life' as masturbation to sexual act; the positivist tradition claims to replace philosophy (metaphysics) with the scientific analysis of the concept; the Heideggerian phenomenologists endeavor to 'pass through philosophy' toward the post-philosophical 'thought.' In short, what is today practiced as 'philosophy' are precisely different attempts to 'deconstruct' something referred to as the classical philosophical corpus ('metaphysics,' 'logocentrism,' etc). One is therefore tempted to risk hypothesis that what Lacan's 'antiphilosophy' opposes is this very philosophy qua antiphilosophy: what if Lacan's own theoretical *practice* involves a kind of *return to philosophy*? (Žižek, 1993, pp. 3–4)

He continues:

> And it is our hypothesis that Lacan opens up the possibility of another repetition of the same gesture. That is to say, the 'postmodern theory' which predominates today is a mixture of neopragmatism and deconstruction best epitomized by names such as Rorty or Lyotard; their works empathize the 'anti-essentialist' refusal of universal Foundation, the dissolving of 'truth' into an effect of plural language-game, the relativization of its scope to historically specific intersubjective community, etc. Isolated desperate endeavors of a 'postmodern' return to the Sacred are quickly reduced to just another language game, to another way we 'tell stories about ourselves.' Lacan, however, is not part of this 'postmodern theory': in this respect, his position is homologous to that of Plato or Kant. The perception of Lacan as an 'anti-essentialist' or 'deconstructionist' falls prey to the same illusion as that of perceiving Plato as just one among the sophists. Plato accepts from the sophists their logic of discursive argumentation, but uses it to affirm his commitment to Truth; Kant accepts the breakdown of the traditional metaphysics, but uses it to perform his transcendental turn; along the same line, Lacan accepts the 'deconstructionist' motif of radical contingency, but turns this motif against itself to assert his commitment to Truth *as contingent.* (Žižek, 1993, p. 4)

In the same vein, for Badiou the sophist, 'the perverted double of the philosopher', must 'only be assigned *to his place*' (Badiou, 1999, p. 133). As other commentators after Žižek have pointed out, Badiou's attempt to renew philosophy must be considered, paradoxically, under the notion of 'philosophy *qua* antiphilosophy'.[9] Or, as Badiou himself puts it, 'inasmuch as there is a philosophy of Lacanianism, it's the philosophy of antiphilosophy' (in Johnston, 2010, p. 154). Elsewhere in *Conditions* Badiou says, 'To clarify the matter of Lacan's anti-philosophy, it is doubtless necessary to refer to "the Plato symptom." The Plato symptom applies universally to every stance our contemporaries hold on what philosophy is' (Badiou, *Conditions*, 2008, p. 229). As Adrian Johnson aptly sums up: 'Badiou's position mandates two inverse yet complementary movements: a philosophical traversal of antiphilosophy (as Lacanian psychoanalysis) and an antiphilosophical traversal of philosophy' (Johnston, 2010, p. 157).

Following these remarks, it can be claimed that, at this time of crisis, there is yet another reiteration of the *will to architecture* by Badiou. But this time around, this other name for philosophy must be qualified under the terms of antiphilosophy. To transpose Karatani's statement above, it can be said that for Badiou, it is not that 'philosophy is another name for the *will to architecture*', but rather, this 'philosophy *qua* antiphilosophy' is another name for the '*will to architecture*'. This return to philosophy again is grounded in the 'ungroundedness' of mathematics and *formalization* and in what Lacan called 'matheme'.[10] 'Today formalism is ubiquitous. No longer useful, perception, affect, nature, life, and the life-world have been dismissed as part of the romanticist reaction against the architectonic', Karatani remarks (Karatani, pp. 18–19). Furthermore, 'Not even philosophy is beyond the reach of formalization. Husserl devoted himself to the question, "What is left for philosophy after formalization?" We might say that if philosophy can be said to exist, it is only in the form of self-referential question, "What is left for philosophy?" Yet this question itself is not left untouched by formalization' (Karatani, p. 101). Still, 'philosophy is a self-referential system where ultimate determination and closure are impossible' (Karatani, p. 103). The Platonist mathematician Kurt Gödel who, in the twentieth century, introduced 'undecidibility' into mathematics, as Karatani informs us, famously proved the impossibility of formalization by a rigorous formalization. The foundation is the absence of foundation. This 'Foundation' is at the base of Badiou's renewal of philosophy. But at the same time, it is important to bear in mind that *formalization* does not derive from mathematics, but from the *will to architecture,* as Karatani claims. It was imposed upon mathematics.[11] He writes:

> Gödel's proof released mathematics from the illusion of the architectonic and showed that, under the guise of accepting mathematics as normative, the architectonic has always concealed the absence of its own foundation. Despite its solid, if tautological, appearances, mathematics continues even today to develop in manifold ways precisely because it is not an edifice. Mathematics, we can say, is essentially historical. (Karatani, p. 56)

In Western thought, let us reiterate Karatani's claim, 'what is crucial is not the edifice of knowledge itself, but the will to architecture that is renewed with every crisis – a will that is nothing but irrational choice to establish order and structure within a chaotic and manifold becoming, a will that is only one choice among many' (Karatani, p. 18). Plato, to recall, was the first to employ the figure of the architect as metaphor. Significantly, Karatani goes to Plato's *Symposium* (which is a discourse on Love) and not to *Republic* (which is the usual reference for pointing to the 'metaphor of architecture' in Platonic philosophy) to note that architecture through the act of 'making' [*poiesis*] is able to 'resists or withstands all "becomings"'. He quotes the relevant passage in *Symposium*: 'By its original meaning [*poiesis*] means simply creation, and creation, as you know, can take very various forms. Any action which is the cause of a thing emerging from non-existence into existence might be called [*poiesis*], and all the processes in all the crafts are kinds of [*poiesis*], and all those who are engaged in them [creator]' (Karatani, p. xxxi).[12] Karatani points out that Plato likened philosophers to the figure of architect who would take the same position, but he despised 'the manual labor involved in building' (Karatani, p. xxxii). Thus he draws the conclusion that 'Platonic architecture is metaphorical' and Plato's use of it, and those who came after him, from Descartes to Kant and Hegel, 'should be understood as the will to construct an edifice of knowledge on a solid foundation' (Karatani, p. xxxii). Badiou, who follows Gödel's proof of incompleteness theorem, goes against all anti-Platonic adversaries, from Nietzsche to Wittgenstein to Lyotard and the rest of postmodern neopragmatists and deconstructive 'poststructuralists', from the old sophists, Gorgias and Protagoras, to the new modern sophists. He renews philosophy based on the critique of architectonics to endorse the 'architecture of philosophy' claiming, as I cited above, 'The architecture of a philosophical idea exists in itself; it has its own autonomy' (Badiou with Tarby, 2013, p. 88). It is the metaphor of architecture that permeates the anti-Platonic texts of postmodern sophists against the Platonic *will to architecture,* which must be evacuated from philosophy proper. This qualified will to architecture even reaches the modern poets. Badiou goes after the poet Mallarmé who (like Paul Valéry) would take up the same Platonic position that had originally excluded them. Reading Valery's *Eupalinos or the Architect*, Karatani writes: 'Valéry clearly defines the poet as an architect. Poets once exiled by Plato could now return armed with the Platonic will to architecture, if only to expose the limit of architecture itself' (Karatani, p. 24).[13] Plato would have never thought that he would be one day in the company of the poets against whom he railed! Badiou towards the end of his *Manifesto for Philosophy* writes: 'Mallermé, again: "every thought emits a throw of the dice," Let us throw the dice of philosophy. When the dice fall, there will still be time to discuss, with modern sophists, what Mallarmé calls, "the total count in the making"' (Badiou, 1999, p. 138).

At this point, I tentatively bring this section to an end with above preliminary remarks, which clearly belong to the field of philosophy. My concern is, however, not with philosophy but with the field of architecture. I deployed Karatani's argument purposefully only to intervene 'architecturally' into Badious's discourse, to locate its singularity in the longer tradition of the invariant of *will to architecture* in philosophical texts. The above remarks are therefore intended only as preface to the critique I want to advance against the recent problematic of the importation of 'philosophy' into the architecture discipline, which I name as antiphilosophy. My critique will begin with the premise that if the *will to architecture* is another name for philosophy in the

Western thought, it is the same *will* that is also at work in architecture itself in so far as both are 'self-referential *differential*' systems. I will return to this later. In the last three decades, it is precisely this *will to architecture* in architecture that, as I will argue, has come under attack and has been weakened. The practice of theory in academy has obsessively and insistently held architecture up to the mirror of 'philosophy' in order to do 'high theory'. My critique is geared to breaking this mirror. As Badiou writes, 'philosophy is always the breaking of the mirror. This mirror is the surface of language, on which the sophist sets everything that philosophy treats in its act. If the philosopher claims to contemplate himself on this sole surface, he sees his double, the sophist, suddenly spring forth from it and thus take himself for the sophist' (Badiou, 1999, pp. 143–4). The act of breaking the mirror to which contemporary architecture is held is, therefore, a double act. Breaking it is *also* breaking the 'philosophy' it has incorporated into its corpus, that we are told by Badiou is in a need of a breaking itself. Looking at the surface of this mirror of architecture we see our double twice over. We look terribly distorted and displaced! The discipline's discursive practice imported from the Outside the 'postmodern theory' of deconstructive 'poststructuralist' neo-pragmatist 'philosophy' – that now must be renamed antiphilosophy – which tried to stabilize itself under the metaphors of architecture. It must be noted that it is the same metaphor of architecture that was widely used in various discourses of structuralism and 'poststructuralism'. While I adopt the term antiphilosophy in Badiou's sense that I will explain further below, I nevertheless put the term into a different sense for my own purpose here. I will contend that this 'metaphor of architecture' transferred from 'philosophy' to architecture must itself be evacuated from discourse of architecture in order to *return* architecture to *itself*, or to return architecture to the Platonic *will to architecture* with the caveat that this *will* must be subjected to the critique of architectonics. In this critique, the Kantian turn to 'transcendental critique' is only a starting point.[14] Against the 'local' sophists nesting in the field of architecture, enjoying themselves in company wit the 'new' sophists of philosophy, I am tempted to repeat Žižek's in his *Tarrying with Negative* for my purpose: 'is it possible today, apropos of the postmodern age of new sophists, to repeat *mutatis mutandis* the Kantian gesture?' (Žižek, 1993, p. 5). Before I enter the discourse of architecture and its misappropriation of philosophy, some reflection on the notion of *suture* as related to Badiou's thoughts on antiphilosophy is in order.

Suture: A mark of antiphilosophy

Famously, for Alain Badiou, four '*generic procedures*' constitute the conditions of 'truths' in philosophy: *matheme* or science, politics, art and love.[15] In his *Manifesto for Philosophy* he states: 'We shall thus posit that there are four conditions of philosophy, and the lack of a single one gives rise to its dissipation, just as the emergence of all four conditioned its apparition' (Badiou, 1999, p. 35). Thus, for Badiou, without 'conditions' there will be no philosophy. As the commentators inform us, 'Philosophy is, properly speaking, *indiscernible*, but can come to be under the pressure and constrains of a particular epoch, an epoch wherein the discursive operation of mathematics (or science), art, politics and love are extant and are engaged in thinking and producing the truth of their time. Philosophy then appears as a discursive operation in its own right, one that is itself the formal composition of these irreducible and disparate truths.'[16] Badiou uses the technical term 'suture' to explain the situation when 'philosophy *delegates* its function to one or other of its conditions, handing over the whole of thought to *one* generic procedure' (Badiou, 1999, p. 61). He gives a precise definition: 'I shall call this type of situation a *suture*. Philosophy is placed in suspension every time it presents itself as being sutured to one of its conditions' (Badiou, p. 61). Before Badiou's deployment of the notion of 'suture' in this particular sense in his *Manifesto for Philosophy* in 1989, the concept of the term had already gone through a complex historical debate to which Badiou himself had contributed. Its first occurrence goes back to the famous circle around the journal *Cahiers pour l'Analyse* at École Normale Supérieure (ENS) in Paris, published in ten issues between 1966 and 1969. A selection of the original essays has recently been translated into English and collected in two volumes titled *Concept and Form*.[17] This circle was primarily formed around the two towering figures, Louis Althusser and Jacques Lacan, and the encounter that took place between Marxism and psychoanalysis at the ENS. The actual debate on the notion of suture originally took place between Jacques-Allan Miler and Alain Badiou who were both active members in this circle during this period. Miller wrote his seminal essays 'Suture (Elements of the Logic of the Signifier)' in the first issue of the journal, to which Badiou responded by his 'Mark and Lack' in the last issue.[18] In the last section of this essay I will come back to discuss more this important circle.

A profound ambiguity surrounds the concept of Suture. To clarify its history Slavoj Žižek has written an excellent piece titled '"Suture," Forty Years Later', printed in the second volume of *Concept and Form*. He illuminates the concept of 'suture' tracing it back to the original debate in the *Cahiers* and its subsequent mutations in cinema theory and its reduction in the discourse of deconstruction.[19] I want here to highlight some of the more salient points in Žižek's otherwise comprehensive treatment of the concept. By referring back to the debate between Miller and Badiou mentioned above, Žižek importantly points out that the debate primarily concerns the status of the 'subject' and 'structure' as *the* key elements in the project of 'structuralism'. We have to keep in mind that the germ of the ideas in what later became known as 'structuralism', 'poststructuralism' and 'deconstruction' goes back to the original debate in the *Cahiers* named by Žižek as the 'nodal point' of these discourses, which was rendered reductively in these discourses. It stands for all of what later became known as the 'French Theory'.[20] Žižek remarks that the founding gesture of structuralism is the notion that 'structure' is a 'self-relational differential' system. The question is this: Is there a subject to this structure? Žižek points out that the answer at that time was 'a resounding no'. He explains: 'Even "post"-structuralist deconstruction, with all its emphasis on gap, rupture, difference and deferral, etc., conceived the subject as the culmination of the metaphysics of the self-presence, an entity whose self-identity was something to be dismantled' (Žižek, 2012, p. 147). Žižek refers to Derrida's early analysis of Husserl's phenomenology in which the 'subject's self-presence and self-identity' whose foundation is 'the experience of *"s'entendre-*

parler (of hearing or understanding-oneself-speaking)', which 'is always already undermined by the process of "writing" that stands for deferral of self-identity, by the "dead letter" in the very heart of living spirit' (Žižek, 2012, p. 148). What is important to bear in mind is that, as Žižek writes, deconstruction by valorizing the thematic of gap, deferral and lack, 'dismisses the subject as the agent and result of the obfuscation of this lack' (Žižek, 2012, p. 148). Miller introduced the notion of 'suture' he took from Lacan (who referred to the word only once) to bring to the fore the elaborate concept of subject belonging to the differential notion of structure. And, Badiou, as Žižek explains, in his opposition to this 'subjectivized structure', would insist on the 'anonymous and asubjective nature of structure per se: analysis of structure offers scientific knowledge of the real, there is no lack in structure, and the place of subject should be strictly limited to the level of ideological or imaginary misrecognition, to the illusory way we live and experience anonymous structural causality' (Žižek, 2012, p. 148). At this point, Žižek brings in another dimension of this debate referring to the Jean-Claude Milner's contribution in his 'The Point of the Signifier', a 'brilliant' interpretation of Plato's *Sophist*.[21] In the centre of Plato's struggle with the sophists, the 'ill-famed Gorgias', who laid their claim on 'self-referential abyss of language which turns in its circle, lacking any external support, such that one can assert whatever one wants; there is no objective measure to the truth of our claims' (Žižek, 2012, p. 148). After breaking with the 'closed' myth of the universe, Plato tried 're-anchoring language in the metaphysical reality of the eternal ideas' (Žižek, 2012, p. 149). That is, as Žižek says, Plato after his *Parmenides,* in which he 'dangerously' came close to the sophists on the variation of the relation between signifier One and the real Being, in the *Sophist* crucially dealt with the question of non-being in trying to mediate between Parmenides's One and the sophists multiplicity of non-being. Žižek writes: 'Plato describes sophistry as the *appearance-making art*. Imitating true wisdom, sophists produce deceptive appearances. In their empty ratiocinations and search for rhetorical effects, they talk about things that do not exists, that are not' (Žižek, 2012, p. 149). Plato's gesture is 'to define Not-Being not as the opposite of Being', Žižek remarks, but as a 'Difference within the domain of Being' (Žižek, 2012, p. 149). His solution is to relativize non-being, to separate it from the absolute negation of being. Žižek then makes the amazing claim that although Plato in his *Parmenides* came close to articulate the notion of 'self-referentiality', but 'he lacked the structuralist concept of *differentiality* which defines the signifying order' (Žižek, 2012, p. 149). It was of course Ferdinand de Saussure who first showed that the identity of a signifier resides in difference; there is no positive term in language, with the crucial consequence that it is the differential identity that denotes the absence that refers to presence, so-called the presence of absence. From these observations Žižek concludes that:

> This paradox introduced self-reflexivity into the signifying order. If the identity of a signifier is nothing but series of its constitutive differences, then every signifying series has to be supplemented – 'sutured' – by a reflexive signifier which itself has no determinate meaning (no signified), since it stands only for the presence of meaning as such, the presence of meaning as opposed to its absence.[22]

Further reflecting on the debate between Miller and Badiou, and in relation to the Althusserian notion of subject as the site of imaginary or ideological (mis)recognition and Lacanian definition of the 'signifier' as that which 'presents the subject for another signifier' and Miller's adherence to it, Žižek judges Miller's theory of 'suture' to be 'mixed with misunderstanding' of the concept. Žižek writes:

> Suture, in other words, designated the operation by means of which the field of ideological experience gets 'sutured,' i.e., closed in its circle, rendering invisible the decentred structural necessity. By this reading 'suturing' means that all the disturbing traces of the radical Outside within the field of ideological experience are obliterated, so that this field is neatly 'sown up,' perceived as seamless continuity. We might illustrate the idea by considering how a large historical process is (over)determined by a complex network of 'anonymous' structural causes, but that this complexity is obfuscated when we posits Subject (humanity, consciousness, life, God . . .) which appears to dominate and run the process. (Žižek, 2012, p. 155)

In respect to the question of 'suture' in Badiou's antiphilosophy, Žižek brings up the conceptual couple of 'presence/representation' and makes some important comments. Within this couple, he says, antiphilosophy develops its own version of the logic of 'suture': 'It conceives suture as the mode in which the exterior is inscribed in the interior, thus "suturing" the field, producing the effect of self-enclosure with no need for an exterior, effacing the traces of its own production. In this way, traces of the production process, its gaps, its mechanism, are obliterated, so that the product can appear as a naturalized organic whole' (Žižek, 2012, p. 156). But then, not only there is no 'interior without exterior', but also 'no exterior without interior', Žižek immediately adds. He introduces the notion of 'reflexivity' in this regard: 'To put it succinctly, "suture" means that external difference is always an internal one, that the exterior limitation of a field of phenomena always reflects itself within this field, as its inherent impossibility to fully become itself' (Žižek, 2012, p. 157).

Now, let me come back to the specific use of the concept of 'suture' in Badiou. In *Manifesto for Philosophy*, he comes back again to Lyotard to say that he cannot grant the 'philosopher' his definition of philosophy as 'a discourse in search of its own rules' (Badiou, 1999, p. 66).[23] He further elaborates: 'There are at least two universal rules, failing which one no longer has any reason to speak of philosophy. The first is that it must set the eventful naming of its conditions, and thus make possible the simultaneous and conceptually unified thinking the matheme, the poem, political invention and the two of love' (Badiou, 1999, p. 66). He continues:

> The second is that paradigm of the course, or of rigor, which establishes a space of thinking wherein all generic procedures find shelter and welcome, must be exhibited from within this sheltering and welcoming. This is another way of saying that philosophy is only de-sutured if it is, on its own, systematic. If *a contrario* philosophy declares the impossibility of the system, it is because it is sutured, and hands thought over to only one of its condition. (Badiou, 1999, p. 66)

The term 'systematic' to which Badiou is referring in fact has to be understood as architectonic, the *sine qua non* on which the philosophic system is constructed. Yet this must be qualified as this 'systematicity' is not a 'metaphor of architecture' as such. It must be remembered that in terms of mathematical formalization in Badiou, or *matheme*, after Gödel's proof, the notion of 'systematic' foundation is at the same time the absence of foundation. As Karatani said: 'Godel's proof presents us with a case wherein the attempt to *architectonize* mathematics results not in a mathematical foundation but in the impossibility of mathematical foundations. Godel's proof of the lack of mathematical foundation is, however, emancipatory rather than restrictive for mathematics' (Karatani, 1995, p. xxiv). This is why Badiou has to 'de-suture' philosophy from the grip of its conditions in order to not lose its *systematicity*. To put it in differently, the *will to architecture* in Badiou comes with its limits, only because this *'will'* itself is an assertion of some 'pure presence', as Žižek would say '(of the real of society for Marx, of existence for Kierkegaard, of the will for Schopenhauer and Nietzsche, etc.)' that 'remains irreducible to and in excess with regard to the network of philosophical concepts and means of representation' (Žižek, 2012, p. 156).

In her stimulating essay titled 'The Firth Condition', Alenka Zupancic takes up Badiou's philosophy and makes compelling argument directly relevant to my main concern here, that is, the state of antiphilosophy in architecture discourse, that I will take up in the next section. She points out that philosophy's conditions, that is, mathematics, politics, art and love, that constitute Badiou's affirmation of philosophy in his polemics against the 'modern sophists' – which is not just reaction against the 'bad' others – are 'just' conditions and not a *'foundation'* for philosophy. She writes: 'should any of the above-mentioned generic procedures be transformed from condition to the foundation of philosophy then this gives rise to what Badiou calls a "suture" that can lead to suspension of philosophy, i.e., to its abandoning itself to one of its conditions' (Zupancic, 2004, p. 191). Therefore, 'one could thus say that there is a fifth condition of philosophy: Philosophy has to pull itself away from the immediate grip of its own condition, while nevertheless remaining under the effect of these conditions' (Zupancic, 2004, p. 191). She further adds that after Hegel, something *did* happen to philosophy: 'in certain sense, Hegel *was* the "last philosopher"' (Zupancic, 2004, p. 191). In making this claim she quotes Badiou from *Manifesto for Philosophy* where he said: 'if philosophy is threatened by suspension, and this perhaps since Hegel, it is because it is captive to a network of sutures to its conditions, especially to its scientific and political conditions, which forbade it from configuring their general compossibility' (Zupancic, 2004, p. 191; also Badiou, 1999, p. 64). Zupancic supplements Badiou's remarks: 'Since Hegel, philosophy thus mostly took place in the element of its own suppression, to the advantage of one of these procedures (science, politics, art). This is also why, according to Badiou, all great philosophers after Hegel were in fact anti-philosophers (Nietzsche, Marx, Wittgenstein, Heidegger . . .)' (Zupancic, 2004, p. 191).

The reflections I offered above on the concept of 'suture' should be adequate at this point to bring the concept into my discussion of architecture that I take up next.

Architecture's suture to philosophy

Philosophy is the singular and privileged *condition* among the multiple conditions making the thought of architecture possible in its general configuration of compossibility. But the moment architecture is abandoned to this privileged condition only to remain in its grip, it is *sutured*. The assertion of the *will to architecture* in architecture itself cannot remain in the state of its *pure presence,* as its assertion is in philosophy, which, as Karatani told us, is another name for the *will to architecture.* In the pure presence of the *will,* architecture becomes its own metaphor, in so far as this metaphor is operative metaphor in both architecture and philosophy. Otherwise, architecture becomes another name for philosophy in excess to the network of the concepts for its representation in disregard to its radical *contingency.* To transpose Marx's remark in his introduction to 'A Critique of Hegel's Philosophy of Right': 'Philosophy cannot be actualized without transcendence [*Aufhebung*] of architecture, architecture cannot be transcended without actualization of philosophy.'[24] It should be noted that the Hegelian concept of *Aufhebung* in the above passage, often translated as 'sublation', must be understood in its difficult but proper meaning.[25] But, in so far as architecture *sutures* itself to philosophy, thus suspending itself, it cannot pull itself from the immediate grip of philosophy as its condition, it instead transforms this condition into *foundation,* in the sense of Zupancic's interpretation above. I call this state of *suspension* of architecture abandoned to philosophy taken as its foundation, the *antiphilosophy of architecture.* In antiphilosophy, the *will to architecture* leaves architectonic as the solid Foundation; it leave the imperative of *systematicity.* Architecture sutured to philosophy, that is, remaining in its grip, not actualized or sublated [*Aufhebung*] in the sense in Marx's passage above, is an architecture emptied of its *will to architecture* in disregard of the 'architectonic of reason' in Kantian sense of the term, as the 'art of [building] system. In its grip to antiphilosophy, architecture might have acted against its own will to architecture, turning to its own *negation.* In this state, architectonic (metaphor) is indispensible as the *critique* of the prevailing 'metaphor of architecture' not only in recent 'philosophy' that is the target of Badiou and Žižek, but also in architecture. In Badiou's sense, we *cannot* grant a definition to architecture as *not* being the art of *system* after the Kantian turn, that is, not being built on 'solid foundation', not being the 'least architectonic', as Badiou would say, no matter how much deconstruction tried to undermine it, when the Derridean notion of the 'metaphysics of presence' again and again was brought up and obsessively discussed in certain circles in academy as the critique of contemporary architecture. This has been the state of affair and what has happened to the disciplinary autonomy of architecture and its discursive practice of theory in academy since the post-1970s to present. Below I will offer a précis of the actual mutations in this theoretical practice. Significantly, during this time, architecture sutured itself to a 'philosophy' as its condition that is already an antiphilosophy on its own term in Badiou's analysis discussed above. Therefore the state of antiphilosophy of architecture found itself in a *double bind.* In other words, it found itself to be in double *suture.* The 'philosophy' to which architecture was sutured itself was the predominant 'postmodern theory' in various brands of 'poststructuralism', deconstruction, and Anglophone neo-pragmatism, all issued from the 'linguistic turn' in the twentieth century that marks antiphilosophy as we are told. The architecture discipline has handed down its theoretical practice to the emerging 'sophists' in the discipline who followed and emulated their master sophists in the field of philosophy. The same characteristics that Badiou articulates in case of the 'new sophists' in the field of philosophy may be applied to their counterpart in the field of architecture. Badiou in his polemic with the new sophists writes: 'asserting the end of philosophy and the irrelevance of Truth is strictly a *sophistic* appraisal of the century. We are attending a second anti-Platonic requital, for contemporary "philosophy" is a generalized sophistry, which is moreover neither without talent nor without greatness. Language games, deconstruction, weak thought, radical heterogeneity, differends and differences, the ruin of reason, promotion of the fragment, discourse reduced to shreds: all this argues in favor of a sophistic line of thinking and puts philosophy in a deadlock' (Badiou, 1999, p. 135). He asks, 'who are the modern sophists?' and writes: 'The modern sophists are those that, in the footsteps of the great Wittgenstein, maintain that thought is held to the following alternative: either effects of discourse, language games, or the silent indication, the pure "showing" of something subtracted from the clutches of language. Sophists are those for whom the fundamental opposition is not between truth and error, or errancy, but between speech and silence, that is between what can be said and what is impossible to say' (Badiou, 1999, p. 116).[26] The role of modern sophists consists, as Bruno Bosteels comments on Badiou's thought: 'in alerting the philosophers to the contemporaneity of their discourse' (Bosteels, 2011, p. 28). He quotes Badiou as saying: 'The great modern sophistics, linguistic, aestheticizing and democratic, exercises its dissolving function, examines impasses and draws the picture of what is contemporary to us. It is essential for us as the libertine was to Blaise Pascal: it *alerts* us to the singularities of the time' (Bosteels, 2011, p. 98). As Bosteels puts it, 'the function of the sophists is not just stylistic or aesthetic but also ethical in nature' (Bosteels, 2011, p. 28). This is what Badiou says in this regard: 'The sophist is required at all times for philosophy to maintain its ethics. For the sophist is the one who reminds us that the category of Truth is void' (Badiou, 1999, p. 134). Further, 'The history of philosophy is the history of its ethics: a succession of violent gestures through which philosophy is withdrawn from its disastrous redoubling' (Badiou, 1999, p. 144). As Bosteels comments, philosophy then must be preventing from 'redoubling' itself as 'its own condition and become a science, an art, or a politics all by itself. For Badiou, this is why the different guises of the sophist must at all times be acknowledged and taken up again and again as part of the self-definition of philosophy' (Bosteels, 2011, p. 29).

The same alertness must be exercised against the sophists of architecture as the same terms, linguistic, stylistic and aestheticizing tendencies, have been prevailing in its discursive practice. The sophists of architecture, amateur rhetoricians, moved architecture closer to the 'self-referential abyss of language', to repeat what Žižek said above, 'which turns in its circle, lacking any external support', without an Outside. They are busy producing 'deceptive appearances', indulging in the '*appearance-making art*', as Plato described sophistry, exercising 'empty ratiocination and search for rhetorical effects.' By the 1970s, notion of the 'text' took ascendency over the 'metaphor of architecture' as the operative metaphor in postmodern theory in various versions of 'poststructuralism' that came to be know as the 'French Theory'. By the

1980s, this theory of the text and the Derridean notion of 'writing' was imported into architecture discursive practice in academy, dislodging 'the critique of architectonic indispensible to the critique of architecture as metaphor' as Karatani put it that was quoted above. He mentions Edward Said who in his *The World, the Text, and the Critic* had already objected to this notion of the Text when it appeared in humanities and literary criticism:

> And yet something happened, perhaps inevitably. From being a bold interventionary movement across lines of specialization. American literary theory of the late seventies had retreated into labyrinth of 'textuality,' dragging along with it the most recent apostles of European revolutionary textuality – Derrida and Foucault – whose trans-Atlantic canonization and domestication they themselves sadly enough to be encouraging [...] My position is that texts are worldly, to some degree they are events, and even when they appear to deny it, they are nevertheless a part of the social world, human life, and of course the historical moments in which they are located and interpreted.[27]

For Said it was the question of 'secular criticism', a criticism of a unitary foundation, or its lack thereof, of all that is 'within' rather than from 'without' (Žižek, 2012, p. 156). Or, as Žižek argued that as I quoted above, it is the 'suturing of the field with no need for an exterior, effacing the traces of its own production'. Beginning with the 1980s, in an inevitable move to remain 'contemporary', discourse on architecture in the academy made the attempt to reconfigure its practice of theory by exploiting 'philosophy' (philosophy qua antiphilosophy) from its outside. In holding architecture to the mirror of philosophy, the discipline made repeated attempts to lay claims to 'high theory' engaging in futile exercise of 'applied' philosophy. In this enterprise, architecture discourse put the disciplinary autonomy of 'theory' aside in order to incorporate 'Theory', theory with capital 'T', from the outside of disciplinary setting, mainly the French Theory. As Peter Osborne has remarked, in the French context, 'theory' was the result of both the development in the discourse of humanities in structuralism and poststructuralism *and* the Marxist critique of philosophy, primarily by Althusser who designated *Théorie*, with capital T, to refer to 'Marxist philosophy' as 'the theory of theoretical practice' to 'reserve the term *philosophy* for ideological philosophies, in line with Marx and Engels's diagnosis of the ideological character of philosophy per se ("self-sufficient philosophy") in the *German Ideology*' (Osborne, 2011, p. 21). Reading the French Theory in this period, the 'theory' internal to architecture discipline proved to be no longer adequate for the task of theorizing. This inevitable move, which continues to the present, has changed the nature of 'theory' that is no longer confined to the disciplinary boundary of architecture, from which we apparently cannot retreat. But this move to remain 'contemporary' was accompanied by adverse effects plaguing 'philosophical theory' in the discipline. Let me enumerate them in a summary fashion:

1. The proponents of the French Theory in the discipline fantastically remained ignorant of the complex philosophical debate in the second half of the twentieth

century that has been named by Alain Badiou as the 'Adventure of French Philosophy'.[28] Postmodern deconstructive theory was imported into the discourse of the discipline in the absence of any knowledge of the origin and birthplace of the debate in France between 1966 and 1969, which as I discussed above, had been formed in the circle around the *Cahier pour l'Analyse*. The general ignorance in architecture discourse of the complexity of the 'French Theory' during this time constitutes the fault line in the discipline. It attempt to do 'high theory' by exploiting a mixture of concepts and categories extracted from the writing of Jacques Derrida (sadly encouraged by Derrida himself who actively participated in certain architectural circles promoting his philosophy), and later from the work of Gilles Deleuze by manipulating his uses of 'architecture metaphor' in his late philosophy, to mention only the two most conspicuous cases of the misuses of the French Theory in the discipline in the last 30 years.[29]

2. One characteristic of the French Theory is its problematic disavowal of the Critique, from the Kantian transcendental critique to the Frankfurt School Critical Theory, Adorno and Benjamin, to the Marxist critical theory. The avowal of this 'theory sans Critique' in architecture discourse not only amounts to the renunciation of the project of the Critique, but also the wholesale renunciation of the powerful militant radical left theory in the late 1960s and early 1970s associated the legacy of '*La pensée* 68'.[30] This is the hallmark of the 'theory' enterprise in the discipline that triumphantly buries the project of *radical* critique in architecture. The discipline ignored *Critique* to do the fashionable Theory abandoning the encounter between Marxism and psychoanalysis, which was the achievement of the *Cahiers pour l'Analyse,* the legacy of which lives now in current radical philosophy, prominently by Alain Badiou and Slavoj Žižek.

3. It is not so much the problem with reductive reading of the French Theory in academic discourse of architecture as it is the naïve assumption about the relation between architecture *and* philosophy which share the same *will to architecture* as its foundational thought. The pedagogy of theory has abandoned the 'architectonic of reason' as the original modern gesture of Critique of the will to architecture. It has thus generated a generation of sophists who have exercised their hegemony over what is defined as 'philosophy' and the practice of theory. What Badiou says for the discipline of philosophy also holds valid for the field of architecture. If, according to Badiou, philosophy must begin to renew itself with a Platonic gesture of Foundation that is based on mathematics as ontology, a foundation without foundation, by the same token, architecture also must organize its discourse with the same gesture of Foundation with the Platonic Idea. In the case of architecture, not unlike philosophy, as Badiou would say, it is the fundamental 'impurity' of its concept which accompanies its *radical contingency.* In this gesture, it must de-suture itself from antiphilosophy. I want to outline this act of de-suturing below.

De-suturing architecture from antiphilosophy

I name the regime of thought that has 'sutured' architecture and theory to the French Theory as *antiphilosophy.* Should we take this antiphilosophy to be anti-

will to architecture, if, as discussed above, philosophy is synonymous to or another name for 'will to architecture' in Western tradition? To address this issue I return to explicate the conjunction between antiphilosophical *sophists* and the architectonic critique in the discourse of architecture. I begin with the thesis that architecture must 'de-suture' itself from this antiphilosophy so that it can begin to *think* in the space of its 'compossibility' (a Badouian term) constituting its multiple 'truths'.[31] This act of de-suturing is *sine qua non* if architecture must (re-)turn to *itself*, to its constitutive *reflexivity*, in what we can call as the signifying structure of 'self-relating differential' system, towards a thought that can be termed as '*pensée* architectural', and its return to radical emancipator project, which must take place within the multiple *conditions* that constitute its actuality and its *contingency*. I return here to the distinction between *foundation* and *condition* that I adopted after Alenka Zupancic. The advocates of the French Theory in architecture, while ignoring architecture's multiple *conditions* for its actuality – to which it occasionally is 'sutured' – have instead taken philosophy as the *foundation* to do theory with it. In this exercise, they *abandoned* architecture theory to philosophy as its foundation, thereby *suspending* its relation to all other conditions that constitute its compossibilities. Against this suspension, I argue, architecture must emphatically pull itself from the immediate grip of philosophy *as foundation* while remaining under its *effects*. This poses the central question as to what condition and in what mode of thought must architecture invoke philosophy in its discourse. This question leads to the problematic tendency in the discipline to do theory with a view onto the 'philosophy *of* architecture'. In insisting on this view, architectural discourse in the academy, to put it in Kantian term, has taken the philosophical thought not as the *condition of its possibility*, that is, the a priori condition of the possibility of architectural thought, but rather, as legitimization of its institutional practice. The fatal consequence of this flawed approach is Political, in the sense that the discipline has sought its legitimacy by conforming to the exigencies of dominant political order while remaining all along *apolitical*, or worse, anti-political. The political factor is primary among the multiple conditions of thought that architecture must compossibilize. The notion of the political must be understood here as synonymous with 'theory' against ideology. It is related to the notion of 'Theoretical Training' in its specific Althusserian sense (Hallward, 'Introduction', 2012). The act of crossing from ideology to the political constitutes the work of theory. A useful lesson can be learned from critical philosophers of our time who have engaged literature, cinema, opera and other visual arts.[32] As Jean-Jacques Lecercle argues, when contemporary radical philosophy attempts to read 'literature', it bases its reading on the fundamental idea that literature *thinks* on its own – some exceptions notwithstanding. For critical philosophers, the idea of 'philosophy *of* literature', a notion they avoid by all means, presupposes a hierarchy whereby philosophy *thinks* and for which literature would be an object of philosophical speculation.[33] This means that they do not take literature as yet another region to impose the jurisdiction of philosophical 'concepts' on the thought of literature; literary text is not a mere pretext for the development of philosophical analyses that are independent of it. They read literature not to apply to literary text the techniques of reading and constructing concepts, which are in the sole province of philosophy. In other words, they do not 'suture' literature to philosophy as its foundation of possibility of thinking, which is reflexively immanent in the literary text itself.

This lesson has largely been ignored in the discipline of architecture. The reverse is the case in the sense of the 'hierarchy' that is tenaciously maintained in the discursive practice of theory in architecture. Architecture discourse in the academy allowed 'philosophy' to impose its jurisdiction on its thought, let it to *think* for it. The notion that the thought of philosophy as such is reflexively *immanent* in the thought of architecture is lost. Confusing the difference between foundation and condition, the project of theory in the discipline has abandoned itself to philosophy as its *foundation*, mistaking speculative philosophical concepts for categories to guide building practice, rather than taking them as the *condition* for generating categories of thoughts towards constructing a *project of critique*, which in my mind is the only legitimacy there is to bring philosophy into architecture. I hazard to put a title on this project: *The transcendental critique of pure architecture.* The 'object' of this critique has yet to be constructed that cannot be discussed here.[34] Not granting architecture its right to *think* on its own, or not letting it to come reflexively to itself, by keeping it under the jurisdiction of philosophy to do the *thinking* for it, the project of experimentation with the French Theory in the last four decades, I claim, is a failed project. The antiphilosophy is the explanatory term I suggest for this putative failure.

I want to come back to the influential intellectual circle that I briefly discussed above, the circle around the *Cahiers pour l'Analyse* at the École Normal Supérieure (ENS) in Paris. I return to the debate in this circle on the concept of 'suture' to support the critique I am advancing and to emphasize the important lessons of this circle that were lost in theoretical endeavours in architecture discourse. An editorial collective of students called '*Cercle d'Épistémologie*' ran this journal. With excellent introductions by the editors, Peter Hallward and Knox Peden, to the two-volume English edition titled *Concept and Form*, this collection sheds much light on the previously neglected role of the *Cahiers* in formation of ideas shaping the contemporary French philosophy. As the editors inform us, the *Cahiers* is the origin of the philosophical movements that later came to be known as 'structuralism' and 'poststructuralism' as I have already discussed above.[35] In its historical context, it is important to keep in mind that the *Cahiers pour l'Analyse* was basically intended to defend Enlightenment rationalism in the tradition of the French eighteenth century 'against a certain phenomenological romanticism which was focused more on interiority or feeling' popular in 1950s and early 1960s French intellectual thoughts.[36] The *Cahiers* was formed, as I mentioned before, around two powerful figures, Louis Althusser and Jacques Lacan. At the centre was the project of bringing Marx to Freud, philosophy to psychoanalysis, which the previous attempt by Frankfurt School had failed to do.[37] This encounter was primarily related to the ideas of 'structure', science, and the question of the 'subject' around the notions of 'lack' and 'absent cause', variably going back to Althusser's reading of Marx and Lacan's reading of Freud. This project was grounded in the 'philosophy of concept', 'formalization' and 'matheme'. It should be mentioned here that on the side line of the *Cahiers pour l'Analyse,* the radical political environment in France before 1968 led the so-called *Cercle d'Ulm* at ENS, headed by Jacques Rancière and Jean-Allan Miller among others, to establish a new student-run journal titled *Cahiers Marxistes-*

Léninistes in 1964.[38] The journal was conceived along the line of Althusser's teaching on 'Theoretical Training' at the time and 'was designed to complement the creation of well-attended "theoretical schools" for transmission of Marxist science' (Hallward, 2012, p. 22).[39]

Emerging from the circle around the *Cahiers pour l'Analyse* significant debates on philosophy, psychoanalysis and political theory came out before the event of May 1968, which interrupted the publication of the journal and eclipsed the debate in the late 1970s 'backlash against anti-humanism and *la pensée 68*' (Hallward, 2012, p. 3). As was mentioned, notable in the entire *Cahiers* project was Althusser's notion of '*formation theorique*'. This project itself was based on the rigorous notion of 'the passion of concept' (Michel Foucault's term) as opposed to 'lived experience'. This project, as Hallward explains, was 'trying to provide that theoretical supplement required to develop the more general "philosophy," left undeveloped both by Marx and his followers, that would secure the science of historical materialism' (Hallward, 2012, p. 22).[40] Significantly, it is the rigorous theoretical ideas in this circle that were later 'restored' in the work of Alain Badiou and Slavoj Žižek, whose radical philosophical and political-aesthetic theories constitute the main core of contemporary radical philosophy today, joined by a certain 'younger' generation of the philosophers in what is called as the 'New French Philosophy' (Hallward, 2012).[41] I should mention that Jacques Rancière, who took a distance from the *Cahiers* project, is one of the original radical thinkers of our time.[42] Significantly, on the question of the Subject, the work of these philosophers, especially Badiou and Žižek, both of whom were influenced strongly by Jacques Lacan, albeit in different ways, must radically be separated from the fashionable trend of 'poststructuralism' and deconstruction. In this respect, as commentators have remarked, poststructuralism when confronted with the question '*How can a modern doctrine of the subject be reconciled with an ontology?*' has showed that 'it has no doctrine of the subject' (Feltham and Clemens, 2005, p. 3). 'Thus in poststructuralism there is no distinction between the general field of ontology and a theory of the subject; there is no tension between the being of the subject and being in general' (Feltham and Clemens, 2005, p. 3).[43]

It is within the psychoanalytical theory in Jacques Lacan's teaching that this doctrine of the Subject, in relation to 'structure' and 'science', informs the work of the *Cahiers*. It is here that the notion of 'suture' enters the discourse of the subject, as we have seen. Commenting on Jacques-Alain Miller's key text in the *Cahiers* titled 'Action of the Structure', in which a distinction between 'structuring' and 'structured' is drawn, Hallward writes: 'to the degree that the structure includes a reflexive elements, "an element that turns back on reality and perceives it, reflects it and signifies it, an element capable of redoubling itself on its own account"'. . . 'This element introduces a gap or absence into the structuring process, something that structure "misses." On the level of what is structured or lived, this absence is generally covered over by imaginary or ideological representation of fullness and coherence' (Hallward, 2012, p. 45). The lack in the structure, of course, cannot be represented but is covered by an element, which 'takes the place of the lack', as Hallward further remarks. Crucially: 'Every structure must incorporate some such placeholder for the lack it includes, which serves to "sew up" or "suture" the lack, and by thus assigning it a place, absorbs it into an imaginary continuum' (Hallward, 2012, p. 45). And in relation to the famous title of the 'logic of signifier' by Miller, Hallward writes: 'In other words, from one link to another of signifying chain, a signifier represents, places or "sutures" (i.e., treats-as-identical or counts-as-one), for another signifier, that essential lack of self or place which is all that can be represented of the subject qua subject. "Suture names the relation of the subject to the chain of its discourse," by treating its absence or lack of place as *a* lack of place, i.e., by subsuming it "in the form of a placeholder [*tenant-lieu*]"' (Hallward, 2012, p. 50). The status of the subject (or lack) and key notion of suture in relation to structure were in the centre of the field of 'structuralism'. Here is Hallward's conclusion about the whole *Cahiers* project in its context of time and space. He writes:

> As for what remains significant about this revolutionary project today, the least that can be said is that the verdict no longer appears as clear-cut as it did to jaded proponents of *la nouvelle philosophie* in the late 1970s and the liberals who followed them in the 1980s and 90s. [...]. But after decades dominated by the myriad forms of a backlash against radical politics (liberalism, deconstruction, 'ethics', historicism, cynicism . . .), many younger thinkers and activists are at least more receptive now to the basic problem that 'theoretical training' was meant to solve in the 1960s: how might we think and work towards radical change in conditions of economic inertia, political complacency and popular disempowerment, compounded by the absence of an appropriately oriented political organization? Today's answer to this old question may depend on a different account of the relation between structure and subject, drawing on a more dialectical conception of the former and a more assertive (if not 'revolutionary') conception of the latter. (Hallward, 2012, p. 55)

The failure of the architecture discipline in its pretentious inroad into the French philosophy, as I have argued, is a case of antiphilosophy. What is at stake is the relation between internal field of architecture to its external, to the 'other' as its *contingency*, in which the traces of its production are obliterated. Going back to the notion of 'reflexivity' of thought in architecture that I mentioned at the outset, we can put it now in relation to 'suture' and production linked to the question of inside versus outside, or interiority versus exteriority. In this regard, what Žižek has said about antiphilosophy in the larger context of contemporary debate about philosophy that I cited before can also be applied to architecture field. To recall what he wrote: 'Anti-philosophy develops here its own version of the logic of "suture": It conceives suture as the mode in which the exterior is inscribed in the interior, thus "suturing" the field, producing the effect of self-enclosure with no need for an exterior, effacing the traces of its own production. In this way, traces of the production process, its gaps, its mechanisms, are obliterated, so that the product can appear as a naturalized organic whole' (Žižek, 2012, p. 156). If we translate this into the notion of reflexivity of thought in architecture, we can claim that this reflexive thought cannot attain 'self-enclosure'. This is exactly what the antiphilosophy of architecture has denied in the production of categories in the thought of architecture.

To conclude: On politico-aesthetic and ethical grounds, I consider the suturing of architecture to philosophy as *aestheticization of theory*, or the 'commodification of theory', committed by the 'sophists' in the discipline. In their erroneous reading of 'multiplicity' and misconception of the 'One', they are representative of antiphilosophy in the discipline. They are in the business of '*appearing-making art*' in the sense of Plato's description of sophistry as Žižek told us. They engage in rhetorical 'self-referential abyss of language', which blocks the outside from the inside. Theirs is a zero-degree aesthetic language game. In this regard, the enterprise of reading philosophy in the discipline is plagued by a lack of 'Theoretical Training' in the academy to use this Althusserian term. To reiterate, 'Theoretical Training' in the academy must be directed, in my mind, to read philosophy for the sole purpose of constructing a radical *project of critique* in architecture and in its critique of the *Idolatrous* role that it has assumed in contemporary culture of late capitalism. De-suturing architecture from antiphilosophy, in this sense, means that reading philosophy must once again be taken up with the view to restore the project of critique and no longer as a mere series of 'concepts' to be 'applied' as *prescription* to practice. In this sense, following the debate of the *Cahiers* and its *radical restoration* which has taken place in the project of contemporary French philosophy in the service of political *emancipatory* project, 'theory' must be conceived as politics to block ideology. Otherwise, the hard work of doing theory within the project of reading philosophy will descent into a legitimizing act of an affirmative ideological-aesthetic operation in support of what Badiou somewhere has called as the 'image brothel' of democratic-liberal capitalism. Architecture must renew its *will to architecture* but only within the elements of the philosophical critique of 'architectonic reason' in Kantian sense of the term, built on a foundation without foundation, beginning with the foundation of the Platonic Idea.

Notes

1   For the cited statement see Jean-Francoise Lyotard, *The Differend: Phrases in Dispute* (Minneapolis: University of Minnesota Press, 1988). Badiou adds, 'Is a "writing of ruins", a "micrologia", a diligent for "graffiti" (which Lyotard considers as metaphors for the style of contemporary thought) still connected to "philosophy", however we understand it, in any relation other than a simple homonymic one?', p. 28. Badiou had reviewed Lyotard's *Differend* that appears in his *The Adventure of French Philosophy* in chapter 13, 'Custos, Quid Noctis?'. See also Alain Badiou's *Pocket Pantheon* in which he devotes a chapter to Lyotard as his contemporary philosopher while maintaining his radical difference from him.

2   More precisely Kant in the first paragraph of 'The Transcendental Doctrine of Method, Third Chapter, the Architectonic of Pure Reason' writes: 'by an *architectonic* I understand that art of system. Since systematic unity is that which first makes ordinary cognition into science, i.e., makes a system out of a mere aggregate of it, architectonic is the doctrine of which is scientific in our cognition in general, and therefore necessarily belongs to the doctrine of method', *Critique of Pure Reason*, p. 691.

3   Karatani in this otherwise undeservedly neglected book regrettably makes no mention of Alain Badiou. Given the impasse that he mentions in the introduction to the English translation of his book he confronted in his intellectual itinerary while

writing his book, I suspect that the great argument he has presented in his book could have entirely been benefitted or rewritten had the author entered the philosophic system of Badiou to his advantage. I would think that Karatani would have revised what he wrote about Wittgenstein in the third part of his book in the light of Badiou's discourse of antiphilosophy, but this does not diminish the intellectual force already displayed in his excellent book.

4   The comments quoted are by Karatani, *Architecture as Metaphor*, p. xli. For more on this point see the other great book of Kojin Karatani, *Transcritique: On Kant and Marx* (Cambridge, MA: MIT Press, 2003), chapter 2: 'The Problematic of Synthetic Judgment'.

5   For an excellent discussion of Gödel see Rebecca Goldstein, *Incompleteness: The Proof and Paradox of Kurt Gödel* (New York and London: W. W. Norton, 2005).

6   Karatani quotes Kant from his *Critique of Aesthetics Judgment* where he employs architectonic as a metaphor: 'For if such a system is some day worked out under the general name Metaphysics – and its full and complete execution is both possible and of the utmost importance for the employment of reason in all department of its activity – the critical examination of the ground for this edifice must have been previously carried down to the very depths of the foundation of the faculty of principles independent of experience, lest in some quarter it might give way, and, sinking, inevitably bring with it the ruin of all.' p. Xlii. Also see Immanuel Kant, *Critique of Aesthetic Judgment*. James Creed Meredith (trans.). Oxford: Clarendon Press, 1911.

7   See Alain Badiou, 'What Is a Philosophical Institution? Or Address, Transmission, Inscription', in *Conditions*.

8   As Bronu Bosteels informs us, Lacan 'in the mid-1970s, had called himself an antiphilosopher after the example of eighteenth-century *antiphilosophes*, a self-applied label that historically refers to the mostly religious and conservative, if not outright reactionary, thinkers who resist the arrival of rationalism, deism, or materialism on the part of French enlightenment thinkers, the so-called *philosophes*, such as Diderot, Voltaire, or d'Holbach', see 'Radical Antiphilosophy', in *Filozofski vestnik*, p. 156.

9   In this regard, see Bruno Bosteels, 'Radical Antiphilosophy', cited above; see Adrian Johnston, 'This Philosophy Which Is Not One: Jean-Claude, Alain Badiou, and Lacanian Antiphilosophy'; See also the 'Introduction' by Bruno Bosteels to Alain Badiou's *Wittgenstein's Antiphilosophy* and Justin Clemens and Adam J. Bartlett, '"the Greatest of Our Dead": Badiou and Lacan', in *Badiou and Philosophy*.

10   See different chapters on mathematics and philosophy in Alain Badiou's *Conditions* and *Alain Badiou: Theoretical Writings*. Also, *Badiou and Philosophy*, specially 'Part I: Philosophy's Mathematical Condition'.

11   For more see the chapter 'Natural Language' in Karatani's *Architecture as Metaphor*.

12   Translator of Karatani follows certain translations of Plato's text to render poet as 'creator' and poetry as *poiesis*. The version of the passage quoted above in *Plato, Complete Works*, reads as the following: 'Well, you know, for example, that "poetry" has a very wide range. After all, everything that is responsible for creating something out of nothing is a kind of poetry; and so all the creations of every craft and profession are themselves a kind of poetry, and everyone who practices a craft is a poet. True. Nevertheless, she said, as you know, these craftsmen are not called poets', p. 488. The translator of this edition of Plato remarks that '"poetry" translates *poiesis*, lit. "making", which used mainly for poets – writers of metrical verses that were actually set to music', p. 488.

13 Karatani is specifically referring to Valery's Platonic Dialogue in *Eupolinos, or the Architect*. William M. Steward (trans.). London: Oxford University Press, 1932. Karatani remarks that 'It was those poets who, in other words, took up the platonic position that had originally ousted them – a group of poets from Edgar Allan Poe to Paul Valery – who attempted to make poetry architectonic by rejecting becoming', p. 23. Comparing Valery to Edgar Allan Poe who attempted to construct poetry rationally in rejecting romanticism, Karatani points out that 'It was, however, who realized that the awareness of the mystical process of poetry – *poiesis* in the narrow sense – leads to the speculation of *techné* in a broad sense', p. 24.

14 In his *Transcritique: On Kant and Marx*, Karatani, defines the Kantian notion of transcendental: 'Simply stated, the transcendental approach seeks to cast light on the unconscious structure that precedes and shapes experience', p. 1.

15 For more see Badiou's *Manifesto for Philosophy*.

16 See Justin Clemens and Adam J. Bartlett, '"The Greatest of Our Dead": Badiou and Lacan', p. 189.

17 Ten issues of the journal appeared between 1966 and 1969. See the two-volume publication in English, *Concept and Form*. Both volumes include excellent introductions by the editors giving overviews of the history of the debate around the journal at the ENS.

18 See Jacques-Allan Miller, 'Suture (Elements of the Logic of the Signifier', and Alain Badiou, 'Mark and Lack', both reprinted in the *Concept and Form, Volume One: Key Texts from the Cahiers pour l'Analyse*.

19 See Slavoj Žižek, '"Suture," Forty Years Later', in *Concept and Form, Volume Two: Interviews and Essays on the Cahiers pour l'Analyse*.

20 As Peter Hallward mentions, besides the figures who were originally involved in the *Cahiers* between 1966 and 1969, including Louis Althusser, Jacques Lacan, Jacques Derrida, Michel Foucault, Luce Irigaray, there were younger students involved in the production of the journal at ENS namely, Jacques-Allan Miller, Jean-Claude Milner, Alan Badiou, Francoise Regnault and many others. Peter Hallward, 'Introduction: Theoretical Training', in *Volume One: Key Texts from the Cahiers pour l'Analyse*.

Moreover, what is important to mention is that several themes that were originally debated in the *Cahiers* have come back with new significance in ongoing debates in philosophy, psychoanalysis and political theory. Hallward writes: 'While the theoretical priorities of the *Cahiers* were eclipsed in the practical aftermath of May 1968 and dismissed in the late 1970s backlash against anti-humanism and *la pensée 68*, new developments in French philosophy and recent critical theory (signaled for instance by interest in the work of Alain Badiou and Slavoj Žižek) have restored some of the issues explored in journal to the top of today's philosophical agenda', in 'Introduction: Theoretical Training', p. 3.

21 See Jean-Claude Milner, 'The Point of the Signifier', in *Concept and Form, Volume One*.

22 Žižek, '"Suture," Forty Years Later', 150. After these remarks, Žižek further traces the history of the concept of 'suture' when it was adopted in late 1960s by the cinema theory, mainly by Jean-Pierre Oudart in his 'La Suture', parts I and II, *Cahiers du Cinema* 211 and 212 (April and May 1969), and later by the English *Screen* theorists in the following decades.

23 See Also Jean-Francois Lyotard's *The Differend, Phrases in Dispute*. The relevant passage from which Badiou cites is in paragraph 98, which reads: 'Philosophical discourse has as its rule to discover its rule: it's *a priori* is what is at stake. It is a matter of formulating this rule, which can only be done at the end, if there is an end', p. 60.

24 The actual phrase by Marx in his 'Toward a Critique of Hegel's Philosophy of Right: Introduction' reads as: 'Philosophy cannot be actualized without the transcendence [*Aufhebung*] of the proletariat. The proletariat cannot be transcended without the actualization of philosophy', in Karl Marx, *Selected Writings*, p. 39.

25 As Stephen Houlgate writes: 'The first thing to be said about *Aufhebung*, then, is that it is a process of negation *and* preservation at one and the same time. The second thing to be noted is that it is nothing beyond the process of *self*-impurification that is initiated and undergone by the categories and forms of being concerned. *Aufhebung* is not an "external" act of negating categories or of raising them up into a "higher" unity carried out by thought [. . .]. Furthermore, *Aufhebung* is a process without any goal or *telos*. It is not guided by any will to synthesize or to overcome differences or by any desire to make strife or conflict yield to harmony and reconciliation. Nor, pace Derrida, is it driven by any "economic" interest in reappropriating and drawing profit from absolute loss. *Aufhebung*, for Hegel, is simply the process whereby purity slips away into, and is lost in impurity – impurity that consists in not just being what one is but in being inextricably bound together', in *The Opening of Hegel's Logic*, pp. 302–3.

26 Badiou further writes: 'Just as Plato wrote the *Gorgias* and *Protagoras* for the major sophists, we should write the *Nietzsche* and the *Wittgenstein*. And for the minor sophists, the *Vattimo* and *Rorty*. Neither more no less polemical, neither more no less respectful', p. 137.

27 Quoted in Karatani, *Architecture as Metaphor*, p. xxxviii. Also see Edward W. Said, *The World, the Text, and the Critic*. Cambridge: Harvard University Press, 1983, pp. 3–4.

28 See Alain Badiou's 'Preface to the Adventure of French Philosophy', in *The Adventure of French Philosophy*, Bruno Bosteels (ed.), (trans.) and (intro.). London and New York: Verso, 2012.

29 I have discussed these cases expensively in my forthcoming, 'Baroque Theory: Adventure and Misadventure of Architecture with French Theory'.

30 Specifically in the Italian context, the Marxist political theory was incorporated into the discourse of architecture in late 1960s and early 1970s which produced powerful theory and criticism of architecture against and within what at that time in Italy was called 'neo-capitalism', within the movement connected to the working class of Autonomia and 'Operaism' led by Mario Tronti in the field of radical political philosophy, and in architecture field by figures such as Manfredo Tafuri and also Rossi among others, see Pier Vittorio Aureli, *The Project of Autonomy: Politics and Architecture Within and against Capitalism*. It must be noted that the Italian school during this period was not so much in dialogues with the French Althusserian and Lacanian discourses in France.

31 I use the term 'compossibility' in the sense Badiou uses it in *Manifesto of Philosophy*. Badiou used this term in relation to his idea of 'truth procedure' related to the 'conditions' of philosophy. In the chapter on 'Condition' in his book, Badiou says this: 'The first philosophical configuration that proposes to dispose these procedures – the set of these procedures –, in a unique conceptual space, thus showing that *in thought* they are compossible, is the one that bears the name Plato, "let no one enters here who is not a geometer," prescribes the matheme as a condition of philosophy', p. 34. In defining this term in the specific sense Badiou uses, the translator of his text, Norman Madarasz, explains: 'The concept of "compossible" stems from Leibniz who held that in God's Understanding there exists a virtual force field of logic completely unlike the space-time field. God's Understanding is said to contain a multiplicity

of contradictory, mutually destructive worlds, whose possibility for co-existing is termed "compossibility." As with another concept that Badiou takes on, the Principle of the Indiscernible, compossibility could not exists in actuality, hence God's choice of the "best of all possible worlds" in which Man is to live', p. 157.

32 See particularly Jean-Jacques Lecercle, *Badiou and Deleuze Read Literature*. As I discussed above, in the case of architecture Deleuze did not follow the protocol, that is, trying to find in architecture what he wanted to find for his philosophical system.

33 For this argument see Lecercle, *Badiou and Deleuze Read Literature*.

34 Among other things, this project of critique entails a Kantian gesture and would begin to discuss the 'impurity' of architecture within its multiple conditions. I take up this project in my forthcoming 'Surplus: Building in the Discourse of Capitalism: A Metacritique of Architecture'.

35 Peter Hallward in his 'Introduction: Theoretical Practice' cites Francois Dosse as saying that structuralism must be recognized as 'the single most symptomatic, most ambitious and most radical manifestation of the structuralist project of the 1960', *Concept and Form, Volume One*, pp. 2–3. Further Dosse writes: '*The Cahiers pour l'Analyse* in the scared ENS on the rue d'Ulm was the most symptomatic emanation of the structuralist flavor of the sixties, in its unbounded ambitions, in its most radical scientific experiments, in its most elitist appearance as an avant-garde/popular dialectic that claimed to speak in the name of the world proletariat, and which is used to legitimate the most terrorist and terrifying of theoretical practice. [. . .] It was this unharmonious mixture that inspired an entire generation of philosophers' (Francois Dosse, *History of Structuralism*, vol. 1, Deborah Glassman (trans.) [Minneapolis: University of Minnesota Press, 1977], 238), nos 6, 3. 'Dosse describes the broad Althusserian project as enabling a "practical combination of an often mad political voluntarism – a desperate activism – and the notion of the subjectless process that resembled a mystical commitment" (299tm)', ibid. Hallward adds that the *Cahiers* must be also recognized as the 'most significant collective participation of some of the theme that would soon be associated with 'poststructuralism' – an emphasis on precisely those aspects of a situation that remained un- or under-structured, on absence, lack, displacement, exception, indetermination, and so on', pp. 2–3.

36 See 'The Chain of Reason: An Interview with Alain Grosrichard', in *Concept and Form, Volume Two*, p. 223.

37 See Knox Peden, 'Introduction: The Fate of the Concept', in *Concept and Form, Volume Two*. Peden writes: 'Like Althusser, Lacan had a specific investment in thinking the relationship between the "concept" and "practice". Indeed, concepts *qua* concepts were central to this period of his teaching, as signaled by the title of seminar, delivered in 1964, that had the most proximate impact on the Cercle d'Épistémologie [Editorial Collective]: *The Four Fundamental Concepts of Psychoanalysis*. There Lacan makes clear that the concept is to be conceived as a mode of praxis: "what is Praxis?", he asked. "It is the broadest term to designate a concerted human action, whatever it may be, which places man in a position to treat the real by the symbolic" (S 11, 6)', p. 11. Further, 'As Lacan famously remarked: "the real can only be inscribed on the basis of an impasse of formalization" (S 20, 93)', p. 11.

38 For comprehensive discussion of this journal see Peter Hallward's 'Introduction: Theoretical Training', *Concept and Form, Volume One*.

39 Hallward writes that 'The most urgent priority, as Althusser had repeatedly insisted, was the "theoretical training [*formation*]" of a new revolutionary generation, one whose grasp of Marxist Science would reverse the disastrous revisionist steps taken

by the older generation and return the party [PCF] to its proper course', p. 22. Hallward further quotes Althusser on the notion of 'Theoretical Training': 'By *theoretical training*, we understand the process of education, study and work by which a militant is put in possession – *not only of the conclusion* of the two sciences of Marxist Theory (historical materialism and dialectical materialism), *not only of their theoretical principles*, not only of some detailed analyses and demonstration, all its principles and all its conclusion, in their indissoluble scientific bond. We literally understand, then, thorough study and assimilation of all the scientific works of primarily importance on which knowledge of Marxist theory rests. . .', p. 23.

40   Further Hallward writes that 'Conceived along rigorously Althusserian lines, the journal was designed to complement the creation of well-attended "theoretical schools" for the transmission of Marxist science', p. 22.

41   See also Ian James, *The New French Philosophy*. As is well known, the first two, Badiou and Rancière, later broke with their teacher Louis Althusser and his famous radical distinction between science and ideology.

42   Rancière stood away from Lacan and opposed his teacher Althusser, see '"Only in the Form of Rupture": An Interview with Jacques Ranciere', in *Concept and Form, Volume Two*. Alain Badiou summarizes the intellectual positions of figures the career of *Cahiers* came to an end with political rupture of May '68: 'Clearly the Althessurean (Baliber, Macherey, my friend Emmanual Terray, in certain respect Ranciere, who is an anti-Althusserian Althusserian), that is to say the non-Lacanians, have followed an entirely different trajectory. They are working in a far more historicist problematic, more in debt with Foucault than with Lacan. They are closer to a debate with classical Marxism, less tied to hypothesis of formalization. Overall, it is a different trajectory, even if on isolated political questions I have often been very close to them. And we should give credit where it is due: unlike Benny Levy, Miller, Milner, and even Regnault, they are not renegades', see 'Theory from Structure to Subject: An Interview with Alain Badiou', p. 289.

43   They further remark that 'Where Badiou sees an essential question for modern philosophy, then, poststructuralism see nothing. [. . .] Poststructuralism typically encounters a number of problems in its theory of the subject. Funnily enough, these problems are quite clearly inherited from the very philosophical tradition whose "death" poststructuralism gleefully proclaims. There was enough life in the corpse to pass something on – and what it passed on were the two fundamental problems in the thought of the subject', namely agency and identity, p. 3.

Bibliography

Aureli, P. V. (2008), *The Project of Autonomy: Politics and Architecture Within and against Capitalism*. New York: Buell Center/FORuM and Princeton Architectural Press.

Badiou, A. (1999), *Manifesto for Philosophy*. N. Madarasz (trans.), (ed.) and (intro.). Albany: State University of New York Press.

— (2004), *Theoretical Writings*. London: Continuum.

— (2005), *Infinite Thought*. London: Continuum.

— (2008), *Conditions*. London and New York: Continuum.

— (2009), *Pocket Pantheon*. London and New York: Verso.

— (2011), *Wittgenstein's Antiphilosophy*. London and New York: Verso.

— (2012), *The Adventure of French Philosophy*. London and New York: Verso.

Badiou, A. with Tarby, F. (2013), *Philosophy and the Event*. Cambridge: Oxford University Press.

Bosteels, B. (2008), 'Radical Antiphilosophy', in *Filozofski Vestnik*, vol. xxix, no. 2.

— (2011), 'Introduction', in A. Badiou, *Wittgenstein's Antiphilosophy*.

Clemens, J. and Adam J. Bartlett, A. J. (2012), '"The Greatest of Our Dead": Badiou and Lacan', in *Badiou and Philosophy*. S. Bowden and S. Duffy (eds). Edinburgh: Edinburgh University Press.

Feltham, O. and Clemens, J. (2005), 'An Introduction to Alain Badiou's Philosophy', in *Badiou, Infinite Thought*. O. Feltham and J. Clemens (eds) and (trans). London and New York: Continuum.

Goldstein, R. (2005), *Incompleteness: The Proof and Paradox of Kurt Gödel*. New York and London: W. W. Norton.

Hallward, P. (2012), 'Introduction: Theoretical Training', in *Concept and Form, Volume One: Key Text from the Cahiers pour l'Analyse*. London and New York: Verso.

Hallward, P. and Peden, K. (eds) (2012), *Concept and Form. Volume One: Key Texts from the Cahiers pour l'Analyse, Volume Two: Interviews and Essays on the Cahiers pour l'Analyse*. London and New York: Verso.

Houlgate, S. (2006), *The Opening of Hegel's Logic*. West Lafayette: Purdue University Press.

James, I. (2012), *The New French Philosophy*. Cambridge: Polity.

Johnston, A. (2010), 'This Philosophy Which Is Not One: Jean-Claude, Alain Badiou, and Lacanian Antiphilosophy', in *Journal of The Jan Van Eyck Circle for Lacanian Ideology Critique*, 3.

Kant, I. (1998), *Critique of Pure Reason*. P. Guyer and A. W. Wood (trans) and (eds). Cambridge: Cambridge University Press.

Karatani, K. (1995), *Architecture as Metaphor: Language, Number, Money*. S. Kohso (trans.), M. Speaks (ed.). Cambridge, MA: MIT Press.

— (2003), *Transcritique: On Kant and Marx*. Cambridge, MA: MIT Press.

Kostka, A. and Wohlfarth, I. (eds) (1999), *Nietzsche and the 'Architecture of Our Minds'*. Los Angeles: The Getty Research Institute for History of Art and Humanities.

Lacour, B. (1999), 'Architecture in the Discourse of Modern Philosophy: Descartes to Nietzsche', in Nietzsche *and the 'Architecture of Our Minds'*. Alexandre Kostka and Irving Wohlfarth (eds).

Lecercle, J.-J. (2010), *Badiou and Deleuze Read Literature*. Edinburgh: Edinburgh University Press.

Lytord, J.-F. (1988), *The Differend, Phrases in Dispute*. Minneapolis: University of Minnesota Press.

Marx, K. (1994), *Selected Writings*. L. H. Simon (ed.). Indianapolis: Hackett.

Miller, J.-A. (2012), 'Suture, Elements of the Logic of the Signifier', in *Concept and Form, Volume One: Key Texts from the Cahiers pour l'Analyse*. London and New York: Verso.

Osborne, P. (2011), 'Philosophy After Theory, Transdisciplinary and the New', in *Theory After 'Theory'*. J. Eliott and D. Attridge (eds). London and New York: Routledge.

Plato (1997), *Complete Works*. J. M. Cooper (ed.). Indianapolis: Hackett.

Žižek, S. (1993), *Tarrying with Negative: Kant, Hegel, and the Critique of Ideology*. Durham: Duke University Press.

— (2012), '"Suture," Forty Years Later', in *Concept and Form, Volume Two: Interviews and Essays on the Cahiers pour l'Analyse*. London and New York: Verso.

Zupancic, A. (2004), 'The Fifth Condition', in *Think Again: Alain Badiou and the Future of Philosophy*. P. Hallward (ed.). London and New York: Continuum.

13

Architecture's Theoretical Death

Gabriel Rockhill and Nadir Lahiji in Conversation with
Slovenian Philosopher Mladen Dolar

Mladen Dolar: I wanted to say, before beginning the conversation, that I do not have a special relation with architecture. I have never written about architecture, so I am speaking as an outsider, with no technical knowledge or involvement with architecture. I have written rather extensively about music. I have some musical training, and I have worked on various conceptual approaches to music. I have also written a number of literary analyses, and music and literature are something I live with in my daily life. But I do not live with architecture in that way. I am an outsider, if indeed one can be an outsider to architecture, or rather I am a naïve user of architecture. You should not, therefore, expect to be dealing with a philosopher who will unveil some hidden truth about architecture. I may just have some reflections, which are not based on an expert knowledge.

Gabriel Rockhill: Perhaps we can begin, then, by relating your work on music to an analogous issue in architecture. You have remarked, in *Opera's Second Death*, that philosophers have paid only a modicum of attention to the opera, and you have sought to redress this limitation in your own work. This collection of essays is similarly concerned with an apparent philosophic blind spot, namely one that obfuscates the role of architecture in the encounters between art and politics. There are, of course, a few rare but important exceptions (Benjamin, Foucault, Lefebvre, Jameson, etc.), and we should avoid harmful generalizations. Nevertheless, it is at least arguable that many of the prominent thinkers participating in the debates on art and radical politics in the long twentieth century have tended to focus on literature and the visual arts – as well as music, in certain instances – instead of architecture and urban design. Do you have any insight into the production of such apparent philosophic blind spots? Where do you think they come from, and how can they best be overcome?

M. D.: I am not very comfortable with this question, which seems to presuppose that philosophers have an obligation to talk about all things, and that they should therefore develop a discourse on architecture. If I am uncomfortable, it is in part because I come to America a lot as a visitor, but I am almost never invited by a philosophy department. This is because the kind of philosophy I do is covered by English departments, comparative literature departments, cultural studies, French and German departments. This conference was rather exceptionally organized by a philosophy department.[1] This is just to say that philosophy does not exist as a clearly established field. I belong to the European continental philosophy tradition, but here in the United States almost the entire enterprise is taken over by the analytic tradition, and continental philosophy is done in other departments. This is just to say that one cannot speak of philosophy in general. Which philosophy? How can one speak of this entity as a whole?

Nadir Lahiji: And, for that matter, of radical philosophy . . .

M. D.:   Radical philosophy is a continuation of either French structuralism and post-structuralism, or a radicalization of Marx, the Frankfurt school etc., so it is a very specific kind of philosophy. I have a certain unease in saying philosophy as such has a blind spot. Is there a philosophical discourse around which one could unify philosophy in such a way as to place it under a heading that everybody would accept? I do not think so. But, quite apart from some qualifications that would need to be made, there is indeed a huge question of the philosophy of art, and in that scope, the question of why literature and the visual arts are actually very often the models when one wants to speak of art.

N. L.:   And specially music and opera.

M. D.:   Music is a particular case. If you look back at the beginnings of philosophy, if you take Pythagoras and his idea of the harmony of the spheres, there you have some basic ontological presuppositions that are linked to music. The same proportion that can be mathematically established also governs musical proportion, astronomical proportion and should also rule over social proportions. There was something like the music of the universe, so a certain theory of music was absolutely fundamental for conceiving the universe at large and our place in it. Plato was entirely influenced by this in his own take on music, and the idea of the harmony of the spheres ruled or haunted the European imaginary up to the eighteenth century. It spelled out the basic proportion at the core of both the cosmos and social life, and modernity can be seen as bidding farewell to this fantasy. The nineteenth century relation to the opera poses different problems. Opera was then a sort of fancy, a glamorous social event to which philosophers would rather not go. It was linked to certain social stratification and the production of a collective imaginary – Kierkegaard and Nietzsche were the ones who took this very seriously. In the twentieth century you have people like Adorno – more than half of his writings are on music – but also a number of others.

N. L.:   And, then Adorno only wrote one piece about architecture.

M. D.:   When was that?

N. L.: He was invited in 1965 by the German Wurkbund to deliver a paper about architecture in which he talked about the Viennese architect, Adolf Loos. His talk was titled 'Functionalism Today', and it was later published.[2] Then, of course, he presented an apology that he does not belong to this field, that he is a 'dilettante' coming to architecture, but he nonetheless said beautiful things about aesthetics, and he criticized Loos and the notion of 'ornament' by going back to Kant's aesthetic philosophy. So he basically wrote one piece on architecture and only sporadically comes across architecture in his other works.

M. D.: Well, I think the basic presupposition of your question is that there is philosophy and it should cover all fields, so why doesn't it cover architecture. I would rather say that there is no philosophy in a global and totalizing sense, yet you have a number of prominent cases where some figures seriously engaged with architecture. You mentioned Benjamin and Jameson, but there is also Derrida and Foucault. These are not minor figures. I would say, do not look at philosophy and expect philosophy to cover evenly and justly every single field. There is no neutral perspective from which one could claim an even and just distribution of attention.

G. R.: Maybe we can talk more specifically, because it is true that the goal of the question was not at all to suggest that philosophy should be a global discourse that encompasses everything. Instead, it was motivated by a concern with what appears to be a major limitation in the critical theory tradition, broadly construed. If we look back on the long twentieth century, we see that an extensive and intensive debate developed on the relationship between art and politics, which stretched roughly from Lukàcs and the Frankfurt School to figures like Sartre, Barthes and Rancière. Within this debate, it is arguable that the fundamental reference point was literature and the visual arts, and many of the major participants did not engage in any extensive manner with architecture and urban design. Much of the controversy between these various thinkers takes place within a field delimited by the museum-based model of art and canonized literature. This strikes me as a significant limitation, particularly because – at a very banal and everyday level – architecture and urban design directly shape and mold the social body. Speaking schematically, and leaving aside the important exceptions that would need to be cited, it is as if the political art *par excellence* was ignored in favour of scrutinizing the ways in which the fine arts, the high arts, could be linked to radical politics. This, then, was the motivation behind the opening question, which could be reformulated as follows: isn't it curious that architecture, urban planning and design have not played a more central role in the critical theoretical debates on art and radical politics through the course of the long twentieth century?

N. L.: And, if I am correct, Hegel is probably the 'last' philosopher who directly and extensively wrote about architecture, with the exception of those who have used the 'architecture metaphor' or discussed, *à la* Kant, the 'architectonic of reason'. I am wondering, therefore, what happened after Hegel. Why do philosophers continue to talk about music and the visual arts, while architecture tends to be relegated to the realm of metaphor?

M. D.:   I do not know if I have any simple answer to this. I think the answer is perhaps not so different from the answer I gave about music, where you have a number of singular figures who have engaged with it with passion. But there is indeed the question of why literature and the visual arts take such a dominant position, defining the universal terms, while everything else was more relegated to particularity. Why do certain arts at a certain time figure as paradigmatic? It is very curious, if you take the case of Rancière, for instance, who is now largely a figure or reference.

G. R.:   Rancière is an excellent example of the tendency to which I am referring. In spite of his prolific writings on art and literature, he has published almost nothing on architecture. When I have had the opportunity to question him about this, he has a justification that is internally consistent with his theoretical framework, but which I find unsatisfactory: he claims that the aesthetic regime of art dissolved the principle of genres, or the *principe de généricité*, and that it does not make sense to separate architecture from other 'genres' of art when discussing this regime. What this ultimately means, then, is that his writings on 'literature' have something important to say about 'architecture'. When you consider his analyses of Victor Hugo's *Notre-Dame de Paris* or Balzac's detailed descriptions of facades, this makes a certain amount of sense. However, it is unclear to me how this justifies the enormous privilege he has accorded to analysing 'literature' in the banal sense of the term rather than exploring the work of architects. He has argued, for instance in works like *The Politics of Aesthetics, Mute Speech* and *The Aesthetic Unconscious*, that literature has ultimately been the generative source at work behind the historical emergence of the social sciences, psychoanalysis, film and contemporary art. And, with the notable exception of *The Nights of Labor* and a few other texts, by 'literature' we can understand – as is clear from his theoretical practice – the canonized works of the long nineteenth century, and particularly the French, male, bourgeois tradition.

M. D.:   This is certainly a problem. What serves as the paradigm is the grand nineteenth century literary tradition extended by the grand and canonized tradition of modernism. And in the case of visual arts, this includes almost exclusively what could be labelled as 'museum art'. This already raises the parallel question of popular culture, which has largely shaped the lives of people in more massive, if more trivial ways, providing the imaginary to live by, taking stock of collective fantasies and social attitudes. No doubt there is a definite choice made by the largest part of radical theory. Adorno is the vintage case for this, or take Badiou, who talks about Beckett endlessly.

G. R.:   As well as Mallarmé . . .

M. D.:   Mallarmé and Beckett, the tradition of high modernism. One can find exceptions. I think Slavoj Žižek insists on making a different choice, or mixing up the canon. He has always addressed popular culture, from the outset, not shying away from addressing even the rather dreadful and banal moments, some things I couldn't bear to watch or read. But dealing with the popular culture is absolutely necessary, essential even. It raises the question of the political impact of culture in an acute way.

N. L.: To what extent can we attribute this to a political factor? If it is not for purely aesthetic reasons, is there a political reason why some people, like Žižek, decide to talk about architecture and popular culture?

G. R.: The theoretical practice that turns a blind eye to the so-called manual arts (as well as popular culture) is in perfect harmony with the liberal tradition of bourgeois education in which one is trained in the high arts and the cultured realm of *Geist*. In fact, such a theoretical practice might, in part, be a direct consequence of the social sculpting of perception that is part and parcel of just such an education, which implicitly trains individuals to focus on valid objects of study and ignore others.

M. D.: Absolutely. Look at Badiou, or Derrida or Foucault, and a number of others. They are all *normaliens*. They received the best education one could possibly get at the École normale supérieure. It is only after living in France for a while that one realizes what a *normalien* is, and how the social, cultural, philosophical elite is reproduced by the so-called *grandes écoles*, like freemasonry. No doubt there is a problem involved in the fact that all these radical thinkers were actually shaped by these very strict social filters of transmission and distribution of knowledge and social positions, that this background is ingrained in their thinking and discourse also in ways which are not visible. So many things are taken for granted even in their highly reflected positions. The choice of a certain type of literature and art as the paradigm is no doubt also the consequence of this.

G. R.: This system creates not only an intellectual elite, but even a theoretical nobility of sorts, and there have been many excellent sociological analyses of the extent to which the theoretical practices that they partake in are undergirded by a series of deep metaphilosophical assumptions (which are ultimately tied up with the perpetuation of very specific social relations).

M. D.: I agree, this is really very extraordinary . . .

N. L.: Badiou actually anecdotally says that when he was a child his parents would take him to Wagner's operas; that was one of his cultural habits . . .

G. R.: It is interesting that a lot of the figures that we are discussing, in spite of their bourgeois upbringing and/or training, either underwent or undertook a political transformation leading them to embrace various forms of Marxism and neo- or post-Marxism. One question that needs to be raised, in this regard, is the following: Have they attempted to link their bourgeois heritage to more or less radical forms of politics by creating a bridge, *in nuce,* between their cultural past and possible political futures? In other words, has the undue focus on literature and the visual arts partially resulted from a desire, on the part of bourgeois intellectuals, to discover a privileged link between the cherished high arts of their upbringing and the higher political aspirations of their adult lives?

M. D.: The question starts already with Marx who had a liberal bourgeois background. Engels' father was a factory owner, Lukàcs had an aristocratic background (not only bourgeois but aristocratic!), Horkheimer from a wealthy family, and Adorno, well look at his musical education . . . All of them actually came from wealthy families and had a very good education, in most cases the best education you could get at the time. The question is how far this argument goes. To what extent is one unwittingly determined by one's social origin and education? Maybe one can argue that they all made their ways, in different manners, to radical politics, while the cultural heritage, their cultural habitus, was deeply ingrained within their social position. Perhaps it is easier to change one's political agenda than the cultural habitus, and it is by cultural habitus that one remains 'spontaneously' defined by class structure. The symptomatic marginal interest in architecture may therefore depend on the liberal arts education and a certain definition of the canon.

N. L.: But, do you think that this might have something to do with the fact that we cannot, when we talk about architecture, situate it within the fine arts, unless it is in terms of a hierarchical system of value? Deleuze, in this regard, says that architecture is the 'first art', exactly like Hegel. Where and when does art 'begin' or have an origin? Do you think that architecture always encounters this sort of difficulty regarding its categorization? If it is an art, what is the 'art factor' in this hierarchical system of high/low? How do elements of kitsch, 'the low', technology, etc. come into architecture?

M. D.: You are asking very large questions. What is the origin of art? How does art relate to technology? What is the relation between the aesthetic value and technology, or the pragmatic 'lowly' aspects? Do you know the work of Huizinga?

G. R.: Huizinga?

M. D.: Johannes Huizinga, *Homo Ludens*, the classic work written in 1938. *Homo Ludens* is about the notion of the game, and what defines a game is a certain division of space and time. One sets apart a certain space and a certain period of time, and within that compound special rules apply. In this special space and time one deals with things that are beyond the everyday economy of survival. If one defines a game in this way, one could see that both art and religion are based on this, a partition of space and time, and establishing a set of codes which are beyond the striving for survival. If we define art in this way, there is a division of space where something is art, because of particular rules, then one can see that architecture is actually this 'zero' art or 'paradoxical' art, because it defines the very parameters of space, so it both inhabits space we inhabit, but partitioning it and dividing it, distributing it in a certain way. Architecture both draws this spatial line and blurs it, the origin of architecture being a monument, the space of the sacred, the temple, the Pyramids. It distributes the space to establish a space which is separate from the economy of survival. At the same time it shapes also the other space, that of economy and survival, it constantly negotiates the line between the pragmatic and the sacred. It makes the disposition of space available, in multiple kinds of ways. Architecture has always been a matter of survival, how to ensure protection against the elements, provide the habitat, but at the same time it massively invested in monuments which are, from the pragmatic point of view, useless. It is the embodiment of the very line between technology of survival and the monument beyond the purposes of survival.

N. L.: This relates to Wagner. Shall we turn to Wagner and the 'total work of art'? Can architecture come to play the role of the 'total work of art'? How do we discuss this when it comes to architecture, given also the fact that, going back to your earlier discussion, Agamben claims, in 'In Praise of Profanation', that architecture is that element of profanation as opposed to what you just said about Huizinga . . .

M. D.: Agamben's argument is very precise. We seem to be living in a profane world, a totally secularized world, 'everything holy is being profaned', as Marx says in the *Manifesto*, thus summing up the process of modernization brought about by capitalism. But there is also the reverse argument already in Marx, namely that the world of commodities is itself imbued with theology and metaphysics, so it is more accurate to maintain that this is not the world of universal profanation, but rather the world of universal sacralization. This is where Agamben continues this argument by saying that the problem is now that there can be no profanation of this universal sacred. Once the sacred is gone we are rather stuck with the universal empty form of sacredness, which is the world of commodity. Marx, if you look at the structure of his argument in *Capital*, constantly uses religious metaphors to describe the world of commodities in what appears to be universal secularization. Benjamin goes even further in his fragment 'Capitalism as religion': there is rather the universalization of religion as an empty form. This goes back to the question of art, to the partition of space and time, to the twin questions of whether art is just another sort of commodity, or how to oppose this, and on the other hand of *l'art pour l'art*, art-for-art's sake, which is a very modern question emerging after the French revolution, once its umbilical cord with the sacred had been severed. So the process of modernity has always been linked with endeavours to blur this partition, to supersede it, to get out of galleries, or out of canonized and codified spaces and rituals that defined art. The partition no longer holds, the very economy of survival has become sacralized, which then calls for a wholly novel positioning of art, no longer tied to the special partitioning of the sacred, yet separating itself from commodity. A large part of modernity aimed at transcending the usual boundaries of arts, their being confined to a place where they had no social and political consequences.

G. R.:   Perhaps we can move on to the question of the social signification of art. One of your arguments concerning opera is that it emerged between incompatible imperatives because it had 'feudal form and bourgeois contents' (*Opera's Second Death* 8). Do you see other artistic practices as beholden to multiple imperatives, caught in a force field of social struggle? This point seems particularly important in the case of architecture insofar as it tends to be embedded in a more functionalized universe. Moreover, the social use of spaces can transform them in significant ways over time, as Foucault has notably argued in his discussion of Jean-Baptiste Godin's *Familistère*. Could you comment in general on the social significance of architecture as well as, more specifically, on the role of reception in the arts?

M. D.:   I think any work of art has multiple social significations. It is not a univocal thing; it always has multiple inscriptions in its very immediacy. One part of it is its inscription into a social division and the regime of distribution, and one should always carefully scrutinize this, although I think that ultimately the work of art is not reducible to the social function it is given or entrusted with. With architecture there is obviously first the massive fact that in order to do proper architecture one needs large amounts of money, as opposed to, say, literature that anyone can write, or most other arts where the capital investment is more modest. Architecture has been linked, since its beginnings, with great state investments.

N. L.:   But also cinema and opera are expensive arts to produce. In that respect maybe architecture and cinema are very similar. One is of course more private as opposed to the other . . .

M. D.:   Opera is a curious case. One can argue that opera was finished in the early twentieth century and that what happens in the last hundred years is like a lavish afterlife, which is underpinned by more money than ever in its history. It's like a postmodern enterprise, based largely on ever more elaborate remakes of a set repertoire, consisting of roughly 50 standard pieces. Of course some new operas are written and produced, but they still function as a supplement. The bulk is formed by canonic set pieces that one has to reinvent with ever more sophisticated means. But to go back to architecture, huge investments are needed, and there is always the moment of the ruler, the state, the private foundation, which want to present their glory in this architectural work. They want it as the celebration of their own status, ideology, the monument they will be remembered by. But the social meaning of architecture can never be quite exhausted by this. If you look at the obvious cases, the grand things in Paris, the Eiffel tower and Centre Pompidou, they were both scandalous at the time, they were built against the will of people and then, after a very short period, they started to serve as icons. They were shaped in such a way so as to become the popular icons which rule people's lives, provide the imaginary, the guiding figures, the figureheads.

N. L.:   But this was also a part of Mitterrand's view. It was not just Georges Pompidou, but projects such as the Grand Arch, the Louvre, the Bibliothèque Nationale . . .

M. D.: Yes, I absolutely agree, Mitterrand was particularly keen on this. He wanted the ideology of state to show up in architecture; he wanted this to be his shrine, his monument for posterity: 'Let me be remembered by this Pyramid . . .' The nineteenth century invested in architecture as the mark of progress and optimism, the marvel of engineering, but one cannot predict what social signification it will take on.

G. R.: What you seem to be suggesting, if I understood correctly your earlier comments, is that there is something inherent in art objects across time rather than there being a battlefield of social forces in which the very status and the sheer existence of art objects and architectural spaces is regularly renegotiated.

M. D.: There is always the battle over meaning and social function, yet something persists, insists in the work of art through these contradictory multiple meanings and functionalities. One can go back to Marx and to this remark he made off-handedly at the end of the introduction to the *Grundrisse*. He brings up, rather curiously and unexpectedly, Greek art and he says that of course Greek art was socially conditioned and you can see how Homer makes sense within these particular historical conditions. Then he says that Homer is no longer possible in the times of gunpowder and in completely changed circumstances. Then he goes on to say that the question is not why and how Greek art relates to society and historical conditions, the question is rather why does Greek art still speak to us and still present an unmatched model, across the centuries, despite the different social structure, technology, different modes of art production and distribution. Everything is changed, so how come it still makes sense, a lot of sense? How come it has a universal address? So, on one side, you have the fact that art responds to a particular social context and intervenes in that social context, and then there is the part of art which actually disentangles itself from the social context, it rather has the capacity to define the social context instead of being defined by it. This part of art produces, within its historical moment, the element of the universal which cannot be exhausted by its historical moment. And this universal appeal doesn't stem from some attempt to disentangle oneself from the social and historical context, but in the midst of full immersion in it. Or to put it in another way, the historical conditions are never simply some given from which one could explain art and account for its function. Art is placed in a break where the historical moment is not equal to itself, the break in historicity.

G. R.: I absolutely agree that this is a fundamental issue. I do not want to reduce the production of works of art to a social determination in any kind of reductive sense. However, the very concept of art that you are relying on when you juxtapose the universal address of art and the historical particularity of its production is a modern, European concept. We should be careful to avoid assuming that a spiritual realm of philosophic ideas and cultural forms transcends history whereas material practices do not. Our conceptual apparatus – including such fundamental notions as the 'universal address' of art – has its own deep-seated historicity and does not escape the flow of time. This is flagrantly the case in the reference to Greek art that you cite, for at least two very good reasons. To begin with, the Greeks had no concept of art as we understand the term. The notion of art in the singular was not part of their theoretical framework, and their terminological matrix – including words such as *poiesis* and *techne* – cannot be easily mapped onto our own. Secondly, Marx was clearly writing in the wake of Winckelmann, Hegel and so many others who were contributing to the formation of both art history and aesthetics (which are modern inventions). The very idea that there is a more or less linear history of art in which the past is autonomous and deserves to be studied for its own sake, and that there are singular masterpieces that speak across the ages – this is a modern idea. It becomes bound up in complex ways with the emergence of the museum at the end of the eighteenth century and a number of other important institutions and practices. In short, our concept and practice of art are far from transcending history. This does not, however, mean that 'art' is somehow reducible to strict historical determinants. On the contrary, as I just suggested, the very notion of art in the singular was produced by an intricate concatenation of various socio-historical agencies.

M. D.:   I agree. I started by saying that one can speak of art, in this massive way, only in the sense of the nineteenth century. Then the term art makes sense in its autonomy, and you know that aesthetics as a discipline is largely an eighteenth century invention. But the moment that art established itself as an autonomous field is also largely the moment when Hegel declared the end of art. This is a great irony. These are the two sides of the same coin: once art was established and canonized, it was finished. I like Agamben's argument about the end of art, namely that what happened with modernity, after Hegel, is largely like art annihilating itself: the end of art started to function as the paramount object of art. This could be one simple (too simple) definition of modernity.

N. L.:   And this is around the time that Wagner was already talking about the 'total work of art'. . .

M. D.:   Well, this comes half a century later, with the romantic cult of genius, with the idea that art should now step into the place that was left empty by religion. So you have then this grandiose project of *Gesamtkunstwerk*. It should be a grandiose thing precisely by its coincidence with the end of art, the grandiose statement of a demise. Nobody would think of *Gesamtkunstwerk* in the eighteenth century. There is, by the way, a wonderful passage in Plato's *Laws*, where he considers how to act if serious poets and tragedians were to ask their admission into the city. This is what we should tell them: 'Most honored guests, we are tragedians ourselves, and our tragedy is the finest and best we can create. At any rate, our entire state has been constructed so as to be a "representation" of the finest and noblest life – the very thing we maintain is most genuinely a tragedy. So we are poets like yourselves, composing in the same genre, and your competitors as artists and actors in the finest drama, which true law alone has the natural powers to "produce" to perfection . . .' (*Laws* VII, 817b–c). So the state is the true *Gesamtkunstwerk*, the supreme theatre dispensing with any other. The state is the best show in town, it beats theatre and all arts at their own game, it is the superior and the true show-business. So the history of art could be ironically placed between two notions of *Gesamtkunstwerk*: Plato's State at its beginning and Wagner's Bayreuth at its demise. But then, we need Beckett to spell out the truth of the latter.

(This interview was conducted on the 13th of April 2013, in Philadelphia.)

Notes

1 The conference in question is Villanova University's 18th Annual Graduate Philosophy Conference, 'Apocalyptic Politics: Framing the Present', which took place on the 12th and 13th of April, 2013.
2 Theodor Adorno, 'Functionalism Today', published in *Oppositions*, no. 17 (1979), translated from 'Funktionalismus heute', in Adorno, *Gesammelte Schriften*, vol. 10, pt. 1 (Frankfurt: Suhrkamp, 1977).

Index